Echoes of Scripture in the
Letter of Paul to the Colossians

Biblical Interpretation Series

VOLUME 96

ECHOES OF SCRIPTURE IN THE
LETTER OF PAUL TO THE COLOSSIANS

Function of OT text in the New 1. *Prophetic* 3. *analogy* 2. *typological*

Echoes of Scripture in the Letter of Paul to the Colossians

BY

Christopher A. Beetham

1. *Common ground is essential for*
   — scripts *OT in NT*
   — schemas
   — knowledge *— shared unique*
   Shared — *vocabulary or*
   — worldview *conceptualizations*

2. *OT text adds relevancy to NT passage*

Society of Biblical Literature
Atlanta

3. *earlier interpretive tradition*
4. *review source context in MT + LXX*

ECHOES OF SCRIPTURE IN THE LETTER OF PAUL TO THE COLOSSIANS

Library of Congress Cataloging-in-Publication Data

Beetham, Christopher A.
  Echoes of Scripture in the Letter of Paul to the Colossians / by Christopher
A. Beetham.
    p. cm. — (Biblical interpretation series ; v. 96)
  Originally published: Leiden ; Boston : Brill, 2008.
  Includes bibliographical references and index.
  ISBN 978-1-58983-499-6 (paper binding : alk. paper)
  1. Bible. N.T. Colossians—Relation to the Old Testament. 2. Bible. O.T.—
Relation to Colossians. I. Society of Biblical Literature. II. Title.
  BS2715.52.B44 2010
  227'.707—dc22
                                    2010018166

To Mindy
ἠγαπημένη τοῦ θεοῦ (Col 3:12)

In previous studies of the NT use of Scripture, far too much emphasis has been placed on actual quotations....Much of the NT abounds with allusions to the OT that have little resemblance to the exact wording. These allusions make up the larger portion of the NT use of Scripture and form the heart of its view of Scripture.

—Leonhard Goppelt, *Typos*

Creation texts

Original   Gen 1:26-28

Prophetic New   Is 41:2-9

inheritance – Deut 10:9

inheritance/ Ex 14:30
New Creation

CONTENTS

ILLUSTRATION

ACKNOWLEDGEMENTS

Having completed this work, there is a sense of both elation in the accomplishment and the realization as to how utterly dependent this work is upon the efforts, finances, and love of others. I first want to offer a deeply heartfelt word of thanks to all those of Wheaton Graduate School who dreamed, planned, and labored to make a Ph.D. in Biblical and Theological Studies at Wheaton a reality.

I want to thank especially those who gave financially to make my doctoral studies possible. Mr. Gene and Mrs. Margaret Logan provided a substantial amount for a fund, the interest of which supplied the stipend necessary for me to study at Wheaton. Gene and Margaret are outstanding models of generosity and excellence of character, and it is an honor to have become acquainted with them. Likewise Mr. Bernard and Mrs. Muriel Tolsma have faithfully supported us for the past six years of seminary and now doctoral studies. Their kind and loving support often arrived on days we didn't otherwise know how the needed groceries were going to be obtained. My parents, Roy and Sharon Beetham, have loved, financially supported, and cheered us on over the past nine years of school. Their encouragement to pursue my passion strengthened me at key junctures along the way. My parents-in-law, Doug and Judy Truer, have likewise supported us in a myriad of ways, including financially creative means such as supplying groceries and purchasing (and then installing!) the needed automotive parts to keep our 1993 Ford Explorer running and safe.

I will never cease to be grateful for the biblical scholars who have shaped my life and taught me the exegetical tools needed for study of the texts. Dr. Scott Hafemann's passion for scripture and his model as a scholar and painstaking exegete have left an indelible mark on me. With a master's hand, he taught me both Greek and NT exegesis, and his in-class investigations of the NT's use of the OT stimulated my own interest in the possibilities for biblical theology. Several hours spent in informal conversation and in a reading group served only to further my deep respect for him as both a person and scholar. Words cannot express my appreciation for the several years that he mentored me.

I owe no less to Professor Greg Beale. Dr. Beale served as my doctoral mentor, but our teacher-student relationship began well before these years, at Gordon-Conwell Theological Seminary (1999–2002). He has poured himself into my life as a scholar and mentor. His intensity, tenacity, and passion are infectious. His work in biblical theology, anchored as it is in rigorous exegesis, served as a model for my own inroads into the discipline. Professor Beale's commentary on the book of Revelation provides a magisterial example of the fruit that labor in the field of 'Old Testament in the New' can bear. I am profoundly grateful for the years that Dr. Beale has guided me through the field of biblical scholarship.

I wish to thank Dr. Doug Moo for serving as my second reader, and Dr. A. Andrew Das of Elmhurst College for serving as my external reader. Both Drs. Moo and Das asked penetrating questions and provided numerous suggestions for improvement of the manuscript. I am grateful for their careful reading. Without question this study is better because of their labor.

Lastly, I wish to thank my wife and children for their constant love. Sam, seven, Kate, four, and Erin Elizabeth, now two, are an immense source of joy for me. Playing with them, holding and consoling them, sharing life and learning about discipleship together—these experiences are unforgettable. Mindy, my life partner and kindred spirit, is an incredible human being who resonates with a refreshing depth of character. From the beginning we vowed not to sacrifice family for this doctorate degree, and we have stayed true to this pledge. Her love, commitment, and enthusiasm for "us," our family, and this work proved invaluable for the completion of this dissertation. It is only fitting that I dedicate it to her.

October 13, 2006   Chris Beetham

*   *   *   *   *

In light of Brill's acceptance of this manuscript for publication, I wish to thank editors Ivo Romein and Wilma de Weert at Brill for their labor and good cheer, and to express my appreciation to the *Biblical Interpretation Series* editor, Professor R. Alan Culpepper, for his willingness to accept this work for the series. The present work is a slightly revised and expanded edition of the original dissertation manuscript.

April 28, 2008   Chris Beetham

LIST OF ABBREVIATIONS

DNTB   *Dictionary of New Testament Background.* Edited by Craig A. Evans and Stanley E. Porter. Downers Grove: InterVarsity, 2000.

DOTP   *Dictionary of the Old Testament Pentateuch.* Edited by T. Desmond Alexander and David W. Baker. Downers Grove: InterVarsity, 2003.

JSJSup   *Supplements to the Journal for the Study of Judaism* (formerly *Studia Post-Biblica*). Edited by John J. Collins. Leiden: Brill.

Lamsa   *The Holy Bible from Ancient Eastern Manuscripts containing the Old and New Testaments translated from the Peshitta.* George M. Lamsa. Nashville: Holman, 1981.

Lust   *A Greek-English Lexicon of the Septuagint.* J. Lust, E. Eynikel, and K. Hauspie. 2 vols. Stuttgart: Deutsche Bibelgesellschaft, 1992–1996.

LXX   Göttingen edition of the Septuagint, unless the book in question is not yet covered by this edition; then it refers to the Cambridge edition (Brooke, McLean, and Thackeray) or to Rahlfs [see bibliography].

NSBT   New Studies in Biblical Theology. Edited by D. A. Carson. Downer's Grove: InterVarsity.

CHAPTER ONE

INTRODUCTION AND HISTORY OF RESEARCH

Investigation of the use of the Old Testament in the New "has long been recognised as an important field of research."[1] The earliest works emphasized textual matters (e.g., text variants), comparison with rabbinic modes of interpretation, and the problems associated with the question of what version or text the NT authors depended upon for their quotations.[2] With the rise of literary criticism and its subsequent influence on biblical studies in the 1970s and 1980s, new approaches to the field of the Old in the New were introduced. In 1989, Richard Hays introduced the literary-critical study of intertextuality into the field, though in reality he limited his study to select readings in Paul.[3] Investigation of OT allusions and echoes in the NT literature burgeoned in the 1990's and in the early years of the new millennium, with works being written on several individual NT books or sections within a NT book. Such monographs and other studies included investigations in Mark, Luke, John, Acts, Romans, 1 Corinthians, Ephesians, and Revelation.[4]

---

[1] E. Earle Ellis, *Paul's Use of the Old Testament* (Grand Rapids: Eerdmans, 1957), 1. Let it be noted here that this study follows the *SBL Handbook of Style* with regard to abbreviations and formatting (supplemented by *The Chicago Manual of Style* when necessary).

[2] Ellis, *Paul's Use*, 2–5; Otto Michel, *Paulus und Seine Bibel* (BFCT 2/18; Gütersloh: Bertelsmann, 1929; repr., Darmstadt: Wissenschaftliche Buchgesellschaft, 1972), 1–4; Richard B. Hays, *Echoes of Scripture in the Letters of Paul* (New Haven: Yale University Press, 1989), 9–10.

[3] Hays, *Echoes of Scripture in the Letters of Paul*.

[4] See e.g., Craig A. Evans and James A. Sanders, *Luke and Scripture: the Function of Sacred Tradition in Luke-Acts* (Minneapolis: Fortress, 1993); Brian S. Rosner, *Paul, Scripture, and Ethics: A Study of 1 Corinthians 5–7* (AGJU 22; Leiden: E.J. Brill, 1994; repr., Grand Rapids: Baker, 1999); Steve Moyise, *The Old Testament in the Book of Revelation* (JSNTSup 115; Sheffield: Sheffield Academic Press, 1995); Rikki E. Watts, *Isaiah's New Exodus and Mark* (WUNT 2/88; Tübingen: J. C. B. Mohr (Paul Siebeck), 1997; repr., *Isaiah's New Exodus in Mark* (Grand Rapids: Baker, 2000); Roy E. Ciampa, *The Presence and Function of Scripture in Galatians 1 and 2* (WUNT 2/102; Tübingen: J. C. B. Mohr (Paul Siebeck), 1998); G. K. Beale, *John's Use of the Old Testament in Revelation* (JSNTSup 166; Sheffield: Sheffield Academic Press, 1998); idem, *The Book of Revelation* (NIGTC; Grand Rapids: Eerdmans, 1999); David W. Pao, *Acts and the Isaianic New Exodus* (WUNT 2/130; Tübingen: J. C. B. Mohr (Paul Siebeck), 2000; repr., Grand Rapids: Baker, 2002); H. H. D.

The reason for the present study is that no monograph or even journal article has probed the use of the Old Testament in Paul's letter to the Colossians. The reason for this neglect is understandable before the 1990s, because before this time the field concentrated upon explicit quotations, and Colossians contains no explicit quotations of Scripture. In light of the intertextual turn that Hays introduced into the field of NT study in 1989, however, the time is appropriate to look again at Colossians to determine whether the Scriptures of Israel have left their mark on the letter nevertheless.

Scholars today have concluded that there are no explicit quotations in Paul's letter to the Colossians. First of all, unlike Romans, 1 and 2 Corinthians, and Galatians, Colossians contains no introductory formulae, that is, markers that introduce and signal a formal quotation (e.g., γέγραπται, "it is written" at Gal 3:10). Moreover, numerous scholars of the past two centuries have compiled lists of OT quotations in the NT (or at least in Paul), and most of these excluded Colossians from their catalogs of quotations. These scholars include Horne (1847), Turpie (1868), Böhl (1878), Toy (1884), Hühn (1900), Swete (1902), Venard (1934), Ellis (1957), Archer and Chirichigno (1983), Bratcher (1984) and Silva (1993).[5]

Williams, *The Wisdom of the Wise: The Presence and Function of Scripture Within 1 Cor. 1:18–3:23* (Leiden: Brill, 2001); Thorsten Moritz, *A Profound Mystery: The Use of the Old Testament in Ephesians* (NovTSup 85; Leiden: Brill, 1996); Timothy W. Berkley, *From a Broken Covenant to Circumcision of the Heart: Pauline Intertextual Exegesis in Romans 2:17–29* (SBLDS 175; Atlanta: SBL, 2000); Margaret Daly-Denton, *David in the Fourth Gospel: The Johannine Reception of the Psalms* (AGJU 47; Leiden: Brill, 2000); J. Ross Wagner, *Heralds of the Good News: Isaiah and Paul "in Concert" in the Letter to the Romans* (NovTSup 101; Leiden: Brill, 2002); Gary T. Manning, *Echoes of a Prophet: The Use of Ezekiel in the Gospel of John and in Literature of the Second Temple Period* (JSNTSup 270; London: T&T Clark, 2004); cf. Andrew H. Wakefield, *Where to Live: The Hermeneutical Significance of Paul's Citations from Scripture in Galatians 3:1–14* (Academia Biblica 14; Leiden: Brill, 2003), which employs intertextual insights to Paul's explicit quotations of Scripture in Galatians 3:1–14.

[5] Thomas Hartwell Horne, *An Introduction to the Critical Study and Knowledge of the Holy Scriptures* (2 vols.; 8th ed.; New York: Robert Carter, 1847), 1:293–310; David M. Turpie, *The Old Testament in the New: A Contribution to Biblical Criticism and Interpretation* (London: Williams and Norgate, 1868), 275–79; Eduard Böhl, *Die Alttestamentlichen Citate im Neuen Testament* (Vienna: Braumüller, 1878), 345–51; Crawford H. Toy, *Quotations in the New Testament* (New York: Charles Scribner's Sons, 1884), 201, 283–300 (offering Prov 2:4 at Col 2:3 as a sort of allusion); Eugen Hühn, *Die alttestamentlichen Citate und Reminiscenzen im Neuen Testamente* (Tübingen: J. C. B. Mohr [Paul Siebeck], 1900), 197–98; Henry B. Swete, *An Introduction to the Old Testament in Greek* (Cambridge: Cambridge University Press, 1902; repr., New York: KTAV, 1968), 389–91; L. Venard, "Citations de l'Ancien

Though scholars have concluded that there are no quotations of Scripture in Colossians, this is not to say that scholars therefore have not seen *any* influence of the OT upon the letter. Indeed, its presence is strong enough that Henry Gough believed that he had possibly ascertained even some quotations in Colossians. In his 1855 work, Gough observed what he understood to be either "direct quotations" or "verbal allusions" of Isa 1:13–14 in Col 2:16, Isa 29:13 in 2:22, Ps 110:1 in 3:1, Ps 78:31 [77:31 LXX] in Col 3:6, Gen 1:26–27 in 3:10, Deut 10:17 (and/or 2 Chr 19:7) in 3:25, Dan 2:8 in 4:5, and Lev 2:13 in 4:6.[6]

Most scholars, however, have maintained that Paul did not quote Scripture in Colossians; nevertheless they have also concluded that his language was impacted by the OT at various points in the letter. In 1848, Grinfield held that Gen 1:27 stood behind Col 3:9–10 and Lev 2:13 behind 4:6; he also proposed numerous other parallels, including the possibilities that Deut 10:16, 30:6, and/or Jer 4:4 influenced Col 2:11, that Isa 29:13 influenced 2:22, and that Ps 110:1 had left its mark on Col 3:1.[7] In 1884, Toy offered evidence that Prov 2:4 and Job 28:21

Testament dans le Nouveau Testament," *DBSup* 2:24–28; Ellis, *Paul's Use of the Old Testament*, 150–52; Gleason L. Archer and Gregory Chirichigno, *Old Testament Quotations in the New Testament* (Chicago: Moody, 1983), xix–xxii; Robert G. Bratcher, ed., *Old Testament Quotations in the New Testament* (3rd rev. ed.; UBS Handbook Series; New York: United Bible Societies, 1984), 58–59 (though offers Col 2:22 as allusion to Isa 29:13 LXX and 3:1 as allusion to Ps 110:1); M. Silva, "Old Testament in Paul," *DPL* 631; cf. Hans Hübner, "New Testament, OT Quotations in the," *ABD* 4:1098, who writes that "no Scripture quotation is found in Colossians, although its author refers back to authentic Pauline letters which contain formal quotations."

Hans Vollmer, in his study entitled *Die Alttestamentlichen Citate bei Paulus: Textkritisch und biblisch-theologisch gewürdigt nebst einem Anhang Ueber das Verhältnis des Apostels zu Philo* (Freiburg and Leipzig: J. C. B. Mohr [Paul Siebeck], 1895), intentionally limits himself to the investigation of the four *Hauptbriefe* (see page vi); this approach to Paul is also taken by Dietrich-Alex Koch, *Die Schrift als Zeuge des Evangeliums: Untersuchungen zur Verwendung und zum Verständnis der Schrift bei Paulus* (BHT 69; Tübingen: J. C. B. Mohr [Paul Siebeck], 1986), 21–23. Michel, *Paulus und Seine Bibel*, 193–201, though he surveys Ephesians and 1 Timothy, does not mention Colossians in his discussion regarding quotations in the so-called NT post-Pauline writings.

[6] Henry Gough, *The New Testament Quotations* (London: Walton and Maberly, 1855), 366. Gough offers both "direct quotations" as well as "verbal allusions" in these tables and makes no distinction between the two for the reader, believing that the differences between the two categories are "self-apparent" (see page v of his PREFACE). See also footnote 23 below for another work that saw actual quotations of the OT in Colossians.

[7] Edward Grinfield, *Scholia Hellenistica in Novum Testamentum* (2 vols.; London: Pickering, 1848), 2:879, 928. His table of citations and parallels of the OT in the NT is found on pp. 859–944.

had influenced Col 2:3 in a sort of allusion.[8] In 1900, Hühn offered several phrases in Colossians as parallels or "reminiscences" of OT texts, including Prov 8:22–30 at Col 1:15–17, Deut 4:6 and Isa 11:2 at 1:9, Deuteronomy's "inheritance" language at 1:12, Deut 10:16, 30:6, and Jer 4:4 at Col 2:11, Isa 29:13b at Col 2:22, Ps 110:1 at Col 3:1, Gen 1:26–27 at 3:10, and Deut 10:17, 1 Sam 16:7, Job 34:19, and 2 Chr 19:7 at 3:25b.[9] He posits several other parallels also, which are too numerous to list here.[10] In 1903, Dittmar proposed that Prov 8:22, Sir 24:9, and/or Jer 2:3 may lie behind Col 1:18. He also offered Isa 45:3 and Sir 1:25 for Col 2:3 and Isa 29:13 for Col 2:22.[11] In 1952, C. Maurer, agreeing with the marginal notes of his Nestle Greek text, asserted that there were eight OT parallels and citations in Colossians.[12] In 1957, Ellis proposed that four allusions to OT texts existed in Colossians: Isa 45:3 at 2:3, Isa 29:13 at 2:22, Ps 110:1 at 3:1, and Gen 1:27 at 3:10.[13]

In his 1965 Yale dissertation, Fred Francis devoted a few sections of detailed study to what he believed was the use of Scripture in Col 2.[14] Francis wrote that he believed that his work was "the first detailed study of the use of Scripture in Colossians."[15] Francis argued that Deut 28:12–13, Exod 19:10–15, Isa 29:13, and Esther influenced the language and thought of the author of Colossians in Col 2.[16] His section on the use of Isa 29:13 at Col 2:22 is quite good, and some of his insights have been incorporated into our present study (see chapter eleven). Francis's other proposals, however, appear to be forced. He lacks any methodological control or criteria with which he can self-

---

[8] Toy, *Quotations in the New Testament*, 201, 292.

[9] Hühn, *Die alttestamentlichen Citate*, 197–98.

[10] Hühn, *Die alttestamentlichen Citate*, 197–98.

[11] W. Dittmar, *Vetus Testamentum in Novo: Die alttestamentlichen Parallelen des Neuen Testaments im Wortlaut der Urtexte und der Septuaginta* (2 vols.; Göttingen: Vandenhoeck & Ruprecht, 1903), ad loc.

[12] C. Maurer, "Der Hymnus von Epheser 1 als Schlüssel zum ganzen Brief," *EvT* 11 (1951/52): 158. Maurer does not state which OT texts he believes are in Colossians, though one could surmise that his list coincides at least roughly with the current edition of Nestle available to him because of his explicit mention of that Greek text edition.

[13] Ellis, *Paul's Use of the Old Testament*, 154.

[14] Fred O. Francis, "A Re-examination of the Colossian Controversy" (Ph.D. diss., Yale University, 1965), 146–50, 155–70, 210–18.

[15] Francis, "Re-examination of the Colossian Controversy," 258.

[16] Francis, "Re-examination of the Colossian Controversy," 146–50 (Deut 28); 155–64 (Exod 19); 164–70 (Isa 29:13); 210–18 (Esther).

critically evaluate his proposals and consequently hedge himself against the bug of "parallelomania."[17] This study has not followed him in the conclusion that Paul alluded to Deut 28:12–13, Exod 19:10–15, or Esther in Col 2.

In 1983, Hanson wrote a brief treatment of the possible use of the OT in Colossians in a chapter devoted to the so-called deutero-Pauline letters and to Hebrews (Hanson's study is an account of the use and interpretation of the OT in the NT as a whole).[18] In his brief treatment, Hanson argues that the Jewish exegetical traditions of Prov 8:22–30 and Gen 1:1 stand behind the hymn of Col 1:15–20, that Gen 1:26 and Ps 89:27 have influenced Col 1:15, and that Col 1:19 "is based on Psalm 132:14."[19] He also wrote that Col 2:3 probably took up Isa 45:3, and that 2:14–15 alluded to Num 25:1–5. He also asserted that Col 2:22 "very definitely echoes" Isa 29:13.[20]

In 1984, Robert Bratcher offered Col 2:22 as an allusion to LXX Isa 29:13 and 3:1 as an allusion to Psalm 110:1.[21] In 1993, the Deutsche Bibelgesellschaft published the 27th edition of the Nestle-Aland Greek New Testament (NA[27]). In the apparatus in the outer margins alongside the text proper, the editors give references to OT quotations and allusions next to the appropriate NT passage. Quotations "are indicated by italics...and allusions by normal type."[22] For Colossians, the NA[27] editors posted no quotations, but they did claim several allusions for the letter. These included: Prov 8:23–27 at 1:17, Sir 1:24–25, *1 En.* 46:3, Isa 45:3, and Prov 2:3–4 at 2:3, Isa 29:13 at 2:22, Ps 110:1 at Col 3:1, Gen 1:26–27 at 3:10, Lev 25:43–53 at 4:1, and Eccl 5:7 at 4:1.[23]

---

[17] S. Sandmel, "Parallelomania," *JBL* 81 (1962): 1–13.

[18] Anthony Tyrrell Hanson, *The Living Utterances of God: The New Testament Exegesis of the Old* (London: Darton, Longman, and Todd, 1983), 90–96.

[19] Hanson, *Living Utterances of God*, 92.

[20] Hanson, *Living Utterances of God*, 93–96 (quotation from p. 96).

[21] Bratcher, *Old Testament Quotations in the New Testament*, 58–59. This 1984 edition is actually the 3rd edition. The 1st edition was printed in 1961 and was unavailable to me, but it may have offered these allusions at this earlier date.

[22] Kurt Aland et al., eds., *Novum Testamentum Graece* (27th ed.; Stuttgart: Deutsche Bibelgesellschaft, 1993), 78*.

[23] In comparison, the 16th edition, published in 1936 and placing quotations in bold and allusions in the outer margins, posted as *quotations* the following: Prov 2:3–4 and Isa 45:3 at 2:3, Isa 29:13 at 2:22, Ps 110:1 at 3:1, and Gen 1:26–27 at 3:10. It also posted as allusions the following: Prov 8:25–27 at 1:17, and Lev 25:43–53 and Eccl 5:7 at 4:1.

In 1994, Barth and Blanke contended that the author of Colossians alluded at least five times to the OT. They argued for allusions of Isa 45:3 and Prov 2:3–4 in Col 2:3, Isa 29:13 in 2:22, Ps 110:1 in 3:1, Gen 1:26–27 in 3:10, and Deut 10:17 in 3:25.[24]

In 1997, Hans Hübner's second volume of *Vetus Testamentum in Novo*, which treats the Pauline corpus, was published.[25] In the work, Hübner offers numerous parallels between NT and OT texts based primarily upon word agreement. He leaves it up to the reader to decide whether the parallels constitute an actual quotation, allusion, or echo, or whether the parallels are merely coincidence.[26] Thus the work offers no evaluative judgment upon the parallels adduced. For his section on Colossians, Hübner presents parallels that are too numerous to list here, but his findings support several of this study's conclusions.[27] His list, however, fails to offer echoes of Gen 1:28 at Col 1:6, 2 Sam 7 at 1:13, Deut 30:6 at 2:11, and Gen 17 at 2:13, for which this study will argue in the following chapters.

In a forthcoming commentary on the use of the OT in the entire NT, Greg Beale has written what will be one of the first serious investigations of the OT in the entire letter to the Colossians.[28] Professor Beale served as my doctoral mentor and the present study was written under his guidance. Our studies on the use of the OT in Colossians were conducted independently, although we approached the task with similar methodologies. In coming together to discuss our research, we were encouraged to discover that several of our findings overlapped. Readers will find that Dr. Beale presents a few more allusions than the present study. He detects and argues for the probability of the following:

1) Genesis 1:28 in Col 1:6, 10
2) Exod 31:3, 35:31–32, Isa 11:2 in Col 1:9–10
3) The exodus motif in 1:12–14

---

[24] Markus Barth and Helmut Blanke, *Colossians: A New Translation with Introduction and Commentary* (trans. Astrid B. Beck; AB 34B; New York: Doubleday, 1994), 64n.98.

[25] Hans Hübner, *Vetus Testamentum in Novo: Band 2, Corpus Paulinum* (Göttingen: Vandenhoeck & Ruprecht, 1997).

[26] Hübner, *Vetus Testamentum in Novo*, xvi–xvii.

[27] Hübner, *Vetus Testamentum in Novo*, 505–47.

[28] See now as G. K. Beale, "Colossians," in *Commentary on the New Testament Use of the Old Testament* (ed. G. K. Beale and D. A. Carson; Grand Rapids: Baker Academic, 2007), 841–870.

4) 2 Samuel 7:12–16 in Col 1:13
5) Genesis 1:27 in 1:15
6) Psalm 89:27 [88:28 lxx] in 1:15
7) Possibly "Wisdom" in Col 1:15–17
8) Psalm 68:16 [67:17 lxx] in 1:19
9) Daniel 2 in 1:26–27
10) Daniel 2 and Proverbs 2:3–6 in Col 2:2–3
11) Isaiah 29:13 in 2:22
12) Genesis 17:10–27 in 2:13
13) Deuteronomy 30:6 in 2:11
14) Psalm 110:1 in 3:1
15) Genesis 1:26–27 in 3:10
16) Possibly Genesis 3:7–21 in 3:9–10
17) Daniel 2:8 in 4:5

Dr. Beale's work provides independent confirmation of several of the allusions and echoes proposed in the present study.

As I finished this work, news reached me that Dr. Gordon Fee had also written an article on the use of the ot in Colossians that was in the early stages for publication. Dr. Fee has kindly granted me permission to peruse and cite this work.[29] In the twenty-four page article, Fee argues for ten echoes of the ot (here offered in the order Fee discusses them):

1) The exodus theme in Col 1:12–14
2) Isaiah 29:13 in 2:22
3) Isaiah 11:2 in 1:9–10
4) Psalm 110:1 in 3:1
5) Deuteronomy 7:6–8 in Col 3:12
6) 2 Samuel 7:14, 18 in 1:13
7) Genesis 1:26, 28 in 1:15
8) Psalm 89:27 in 1:15
9) Genesis 1:1 in 1:18
10) Genesis 1:26, 28 in Col 3:9–10

---

[29] See now as Gordon D. Fee, "Old Testament Intertextuality in Colossians: Reflections on Pauline Christology and Gentile Inclusion in God's Story," in *History and Exegesis: New Testament Essays in Honor of Dr. E. Earle Ellis on his 80th Birthday* (ed. S. Aaron Son; T&T Clark, 2006).

Dr. Fee's work has likewise offered independent confirmation of several of the allusions and echoes proposed in this study. He does, however, also argue vigorously against any allusion to Wisdom in Col 1:15–20 (such as from Prov 8:22–31), and thus against one of the allusions proposed in this investigation. According to the present study's conclusions, Fee has therefore not detected five of the allusions and echoes that are in Colossians (Gen 1:28 at Col 1:6, 10; the Prov 8:22–31 exegetical tradition in Col 1:15–20; Ps 67:17 LXX [68:16] in 1:19; Deut 30:6 at 2:11; Gen 17:11 at Col 2:13).

Various commentaries, if the data were compiled, would offer an extensive expansion to this brief history of research of the OT in Colossians. The following study in fact offers such a collection of data, since a footnote at the beginning of each of the relevant chapters provides information on those commentators who have also observed the allusion or echo in question. Most of the commentators are from the twentieth century, though a few are earlier (including Calvin and Lightfoot). The early church fathers (through the third century C.E.) were also investigated to see if they demonstrated awareness of the various proposed allusions or echoes. We therefore refer the reader to the beginning of the appropriate chapters that follow for further information on the history of research on the use of the OT in Colossians.

This dissertation seeks to contribute to "Old Testament in the New" studies in the following ways: 1) to offer a thorough methodology and precise definitions of terms in order to detect and verify allusions and echoes of Scripture in Colossians, 2) to put forward and defend the eleven allusions and echoes detected by the methodology, 3) to discuss how Paul has used the detected allusions and echoes hermeneutically and theologically, 4) to analyze how early Jewish, later Jewish, and early Christian exegetical tradition of the same Scripture might shed light on Paul's use, and 5) to demonstrate how detection of the allusions and echoes in Colossians contributes to the overall understanding of Colossians and of the relationship between the testaments. The study will discuss the implications of the investigation for understanding Paul's Colossian audience and their ability to overhear what Paul had done. It will also touch on the question of Paul's faithfulness to the original context of the passages to which he refers, as well as probe briefly as to why Paul did not explicitly quote Scripture in Colossians. Finally, the investigation will look briefly at what insight might be gained with regard to the question of the authorship of the letter, as well as to the relationship between Colossians and Ephesians.[30]

---

[30] The authenticity of Colossians as a letter from the apostle Paul is disputed. Raymond E. Brown, *An Introduction to the New Testament* (ABRL; New York: Doubleday, 1997), 610, wrote that "at the present moment about 60 percent of critical scholarship holds that Paul did not write the letter." Most of these scholars, however, do consider it "Pauline," i.e., as stemming from a school of disciples of Paul or a close companion of Paul, such as Timothy. Since the exegesis of the present study is not substantially impacted either way, a full discussion of the issue is not necessary at this point. For a defense of Pauline authorship, see, e.g., Werner Georg Kümmel, *Introduction to the New Testament* (trans. Howard Clark Kee; rev. ed.; Nashville: Abingdon, 1975), 340–46; Peter T. O'Brien, *Colossians, Philemon* (WBC 44; Waco: Word, 1982), xli–xlix. For the view that Paul did not write the letter, see, for example, Brown, *Introduction*, 610–17 (with caution); Eduard Schweizer, *The Letter to the Colossians: A Commentary* (trans. Andrew Chester; Minneapolis: Augsburg, 1982), 15–24. Although it would not directly impact this study, and furthermore, while there is no place for dogmatism on the issue, I am of the opinion that Paul dictated the letter while in prison, employing an amanuensis (Timothy?; see Col 1:1, 4:18). The argument for the authenticity of the letter, based upon its subtle yet certain relationship with the authentic letter of Paul to Philemon, provides a solid basis for holding to Pauline authorship of the letter to the Colossians. In my opinion, this relationship between Colossians and Philemon has not been explained away in any convincing fashion by those who hold to non-Pauline authorship. It is much more likely that the same author stands behind both and that both were composed at roughly the same time in Paul's missionary career.

CHAPTER TWO

ON DETERMINING ALLUSIONS AND ECHOES:
DEFINITIONS AND METHODOLOGY

Interpreters have long been drawn to source investigation. The wealth
of meaning that is uncovered when a literary allusion is detected draws
interpreters to the occupation. They are eager to find allusions to prior
texts in order to cash in on such rich resources of meaning. It is, however, on account of such scholarly eagerness that the good examples of
source investigation were nearly outweighed by the poor and embar-
rassing ones written in the past century and beyond in literary circles
generally.[1] Richard Altick cites Alfred Lord Tennyson's comments on
the appalling situation already in his own day in 1882:

> But there is, I fear, a prosaic set growing up among us, editors of booklets,
> book-worms, index-hunters, or men of great memories and no imagina-
> tion, who *impute themselves* to the poet, and so believe that *he*, too, has no
> imagination, but is for ever poking his nose between the pages of some
> old volume in order to see what he can appropriate. They will not allow
> one to say "Ring the bell" without finding that we have taken it from Sir
> P. Sidney, or even to use such a simple expression as the ocean "roars,"
> without finding out the precise verse in Homer or Horace from which
> we have plagiarized it (fact!).[2]

The reason for such outlandish "parallelomania" was because strict
controls of methodology were not rigorously followed.[3]

Despite the abuses that source research has had to endure over the
years, there is no reason to throw the whole enterprise out the window.
In fact, NT studies have witnessed an explosion of research in recent
years in this area, as literary-critical methods slowly but surely carved
their niche into the discipline. The research especially revolves around

---

[1] Richard D. Altick and John J. Fenstermaker, *The Art of Literary Research* (4th rev.
ed.; New York: W. W. Norton, 1993), 107–8.
[2] Hallam Tennyson, *Alfred Lord Tennyson: A Memoir* (New York: MacMillan, 1898)
1:258, cited by Altick, *The Art of Literary Research*, 107.
[3] Altick, *The Art of Literary Research*, 108.

the use of the Old Testament in the New, but not exclusively so.[4] The reason that the enterprise continues to grow is that the research has untapped rich reservoirs of meaning in passage after NT passage.[5]

The logical conclusion that should be held on account of 1) the deplorable abuses and excesses in this area in the past, yet 2) the rich dividends of meaning such study has uncovered, is that such investigations should *continue*. However, they must be done under the watchful eye of a strict methodology, rigorously and consistently carried out. What follows is a proposal of such a methodology as we prepare to hunt for allusions and echoes in Paul's letter to the Colossians.

An Author-Oriented or Reader-Oriented Approach?

One of the questions that scholars face in proposing allusions, especially of the elusive kind, is "But would the audience have recognized your proposed allusion?"[6] The question is a good one and requires a studied response. As we will see below, an *allusion* by definition must be overt enough to be recognized by the audience. An author has failed in his use of allusion as a literary device if the audience does not catch the reference. If the audience fails to recognize the allusion, however, it does not follow that the attempt to allude was not made by the author. The allusion may be there, embedded in the text, even though the audience missed it.

The question becomes acute when we consider the ad hoc orientation of Paul's letters. His letters are not general treatises, but are written to address specific situations and concerns at local churches for which the apostle held some pastoral responsibility. J. C. Beker raises this question in regard to Richard Hays's work *Echoes of Scripture in the Letters of Paul.*[7] Hays's response is that

---

[4] For example, the work of Michael Thompson, *Clothed with Christ: The Example and Teaching of Jesus in Romans 12.1–15.13* (JSNTSup 59; Sheffield: JSOT Press, 1991), seeks to trace Jesus tradition (JT) in Paul's letter to the Romans.

[5] See, for example, the now standard work in the field by Hays, *Echoes of Scripture in the Letters of Paul.* One may not agree with all of Hays's findings or interpretations, but the work is an excellent example of the possibilities that literary approaches have opened up for NT research.

[6] A. Andrew Das, for example, mildly criticizes Hays, asking this question of a particular echo that Hays had proposed in his *Echoes of Scripture.* See Das's *Paul, the Law, and the Covenant* (Peabody, Mass.: Hendrickson, 2001), 188n.57.

[7] J. Christiaan Beker, "Echoes and Intertextuality: On the Role of Scripture in Paul's Theology," in *Paul and the Scriptures of Israel* (eds. Craig A. Evans and James A. Sanders; JSNTSup 83; Sheffield: JSOT Press, 1993), 65.

the fact that Paul was trying to communicate in contingent situations does *not* mean that he could not have used allusive echoes in his letters. When they are understood, allusions are potent strategies of communication.[8]

Hays's point is that even the contingent nature of Paul's letters does not preclude the possibility that Paul alluded back to the Scriptures, which so determined his worldview.

The question "But would the audience have recognized your proposed allusion?" reveals an *audience or reader-orientation* to interpretation. Such a question does have a smaller but important place even in an *author-oriented* approach. By definition an author's effort to employ allusion is only effective if it is overt enough to be recognized by the audience. The purpose of this study, nevertheless, is to "orient one's discussion to the language of the author" of the letter to the Colossians in an author-oriented approach:

> Although investigation of an audience-oriented approach has merit in establishing the shared assumptions and biblical knowledge of the audience (in fact, much more could and should be done in this area), it is questionable whether it provides the proper basis for establishing the *author's* use of the Old Testament. If one is interested in establishing a given author's use of the Old Testament, it would appear imperative to orient one's discussion to the language of the author, rather than supposed, reconstructed "knowledge" of the audience.[9]

The purpose of the present investigation is to discern Paul's biblically rooted allusions and echoes in his letter to the Colossians. This study therefore appropriates the *author-oriented* approach mentioned by Porter, the kind that will "orient one's discussion to the language of the author." This will be the approach even with echo, which can be either consciously or unconsciously executed (see below). Even if Paul only unconsciously echoed a text simply out of his saturation with Scripture, we can still speak of Paul "doing" something as an author with and in the words he wrote. In such a case, Paul still expressed himself with phraseology whose language stems from a particular text that he had read on a previous occasion, whether he himself was aware that he was

---

[8] Richard B. Hays, "On the Rebound: A Response to Critiques of *Echoes of Scripture in the Letters of Paul*," in *Paul and the Scriptures of Israel* (eds. Craig A. Evans and James A. Sanders; JSNTSup 83; Sheffield: JSOT Press, 1993), 86.

[9] Stanley E. Porter, "The Use of the Old Testament in the New Testament: A Brief Comment on Method and Terminology," in *Early Christian Interpretation of the Scriptures of Israel: Investigations and Proposals* (eds. Craig A. Evans and James A. Sanders; JSNTSup 148; vol. 5 of *Studies in Scripture in Early Judaism and Christianity*; Sheffield: Sheffield Academic Press, 1997), 95 (emphasis mine).

doing it or not. And this written expression rendered by the author can be compared with the earlier OT material to discern whether its origins may be found in a particular OT text or tradition.[10]

Despite this author-oriented approach, the present study will also apply literary-critical tools in its investigation. Recently, literary-criticism has often presupposed an *audience-oriented* approach. In light of this, the question arises whether an interpreter may legitimately use literary-critical tools if a central presupposition of the approach is disregarded. This is a criticism that William Scott Green levels at Hays's *Echoes of Scripture*.[11] Hays replies:

> While I am well aware of the philosophical context in which these [literary critics] employ intertextual analysis, I fail to see why my interest in intertextual echo should compel me to accept their ideological framework. As I argued in a long footnote in *Echoes* [227n.60], the literary-critical operation of tracing the meaning-effects created by Paul's intertextual figurations is "in principal neutral with regard to metatheories about language and truth."[12]

Hays does not feel the need to adopt the presuppositions that typically drive intertextual analysis, and he believes that this stance does not hinder his employment of the tool.

Green argues, however, that Hays's minimalist baptism into literary methodology has rendered his analysis as "insufficiently suspicious," making Hays capable of seeing only what Paul wanted his readers to see.[13] His analysis "falls into mere descriptiveness."[14] Hays, however,

---

[10] Therefore, in this study we are not trying to get into the "mind" of the author (as if that were possible). All we have is the written expressions of the author, which in this study are taken as an author's attempt to render meaning in written form. See E. D. Hirsch, Jr., *Validity in Interpretation* (New Haven: Yale University Press, 1967), 1–19. If in seeking to ascertain the author's intention via his written communication, we find that his language is expressed and colored in the expressions and language of a text previously read by the author, this does not suddenly throw the study of these influences back into the realm of the unknowable "mind" of the author. Again, the expressions are public (in that they are written out for anyone who wishes to read them) and originate with an author intending to communicate, so that we as interpreters can legitimately adjudicate between the variously proposed influences (if any) upon a writer and his written expressions.

[11] William Scott Green, "Doing the Text's Work for It: Richard Hays on Paul's Use of Scripture," in *Paul and the Scriptures of Israel* (eds. Craig A. Evans and James A. Sanders; JSNTSup 83; Sheffield: JSOT Press, 1993), 59, 62–63.

[12] Hays, "On the Rebound," 79–80.

[13] Hays, "On the Rebound," 83.

[14] Green, "Doing the Text's Work for It," 63.

takes this as "unintended praise," because that was precisely what he set out to do. He desired to describe what Paul had done with the Scriptures of Israel.[15] Hays did not set out to evaluate whether Paul's appropriations of Scripture were "power moves," made to advance his interpretive community's ideological interests against another's (in this case the Jewish community) and *their* understanding of Scripture.

The present study seeks to combine the best of historical-critical and literary-critical methodology in a robust approach that will help us to overhear Paul's biblical allusions and echoes.[16]

Literary Modes of Reference: Quotation, Allusion, and Echo

What is the difference between a quotation, an allusion, an echo, and a parallel? Clear definitions are necessary to differentiate between these various categories and to clear away cobwebs of confusion. The following definitions are therefore offered and will be strictly followed throughout the body of this investigation.[17] Our demarcation of definitions has attempted to take its cues from literary-critical circles.

Quotation

This study makes no distinction between the terms *quotation* and *citation*. According to Harry Shaw, a citation is a "reference to an authority or precedent. The term usually refers to the act of *citing verbatim* the written or spoken words of another."[18] John Hollander offers the same in a roundabout manner: "Actual quotation, *the literal presence of a body of*

---

[15] Hays, "On the Rebound," 84.

[16] With Hays, I feel no obligation to begin from an *audience-oriented* approach or to relegate the role of the author to that of the reader. I do appreciate literary-criticism's emphasis on the final form of the text and for its insistence that interpreters take care to be sensitive to works as pieces of *literature*, written in particular genres. I also appreciate its attention to literary modes of reference such as allusion and echo and the definitions they offer for such modes.

[17] Cf. Porter, "The Use of the Old Testament in the New Testament," 94–95, who writes: "In order to undertake any such investigation [of the OT in the New] it is imperative that one define the categories under discussion, and then apply them rigorously. Ideally, a common language would be found that all could willingly use, but this is an unreasonable expectation. Therefore, short of a common language, *interpreters should be clear in their own terminology and the application thereof*" (emphasis mine).

[18] Harry Shaw, *Dictionary of Literary Terms* (New York: McGraw-Hill, 1972), 76 (emphasis mine).

text, is represented or replaced by allusion, which may be fragmentary or periphrastic."[19]

Quotations may be further divided up into two categories: *formal* and *informal*.[20] A *formal* quotation is a quotation that is accompanied by a *quotation formula*, which serves as a clear marker to the reader that what follows (or immediately precedes) is a citation from a previous source. In the NT, examples of such formulae include καθὼς γέγραπται ὅτι ("as it is written (that)"; Rom 3:10), εἶπεν Ἡσαΐας ("Isaiah said"; John 12:39), and λέγει ὁ θεός ("God says"; Acts 2:17). The phenomenon of formal quotation does not occur in the letter to the Colossians. An *informal* quotation, on the other hand, is a quotation that lacks a quotation formula. An informal quotation is just as much a quotation as a formal one; it merely wants for an explicit introductory marker.

Hollander speaks of a "kind of rhetorical hierarchy" between quotation, allusion, and echo.[21] The strongest, most explicit mode of reference is quotation. The citation of the former reference is verbatim or nearly so, and is long enough to be recognized as such.[22] An allusion, while still overt by definition, is less explicit, being more "fragmentary or periphrastic."[23] J. Fekkes writes that "the more a text is broken up and woven into the passage, the less likely it is to be a quotation."[24] However, there is some gray area. For example, what if we come across a subtle four-word reference that is a word-for-word rendering of its previous text? It is subtler than many quotations, yet is a precise rendering. Is it a strong allusion or subtle quotation?

The example above shows that the *length* of the reference plays a role in its classification.[25] Therefore, for this study a rule shall be arbitrarily

---

[19] John Hollander, *The Figure of Echo: A Mode of Allusion in Milton and After* (Berkeley: University of California Press, 1981), 64 (emphasis mine).

[20] Jan Fekkes III, *Isaiah and Prophetic Traditions in the Book of Revelation: Visionary Antecedents and their Developments* (JSNTSup 93; Sheffield: JSOT Press, 1994), 63–64. Cf. Porter "The Old Testament in the New Testament," 88–94.

[21] Hollander, *The Figure of Echo*, 64.

[22] With a quotation, the author will either offer an explicit marker of some kind to signal to the reader that a quotation is about to take place (or, if following the quotation, that one has just taken place) or cite enough of the predecessor to indicate clearly that a quotation of another work is taking place (often accompanied by a shift in vocabulary, tone, or style). Despite all of this the possibility exists that a quotation could still be missed by the reader.

[23] Hollander, *The Figure of Echo*, 64.

[24] Fekkes III, *Isaiah and Prophetic Traditions in the Book of Revelation*, 65.

[25] I owe this insight to Porter, "The Use of the Old Testament in the New Testament," 95. I am, however, responsible for the direction I take here.

set that a verbatim or near verbatim reference back to a previous text of six words or more will be considered a *quotation*. A reference of five or less—even though verbatim—will be labeled an *allusion*. An obvious exception is the case where a *quotation formula* introduces a reference that is less than five words. For example, in John 19:37 the author introduces a four-word quotation of Zech 12:10 with the formula καὶ πάλιν ἑτέρα γραφὴ λέγει ("and again another scripture says").[26] This phenomenon is rightly labeled as a quotation; the quotation formula makes it such.

In light of the above, the following definition is offered for quotation.

Quotation: An intentional, explicit, verbatim or near verbatim citation of a former text of six or more words in length. A *formal* quotation is a quotation accompanied by an introductory marker, or *quotation formula*; an *informal* quotation lacks such a marker.

Allusion

We have already begun to demarcate our understanding of what constitutes an allusion in the discussion above. In the "rhetorical hierarchy" of modes of reference, allusion stands below quotation and above echo in strength and explicitness. Also already indicated above was the decision that any phrase of five words or less, even though it may be an exact expression of the previous text, will be considered an allusion.[27] Unlike a quotation, however, an allusion is not limited to the form of a linear phrase. It can be more periphrastic and fragmentary, more "broken up and woven into the passage," to repeat Fekkes's words. An allusion can exist in the form of a "word cluster," where several uncommon words, phrases, and/or images from a section of an older text are incorporated and scattered in a paragraph or section of a new text.

---

[26] The four-word quotation is ὄψονται εἰς ὃν ἐξεκέντησαν, "They shall look on him whom they have pierced" (RSV). The quotation is four words in Greek, not in English!

[27] Ziva Ben-Porat, "The Poetics of Literary Allusion," *PTL* 1 (1976): 107, rightly counters that, against the common assumption, literary allusions "are neither tacit nor necessarily brief." The line, however, between quotation and allusion, however gray, needs to be drawn somewhere and therefore is drawn at the five- and six-word range for this study.

Four items are essential to the definition of an allusion. First, an
allusion is an intentional, conscious attempt by an author to point
a reader back to a prior text. Hollander writes: "Intention to allude
recognizably is essential to the concept, I think, and that concept is
circumscribed genetically by earlier sixteenth-century uses of the word
alluding that are closer to the etymon *ludus*—the senses of "punning" and
"troping." Again it should be stated that one cannot in this sense allude
unintentionally—an inadvertent allusion is a kind of solecism."[28] Green
likewise writes that an allusion "usually connotes a conscious authorial
act and perhaps a knowing audience," while an echo "requires neither."[29]
Carmela Perri similarly remarks concerning allusion that "the author
intends that the allusion-marker's echo will identify the source text for
the audience."[30] Earl Miner defines an allusion as "a poet's *deliberate*
incorporation of identifiable elements from other sources, preceding or
contemporaneous, textual or extratextual."[31] Ben-Porat's entire article
on the theory of how allusion works presupposes that allusion is an
intentional, conscious activity of an author.[32]

The second item that is essential to allusion is that an allusion has "in
each instance, a single identifiable source."[33] With the employment of
allusion, the author attempts to point the audience to a specific predecessor. One particular object, whether a text, event, tradition, person, or
thing (whether concrete or abstract) is in view.[34] When it is a *text* that is
in view, "the literary allusion is a device for the simultaneous activation
of [only] two texts," that is, the alluding and the alluded.[35]

Third, an allusion must adequately stand out in order to be perceived by the audience. Perri writes that it is "generally assumed that
allusion-markers are possible to recognize, an assumption which entails
that [it] be sufficiently overt to be understood."[36] This presupposes that
the author and reader share a common language and tradition. For an
allusion to be successful, the prior text must be "...part of the portable

---

[28] Hollander, *The Figure of Echo*, 64.
[29] Green, "Doing the Text's Work for It," 59.
[30] Carmela Perri, "On Alluding," *Poetics* 7 (1978): 300.
[31] Earl Miner, "Allusion," in *The New Princeton Encyclopedia of Poetry and Poetics* (eds.
Alex Preminger and T. V. F. Brogan; Princeton, N.J.: Princeton University Press, 1993),
38–39 (emphasis mine).
[32] Ben-Porat, "The Poetics of Literary Allusion," 105–128.
[33] Miner, "Allusion," 39 col. 1.
[34] Cf. Miner, "Allusion," 38–40.
[35] Ben-Porat, "The Poetics of Literary Allusion," 107.
[36] Perri, "On Alluding," 290.

library shared by the author and his ideal audience."[37] If the work is unfamiliar to the reader, the allusion will race past the ear like an arrow that missed its target. If the allusion-marker itself is obscure, the audience may easily miss it also, comprehending only the surface-level meaning (what Perri labels the "un-allusive" sense).[38] Even if the audience does miss the allusion, however, contextual clues may be present to help the reader piece together a partial understanding of what the author has signified. The amount of meaning lost to a reader when he or she misses an allusion will depend in part upon the number of contextual "helps" present in the text.

The final item essential to allusion is that an author employing it expects that the audience will remember the original sense of the previous text and link the appropriate components that the new context requires in order to be most fully understood. Michael Thompson succinctly summarizes Perri on what constitutes an effective allusion: "In order for the allusion to be successful, the audience must *recognize* the sign, *realize* that [it] is deliberate, *remember* aspects of the original text to which the author is alluding, and *connect* one or more of these aspects with the alluding text in order to get the author's point."[39] Perri herself writes, "Recognizing, remembering, realizing, connecting: these are the effects of a successfully performed allusion for its audience."[40] The nature of an allusion is such that though it is the *author* who alludes, the success of the employment of such a literary device depends upon the *audience*. The author's attempt to "do" something with language fails if the reader does not fulfill any of the requirements which, according to Perri, comprise a "successfully performed allusion."

Perri argues that an allusion marker requires certain aspects of the original text to be recalled and brought forward into the new for the alluding text to be understood fully. Perri goes on further to argue, moreover, that an allusion may suggest other aspects that can be connected, which are neither explicit nor essential to understanding, but nevertheless offer an even fuller meaning when recognized and linked. She writes that "contemplation of the linked texts may activate further meaning patterns between them, or the marked text may evoke

---

[37] Hollander, *The Figure of Echo*, 64.
[38] Perri, "On Alluding," 295.
[39] Thompson, *Clothed with Christ*, 29.
[40] Perri, "On Alluding," 301. Cf. Ben-Porat, "The Poetics of Literary Allusion," 109–111.

properties of texts other than itself ("intra-textual patterns"), any of which affect the significance...of the alluding text."[41] Ben-Porat even claims that this "further activation of elements is the particular aim for which the literary allusion is characteristically employed."[42]

In light of the above discussion within literary scholarship, the following definition is offered for what constitutes an allusion.

Allusion: A literary device intentionally employed by an author to point a reader back to a single identifiable source, of which one or more components must be remembered and brought forward into the new context in order for the alluding text to be understood fully.[43] An allusion is less explicit than a *quotation*, but more explicit than an *echo*. In this study, a linear marker of five words or less is considered to be an allusion.

Echo

An echo stands at the bottom of the "rhetorical hierarchy" of literary modes of reference.[44] It is the least explicit of the three modes. Like allusion, there are four essential items that need to be understood in order to grasp the nature of echo.

First, unlike allusion, an echo may be either a conscious or unconscious act. According to Green, while allusion "usually connotes a conscious authorial act and perhaps a knowing audience" an echo "requires neither."[45] Echoes are faint enough that often it is impossible to gauge whether its appearance in the text was consciously or unconsciously performed by the author. The nature of this literary mode of reference is such that Carlos Baker can quip that echo is a "flash in the brainpan."[46] This does not diminish the importance of echo,

---

[41] Perri, "On Alluding," 296.

[42] Ben-Porat, "The Poetics of Literary Allusion," 111.

[43] We qualify with "fully" because a reader may be able to piece together a partial understanding due to the presence of contextual clues within the immediate context of the allusion. Perri calls this partial understanding the "un-allusive" sense ("On Alluding," 295).

[44] Hollander, *The Figure of Echo*, 64.

[45] Green, "Doing the Text's Work for It," 59.

[46] Carlos Baker, *The Echoing Green: Romanticism, Modernism, and the Phenomena of Transference in Poetry* (Princeton, N.J.: Princeton University Press, 1984), 8, as previously picked up by Jon Paulien, "Elusive Allusions: The Problematic Use of the Old Testament in Revelation," *BR* 33 (1988): 40.

however. Hollander writes that "in contrast with literary allusion, echo is a metaphor of, and for, alluding, and does not depend on conscious intention. The referential nature of poetic echo, as of dreaming...may be unconscious or inadvertent, but is no less qualified thereby."[47]

Second, *like* allusion, echo has "in each instance, a single identifiable source." Hollander states that echo is a form of citation in that it refers back to a particular precursor.[48] Every echo derives from one specific text, event, tradition, person, or thing (whether animate or inanimate, concrete or abstract). If the echo is a textual or literary echo, it stems from a text that the author has read (or heard) at some point in the past.

Third, unlike allusion, by echo the author does *not* intend to point the audience to the precursor. Intention implies a conscious activity, and echo is often but not always a conscious act. Echo is a linking of texts accomplished without the aim to render a communication for public consumption. Perri writes concerning echo that "such subtle incorporations of markers may appear to be for the poet himself, something we 'overhear,' thereby contributing to a quality of lyrical privacy."[49] Hollander writes that "...a pointing to, or figuration of, a text recognized by the audience is not the point" of an echo.[50] Nevertheless, a reader with a deep familiarity of the texts read by the author may overhear the author's otherwise private "flashes in the brainpan" with their well-attuned ear. Echoes surface in a text largely because the author's mind is saturated with the source text. For the apostle Paul, the sacred Scriptures of Israel constituted such a source text.

Fourth, unlike allusion, an echo is not dependent upon the original sense of the precursor to be understood. The meaning in the new context is not tied to the previous context; that is, the audience does not need to "recognize, remember, realize, and connect" the two texts to grasp the author's intended public communication in the new context. The original context may or may not have been taken into consideration. Baker writes that echo can occur "with or without their original contexts" in mind.[51] Therefore, the reader may miss an echo of a previous text yet still can comprehend the text within which the

---

[47] Hollander, *The Figure of Echo*, 64.
[48] Hollander, *The Figure of Echo*, 72.
[49] Perri, "On Alluding," 304.
[50] Hollander, *The Figure of Echo*, 64.
[51] Baker, *The Echoing Green*, 8.

echo is embedded. We cannot speak of a loss of intended-for-the-*public* authorial meaning when the echo is missed by the reader. The component intended as public communication is adequately conveyed apart from recognition of the echo. As we will see, however, discovery of the echo unveils a new horizon to the reader's understanding, because then an attuned ear is overhearing whispers of a vast textual world that lies behind the text and suffuses it.

Thus, although an echo is not dependent upon the original sense of the precursor to be understood, there are three significant reasons why this study will nevertheless investigate the original sense of the parent text of an echo. In his work *The Figure of Echo*, Hollander has shown repeatedly that an investigation of the source text of an echo deeply enhances and colors the understanding of the new context. One might quibble over specific examples that Hollander offers in his study, but the cumulative argument for his thesis is almost unassailable. Richard Hays, who has built upon Hollander's work, writes that an echo often "places the reader within a field of whispered or unstated correspondences."[52] Upon first discovery of an echo by a reader, the author may appear to have done nothing more than borrow a rich or rare expression, word, or concept due to its particular attractiveness in the way it looks, sounds, or turns a phrase. If, however, a reader also recollects the source text, he or she may discover unexpressed links that suggest rich stores of otherwise unnoticed insight. This is what Hays means when he states that echo frequently provides "a field of whispered or unstated correspondences." Elsewhere Hays labels this phenomenon with the technical literary term *metalepsis*. According to him, metalepsis is

> a rhetorical and poetic device in which one text alludes to an earlier text in a way that evokes resonances of the earlier text *beyond those explicitly cited*. The result is that the interpretation of a metalepsis requires the reader to recover unstated or suppressed correspondences between the two texts.[53]

Therefore, the first reason that the original sense of the OT source text of an echo will be investigated is because it frequently leads to a deeper understanding of the echoing text. The unstated correspondences only come to light when the echoed and the echoing texts are compared and the original context of the echoed text explored. For those with

---

[52] Hays, *Echoes of Scripture in the Letters of Paul*, 20.
[53] Richard B. Hays, *The Conversion of the Imagination: Paul as Interpreter of Israel's Scripture* (Grand Rapids: Eerdmans, 2005), 2 (emphasis his).

ears that overhear them, echoes provide entry into the vast symbolic world of the text that stands behind and imbues the echoing text. An echo is an easily overlooked opening that offers access to the rich yet otherwise hidden textual world that shapes the echoing text.

A modest, nonscriptural example may help to illustrate the point. The title of the present study, *Echoes of Scripture in the Letter of Paul to the Colossians*, is my intentional echo of the title of Richard Hays's seminal study, *Echoes of Scripture in the Letters of Paul*. It is true that the reader experiences no loss of intended-for-the public meaning if he or she remained unaware of my echo. My title adequately conveys the contents of the study in the pages that follow, apart from any awareness of my echoing activity. However, if a well-attuned reader overhears my echo of Hays' title and recalls the type of study that it represents, the discovery unveils a new horizon to the reader's understanding of the present work. My reader is overhearing whispers of a vast textual world that lies behind my title and shapes it.

Upon further reflection a perceptive reader may discern that the two titles share an unspoken correspondence or metalepsis. A reader that recollects the echoed text may recall the literary corpus within which Hays conducts his study. It is as his title states, namely, "...*the Letters of Paul*." For the audience for which Hays was writing—critical NT scholarship—this signals that Hays will deal especially with the undisputed letters of Paul, like Romans and Galatians and the Corinthian correspondence. And indeed, it is the undisputed letters of Paul from which Hays selects his readings. Most critical NT scholarship considers Ephesians, 2 Thessalonians, the Pastorals, and often even Colossians to be inauthentic letters of Paul. In my echo of the clause "...*the Letters of Paul*" of Hays's title in my own, the reader may recover an unexpressed but genuine link between the two titles that serves as my playful whisper in support of the minority report. In echoing the phrase, I suggest by the metalepsis that the letter to the Colossians is—like Romans and Galatians and the Corinthian correspondence—an authentic letter of Paul.[54]

The second reason why significant space will be devoted to investigation of the original meaning of the OT source text of detected echoes will be because such study can uncover important unspoken *hermeneutical*

---

[54] About 60% of NT scholars are of the opinion that the letter to the Colossians is not of Paul (see p. 9n.30 of this study). For another, quite excellent example of a nonscriptural metalepsis, see Hays, *Conversion of the Imagination*, 32–33.

presuppositions of the author concerning that original text. For example, in chapter four I argue that the apostle echoed Isa 11:1–9 in Col 1:9–10. If I have overheard correctly, then I have also uncovered his unmentioned hermeneutical presupposition that Isa 11:1–9 read ultimately as a prophecy of the messiah and his end-time rule.

Thirdly, investigating the OT source text of an echo is significant even if Paul's audience never detected the echo, because such investigation can still reveal clues as to *how the apostle understood the OT context of the echoed text*. Again, the study is more concerned with Paul as an author and less concerned with the meaning-effects created by the echo upon an ideal reader, although this latter concern is a legitimate and worthwhile enterprise in its own right.

Echo: A subtle, literary mode of reference that is not intended for public recognition yet derives from a specific predecessor. An author's wording may echo the precursor consciously or unconsciously and/or contextually or non-contextually.

Parallel

Unlike quotation, allusion, or echo, a parallel is *not* a literary mode of reference. Altick's comments on the phenomenon of literary parallel serve well as an introduction to the category:

> When we speak of a direct source, we usually mean that certain elements in poem *y* are found elsewhere only in the antecedent poem *x* and therefore, barring independent investigation, must have been derived from *x*. But even if the elements that suggest the relationship are earlier found in other places besides *x*, it may still be likely that *x* was the immediate source; we may know, for instance, that the poet was reading *x* shortly before he wrote *y*, and hence the reasonable presumption is that he got his idea there rather than anywhere else. "Parallel" and "analogue," on the other hand, imply that neither internal nor external evidence is strong enough to make us confident that *y* derives from *x*. While certain features of poem *y* are indeed found in *x*, they occur fairly often in preceding or concurrent literature, and the fact that they are found in *y* may equally well—in the absence of more specific indications—be due to antecedents floating at large in the nebulous realm of literary tradition or intellectual milieu.[55]

---

[55] Altick, *The Art of Literary Research*, 110–11.

T. L. Donaldson breaks the category of parallel up into two categories, the *genealogical* and the *analogical*. He breaks the former down further into two sub-categories, "strong" and "weak." Altick's comments above overlap with Donaldson's "weak" genealogical parallel and his "analogical" parallel, but do not pertain to Donaldson's "strong" genealogical parallel. Therefore some elaboration upon Donaldson's categories is required.

Strong Genealogical Parallel

Donaldson writes that for a genealogical parallel to be genuine "it is first of all necessary to show a substantial similarity between the two elements under discussion when seen in their contexts. Imaginary parallels, drawn on the basis of highly selective use of source material ignoring wider contexts, are no parallels at all."[56] Moreover, a genealogical parallel is one in which an organic relationship exists between the two texts. In this regard, the sub-category of strong genealogical parallel

> can be said to exist where there is a direct, straight-line influence from one element of the parallel to the other; one religious tradition has been directly influenced by, or has clearly appropriated something from, the other at this point.[57]

Another way that Donaldson puts it is that "religious cargo has passed over the [historical] bridge."[58] This necessarily implies that the borrowed element must chronologically precede the borrowing element.

In this study, the category of strong genealogical parallel covers broader elements (such as a theme or doctrine) rather than a specific textual relationship, which is adequately covered by our categories of quotation, allusion, and echo.[59] An example of a strong genealogical parallel between the OT and the NT is the doctrine of monotheism. Christianity directly inherited its monotheistic outlook from the OT religion. See Figure 1 for the visual depiction of this relationship.

---

[56] T. L. Donaldson, "Parallels: Use, Misuse and Limitations," *EvQ* 55 (1983): 198.

[57] Donaldson, "Parallels," 200.

[58] Donaldson, "Parallels," 199.

[59] Donaldson, however, throws the net of *strong genealogical parallel* wider, so that it would include my category of *echo* and possibly even my category of *allusion* (cf. "Parallels," 199–200). But I think it is important to distinguish these literary modes of reference from his broad (and less incisive) category of parallel.

Weak Genealogical Parallel

An organic relationship also exists between the elements of a "weak" genealogical parallel, as it does in a "strong." However, the element of direct influence is lacking.[60] Instead, the organic relationship essential to a genealogical parallel exists in a diffuse, indirect form. The parallel arises when two works jointly participate in the "common stock" of a tradition and independently employ the same element from this shared tradition.[61] For example, both Paul (Rom 4:1–25) and the author of the letter to the Hebrews (11:8–12) offer Abraham as a paradigm of faith for the believer to emulate. Yet almost certainly the two have employed the same OT narrative independently (Gen 12–17). Paul at Romans 4 is not dependent on Hebrews 11, and vice-versa. See Figure 1 for the visual depiction of this relationship.

Analogical Parallel

An analogical parallel occurs when a strong, contextual similarity arises out of universal human experience. The two elements emerge in their own traditions independently of each other, yet bear a striking resemblance when observed in their respective contexts. Take, for example, the universal experience of the cleansing property of water. This universal element plays a key role in ritual ceremonies that signify purification in both Hinduism and Christianity. Nevertheless, no geographical or historical bridge exists between the two rituals. The parallel arose solely out of the universal human experience that water cleanses.[62] See Figure 1 for the visual depiction of this relationship.

Another example of an analogical parallel, this time observed *within the same tradition*, is that of the moral categories "light" and "darkness" that are found in the Gospel of John and some Qumran documents (e.g., John 1:5, 3:19–21, 12:35–36; cf. 1 John 1:5, 7, 2:8–10; 1QM I, 1, XIII, 5–7; 1QS III, 19–25).[63] The words are common and are used as dualistic categories in other religions (cf. the "yin and yang" of Chinese philosophy and religion). Rather than positing that a dependent relationship exists between John and the Qumran community (a *genealogical* parallel), the striking resemblance is better chalked up as

---

[60] Donaldson, "Parallels," 200.
[61] Donaldson, "Parallels," 200.
[62] I owe this example to Donaldson, "Parallels," 199.
[63] Cf. Donaldson, "Parallels," 204.

an *analogical* parallel, deriving from the universal human experience of light and darkness.

A visual depiction may help to illuminate the similarities and differences between quotation, allusion, echo, and parallel at this point:[64]

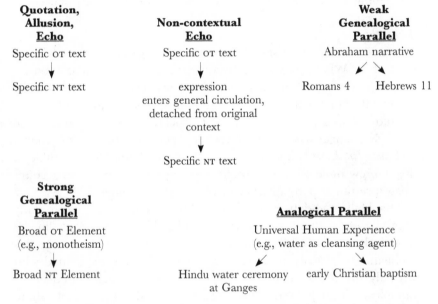

Figure 1. Similarities and differences between quotation, allusion, echo (contextual and non-contextual), and strong, weak, and analogical parallel.

Criteria for Determining the Existence of an Allusion

The necessity of a strict methodology in determining the existence of an allusion has already been discussed above. To move forward properly, a methodology based upon observable data is needed. Such a methodology is introduced below and will be employed consistently and explicitly throughout the study.

---

[64] The visual chart is borrowed in part from Altick, *The Art of Literary Research*, 112. However, I have modified his model to fit both my more incisive definitions and my topic.

First Tier of Evidence: Essential Criteria

The following three criteria must be met if a proposed *allusion* is to
be verified as genuine. Following these three criteria of the first tier of
evidence are five observations of a second tier, which offer some aid in
confirming an allusion that has successfully passed the first tier.

Availability

The methodology must start here. Was the alleged source available to
the author? What is the scholarly consensus on the date of the source,
and what is it for the alluding text? Does the alleged source historically
precede the latter text? This question is much more important for OT in
OT study (as well as for the search of Gospel tradition in the rest of the
NT). Lyle Eslinger has criticized Michael Fishbane's *Biblical Interpretation
in Ancient Israel*, a work that studies the re-use of the Hebrew Bible in
the Hebrew Bible, for not sufficiently taking this question into account
when asserting a particular vector of literary dependence.[65]

Thankfully, the dating question does not plague OT in the NT study
generally or its study in Paul in particular. Hays writes that "in the
case of Paul's use of Scripture, we rarely have to worry about this
problem. His practice of citation shows that he was acquainted with
virtually the whole body of texts that were later acknowledged as
canonical within Judaism, and that he expected his readers to share
his acknowledgment of these texts as Scripture."[66] This is the working
position assumed throughout the present study (although it is unclear
as to whether Paul considered the books of Esther, Song of Songs, or
Ecclesiastes as Scripture).[67] This working assumption is not, however,
necessarily my *reader's* position. In every chapter, therefore, quotation
evidence will be presented from the apostle's other letters that demonstrate his familiarity with the particular work in question and his
regard for it as Scripture.

Altick grounds the availability criterion upon the question of whether
the author had *read* the book in question.[68] The question is readily

---

[65] Lyle Eslinger, "Inner-Biblical Exegesis and Inner-Biblical Allusion: The Question
of Category," *VT* 42 (1992): 48–56. See, however, the excellent response to Eslinger
by Benjamin D. Sommer, "Exegesis, Allusion and Intertextuality in the Hebrew Bible:
A Response to Lyle Eslinger," *VT* 46 (1996): 479–89.

[66] Hays, *Echoes of Scripture in the Letters of Paul*, 29–30.

[67] These works appear to have been considered "on the fringe" by at least some Jewish
experts of the law in the first century C.E. (James A. Sanders, "Canon," *ABD* 1:840).

[68] Altick, *The Art of Literary Research*, 115.

answered in Paul's case. Born a Hebrew of Hebrew parentage, trained as a Pharisee in Judaism, and zealous for his ancestral traditions (Gal 1:13–14; Phil 3:4–6), Paul would have read, studied, and memorized Scripture.[69] It was the air he breathed, the food he ate, the essence he bled. No other corpus saturated Paul's mind more than the sacred Scriptures of Israel.

Word Agreement or Rare Concept Similarity

For a proposed allusion to be validated as authentic, it must meet one or the other aspect of this requirement. Does the proposed allusion share identical words with the alleged source text? The rarer the words are that are held in common, the more likelihood that a relationship exists. Ordinary words ought to be considered suspect and judged unintentional unless strong reasons indicate otherwise. Furthermore, the greater the number of words shared by the two texts, the greater the likelihood that a genuine relationship exists. Nevertheless, even single words can be allusions to a prior text if they are rare and prominent enough. Moreover, the span of text must also be taken into account. "The more shared vocabulary there is within a shorter span of text the more likely that influence is in fact present."[70]

Nevertheless, a proposed allusion can also fulfill this second criterion if both texts have a "rare concept" in common. Miner writes that "although poetic [allusion] is necessarily manifested in words, what it draws on in another work need not be verbal. The words of the alluding passage may establish a conceptual rather than a verbal connection with the passage or work alluded to."[71] For example, we will later propose that Col 2:11 is a look back to Deut 30:6, even though Col 2:11 and Deut 30:6 do not have any actual words in common. Nevertheless, the rare concept of a divinely wrought circumcision is shared by both texts. This example also raises the importance of checking versional differences, for in this case Col 2:11 is closer to the Hebrew of Deut 30:6 than to the LXX.

It is also possible that a proposed allusion could meet this criterion by combining components of both requirements—word agreement as well as that of rare concept. Yet all this said, a proposed allusion may still disqualify *as an allusion* if it fails to meet the third criterion below.

---

[69] See the discussion of Paul's education on pp. 258–260 of this study.

[70] Matthew S. Harmon, "The Influence of Isaiah 40–66 in Galatians" (Ph.D. diss. proposal, Wheaton College Graduate School, Wheaton, Illinois, 2004), 8.

[71] Miner, "Allusion," 39 col. 1.

Essential Interpretive Link

The reader will recall at this point our discussion concerning the definition of allusion. Fundamental to allusion is that the alluding text depends upon the parent text for its marker to be understood fully. The author *intends* for the reader to recognize the marker, remember the original context, and connect one or more aspects of the predecessor to the new context in order for the latter to be understood. *This interpretive link is fundamental to allusion and distinguishes it from echo.*

The recognition of this "essential interpretive link" is a phenomenon that scholars can observe and verify as to whether it exists for any proposed allusion. Does the alleged source have a component that, when brought forward to the alluding text, unlocks the riddle of the alluding text? If it does not, then the proposed source fails to meet this criterion and the proposed allusion is disqualified in the case of that particular source. Another text may yet qualify as the source text, and so the search may continue. Or the proposed allusion is in fact an echo or merely a parallel, and requires reconsideration under those categories.

The following example illustrates this criterion for allusion. In 2 Kgs 9, the prophet Elisha sends a servant to anoint Jehu as king over Israel (9:1–6). The servant relays YHWH's message to Jehu that he is to strike down the entire dynasty of the apostate king Ahab, including his infamous wife Jezebel (9:7–10). Jehu therefore rallies his compatriots and proceeds to Jezreel. There he shoots down Joram, king of Israel and son of Ahab (9:11–26) as well as Ahaziah, king of Judah (9:27–29). Jehu then advances to the residence of Jezebel to kill her (9:30–31). As Jehu enters the gate of her terrace, Jezebel calls down to him through the window, "Is it peace, Zimri, murderer of his lord?"[72]

Yet Jezebel's greeting of Jehu has left us with a puzzle to solve. Why does Jezebel call Jehu by the name of "Zimri"? He is called that nowhere else in any text that concerns him, and thus Zimri is neither a throne- nor a nick-name. His father's name was not Zimri but Jehoshaphat, himself the son of Nimshi (2 Kgs 9:2). The riddle remains and leaves us without a full understanding of the text.[73]

---

[72] The translation is mine.

[73] Due to contextual clues, we do grasp a partial understanding of the text (what Perri calls the "un-allusive" sense ["On Alluding," 295]). "Zimri" is someone who committed treason and murdered his master. Nevertheless, we are still left scratching our heads. Who exactly is "Zimri"? We are still left without a full understanding of Jezebel's *intended* communication.

A concordance search upon the name Zimri reveals a concentration of the use of the name earlier in 1 Kgs 16:8–20. Turning there, we find a narrative about one Zimri, a military commander over half the chariot regiment of Elah, king of Israel and son of the apostate Baasha. Zimri, posing as a loyal compatriot, conspires against and murders Elah, his king, while his victim is drinking himself drunk (16:9–10). In the coup, Zimri usurps the throne and subsequently proceeds to destroy the entire dynasty of Baasha, in accordance with the word of God (16:11–14). Nevertheless, Zimri's reign is short-lived. He rules for seven days before the overwhelming pressure of a countercoup compels him to incinerate himself by burning his palace down upon his own head (16:15–20).

When we recognize "Zimri" as a marker to a previous text, realize that construal is required, recall the components of the predecessor required by the context of the new, and then connect them to the new context, suddenly our puzzle is solved and our text fully unlocked. By calling Jehu "Zimri," Jezebel alludes to a famous person and momentous event in the life of her country that took place roughly a half-century earlier.[74] Like Zimri before him, Jehu, also a captain in the army of the king of Israel, has arisen, conspired against, and killed his own king in a coup. The "essential interpretive link" that unlocks the allusion embedded in our text has been discovered, and is in this way also verified as an allusion.

There is more. Recall that Perri wrote that contemplation of the linked texts could "activate further meaning patterns between them."[75] That is, further reflection may suggest that other aspects of the two texts may be properly connected that are neither explicit nor essential to understanding, but nevertheless offer an even fuller meaning when recognized and linked. In the case of 2 Kgs 9:31, Jezebel almost certainly intended her words as an insult to degrade Jehu. The reader will recall the second half of her statement, "Zimri, *murderer of his lord*," as confirmation of this interpretation. It will also be recalled that Zimri's reign lasted all of seven days, ending in a horrific death. The allusion further suggests that contempt and mockery lie behind Jezebel's words.

---

[74] Zimri probably reigned in 885 or 884 B.C.E., while Jehu confronted Jezebel in 841 B.C.E. See Edwin R. Thiele, *The Mysterious Numbers of the Hebrew Kings* (rev. ed.; Grand Rapids: Eerdmans, 1965), 62–63 (for Zimri); 67 (for Jehu).

[75] Perri, "On Alluding," 296.

By metalepsis she expresses her hope that Jehu's reign will be violently and abruptly terminated just as Zimri's reign was terminated.

The above example demonstrates the central role that the "essential interpretive link" plays in allusion. Without it, one is without the key that unlocks the full meaning of the alluding text.

Second Tier of Evidence: Confirmatory Observations

The three criteria within the first tier of evidence must be met for a proposed allusion to be verified as genuine. Offered here in this section is a second tier of evidence that offers help to confirm or support the findings that have met the three criteria of the first tier. These are supplemental in character, and are of limited help in some instances.

Scholarly Assessment

Have other scholars observed the proposed allusion? If so, what are their remarks concerning it? Did they classify it as an example of quotation, allusion, echo, parallel, or something comparable to our categories listed above? A long history of biblical scholarship exists upon every book of the Bible, and to ignore the work of previous scholars would be both arrogant and hazardous at best. The study will be careful to take into consideration what others have said about every passage proposed. This check offers confirmatory support if other scholars have also detected the allusion. Yet it also provides a note of caution if no one has observed the proposed allusion heretofore. This would not necessarily mean that the allusion is not there (it may well be), but this benchmark serves as a hedge against error and forces the scholar to reconsider the strength of the proposed allusion.

Old Testament and Jewish Interpretive Tradition

Does the proposed OT text already have a history of interpretive tradition within later OT books, as well as within early and late Judaism? If so, does it shed light upon whether the NT text is an allusion?[76] Many OT

---

[76] Craig Evans's main critique of Hays's *Echoes of Scripture in the Letters of Paul* concerns this area. For example, Evans argues that Hays's reading of Deut 30:12–14 in Rom 10:5–10 is a good start but fails to take into consideration that Jewish exegetes had already studied Deut 30:12–14 before Paul's day and offered interpretations that shed light on what Paul had done with the same text. Evans offers Bar 3:29–30 and the Targum of Deuteronomy as examples of this for Rom 10. He writes "...the echo that we hear in Romans 10 is made up of Scripture *and its exegesis* in late antiquity. It

texts resurface later in subsequent OT books and in the extant writings of early Judaism. These examples of later exegesis offer a trajectory of interpretative tradition that may corroborate a proposed NT allusion and the way it employs the prior OT text. Paul's use, for example, may be more in line with the interpretive tradition than with the OT text itself. Paul may also make his point over against the accepted interpretive tradition of a given OT text.

In the following study, priority will be given to the early Jewish literature: the OT pseudepigraphical writings, the Dead Sea Scrolls, the Apocrypha (or deutero-canonical literature), Josephus, and Philo, most (but not all) of which was written prior to 70 C.E. The later Jewish literature—the Targums, Mishnah, the rabbinic commentaries, etc.—will be checked to see if their interpretive trajectories of the OT texts in question illuminate our study. Although most of them do contain traditions that predate the destruction of the temple, the later Jewish literature was written after 70 C.E. and is consequently less relevant to NT study than the early Jewish literature.

Other Verified References from the same OT Context in Colossians
Are there other allusions or echoes from the same OT context in the letter, whose probability has already been established? If so, this increases the chance that Paul has pulled another reference from that same OT section. This criterion is especially useful for authenticating new allusions that have previously gone unnoticed.

Occurrence Elsewhere in the Pauline Corpus
Has Paul quoted, alluded to, or echoed the proposed OT passage in any of his other letters? Asking this question is helpful because *"when we find repeated Pauline quotations of* [and I would add, allusions to] *a particular OT passage, additional possible allusions to the same passage become more compelling."*[77] The deutero-Pauline letters are also to be included in such a check, because in their case a Pauline disciple would have attempted to imitate his master in thought and theology. The disciple

---

is for this reason that I think that it would be more accurate to speak of the echoes of interpreted Scripture in the letters of Paul" (Craig A. Evans, "Listening for Echoes of Interpreted Scripture," in *Paul and the Scriptures of Israel* (eds. Craig A. Evans and James A. Sanders; JSNTSup 83; Sheffield: JSOT Press, 1993), 49–50). Hays embraces the criticism and builds upon it. See Hays, "On the Rebound," 70–75.

[77] Hays, *The Conversion of the Imagination*, 37 (emphasis his).

would have known Paul's thought well, including his favorite texts of Scripture, both broadly (e.g., Isa 40–54) and specifically (e.g., Hab 2:4; see Gal 3:11; Rom 1:17). The letter to the Ephesians is to be carefully checked due to its particularly close relationship with the letter to the Colossians.

Thematic Coherence

Richard Hays offers this as one of his seven criteria for the detection and verification of an echo.[78] I rather see it as a confirmatory criterion and want to combine it with a little of what Hays discusses under another criterion, "satisfaction."[79] My thematic coherence criterion asks, with Hays, "How well does the alleged [allusion] fit into the line of argument that Paul is developing?...Do the images and ideas of the proposed precursor text illuminate Paul's argument?" "Does the proposed reading make sense? Does it illuminate the surrounding discourse?"[80] Does it "fit"?

Criteria for Determining the Existence of an Echo

We separate the criteria for determining an echo from that of allusion to reiterate that the two are quite different in nature, while having similarities. If a proposed allusion has failed to pass the criteria of the first tier, the proposed text may still be tested to see if it qualifies as an echo. A proposed echo will be put through the first tier of criteria for allusion, but need not meet criterion three, *essential interpretive link*. This is because an echo is not an author's public attempt to point an audience to a prior text. It will be remembered that if the author's attempt to allude fails, then the alluding text will not be fully understood.[81] An echo is neither a public act nor a reference that is dependent upon its predecessor for its meaning. Often a reader will miss an echo; nevertheless, he or she can still make more sense of an echoing text than when one fails to recognize an allusion.

If an echo passes the (now truncated) first tier of criteria, it must then be put through the second tier. The second tier is important for

---

[78] Hays, *Echoes of Scripture in the Letters of Paul*, 30.

[79] *Echoes of Scripture in the Letters of Paul*, 31–32.

[80] *Echoes of Scripture in the Letters of Paul*, 31–32.

[81] Though again we repeat that a partial understanding of the author's intended meaning can usually be pieced together due to embedded clues in the immediate context.

confirming an echo, since echoes are by nature subtle. Nevertheless, an echo may be genuine even if none of the second tier's observations apply. The second tier is an aid, but is limited in its applicability.

At this point we affirm that there is an element of intuition and judgment in the detection and verification of echo. Such is the nature of this type of investigation, that it is both art as well as science.[82] The scholar looking for an airtight, mechanical methodology that churns out all the right answers will not find one, for it does not exist. Even textual criticism, an approach governed by numerous and well-established rules, is yet both an art and a science. We submit that an ear well-attuned to the Scriptures of Israel may pick up echoes that the less-attuned ear will not, and while there needs to be a constant care and caution in positing echoes, we need not shy away from presenting what we hear, that is, what we think an author has done, in the text. A worthy goal, therefore, for interpreters to pursue in this area of study is to become like Paul and become saturated with the sacred Scriptures of Israel. In this way our ears can become better attuned to overhear Paul's allusions and echoes.

Classification

Each text to be studied will, at the beginning of its investigation, be placed side-by-side with its OT text in a chart for convenience. The chapter title and first sentence of each chapter will identify for the reader the conclusion as to what type of reference the text is, whether it is an allusion or echo. This study will not be investigating parallels of any sort. Moreover, the reader will notice that we have omitted the category of quotation, because we have already concluded (on account of our definitions demarcated above) that there are no instances of quotation in the letter to the Colossians. Even though there are no quotations of the OT in Colossians and this study will not be studying parallels, to have defined "quotation" and "parallel" is exceptionally helpful because it increases the reader's knowledge base and thereby

---

[82] Hays, *Echoes of Scripture in the Letters of Paul*, 29, writes that "we must reckon with varying degrees of certainty in our efforts to identify and interpret intertextual echoes. Sometimes the echo will be so loud that only the dullest or most ignorant reader could miss it...other times there will be room for serious differences of opinion.... Precision in such judgment calls is unattainable, because exegesis is a modest imaginative craft, not an exact science." Cf. Sommer, "Exegesis, Allusion and Intertextuality," 485–86.

provides a relief for a better understanding of what constitutes an allusion and an echo.

Methodological Approach for Interpreting the Old Testament in the Letter to the Colossians

Once we have verified a proposed allusion or echo as probable, the investigation then proceeds to the second major methodology of investigation. We want not only to detect and verify the proposed allusion or echo that Paul may have embedded in the text, but also we want to investigate what Paul has done by the use of such literary modes of reference. What is the meaning of the text in light of the verified allusion or echo? What ripples does the predecessor make in the new? What new figuration has Paul created in alluding to or echoing the past text? To unravel this, each verified allusion or echo will be put through the following six steps.

Exegesis of the Old Testament Passage Alluded to or Echoed in both its Broad and Immediate Context

This step is imperative for allusion, but it is also crucial for echo to see if there are, to borrow Hays's words again, any "whispered or unstated correspondences." Here we bring to bear all the relevant methods, sources and tools for carrying out an adequate exegesis of the referenced passage in the OT. The exegesis will not be conducted merely on the MT, but both the MT and the LXX will be carefully investigated and given due weight, with differences duly noted. The exegesis will be based upon the texts of the standard critical editions. The *BHS* will be used for the Masoretic text-form. For the LXX text-form, the Göttingen or, if the book in question is not yet available in that series, the Larger Cambridge edition will be employed. If the book in question is also not in the Cambridge edition, Rahlfs's edition will be used. All significant variant readings from the critical apparatuses will be assimilated into the discussion.

A key find that the Qumran scroll discoveries revealed is that the biblical text was in a fluid state in Paul's day. While there were certainly at least two text-forms available (the proto-MT and the proto-LXX),[83] the

---

[83] Some scholars may want to add the proto-Samaritan Pentateuch as a third text-form that was available in Paul's day. It is probably better, however, to view it

Qumran evidence has suggested to some that there were others circulating in the environs in the mid-first century C.E.[84] Because of this situation, the Qumran biblical texts will also be checked for possible variant readings that may have existed within Paul's lifetime.[85] The OT quotations within the OT pseudepigraphical literature, Josephus, Philo, and elsewhere in the NT will also be carefully checked for possible relevant biblical variants.

Because the OT quotation data embedded in his letters so often mirrors the LXX, scholars concur that Paul was well acquainted with the (proto-) LXX text-form family. This study will also work on the reasonable assumption that Paul knew Hebrew and was probably familiar with at least one witness from the proto-MT text-form family.[86] By the end of the first or beginning of the second century C.E., most scholars believe that the proto-MT text-form had become the standard and "official" text for the Jews of Palestine.[87]

---

as a witness of the proto-MT family. The Qumran discoveries demonstrated that "the Sam. Pent. was based on one of the so-called proto-Masoretic texts" (Emanuel Tov, "Textual Criticism," *ABD* 6:406; cf. Bruce K. Waltke, "Samaritan Pentateuch," *ABD* 5:932–38).

[84] E.g., Tov, "Textual Criticism," 6:396 (Tov, however, does not believe it is accurate to label these as different text-forms but merely as "texts" [6:404]); Martin Jan Mulder, "The Transmission of the Biblical Text," in *Mikra: Text, Translation, Reading, and Interpretation of the Hebrew Bible in Ancient Judaism and Early Christianity* (ed. M. J. Mulder; CRINT 2.1; Assen/Maastricht: Van Gorcum, 1988), 96–99.

[85] To get at the relevant biblical DSS material, Washburn's catalogue is employed to navigate the DJD series (David L. Washburn, *A Catalog of Biblical Passages in the Dead Sea Scrolls* [SBL Text-Critical Studies 2; Atlanta: SBL, 2002]).

[86] According to the tally by Silva (M. Silva, "Old Testament in Paul," *DPL* 631), of Paul's 107 OT quotations (Silva includes six from the so-called deutero-Pauline letters), 42 agree with both the LXX and the MT, 31 do not follow either the LXX or the MT, 17 agree with the LXX against the MT, and 7 agree with the MT against the LXX (Silva also offers 10 that are debated). Cf. the catalogue of Paul's quotations by E. E. Ellis, *Paul's Use of the Old Testament* (Grand Rapids: Eerdmans, 1957), 11–12. That even just seven (Ellis catalogs four) of Paul's quotations agree with the MT against the LXX suggests that the apostle knew at least sections of the proto-MT text-form that existed in his day in Hebrew. In my final chapter, I discuss Paul's education and defend the thesis further that Paul probably did know Hebrew, had studied his Hebrew Bible, and had sections of it memorized (pp. 258–260). If I have overheard it rightly, the echo of MT Deut 30:6 in Col 2:11, discussed in chapter nine of this study, offers some further support to this thesis. In light of the quotation data above, it goes without saying that Paul had possessed a competent knowledge of the proto-LXX text-form that had been available to him.

[87] Tov, "Textual Criticism," 6:396; Cf. Karen H. Jobes and Moisés Silva, *Invitation to the Septuagint* (Grand Rapids: Baker Academic, 2000), 38:

The recently discovered Dead Sea Scrolls provide indisputable evidence that at the turn of the era, before the birth of Christianity, the text of at least some books of

Investigation of the Interpretive Tradition of the Old Testament Text

Here we will ask how later interpreters understood the OT text in question. Did the OT text resurface again in later OT tradition? Is the text itself already part of an OT interpretive tradition? With this question, the investigation will have to be careful to check dating of material to verify the vector of literary dependence. How did later interpreters within both early and late Judaism understand the text? What kind of continuity or discontinuity with Judaism does Paul's use express? Do any of these findings shed light upon Paul's use of the same text?

Comparison of the Versions and Analysis of Paul's Textual Use

The relevant versions (including any important text variants) will be compared by being placed side-by-side in a chart. This will always include the NT, the LXX, and the MT, and may also at times include any relevant Jewish tradition (e.g., the Targums, DSS, OT pseudepigraphical literature).[88] Words that recur verbatim will be underlined and words that recur as a synonym or are similar conceptually will be underlined with a broken dash. Here the probable text-form upon which Paul appears to be dependent will be stated, or a discussion will be given in light of a free rendering (see also appendix three on p. 275 of this study). How these aspects bear upon the interpretation of the text will also be discussed, when applicable.

Exegesis of the Appropriate Text in Colossians

The study will pay special attention to the way the alluded or echoed OT text is employed in the immediate context of Colossians. Here we bring to bear all the relevant methods, sources, and tools necessary for carrying out an adequate exegesis of the appropriate passage in Paul's letter to the Colossians.

---

the Hebrew Bible circulated in more than one form. One of these textual forms [i.e., the proto-MT], however, emerged as *the* standard text by the beginning of the second century C.E., apparently supplanting all previous Hebrew texts.

[88] Again, to get at the relevant DSS biblical texts, Washburn's work is employed (see n.85 above). To get at any possible relevant biblical quotations within the pseudepigraphical writings, Delamarter's catalogue is employed (Steve Delamarter, *A Scripture Index to Charlesworth's The Old Testament Pseudepigrapha* [London: Sheffield Academic Press, 2002]). The OT quotations within Josephus, Philo, and elsewhere in the NT are also carefully checked for possible relevant biblical variants.

We must at the same time situate the text in its broad literary context. What has Paul said in the previous paragraph? What has Paul argued up to this point in the letter as a whole? What follows in the next paragraph? What does Paul state in the remaining portions of the letter?

Examination of the other Uses of the same OT Text Elsewhere in the NT as well as in the Early Church Fathers

Have other NT authors understood the OT text in the same way? Have they employed it for a different purpose? Have any early church fathers employed it and how (by "early," this study means the fathers up through the third century C.E.)? How does Paul's understanding of the OT relate to that of the second and third century's perspective on the same texts? Is there continuity or discontinuity? How so? Do any of these findings shed light upon Paul's use in Colossians?

Analysis of Paul's Hermeneutical Use of the OT

Has Paul alluded to the OT text to indicate a prophetic fulfillment? Does he see a historical correspondence or typological fulfillment?[89] Has he drawn an analogy? Is there a realization of an OT ideal? Or has he merely employed the language of the OT predecessor rhetorically, without having the context in mind at all? Since echo, in contrast to allusion, can occasionally be an unconscious activity, therefore "use" may be too strong a word to describe what Paul has done when he has echoed a previous text. We can still ask in light of an echo, however, what presuppositions (if any) of Paul undergird and are revealed in

---

[89] Space limitations forbid a detailed discussion of typology. This study borrows Baker's definition of typology, described as "a biblical event, person, or institution which serves as an example or pattern for other events, persons, or institutions" (David L. Baker, "Typology and the Christian Use of the Old Testament," in *The Right Doctrine from the Wrong Texts?: Essays on the Use of the Old Testament in the New* (ed. G. K. Beale; Grand Rapids: Baker, 1994), 327; repr. from *SJT* 29 [1976]). According to Baker, typology is neither an exegetical method nor allegory, but "a way of understanding history" based upon the conviction that "God is consistently active in the history of the world (especially in the history of his chosen people) and that as a consequence the events in the history tend to follow a consistent pattern" (324, 327). Leonhard Goppelt, *Typos: The Typological Interpretation of the Old Testament in the New* (trans. Donald H. Madvig; Grand Rapids: Eerdmans, 1982), 18, further insists that a type's antitype must be a "heightening of the type," and must be "greater and more complete."

his echoing activity. How Paul echoes a text may reveal fundamental presuppositions of how the apostle understood that text or concept in light of the Christ-event.[90]

Conclusion

Though source study has had to endure abuse in the past, there is no reason to abandon the enterprise. With clear definitions of key terms and the employment of a sound method, the investigation can avoid the peril and realize the promise of such study.

In summary, this work will take an author-oriented approach to literary-source investigation. The purpose is to "orient one's discussion to the language of the author" in order to try to overhear any allusions and echoes of Scripture in Paul's letter to the Colossians. The key terms quotation, allusion, and echo have been defined and contrasted with the categories of strong, weak, and analogical parallel. A methodological approach for verifying allusions and echoes has been set forth in two tiers, one essential and the other supplemental in nature.

Once a proposed allusion or echo has qualified as probable, it will be put through a second methodological approach. This second methodological approach is employed to interpret the "use" of the OT text in Paul's letter to the Colossians. The investigation seeks ultimately to answer the question of what Paul has done with the Scriptures of Israel in his letter to the church in Colossae.

---

[90] Cf. Hays, *Conversion of the Imagination*, 12, where he writes that his investigation of Paul's echoes in 1 Cor 10 has uncovered "the hermeneutical assumptions that govern Paul's references to Scripture throughout the letter." For his study of the OT echoes in 1 Cor 10, see pp. 8–12 of *Conversion of the Imagination*.

CHAPTER THREE

THE SCRIPTURES OF ISRAEL IN COLOSSIANS 1:3–8: THE ECHO OF GENESIS 1:28 IN 1:6

Comparison of Textual Versions and Evaluation

Genesis 1:28 MT	Genesis 1:28 LXX	Colossians 1:6
פְּרוּ וּרְבוּ וּמִלְאוּ אֶת־הָאָרֶץ	αὐξάνεσθε καὶ πληθύνεσθε καὶ πληρώσατε τὴν γῆν	καρποφορούμενον καὶ αὐξανόμενον ἐν παντὶ τῷ κόσμῳ

This proposal meets the two criteria necessary for echo: 1) availability, and 2) word agreement and/or rare concept similarity. Regarding *availability*, Genesis 1–3 was certainly known and read by Paul.[1] Regarding *word agreement or rare concept similarity*, the two texts share both a verbal as well as a conceptual agreement. The texts share two words verbatim (αὐξάνω; καί) and two that are synonymous: the verb פרה ("to bear fruit, be fruitful"), translated with πληθύνω ("to multiply") in the LXX, is semantically equivalent to καρποφορέω ("to bear fruit"), and likewise Paul's use of κόσμος at 1:6 covers the same ground as the LXX γῆ. The two texts also share a verbal hendiadys that accentuates the theme of worldwide increase and expansion via imagery of botanical growth.[2]

---

[1] See, e.g., Rom 5:14; 1 Cor 11:7–9; 15:45; 2 Cor 4:6, 11:3; cf. Col 3:10.

[2] Some scholars have already argued for this echo: Ralph Martin, *Colossians and Philemon* (rev. ed.; New Century Bible; London: Oliphants, 1978), 49; O'Brien, *Colossians*, 13; N. T. Wright, *Colossians and Philemon* (TNTC; Grand Rapids: Eerdmans, 1986), 53–54, 59; Beale, "Colossians," ad loc.; Schweizer, *Colossians*, 36–37, ponders it as a possibility, stating that "the phrase could be influenced by the usage in Gen 1:22, 28 etc....although there admittedly it is not metaphorical."

Others have acknowledged the similarity of phraseology with Gen 1:28 but do not necessarily view it as an echo or allusion: Josef Ernst, *Die Briefe an die Philipper, an Philemon, an die Kolosser, an die Epheser* (RNT; Regensburg: Pustet, 1974), 158; Ernst Lohmeyer, *Die Briefe an die Philipper, Kolosser und an Philemon* (KEK; Göttingen: Vandenhoeck & Ruprecht, 1964), 27n.4; Eduard Lohse, *Colossians and Philemon* (trans. William R. Poehlmann and Robert J. Karris; Hermeneia; Philadelphia: Fortress, 1971), 19–20 (and n.60); Roy Yates, *The Epistle to the Colossians* (Epworth; London: Epworth, 1993),

Old Testament Context: Genesis 1:24–31

Genesis 1 continues to remain one of the most intimidating texts a biblical exegete could face. This study can only touch upon the absolute necessities important for the study at hand. While the chapter is familiar, a chart may yet help to summarize God's activity in the chapter and provide some context and orientation:

First Day:	Creation of Light: "Day" and "Night"	(vv. 3–5)
Second Day:	Creation of the Heavens	(vv. 6–8)
Third Day:	Creation of Seas and Land, Vegetation and Trees	(vv. 9–13)
Fourth Day:	Creation of the Sun and Moon	(vv. 14–19)
Fifth Day:	Creation of Sea Creatures and Birds	(vv. 20–23)
Sixth Day:	**Creation of Land Animals and Man**	**(vv. 24–31)**
Seventh Day:	The Sabbath Rest of God	(vv. 2:1–3)

The chapter has been intentionally structured to highlight the sixth day as the climactic finale of God's creating activity, with humanity as the pinnacle of his work. The purpose of the chapter is to shape worldview with regard to humanity's place with respect to the one God, as well as to the animal world and the rest of creation. It provides the purpose for the existence of humanity: to fill the earth with God's benevolent rule over the rest of the created order as his representative or vicegerent.[3]

At 1:24, God begins his sixth day of work. As in the previous verses of the chapter, God speaks creation into existence. He commands the earth to "bring forth" all kinds of living creatures to live on the land, and so it does (1:24b). The magnitude of power displayed and the perfection of the created result is understated as God looks over what he has made and declares it "good" (1:25b).

7; Barth and Blanke, *Colossians*, 158n.29; J. D. G. Dunn, *The Epistles to the Colossians and to Philemon* (NIGTC; Grand Rapids: Eerdmans, 1996), 62n.12.

[3] For defense of this interpretation, see the exegesis in chapter thirteen.

Having created the land animals, God next wills to create man "in our image, as our likeness" (1:26). Here for the first time he states his intention in the plural ("Let *us* make"). A definite structure frames the section of vv. 26–28 and provides insight into its central concern:

A. "Let us make man in our image, as our likeness"
    B. *Given to rule* over the fish, birds, animals, creeping creatures: "all the earth"
A¹. God *created* (a) man (b) in his *image* (c) in the *image* of God (c¹) he *created* (a¹) him (b¹) male and female (b²) he *created* (a²) them (b³)
    B¹. *Given to rule* over the fish, birds, and every creature creeping on the earth

Though the interpretive options of the phrase "the image of God" are many,[4] the immediate context is clear that the *consequence* for humanity's creation in the image of God is that they are to fill the earth and rule over all the rest of creation as God's representative or vicegerent (cf. Ps 8). Moreover, God also commands *the way* in which humanity is to fill the earth for dominion. In language reminiscent of the fruit-bearing trees of Gen 1:11, 29,[5] humanity is to "bear fruit/be fruitful and multiply" (פְּרוּ וּרְבוּ; LXX: αὐξάνεσθε καὶ πληθύνεσθε). Thus procreation becomes the ordained means for the fulfillment of the mandate. This outcome of filling the earth with human progeny is assured because God endues them with the power to complete their task (he "blessed them"; cf. v. 22).[6]

God truly exalted "man" by making him "in the image of God." Humanity nevertheless remains creature and therefore dependent upon the Creator for what is needed to fulfill the mandate. The text at vv. 29–31 demonstrates that God has already made provision for humanity to carry out their commission successfully. God has given all vegetation and fruit to them for nourishment. This greenery covers "all the earth," so that as humanity spreads out in ever-increasing circles, there will

---

[4] For the interpretive options with reference to the "image," see Claus Westermann, *Genesis 1–11: A Commentary* (trans. John J. Scullion; Minneapolis: Augsburg, 1984), 147–55.

[5] Gen 1:11: עֵץ פְּרִי עֹשֶׂה פְּרִי; LXX: ξύλον κάρπιμον ποιοῦν καρπόν ("fruit-bearing trees producing fruit"); Gen 1:29: פְּרִי־עֵץ זֹרֵעַ זֶרַע ("fruit trees yielding seed").

[6] See *HALOT*, "ברך II," (piel).

always be provision for them to fulfill the mandate. With humanity in place as the "image of God," with the mandate given and the provision for its completion in place, creation is complete and now declared "exceedingly good" (v. 31).

"Be Fruitful and Multiply": the Interpretive Tradition in the OT

The mandate given to humanity in Genesis 1:28 to "be fruitful and multiply" is reiterated at several key junctures in the Genesis narrative and beyond. Whatever editing has taken place, the theme weaves like a thread through the final edition by intentional design:[7]

God to Noah and his sons:

Gen 9:1: God blessed Noah and his sons, and said to them, "Be fruitful and multiply, [פְּרוּ וּרְבוּ; LXX: αὐξάνεσθε καὶ πληθύνεσθε] and fill the earth."[8]

God to Abraham:

Gen 17:2, 6: "And I will make my covenant between me and you, and will make you exceedingly numerous [רבה; LXX: πληθυνῶ]....I will make you exceedingly fruitful [פרה; LXX: αὐξανῶ]; and I will make nations of you, and kings shall come from you."[9]

---

[7] Upon the completion of this chapter, I came across the work of Jeremy Cohen, *"Be Fertile and Increase, Fill the Earth and Master It": the Ancient and Medieval Career of a Biblical Text* (Ithaca: Cornell University Press, 1989), 25–35, who likewise had observed that the "be fruitful and multiply" hendiadys is intentionally picked up in the passages that follow. Cohen writes, "Echoes of Gen 1:28 extend throughout the Hebrew Bible and are hardly confined to its opening chapter" (25).

[8] Cohen, *Be Fertile and Increase*, 25: "Once again God blesses the first humans of a cosmic epoch with fertility and dominion, using the terminology of Gen 1:28 to denote procreation."

[9] Cohen, *Be Fertile and Increase*, 28: "As the narrative of Genesis emerges from its primeval history and focuses on Abraham and his Israelite descendants, the blessing of "be fertile and increase" [from Gen 1:28] continues to reappear.

Midr. Tanhuma Genesis 35:9ff., Part III quotes Gen 17:1 and reads, "I am God Almighty; be fruitful and multiply," making the connection between Gen 1:28 and Abraham even more explicit.

God concerning Ishmael:

Gen 17:20: "As for Ishmael, I have heard you; I will bless him and make him fruitful and exceedingly numerous [פרה and רבה; LXX: αὐξανῶ αὐτὸν καὶ πληθυνῶ]."

God to Isaac:

Gen 26:22, 24: "Now the LORD has made room for us, and we shall be fruitful [פרה; LXX: ηὔξησεν] in the land."... [and the LORD said], "I am with you and will bless you and make your offspring numerous [רבה; LXX: πληθυνῶ] for my servant Abraham's sake."

Isaac to Jacob:

Gen 28:3: "May God Almighty bless you and make you fruitful and numerous [פרה and רבה; LXX: αὐξήσαι σε καὶ πληθῦναι], that you may become a company of peoples."

God to Jacob:

Gen 35:11: God said to him, "I am God Almighty: be fruitful and multiply [פְּרֵה וּרְבֵה; LXX: αὐξάνου καὶ πληθύνου]; a nation and a company of nations shall come from you, and kings shall spring from you."[10]

With this reference, the Genesis mandate has been passed on in succession to each of the three patriarchs, Abraham, Isaac, and Jacob by God himself.

---

[10] Cohen, *Be Fruitful and Increase*, 30, penetratingly observes that "both these blessings of Jacob [i.e., Gen 28:3 and Gen 35:11] reiterate God's bequest of the land to Abraham in Gen 17, and like the commitments to Abraham and Ishmael, Gen 35:11 includes the promise of royal progeny—additional echoes of the conferral of dominion on the sixth day of creation [of Gen 1:26–28]."

The Hebrews in Egypt:

Gen 47:27: Thus Israel settled in the land of Egypt, in the region of Goshen; and they gained possessions in it, and were fruitful and multiplied exceedingly [וַיִּפְרוּ וַיִּרְבּוּ; LXX: ηὐξήθησαν καὶ ἐπληθύνθησαν].[11]

Here, the promise to the patriarchs has become initially realized.

Jacob recounts God's promise:

Gen 48:4: [God] said to me, "I am going to make you fruitful and increase your numbers [פרה and רבה; LXX: αὐξανῶ σε καὶ πληθυνῶ]; I will make of you a company of peoples...."[12]

The Hebrews in Egypt:

Exod 1:7: But the Israelites were fruitful and prolific; they multiplied [פָּרוּ....וַיִּרְבּוּ; LXX: ηὐξήθησαν καὶ ἐπληθύνθησαν] and grew exceedingly strong, so that the land was filled with them.[13]

The mandate to humanity, and its subsequent transformation to a promise made to the patriarchs, is reiterated here as initially realized in Egypt. Note also the language that "the land was filled with them" (וַתִּמָּלֵא הָאָרֶץ אֹתָם), which in light of the allusion to the Genesis 1:28 "be fruitful and multiply" tradition is almost certainly another allusion to Gen 1:28 and its "and fill the earth" (וּמִלְאוּ אֶת־הָאָרֶץ).[14]

---

[11] Cohen, *Be Fruitful and Increase*, 30: "The biblical narrator indicates (Gen 47:27) that God's promises to the patriarchs remain in force when Jacob moves his family to Egypt...."

[12] Cohen, *Be Fruitful and Increase*, 31: "Willing his special affinity with God to yet another generation, Jacob has here altered the language of Gen 35:11, to which he refers. But in quoting Jacob's own direct quotation of God's words to him, Scripture removes all doubt of the formulaic importance of Gen 1:28's key verbs; according to the narrative, the patriarchs themselves recognized their technical significance."

[13] Cohen, *Be Fruitful and Increase*, 31: "The progression of biblical history may have moved to a new book and altered its focus, but Scripture here reminds its readers that even in Egypt, years after the death of Jacob, Joseph, and their children, the divine commitment to Israel's forefathers stood firm."

[14] So too Cohen, *Be Fruitful and Increase*, 31: "It is interesting that the verb *šrz*, which here stands between *prh* and *rbh*, also appears in conjunction with them in Gen 8:17 and 9:7; and the verb for filling (*ml'*) the land recalls the language of Gen 1:28 and 9:1. As Bezalel Porten and Uriel Rappoport pointed out, the sequence of five verbs in Ex. 1:7 also reproduces the poetic rhythm of Gen 1:28."

God to his covenant people Israel:

Lev 26:9: "I will look with favor upon you and make you fruitful and multiply you [פרה and רבה; LXX: αὐξανῶ ὑμᾶς καὶ πληθυνῶ]; and I will maintain my covenant with you."[15]

God passes on the original mandate as a blessing conditioned upon Israel's obedience to the Mosaic covenant.

God to unfaithful Israel concerning the Time of her glorious Restoration from Babylonian exile:

1) Jer 3:16, 18: "And when you have multiplied and increased in the land [רבה and פרה; LXX: πληθυνθῆτε καὶ αὐξηθῆτε], in those days, says the LORD,...the house of Judah shall join the house of Israel, and together they shall come from the land of the north to the land that I gave your ancestors for a heritage."

2) Jer 23:3: "Then I myself will gather the remnant of my flock out of all the lands where I have driven them, and I will bring them back to their fold, and they shall be fruitful and multiply [וּפָרוּ וְרָבוּ; LXX: αὐξηθήσονται καὶ πληθυνθήσονται]."

This passage includes a promise of the Davidic messiah (vv. 5–6).

3) Ezek 36:11a: [God to the mountains of Israel] "I will multiply human beings and animals upon you. They shall increase and be fruitful [וּפָרוּ וְרָבוּ; LXX: omits; α' θ': καὶ αὐξηθήσονται καὶ πληθυνθήσονται]; and I will cause you to be inhabited as in your former times...."[16]

Paul almost certainly knew the creation mandate of Gen 1:28. It is also likely that he was aware of its subsequent repetitions elsewhere in Genesis and the OT. Paul may have held that the original creation mandate was passed on to Noah, then to Abraham and his descendants,[17]

---

[15] Cohen, *Be Fruitful and Increase*, 33, argues that this text itself "had constituted a reinterpretation of the blessings of Gen 1:28."

[16] Cohen, *Be Fruitful and Increase*, 32–33, argues that this text alludes to Lev 26:9, the text that I have listed above.

[17] See too N. T. Wright, *The Climax of the Covenant: Christ and the Law in Pauline Theology* (Minneapolis: Fortress, 1993), 21–23; Wright has also observed that the Adamic commission of Gen 1:28 is intentionally picked up throughout Genesis and into Exodus.

then to Israel as a promise at the time of her glorious restoration from exile (Jer 3:16, 23:3; Ezek 36:11). All of the above references describe a numerical growth of the people. Cohen agrees and yet argues further that the repetitions of Gen 1:28 "assume an additional function: Comprising the divine blessing of humans par excellence, they become a metaphor, a formularized guarantee of divine protection, divine election, and the divine covenant. No wonder the blessing of *prh/rbh* is repeated for Noah, Abraham, Isaac and Ishmael, Jacob, Joseph and his sons, the children of Israel in Egypt, and those who would ultimately enjoy the future redemption...."[18]

The Genesis 1:28 Tradition in Early and Late Judaism

The "be fruitful and multiply" language explicitly appears in several texts of early Judaism. In others, the concept is reflected without the actual use of the hendiadys. Like the OT references themselves, most of the texts communicate a numerical increase of physical offspring. Some deal with the increase of humanity's progeny generally[19] while others describe the numerical growth of Israel in particular,[20] including the increase to occur in the restoration from exile.[21] A few texts state that righteous Israel will numerically increase until she fills the world with righteousness.[22] The race will proliferate and inherit the entire earth, ruling over it forever.[23] Botanical imagery is sometimes combined with this language to enhance the growth metaphor.[24]

However, some texts do employ the language to express types of increase different than numerical growth of physical progeny. According to *1 En.* 5:7, 10, when the elect will inherit the earth, "their lives shall be **increased** [αὐξηθήσεται] in peace and the years of their happiness shall be **multiplied** [πληθυνήσεται] forever in gladness and peace."

---

[18] Cohen, *Be Fruitful and Increase*, 33.

[19] *Sib. Or.* 1.55–58, 272–74; *1 En.* 67:1–3; *2 Esd* 3:12; *Jub.* 6:5, 10:4. cf. *Hel. Syn. Pr.* 12:44–45, 49–52 (2nd–3rd cent. C.E.).

[20] *T. Isaac* 3:7–8; *1 En.* 89:49; *2 Esd* 3:16; 4Q158 1–2, 7–8. This last reference states, "[And he bless]ed him.... And said to him: May YH[WH] *make you fertile and [make] you [numerous....* May he fill you with] [know]ledge and intelligence (or: "understanding"; בינה)...." Cf. Col 1:6, 9–10! I owe this Qumran reference to Beale, "Colossians," ad loc.

[21] Bar 2:34; 11Q19 LIX, 5b–13.

[22] *1 En.* 10:16–22; *Jub.* 36:6; Josephus, *Ant.* 4.112–117; cf. CD-A II, 11–13a.

[23] Sir 44:21; *Jub.* 32:17b–19.

[24] *1 En.* 10:16–22 (combining spiritual botanical growth with literal); *Jub.* 36:6.

One text from Qumran probably describes the sectarian community as a tree planted in God's "garden," whose branches "bear fruit and multiply [רבה and פרה]" and produce good fruit.[25] Elsewhere, Philo allegorically interprets the "be fruitful and multiply" tradition found at Gen 9:1–2. He writes that God desires that souls should increase and multiply in virtue and rule over the earthy body and its senses.[26] In another place and along lines remarkably similar to Col 1:6, 10, *T. Levi* 18:9–14 declares that in the days of Messiah

> the *nations* shall be multiplied in knowledge on the earth [τὰ ἔθνη πληθυνθήσονται ἐν γνώσει ἐπὶ τῆς γῆς] and they shall be illumined by the grace of the Lord, but Israel shall be diminished by her ignorance and darkened by her grief. In his priesthood sin shall cease.... And he shall open the gates of paradise; he shall remove the sword that has threatened since Adam, and he will grant to the saints to eat of the tree of life. The spirit of holiness shall be upon them. And Beliar shall be bound by him.... And the Lord will rejoice in his children; he will be well pleased by his beloved ones forever. Then Abraham, Isaac, and Jacob will rejoice...and all the saints shall be clothed in righteousness.[27]

The rabbis asserted that no man could abstain from the creation mandate to "be fruitful and multiply"; the minimum requirement was either two sons or a son and daughter.[28] The man who disobeys the mandate is as one who has murdered, for the image of God has been tarnished.[29] With regard to a proselyte who had children when he was a pagan, there was debate whether such a one had fulfilled the mandate, for in joining with Israel the gentile had become "like a newly-born child" (i.e., as one who had not yet begotten children; an entirely new man had been born).[30]

Of note is that God needed to make Abraham a "new creation" before the patriarch could "be fruitful and multiply" and beget the nation Israel. This possibly refers to Abraham's circumcision.[31] However, God will only finally fulfill this promise of great fruitfulness to Abraham

---

[25] 4Q433 2, 1–9.

[26] Philo, *QG* 2.56.

[27] H. C. Kee, "Testaments of the Twelve Patriarchs," in *The Old Testament Pseude-pigrapha* (ed. James H. Charlesworth; 2 vols.; ABRL; New York: Doubleday, 1983), 1:795, emphasis mine.

[28] *m. Yevamot* 6:6.

[29] *Midr. Rabbah Genesis* 34.14. See also 17.2.

[30] *b. Bekhorot* 47a.

[31] *Midr. Rabbah Genesis* 39.11. See p. 319n.5.

in the Messianic era. Exodus 1:7 is combined with Hos 2:1 [MT; ET: 1:10] to make this point.[32] Elsewhere, Lev 26:9 is used likewise; in this latter rabbinic text this age is referred to as "the time to come when the era of the redemption arrives."[33]

New Testament Context: The Genesis 1:28 Exegetical Tradition in Colossians 1:6

As so often with his correspondence to local churches, Paul begins his letter with a statement of thanksgiving after his initial greeting (1:1–2). The language of the thanksgiving is similar to what is found in Paul's other letters, as is the reason given for why he thanks God for the readers.[34] The typical Pauline pattern is to render thanks *to God* after he hears about (or has himself witnessed) the readers' faith and/or love. His letter to the Colossians maintains this pattern. Paul thanks God for the Colossians after Epaphras brought him news of their faith in Messiah Jesus and of their love for their fellow believers (1:3–4). On account of their faith and love, Paul offers a prayer-report explaining what he asks of God for them (1:9–14). This report gives way to the celebrated hymn that exalts Christ as preeminent in both creation and the new creation (1:15–20).

Paul states that the Colossians' love has freely flowed due to their expectation[35] of sharing in the glory of God as promised in the gospel (1:5a, 23, 27).[36] Their certainty of partaking of God's glory *in the future* has enabled and freed the Colossian faithful to exert love toward their fellow believers *in the present*. Though their faith is mentioned first, love becomes Paul's emphasis in vv. 4–5a, as can be seen from v. 8, where he mentions only their love again (forming a rough *inclusio*). Their love, Paul says, is "in the Spirit" (v. 8b; ἐν πνεύματι).[37] The phrase does not

---

[32] *Midr. Rabbah Numbers* 2.14.

[33] *Midr. Rabbah Lamentations* 3.21, § 7.

[34] See Rom 1:8; 1 Cor 1:4; 1 Thess 1:2–3; 2 Thess 1:3; Phlm 4–5; Eph 1:15–16.

[35] Gk.: διὰ τὴν ἐλπίδα.

[36] The faith/hope/love triad seen in 1:4–5a is thoroughly Pauline: see 1 Cor 13:13; 1 Thess 1:3, 5:8.

[37] The word πνεῦμα occurs only twice in Colossians (1:8, 2:5). While the use in 1:8 could possibly be taken to mean a human disposition or spirit, it is more probable that Paul is referring to the Holy Spirit. That the noun is anarthrous matters little; Paul mentions the Spirit numerous times without the article (and with or without other modifiers): Gal 3:3, 4:29, 5:5, 16, 18, 25 (2x); 1 Thess 1:5, 6; 1 Cor 2:4, 13, 7:40, 12:3

merely denote sphere; Paul meant that the love the Colossians were displaying was enabled *by* the Spirit. Paul thanks God for the Colossian faithful because the existence of love among them testifies that God had been (and continued to be) at work there and that the gospel proclamation was still advancing among the nations even though Paul, the apostle commissioned to the nations, was imprisoned (4:3).

Elsewhere, at Gal 5:22–23, Paul has asserted that love is a "fruit of the Spirit." There, love heads the list of nine virtues that Paul expected the saints to exhibit as the Spirit worked in them. Love thus holds a prominent place in the list. In fact, love is inextricably tied to the eschatological reality of the new creation in the letter to the Galatians:

> Gal 5:6: For in Christ Jesus neither circumcision nor uncircumcision means anything, *but faith working through love.*   (NASB)

> Gal 6:15: For neither is circumcision anything, nor uncircumcision, *but a new creation.*   (NASB)

> Gal 5:13–14: For you were called to freedom, brothers and sisters; only do not use your freedom as an opportunity for self-indulgence, but through *love* become slaves to one another. For the whole law is summed up in a single commandment, "You shall *love* your neighbor as yourself."

> Gal 5:22: By contrast, the fruit of the Spirit is *love*, joy, peace…

For Paul, the new creation had been inaugurated in Christ and is evidenced by the work of the eschatological Spirit producing fruit, like love, in believers' lives.

The same theological undercurrent flows just under the surface of Colossians, subtly emerging at several points. It is significant, for instance, that six of the nine "fruits of the Spirit" mentioned in Gal 5:22–23 show up in Col 3:12–17, immediately after Paul exhorted his audience to "put on" the "new man" Christ, the new Adam (3:9–11):

(2x), 14:2; 2 Cor 3:3, 18, 6:6; Phil 3:3; Rom 1:4, 2:29 (ἐν πνεύματι), 5:5, 7:6, 8:4, 9 (3x; 1x: ἐν πνεύματι), 13, 14, 9:1, 14:17, 15:13, 16, 19. Cf. Eph 2:22, 3:5, 5:18, 6:18 (all are ἐν πνεύματι). Cf. LXX Ezek 11:24; Mic 3:8; Zech 1:6, 4:6, 7:12; Neh 9:30; Matt 3:11, 12:28, 22:43 (ἐν πνεύματι); Mark 1:8; Luke 3:16; John 1:33; Acts 1:5, 11:16; 1 Pet 1:12; Jude 20. Several major translations also understand πνεύματι at Col 1:8 to be a reference to the divine Spirit (NRSV; NJB; NIV; NAB; NASB; NKJV; NLT; NET; ESV).

Galatians 5:22–23	Colossians 3:12–17
1) ἀγάπη ("love")	ἀγάπη ("love")
2) χαρά ("joy")	εὐχαριστοῦντες τῷ θεῷ πατρί as shorthand for: Μετὰ χαρᾶς εὐχαριστοῦντες τῷ πατρί ("with joy giving thanks to the Father"; Col 1:11b–12)
3) εἰρήνη ("peace")	εἰρήνη ("peace")
4) μακροθυμία ("patience")	μακροθυμία ("patience")
5) χρηστότης ("kindness")	χρηστότης ("kindness")
6) πραΰτης ("gentleness")	πραΰτης ("gentleness")

Neither list is intended to be exhaustive; it is probable that Paul has tailored both to address the situation of their respective audience. Nevertheless, the extensive overlap is hardly coincidental. What Paul expressed as "fruit of the Spirit" in Galatians is in Colossians referred to as virtues the believers are to "put on" (3:12) now that they have "put on" the new humanity of the new creation (3:9–11). Paul, as at Gal 5:22–23, grants to love prominence of place in the Colossian list (see v. 14). At Col 1:8, Paul had already stated that love—like he had at Gal 5:22a—was produced by the Spirit. This may suggest that the rest of the virtues mentioned in Col 3:12–17 likewise stem from the enabling inner work of the Holy Spirit.[38] This closeness of thought to Gal 5:22–23 (see 5:6, 6:15) further supports the suggestion that new creation theology does not run far underneath Colossians, even though the words καινὴ κτίσις do not appear (as in 2 Cor 5:17; Gal 6:15). In fact, there are several places where new creation imagery surfaces in Colossians.[39]

As at Galatia, the gospel is bearing fruit at Colossae (1:6). The phrase "bearing fruit and increasing" in Col 1:6 displays a remarkable similarity in wording, thought, and cadence to the celebrated phrase found in Gen 1:28 "be fruitful and increase." The LXX reads αὐξάνεσθε καὶ πληθύνεσθε, while Paul writes ἐστὶν καρποφορούμενον καὶ αὐξανόμενον. If Paul has echoed Gen 1:28, why then the change from πληθύνω to καρποφορέω ("grow" to "bear fruit")?[40]

---

[38] Or in the letter's own language, from "Christ in you" (see 1:27).

[39] Besides this chapter, see also chapters four, seven, and thirteen.

[40] Paul has also used καρποφορέω twice in Rom 7:4–5; those who belong to Christ are to "bear fruit" to God whereas those who are still in the flesh "bear fruit" unto

First, it should be noted that elsewhere in the Greek tradition καρποφορέω has replaced πληθύνω. The verb καρποφορέω is rare in the LXX, occurring twice (Hab 3:17; Wis 10:7). Yet it does also occur at Ps 91:15 [ET 92:14] in the versions of Symmachus and Theodotian instead of LXX's πληθύνω. With the change the meaning is slightly altered and the botanical imagery of the passage is enhanced. Here in Ps 91:13–15 LXX, the righteous are depicted as trees that flourish and remain luxuriant even in old age. The alteration by Symmachus and Theodotian changes the imagery from merely "growing," (already stated anyway at v. 13 with the same verb), to the richer variation "bearing fruit." Thus Paul's exchange of πληθύνω with καρποφορέω is observed also within the Greek tradition and demonstrates that the exchange of the former for the latter word has occurred elsewhere.

Second, it is possible that Paul has made his own translation from the Hebrew text. It is noteworthy that both the Greek OT and the Aramaic Targums are a step removed from the Hebrew in their translations of Gen 1:28 and, indeed, in all their renderings of the be-fruitful-and-increase tradition. Specifically, they all fail to capture as precisely the botanical imagery of the verb פרה, "to be fruitful/bear fruit" (cf. the noun פְּרִי, "fruit"). The LXX consistently translates the verb with αὐξάνω, thus failing to retain the explicit "fruit" imagery, while the Targumic tradition consistently translates it either as "increase" (*Targum Pseudo-Jonathan*), "be strong" (*Targum Neofiti*),[41] or "be many" (*Targum Onqelos*),[42] thereby dropping fully the botanical metaphor.

From all this it therefore appears that the major translations of Gen 1:28 (etc.) that were probably in circulation in Paul's day offered renderings of the verb פרה that were a step removed from the original Hebrew. It is therefore possible that Paul rendered his own translation of the Hebrew to bring it more in line with the Hebrew imagery. He chose καρποφορέω, a combination of the noun καρπός ("fruit") + the

---

death. For the former, the fruit appears as a result of the Spirit (v. 6)—a theme hit again in Gal 5:22–23 and also in Col 1:6–8.

[41] Martin McNamara, *Targum Neofiti 1: Genesis* (The Aramaic Bible 1A; Collegeville, Minn.: Liturgical Press, 1992), 54n.14, writes that "Nf almost invariably translates [פרה] as "be strong." Thus Gen 1:22; 2:8; 8:17; 9:1,7; 26:22; 35:11; 47:27; 49:22; Exod 1:7; even in causative (Hiphil): Gen 17:16, 20; 28:3; 48:4; Lev 26:9.

[42] Bernard Grossfeld, *The Targum Onqelos to Genesis* (The Aramaic Bible 6; Wilmington, Del.: Michael Glazier, 1988), 43n.9, writes that "the Hebrew 'be fruitful' is a metaphor, which is transformed by [*Targum Onqelos*] into its concrete meaning—the propagation and the numerical increase of the species."

verb φέρω ("to bear") to translate פרה, "be fruitful," thus expressing more literally the sense of the original.[43] If this is the case, Paul even maintained the word order of the MT, since פרה comes first at Gen 1:28 (as well as in the rest of the tradition), following it up by the conjunction and the second verb of the phrase:

Gen 1:28 MT (left to right): פְּרוּ וּ רְבוּ

Col 1:6 καρποφορούμενον καὶ αὐξανόμενον

It is true that it is unusual for Paul to follow the MT against the LXX. If this is the case here, it would nevertheless not be the first time he has done so.[44]

The final question that must be addressed is why Paul went with αὐξάνω instead of πληθύνω in translating the second verb of the phrase (רבה), πληθύνω being much more commonly used to translate רבה than αὐξάνω (only once), and always so within the be-fruitful-and-increase tradition. First, it must be noted that there is significant semantic overlap between the two verbs; they are synonyms and the change yields little or no difference in meaning. Second, it is noteworthy that αὐξάνω is much less common in the LXX,[45] and its claim to fame is as part of the be-fruitful-and-increase tradition that threads its way through Genesis and beyond. Perhaps then, Paul was drawn to αὐξάνω

---

[43] The word καρποφορέω does not appear in the pseudepigraphal literature and only once in Josephus (Ag. Ap. 1.306). Philo employs it twelve times, some of which shed light on Paul's use. As a vine bears fruit, so the soul (ψυχή) bears joy, gladness, and hope when good is hoped for (Names 161–63; cf. Gal 5:22–23). At another place, Philo cites Isa 5:7, "The vineyard of the Lord Almighty is the house of Israel," and by allegory states that the house of Israel is the soul, which is a "most holy vineyard" that bears for its fruit the divine growth known as virtue (Dreams, 2.172–73; cf. 2.272; Drunkenness 8–9; Planting 31). Elsewhere, Philo allegorizes Gen 2 and the Garden of Eden (Planting 28–46). The Garden figures the growths of a reasonable soul, planted by God, growing the trees (= virtues) of life, immortality, knowledge, apprehension, understanding, the conception of good and evil, joy, wisdom, and the worship and service of God (36–40). Indeed, Philo argues that "the man stamped with the spirit which is after the image of God differs not a whit, as it appears to me, from the tree that bears the fruit (καρποφοροῦντος) of immortal life" (44).

Both Philo, Planting 34 and Herm. Sim. 2.3–4 show that καρποφορέω is synonymous with the phrase φέρω καρπόν; the change is merely stylistic. Therefore John 15 is also close background, wherein φέρω καρπόν appears six times (vv. 2 [3x], 4, 5, 16 [cf. 12:24]). Jesus is the vine, his followers the branches; apart from him they can "bear no fruit." The fruits in mind include keeping Jesus' commandments (v. 10), love for fellow saints (v. 12), and joy (v. 11).

[44] See p. 37n.86 of this study.

[45] Forty occurrences compared to roughly two hundred for πληθύνω.

because it was the more prominent of the two words of the hendiadys. Another possibility is that Paul rendered רבה in his own words, apart from any influence from the LXX.

In summary, Paul has probably rendered his own Greek translation of the original Hebrew of the be-fruitful-and-multiply-tradition, under the partial influence of the LXX wording, in order to recapture the image of humans as "fruit-bearers."

If this is the case, then what has Paul done in Col 1:6, 10? Why has he tapped into the Gen 1:28 tradition?[46] In echoing Gen 1:28 and possibly its OT interpretative tradition, Paul implies that the word of the gospel is creating a people who will fulfill the purpose of the original creation mandate. The inference is that this people, recreated "in the image of God" (see Col 3:9–10!) will fill the earth and rule over all the rest of the renewed creation as God's representatives or vicegerents (cf. Ps 8; Rom 8:18–23, 29; 1 Cor 4:8). While Paul does intend to highlight initially the numerical growth and worldwide expansion of the gospel with the phrase (1:6a; ἐν παντὶ τῷ κόσμῳ), the emphasis shifts when he brings it to bear upon the church at Colossae (1:6b). The gospel is not only bearing fruit and increasing *numerically* as it rings out in expansion across the world; at Colossae it also bore fruit and increased *internally* when the Colossians heard and embraced the message. From that day on, the "word of truth" had begun to bear internal spiritual fruit among them, like faith (1:4a) and especially love (1:4b, 8; by the Spirit, 1:8b).[47] Paul thus expresses both an external expansion and an internal, spiritual growth by the phrase.

---

[46] Some (e.g., C. F. D. Moule, *The Epistles of Paul the Apostle to the Colossians and to Philemon* (CGTC; Cambridge: University Press, 1968), 50–51; F. F. Bruce, *The Epistles to the Colossians, to Philemon, and to the Ephesians* (NICNT; Grand Rapids: Eerdmans, 1984), 42) have mentioned the Parable of the Sower [Mark 4:3–20 = Matt 13:3–23 = Luke 8:5–15] as perhaps the closest background to Col 1:6, 10. There, the sower sows the seed of the word (λόγος; Mark 4:14), which, when it falls on the good soil of human hearts, "bear fruit, growing up and increasing" (ἐδίδου καρπὸν [= καρποφοροῦσιν, v. 20] ἀναβαίνοντα καὶ αὐξανόμενα), yielding thirty, sixty and a hundredfold. While this parable provides a definite parallel to Col 1:6, it is impossible to know whether Paul was acquainted with it. The cadence and language of Col 1:6 remain closer to the be-fruitful-and-increase tradition of the OT, which Paul had certainly read and knew. Nevertheless, it need not be an either/or choice; the background that gave birth to Paul's words may have been influenced by more than one tradition.

[47] Cf. 2 Esd 3:20–21 (late first century C.E.): "Yet you did not take away their evil heart from them, so that your law might *produce fruit* in them. For the first Adam, burdened with an evil heart, transgressed and was overcome, as were also all who were descended from him."

Internal, spiritual growth becomes the focus in v. 10, where the hendiadys is repeated. Here the two participles serve as the first two of four that explain how the Colossians are to "walk worthily of the Lord." They are to bear fruit "in every good work" and increase "in the knowledge of God." Note that despite these prepositional phrase modifiers Paul has kept the hendiadys tightly together at the center of v. 10b (cf. the structure of Acts 6:7; see below):

ἐν παντὶ ἔργῳ ἀγαθῷ καρποφοροῦντες καὶ αὐξανόμενοι τῇ ἐπιγνώσει τοῦ θεοῦ

This exact repetition in word selection and order as it is found in v. 6 highlights the phrase and reinforces the argument that Paul had the hendiadys from Gen 1:28 in mind.

The Genesis 1:28 Tradition in the Rest of the NT

The be-fruitful-and-multiply tradition appears explicitly in Acts 7:17 in an allusion to Exod 1:7, which was the initial fulfillment of the tradition:

> But as the time drew near for the fulfillment of the promise that God had made to Abraham, our people in Egypt increased and multiplied [ηὔξησεν ὁ λαὸς καὶ ἐπληθύνθη].

This explicit connection to the tradition provides an important clue that the other two instances of the hendiadys in Acts are to be read in light of the tradition as well:

> Acts 6:7: Καὶ ὁ λόγος τοῦ θεοῦ ηὔξανεν καὶ ἐπληθύνετο ὁ ἀριθμὸς τῶν μαθητῶν ἐν Ἰερουσαλὴμ σφόδρα ("and the word of God increased and the number of the disciples multiplied greatly in Jerusalem").

> Acts 12:24: Ὁ δὲ λόγος τοῦ θεοῦ ηὔξανεν καὶ ἐπληθύνετο ("But the word of God increased and multiplied").

J. Kodell and now David Pao, who partly builds upon Kodell's work, have both argued that Luke intentionally crafted these two statements to recall the OT be-fruitful-and-multiply tradition.[48] Kodell writes:

---

[48] J. Kodell, "'The Word of God Grew': The Ecclesial Tendency of Λόγος in Acts 1,7; 12,24; 19,20," Bib 55 (1974): 505–12; David W. Pao, Acts and the Isaianic New Exodus (Grand Rapids: Baker, 2002), 147–80 (esp. 167–71). Pao includes Acts 19:20 also.

Thus the αὐξάνειν—πληθύνειν compound is a classic LXX usage to express the promise and realization of the growth and expansion of God's covenant People. Luke takes up this theological formula from LXX to fit his presentation of the growth and expansion of the New Testament People of God.[49]

Pao adds that the word of God (ὁ λόγος τοῦ θεοῦ) fits into this program as the active agent that "travels to the end of the earth...to conquer the world and create a community as the true people of God."[50] This use of the be-fruitful-and-multiply tradition in Acts further supports the contention that Col 1:6 (and 10) echoes the same OT tradition.

The Genesis 1:28 Tradition in the Early Church Fathers

The early Fathers did occasionally quote the creation mandate from Gen 1:28, often for apologetic purposes. Tertullian used it to defend sexual relations between a male and female in marriage as a right and blessed activity,[51] yet also argued elsewhere that the apostle Paul effectively abolished the creation mandate with his words, "let even those who have wives be as though they had none" (1 Cor 7:29). This allows virgins to remain single and devote themselves to Christian service.[52] Methodius, however, contended that the creation mandate remained perpetually valid until the end of all things should come.[53] He also, however, viewed the creation mandate to be "duly fulfilled" in an eschatological sense in Christ as a second Adam:

> Whence it was that the apostle directly referred to Christ the words which had been spoken of Adam....the Word, leaving His Father in heaven, came down to be "joined to His wife"...and willingly suffered death for her, that He might present the Church to Himself glorious and blameless...for the receiving of the spiritual and blessed seed, which is sown by Him who with whispers implants it in the depths of the mind; and is conceived and formed by the Church, as by a woman, so as to give birth and nourishment to virtue. For in this way, too, the command, "increase and multiply," is duly fulfilled, the Church increasing daily in

---

[49] Kodell, "The Word of God Grew," 511.

[50] Pao, *Acts and the Isaianic New Exodus*, 176.

[51] *The Soul* 27 (*ANF* 3:208); *Against Marcion* 1.29 (*ANF* 3:294). Cf. the *Apostolic Constitutions* 6.27 (*ANF* 7:462).

[52] *Exhortation to Chastity* 6 (*ANF* 4:53); *Monogamy* 7 (*ANF* 4:64). The pseudepigraphal *Two Epistles Concerning Virginity* 1.3–4 (*ANF* 8:55–56) argues along the same lines.

[53] *The Banquet of the Ten Virgins* 2.1 (*ANF* 6:313).

greatness and beauty and multitude, by the union and communion of
the Word...[54]

The Epistle of Barnabas (ca. 70–135 C.E.) contains the most provocative
use of the creation mandate. The author writes that those who hope in
Jesus have been recreated in his image or pattern (6:11–12, 14).[55] God
has made a second creation in the last days and is making the last things
as the first (6:13).[56] The creation mandate of Gen 1:28 is quoted twice
in this context and is applied typologically to Christians:

> For the Scripture speaks about us when [God] says to the Son: "Let us
> make man according to our image and likeness, and let them rule...."
> And when he saw that our creation was good, the Lord said: "Increase
> and multiply and fill the earth.... So in a similar manner we too, being
> nourished by faith...will live and rule over the earth [κατακυριεύοντες
> τῆς γῆς; an echo of Gen 1:28 LXX]. Now we have already said above:
> "And let them increase and multiply and rule over the fish." But who is
> presently able to rule over beasts or fish or birds of the air?...If, however,
> this is not now the case, then he has told us when it will be: when we
> ourselves have been made perfect, and so become heirs of the Lord's
> covenant.[57]

The author asserts that, just as all humanity was originally commanded
to increase and multiply so as to rule over the first creation, the new
humanity—those recreated in Christ—are to increase and multiply and
rule over the second creation.

Hermeneutical Reflections

It is difficult to know for certain what hermeneutic Paul presupposed
when he echoed Gen 1:28 in Col 1:6, 10. Did he have the whole interpretive tradition assumed, so that the restoration promises of Jer 3:16,
23:3 and Ezek 36:11 are coming to be realized through the gospel of
Christ? Then this would be a case of a prophetic fulfillment for Paul.
If, however, Gen 1:28 is the text influencing Paul's language, then
perhaps the apostle presupposed a typological framework. Paul would

---

[54] *The Banquet of the Ten Virgins* 3.8 (Clark, *ANF* 6:319).

[55] It is noteworthy that the Ezek 11:19, 36:26 tradition of the divine transplant of
a heart of flesh for the heart of stone is quoted in the immediate context at v. 14. On
this theme, see chapter nine of this study.

[56] Cf. *Odes Sol.*, Ode 11 (ca. 100 C.E.).

[57] *Barn.* 6:12, 17b–19.

then have seen in the creation mandate a type for the new creation that had been inaugurated in Christ (cf. Gal 6:15; 2 Cor 5:17). It is possible and even likely that, along with this, Paul believed that God's originally intended design for the Gen 1 humanity was finally being realized through the re-creating agency of the gospel, "the word of truth" (Col 1:5). This is the line of thought that is most attractive in light of the other new creational echoes that run throughout the rest of the letter to the Colossians.[58]

Another alternative, however, is that Paul may have produced the phrase in a rhetorical maneuver. There was neither any thought toward making a contextual statement about Gen 1:28, nor was there any attempt to hint at its extended meaning in the light of the inaugurated new age in Christ. Accordingly, Paul drew on the language to highlight with rhetorical flourish the exponential growth of his gospel across the world.

---

[58] See chapters four, seven, and thirteen of this study.

CHAPTER FOUR

THE SCRIPTURES OF ISRAEL IN COLOSSIANS 1:9–14:
THE ECHO OF ISAIAH 11:2, 9 IN 1:9–10

Comparison of Textual Versions and Evaluation

Isaiah 11:2, 9 MT	Isaiah 11:2, 9 LXX	Colossians 1:9–10
...רוּחַ חָכְמָה וּבִינָה רוּחַ דַּעַת.... מָלְאָה הָאָרֶץ דֵעָה אֶת־יְהוָה	πνεῦμα <u>σοφίας</u> καὶ <u>συνέσεως</u>...πνεῦμα <u>γνώσεως</u>....ἐνεπλήσθη ἡ <u>σύμπασα</u> τοῦ <u>γνῶναι</u> τὸν <u>κύριον</u>	...<u>πληρωθῆτε τὴν ἐπίγνωσιν</u> τοῦ θελήματος αὐτοῦ ἐν πάσῃ <u>σοφίᾳ καὶ συνέσει</u> <u>πνευματικῇ</u>...αὐξανόμενοι τῇ <u>ἐπιγνώσει τοῦ θεου</u>
		See also Col 1:6, which states that this "knowledge of God" via the gospel of truth is increasing throughout "the entire world" (<u>ἐν παντὶ τῷ κόσμῳ</u>).

This proposal meets the two criteria necessary for an echo: 1) availability and 2) word agreement and/or rare concept similarity. Regarding *availability*, Paul had read and knew the first section of the book of Isaiah (see Rom 9:27, 29, 32–33; 15:12 [= Isa 11:10]). Regarding *word agreement*, the two texts share an explicit verbal agreement of four words (Isa 11:2 with Col 1:9; though one word is slightly modified in Col 1:9; see discussion below) as well as a *rare conceptual similarity* (God is filling the world with the knowledge of himself through his messiah and the Spirit).[1] The text makes adequate sense apart from any reader

---

[1] Gordon Fee, *God's Empowering Presence: The Holy Spirit in the Letters of Paul* (Peabody, Mass.: Hendrickson, 1994), 642–43 (including notes 29–31), 675, 908–9, 913, has already argued for this direct and specific influence. See now especially Fee, "Old Testament Intertextuality in Colossians," ad loc. for his more thorough discussion; see also Beale, "Colossians," ad loc.

Others have cited Isa 11:2 as one passage among a few other OT texts that serve as background to Col 1:9: Hühn, *Die alttestamentlichen Citate*, 197 (with Deut 4:6 the only

awareness of Isa 11, so that the reference should be classified as an
echo. Nevertheless, recognition that Isa 11 lies behind Col 1:9–10
deeply enhances our understanding of both the letter and of Paul as
a biblical theologian.

Old Testament Context: Isaiah 11:1–9

The prophecy of Isa 11:1–9, in the form of an announcement of a
royal savior,[2] was perhaps uttered by the prophet Isaiah about 732 b.c.e.[3]
Assyria had become a world power that threatened the independence
of the states located in the coveted "land bridge" region of Syro-
Palestine. King Rezin of Aram (Syria) and King Pekah of Israel formed
a coalition to withstand the Assyrian threat, and pressured King Ahaz
of Judah to join them in the rebellion. The two kings threatened war
if Ahaz refused to join them (Isa 7:1–6; 2 Kgs 15:37). Ahaz wavered,
so the LORD sent the prophet Isaiah to encourage him to trust in the
LORD's promises of protection for the house of David (Isa 7:3–9; see 2
Sam 7:8–16). In spite of this, Ahaz refused to heed Isaiah's word and
instead turned to Assyria for help against the rebelling coalition (2 Kgs
16:5–9). Indignant with Ahaz's unbelief, a king of the Davidic line who
should have modeled faith, Isaiah declared that Assyria, in its sweep of
the rebellious states north of Judah, would come as far south as Judah

---

other text mentioned); Lohmeyer, *Kolosser*, 33n.1; Lohse, *Colossians*, 25–26n.17; Ernst,
Kolosser, 161; O'Brien, *Colossians*, 21; Petr Pokorný, *Colossians: A Commentary* (trans.
Siegfried S. Schatzmann; Peabody, Mass.: Hendrickson, 1991), 47; Daniel Furter, *Les
Épîtres de Paul aux Colossiens et à Philémon* (CEB; Vaux-sur-Seine: Edifac, 1987), 89n.3;
Barth and Blanke, *Colossians*, 176n.19; Jean-Noël Aletti, *Saint Paul Épître Aux Colossiens*
(ÉB; Paris: Gabalda, 1993), 71n.84; C. Marvin Pate, *The End of the Age Has Come: the
Theology of Paul* (Grand Rapids: Zondervan, 1995), 162: "This conjunction of the Spirit
and knowledge/wisdom is rooted in the Old Testament (Ex 31:3; 35:31, 35; Deut 34:9;
1 Chron 22:12; Isa 11:2)"; Dunn, *Colossians*, 70–71; Hübner, *Vetus Testamentum in Novo*,
508–9; Margaret Y. MacDonald, *Colossians and Ephesians* (SP 17; Collegeville, Minn.:
Liturgical Press, 2000), 48.

[2] Marvin A. Sweeney, *Isaiah 1–39: with an Introduction to Prophetic Literature* (FOTL 16;
Grand Rapids: Eerdmans, 1996), 201, 514.

[3] For the view that the passage stems from the time of King Josiah, see Sweeney,
Isaiah 1–39, 204–5; idem, "Jesse's New Shoot in Isaiah 11: A Josianic Reading of the
Prophet Isaiah," in *A Gift of God in Due Season: Essays on Scripture and Community in Honor
of James A. Sanders* (eds. Richard D. Weis and David M. Carr; JSOTSup 225; Sheffield:
Sheffield Academic Press, 1996), 103–118.

and humiliate the people and ravage the land. Judah and Jerusalem would barely escape total destruction (Isa 7:18–23, 8:5–8).

It is within this literary context of Ahaz's moral failure and loss of nerve, as well as the looming threat of the Assyrian juggernaut (Isa 10:28–32), that Isaiah announces 11:1–9 (and 9:1–7). The oracle's promise of a coming Davidic king, who would establish justice, destroy the wicked, bring peace in a renewed creation, and fill the idolatry-riddled land with the "knowledge of YHWH," was announced to instill hope in a people burdened with fear in an uncertain time.

The section begins on the heels of the promise that the LORD would cut down the "thickets of the forest," i.e., the Assyrian war machine, for its arrogance (10:34; see 10:12–19). While the Assyrian king falls like a great cedar, a "shoot from the stump of Jesse," a king from the lineage of David, will arise from what remains of the monarchy. This Davidic king would be endowed with the Spirit of God, a statement that is further interpreted in a three-fold structure as

> the Spirit of wisdom and understanding,
> the Spirit of counsel and strength,
> the Spirit of knowledge and the fear of YHWH

The last line of the three-fold structure is changed by the LXX to "the Spirit of knowledge and piety."[4] The LXX then adds the line, "He will fill him with the Spirit of the fear of God." This move creates a seven-fold endowment of the Spirit in the LXX translation instead of the six of the MT (seven viewed as the number of completeness or perfection).

Endowed with such gifting from above, this ideal king will render judicial decisions impartially, especially for the poor and lowly of the land (cf. Ps 72; Prov 31:9; Jer 23:5–6). Ancient Near Eastern kings typically not only ruled their land but served as the highest ranking judge in their kingdom, adjudicating disputes for their people, often in the gate of the city (cf. 2 Sam 15:1–6).[5]

Because of such great ruling and juridical responsibility, the king needed to have great wisdom, as David (2 Sam 15:20) and Solomon did (1 Kgs 3:5–28, esp. v. 28). Empowered with "the Spirit of wisdom and

---

[4] Gk.: πνεῦμα γνώσεως καὶ εὐσεβείας.

[5] Hans Wildberger, *Isaiah 1–12* (trans. Thomas H. Trapp; CC; Minneapolis: Fortress, 1991), 474–75. He states in comments on 11:3–5 that "...there can be absolutely no doubt that the king was the highest judicial authority and carried the ultimate responsibility for functions connected with the administration of justice" (474).

understanding," the promised king from David's line will successfully
mete out judgment, putting the wicked to death and thus eradicating
them from his land.

The abundant endowment of the Spirit enables the promised king not
only to judge his land with righteousness (vv. 3b–5) but also to establish
peace in a renewed creation (vv. 6–8).[6] By his rule he will abolish the
enmity between humanity and the animal kingdom.

In v. 9, Isaiah describes the climactic result of the promised king's
reign for God's dwelling place on earth. The "mount of holiness" is
Mount Zion located in Jerusalem, the location of the temple built by
Solomon and the locus of YHWH's presence in Israel. Neither the wicked
(v. 4b) nor violent animals (vv. 6–8)[7] will do any more harm there to
the people of God (v. 9a), because the coming king through his Spirit-
empowered rule will fill the earth with the "knowledge of YHWH" even
as the waters cover the sea (v. 9b).[8] Foreign, tyrannical rulers like those
of Assyria will never threaten Zion again.

What exactly, however, is meant by the phrase "the knowledge of
God"? Elsewhere in the OT, the phrase is equated with "the fear of
YHWH," suggesting that such knowledge is more than merely facts *about*
the deity (see Prov 2:5). Hosea employs the phrase "knowledge of God"
as a synonym for אֱמֶת ("faithfulness"; 4:1) and חֶסֶד ("covenant loyalty";
4:1, 6:6).[9] The phrase thus entails not merely a cerebral recognition of
facts about God, but a true understanding of what he requires from his
covenant people wed to a genuine commitment on their part to fulfill
those obligations.[10] In light of this, it is probably best to understand

---

[6] Cf. *Tg. Isa.* 11:6a, "In the days of Messiah of Israel shall peace increase in the
land"; Isa 9:6b–7; Mic 5:5; Ps 72:7; Zech 9:10; *T. Levi* 18:4.

[7] Christopher R. Seitz, *Isaiah 1–39* (Interpretation; Louisville: John Knox, 1993),
106–7, offers evidence that the violent animals are to be taken "in a symbolic sense
(cf. here Daniel 7–8). The predator animals are symbols of nations in their devour-
ing capacities.... The chief burden of the section is that hostility *directed at Israel* will
cease. The hostile powers will be neutralized, such that a little child can lead them"
(emphasis his).

[8] Cf. Hab 2:14: "But the earth will be filled with the knowledge of the glory of the
LORD, as the waters cover the sea" (NRSV).

[9] The prophet Hosea was a rough contemporary with Isaiah. See the convenient
timeline in John Bright, *A History of Israel* (3rd ed.; Philadelphia: Westminster, 1981),
471 [Chart VI].

[10] With regard to the instances in Hosea, Douglas Stuart, *Hosea–Jonah* (WBC 31;
Waco, Tex.: Word, 1987), 75, writes that "the term [i.e., דעת אלהים] represents the
essence of the covenant relationship between God and his people.... The term derives
in part from the language of the ancient Near Eastern treaties, where ידע represents
the acknowledgement of the binding relationship between the parties, especially the
loyalty of the vassal to the suzerain."

Isa 11:9 and the phrase "knowledge of YHWH" within it as stating that the endowment of the Spirit will enable the promised Davidic king to establish full and exclusive covenant allegiance to YHWH throughout his dominion in the coming new age. Idolatry will never be seen in the land again and glad covenant obedience will fill the earth.

The Spirit of Wisdom and Understanding Elsewhere in the Old Testament

There are other passages in the OT that employ the language found in Isa 11:2. This situation therefore requires some discussion as to why Paul in Col 1:9 would or would not have these other passages in mind instead of Isa 11:2. For example, synonymous wording with that found in Isa 11:2 is found twice in the book of Exodus, at Exod 31:3 and 35:31 (given in order below):

> And I have filled him with the Spirit of God, with wisdom and with understanding (LXX: πνεῦμα θεῖον σοφίας καὶ συνέσεως) and with knowledge and with every skill.

> And he has filled him with the Spirit of God, with wisdom and with understanding (LXX: πνεῦμα θεῖον σοφίας καὶ συνέσεως) and with knowledge and with every skill.

The reference is to the same man in each case. The LORD had chosen Bezalel to build the tent of meeting, the ark, and all their furnishings. To endow him with the ability necessary for such a task, God filled him with the Spirit, which is immediately interpreted as a bestowal of great wisdom, understanding, and skill. As Isa 11:2, the LXX wording of these two passages is extremely close to Col 1:9. So why are these not in mind instead of Isa 11:2?

There are three reasons why Isa 11:2 is more likely to have been behind Paul's writing at Col 1:9 than Exod 31:3, 35:31. First, Isa 11:2 was understood as a towering messianic text in Paul's day among the OT Scriptures (see below), whereas the two texts in Exodus were obscure by comparison. Second, the concept of a universal filling of the earth with the "knowledge of God" is present in both Isa 11 and Col 1 in their respective immediate contexts. Third, new creation imagery exists in Isa 11:6–9, a theme that has already surfaced in the immediate context of Col 1:9 (see chapter three of this study). These indicators point to Isa 11:2 as the more probable text influencing the apostle's thought at Col 1:9.

Do we need to go so far as to say, however, that Isa 11:6–9 refers to the new creation? A piece of evidence that supports the assertion that Isa 11:6–9 offers a glimpse of the new creation is the fact that the text is later picked up and quoted at Isa 65:25, which reads:

> The wolf and the lamb shall feed together, the lion shall eat straw like the ox; but the serpent—its food shall be dust! They shall not hurt or destroy on all my holy mountain, says the LORD.

The text is a shortened quotation of Isa 11:6–9.[11] Set within a pronouncement of the new heavens and earth that the LORD promises to create (65:17–25), Isa 11:6–9 acquires significant color in this new context. What perhaps was unclear in Isa 11 is here made explicit: the era of peace and justice foreseen in Isa 11 is nothing other than the age of the "new heavens and new earth" (Isa 65:17). Noteworthy is that the "viper" language of Isa 11:8 has been transformed into an allusion to Gen 3:14, thus establishing a direct connection to the original creation account. The portrayal of Isa 11:8 that pictures young children innocently playing around the holes of vipers is replaced with the Hebrew וְנָחָשׁ עָפָר לַחְמוֹ: "but the serpent—dust shall be his food!" This is a direct allusion to Gen 3:14 and the curse that God spoke upon the serpent for deceiving Eve and plunging God's pristine creation into sin and ruin. The implication of the allusion at Isa 65:25 is that God has fully thwarted and reversed the effects of the serpent's treachery in his establishment of a renewed and perfected creation. The serpent himself remains cursed and unredeemed as perpetual punishment for his rebellion.

Two other OT texts employ language similar to Isa 11:2 and should also be mentioned. The first is Deut 34:9, which states that Joshua son of Nun was full of "the Spirit of wisdom" (רוּחַ חָכְמָה; LXX: πνεύματος συνέσεως) because Moses had laid his hands upon him. This passage, however, lacks the σοφίας καὶ συνέσεως hendiadys that Isa 11:2 and Col 1:9 share, was not interpreted messianically in the first century C.E., and makes no mention of the "knowledge of God" filling the earth. The second passage that shares similar language with Isa 11:2 is the Theodotian rendering of Daniel 5:14. King Belshazzar declares to Daniel:

---

[11] See J. T. A. G. M. van Ruiten, "The Intertextual Relationship Between Isaiah 65,25 and Isaiah 11,6–9," in *The Scriptures and the Scrolls: Studies in Honour of A. S. Van Der Woude on the Occasion of His 65th Birthday* (eds. F. García Martínez, A. Hilhorst, and C. J. Labuschagne; VTSup 49; Leiden: Brill, 1992), 31–42.

I have heard concerning you that a spirit of God [πνεῦμα θεοῦ] is in you and alertness and understanding and wisdom in abundance [σύνεσις καὶ σοφία περισσή] is found in you.

This text contains both the hendiadys found in Isa 11:2 and Col 1:9 as well as an explicit mention of the Spirit of God. It lacks, however, any reference to a universal filling of the earth with the knowledge of God, nor is the statement as conducive to a messianic interpretation as Isa 11:1–9. Moreover, the text is found in the Theodotian version, which poses a possible dating issue, since this Greek version was written *after* the time of Paul. Moreover, Daniel 5:14 is not found in the LXX rendering of Daniel (though it does exist in the Aramaic of the MT).

Isaiah 11:2, 9 in Early and Late Judaism

Five texts of early Judaism explicitly cite or allude to Isa 11:2. Four out of the five clearly identify the promised Davidic king as the messiah. The first text, *1 En.* 49:3–4b, alludes to Isa 11:2 and mentions five characteristics of the Spirit that indwells messiah:

> In him dwells the spirit of wisdom, the spirit which gives thoughtfulness, the spirit of knowledge and strength, and the spirit of those who have fallen asleep in righteousness. He shall judge the secret things. And no one will be able to utter vain words in his presence.[12]

The emphasis on the ability of messiah to judge even what is hidden in secret, and that no "vain words" can be spoken in his presence confirms that Isa 11:2 is in view (see Isa 11:3). The immediate context shows that the judgment referred to is that of humanity at the end of time (chs. 48–51).

The second text, *Pss. Sol.* 17:35–43 (1st cent. B.C.E.) also alludes to Isa 11:2–4:

> [*Lord Messiah*] shall be compassionate to all the nations (who) reverently (stand) before him. *He will strike the earth with the word of his mouth* forever; he will bless the Lord's people with *wisdom* and happiness. And he himself (will be) free from sin, (in order) to rule a great people. He will expose officials and drive out sinners by the strength of his word. And he will not weaken in his days, (relying) upon his God, for God made him powerful in the holy *spirit* and *wise* in the *counsel of understanding*, with *strength* and

---

[12] E. Isaac, "1 (Ethiopic Apocalypse of) Enoch," in *The Old Testament Pseudepigrapha* (ed. James H. Charlesworth; 2 vols.; ABRL; New York: Doubleday, 1983), 1:36.

righteousness.... Then who will succeed against him, *mighty* in his actions
and strong in the *fear of God*? Faithfully and righteously shepherding the
Lord's flock, he will not let any of them stumble in their pasture. He will
lead them all in holiness and there will be no arrogance among them,
that any should be oppressed. This is the beauty of the king of Israel
which God knew, to raise him over the house of Israel to discipline it.
His words will be purer than the finest gold, the best. *He will judge the
peoples* in the assemblies, the tribes of the sanctified. His words will be as
the words of the holy ones, among sanctified peoples.[13]

In context, the figure is clearly identified as the messiah (v. 32), who
will deliver the Jews from their Roman occupiers and purge Jerusalem
(vv. 22, 30, 45). It is by God's Spirit that the messiah will be enabled
to end the occupation (v. 22) and shepherd both Israel and the nations
who reverently stand before him (vv. 34, 40).[14]

The third text that alludes to Isa 11:2 is 1Q28b (or: 1QSb) V, 20–29.
It is a benediction for the "prince of the congregation" (נשׂיא העדה).[15]
This blessing is a collage of OT passages, including especially Isa 11:2–4,
Num 24:17, and Gen 49:9.[16] The amount of wording from Isa 11:2–4
make it the longest text cited in the benediction. The community views
the OT prophecies as yet unfulfilled and looks for their fulfillment in a
messianic figure.

The fourth text from the second temple period that alludes to Isa
11:2 is the "Prayer of Levi." The Prayer of Levi is found in two places,
in Aramaic in 4Q213 (= 4QTLevi[a]) and in Greek, inserted after *T. Levi*
3:2 in manuscript Athos from the Monastery of Koutloumous.[17] The
language of Isa 11:2 shows up in lines 8–9 of the Greek text:

> Let it be shown to me, Lord, the Holy Spirit, and counsel and wisdom
> and knowledge and strength give to me [τὸ πνεῦμα τὸ ἅγιον καὶ βουλὴν
> καὶ σοφίαν καὶ γνῶσιν καὶ ἰσχὺν δός μοι], in order to do the things
> pleasing to you...

---

[13] R. B. Wright, "Psalms of Solomon," in *The Old Testament Pseudepigrapha* (ed. James
H. Charlesworth; 2 vols.; ABRL; New York: Doubleday, 1983), 2:668. Italics are mine
and indicate where the text intersects with Isa 11:2–4.

[14] See also *Pss. Sol.* 18:5–7.

[15] D. Barthélemy and J. T. Milik, *Qumran Cave 1* (DJD 1; Oxford: Clarendon, 1955),
128–29, believe this to be a reference to the Messiah.

[16] Barthélemy and Milik, *Qumran Cave 1*, 129.

[17] Michael E. Stone and Jonas C. Greenfield, "The Prayer of Levi," *JBL* 112 (1993):
247. They cautiously date the Aramaic text to the 3rd cent. B.C.E. (p. 252).

Stone and Greenfield write that the terms "are presumably derived from Isa 11:2."[18] Of note is that Levi, having undergone (cultic?) purification, asks in line 18 for the Lord to enable him to render true judgment, a central result of the Spirit coming upon the Davidic figure of Isa 11:1–5. Levi expresses the goal of his request for the Spirit to be the empowerment to do τὰ ἀρέσκοντά σοι ("the things pleasing to you"). This language parallels Col 1:9–10, where the goal of Paul's prayer for the Colossians to be "filled...in all Spirit-given wisdom and understanding" is that they might "walk worthily of the Lord in *all that pleases* [εἰς πᾶσαν ἀρεσκείαν]."

The fifth text is *T. Levi* 18:5, 7 (second century B.C.E.). *T. Levi* 18:5 is a citation of Isa 11:9, and 18:7 is an allusion to Isa 11:2. The text is extremely relevant for the purpose of this chapter and so shall be quoted at length:

> And then the Lord will raise up a new priest to whom all the words of the Lord will be revealed. *He shall effect the judgment of truth over the earth* for many days. And his star shall rise in heaven like a king; kindling *the light of knowledge* as day is illumined by the sun. And he shall be extolled by the whole inhabited world. This one will shine forth like the sun in the earth; he shall take away all darkness from under heaven, and there shall be peace in all the earth. The heavens shall greatly rejoice in his days and the earth shall be glad; the clouds will be filled with joy and *the knowledge of the Lord will be poured out on the earth like the water of the seas*....The heavens will be opened, and from the temple of glory sanctification will come upon him....And the glory of the Most High shall burst forth upon him. And *the spirit of understanding and sanctification shall rest upon him*....And there shall be no successor for him from generation to generation forever. And in his priesthood *the nations shall be multiplied in knowledge on the earth*, and they shall be illumined by the grace of the Lord....In his priesthood sin shall cease....And he shall open the gates of paradise; he shall remove the sword that has threatened since Adam, and he will grant to the saints to eat of the tree of life. The spirit of holiness shall be upon them.[19]

At the end of time, God will raise up a new priest, the messiah, upon whom the Spirit of understanding and sanctification will rest.[20] He will fill the earth—especially the nations—with the knowledge of God, and will reopen the Garden of Eden for God's people (18:5, 9–10).

---

[18] "The Prayer of Levi," 261.

[19] H. C. Kee, "Testaments of the Twelve Patriarchs," *OTP* 1:794–95 (emphases mine).

[20] Gk.: πνεῦμα συνέσεως καὶ ἁγιασμοῦ καταπαύσει ἐπ' αὐτόν.

Significant for our study is the explicit statement that the messiah's
people *will share in the gift of this same Spirit* (v. 11: "the spirit of holiness
will be upon them"; Gk.: πνεῦμα ἁγιωσύνης ἔσται ἐπ᾽ αὐτοῖς).

While these five texts above show clear influence from Isa 11:2, other
texts exist that have been influenced by the OT "Spirit of wisdom" tradition generally. These are offered here in order to be able to provide a
fuller picture for our study. These texts provide a background against
which Col 1:9 may be evaluated: Is Isa 11:2 especially in mind, or has
Paul's thought only been influenced by the OT background generally?

Some texts show that one can ask in prayer to be filled with the
Spirit of understanding or wisdom.[21] The results of such a filling
include a penetrating grasp of the realm of the spirit world,[22] a heart
and tongue that pour forth wisdom,[23] understanding,[24] cleansing from
sin,[25] discernment into the will and counsel of God,[26] insight into the
deceitfulness of humanity's ways,[27] the ability to speak in the presence
of the Most High,[28] strength for battling spirits of iniquity,[29] and the
capacity to oversee and rule.[30] Philo, commenting upon Exod 31:3 and
Num 11:17, wrote that the Spirit upon Moses and the seventy elders was
the πανσόφου πνεύματος ("all-wise Spirit"), τὸ σοφόν τὸ θεῖον ("the wise,
divine") Spirit without which they could not excel in leadership.[31]

Some texts that mention a "spirit of wisdom" or "understanding,"
however, may not necessarily refer to the divine Spirit but only to
the human spirit. Such difficulty, for example, is encountered in the
interpretation of the "Treatise of the Two Spirits" (1QS III, 13–IV,
26), especially the section of IV, 2–7. This text, however, does appear
to employ the language of Isa 11:2 to describe the [S or s?]pirit of
the sons of righteousness.[32] Other Qumran texts clearly indicate that

---

[21] Sir 39:6; Wis 7:7.
[22] *T. Sol.* 22:1 with 26:6.
[23] Sir 39:6; 2 Esd 14:39–41 (= the giving of the Holy Spirit in response to Ezra's
request, see v. 22).
[24] Wis 7:7.
[25] 1QS IV, 21.
[26] Wis 9:13–17.
[27] *T. Levi* 2:3.
[28] 2 Esd 5:22.
[29] 4Q444 1, 1–4 (רוח דעת ובינה אמת וצדק שם אל בלבבי). Cf. Isa 11:2, 5! This
spirit is explicitly mentioned as the Holy Spirit (רוח קודשו) at 1, 1b.
[30] *Jub.* 40:5b.
[31] Philo, *Giants*, 23–28.
[32] See the discussion by A. R. C. Leaney, *The Rule of Qumran and Its Meaning: Introduction, Translation, and Commentary* (NTL; Philadelphia: Westminster, 1966), 37–56,

the spirit in view is the divine Spirit and connect the reception of this Spirit with the acquisition of the knowledge of God, like Isa 11:2.[33] Of note is that a couple of other texts from early Jewish literature indicate that the messiah would usher in a new age of "knowledge" (i.e., knowledge of God) to Israel and the nations upon his arrival.[34] He would be sinless and would pour out the Spirit on his people upon his arrival, with the result that Israel would become true sons, who walk faithfully in God's ways.[35]

In late Judaism, the figure of Isa 11:2 upon which "the Spirit of wisdom and understanding" rests is explicitly understood as the messiah.[36] In fact, Isa 11:2 is used to support the messianic interpretation of Ps 72:1.[37] This figure of Isa 11:2 is of the line of David from the tribe of Judah and will be the one to redeem Israel.[38] The Spirit, however, that rests upon the figure of Isa 11:2 has not alighted upon him only. This Spirit is also "the spirit of prophecy" and as such has rested upon other people of God, including Moses and Joshua (Deut 34:9 is probably in view), Elijah and Elisha (2 Kgs 2:15), the seventy elders (Num 11:25) and Eldad and Medad (Num 11:26).[39] Solomon fasted for forty days to receive from God "the spirit of wisdom and understanding," and as a result became the "wisest of all men."[40] Elsewhere, Isa 11:2 is connected with the spirit of God that hovered over the face of the waters as described at Gen 1:2, to support the assertion that messiah "existed from the beginning of God's creation of the world."[41] In another text, the mention of the "knowledge of God" filling the earth

---

especially the chart on p. 52, where he indicates that the language of Isa 11:2 has influenced 1QS IV, 4. There are other such "spirit" texts difficult to interpret, e.g., *Jos. Asen.* 19:11, *T. Judah* 20:5, *Jub.* 25:14.

[33] 1QS IV, 20b–23a; 1QH^a V, 25; XX, 10b–13 (= 4Q427 2+3 II, 10b–13).

[34] *T. Levi* 18:2–3, 5, 9a; *T. Benj.* 11:2; cf. *1 En.* 51:3.

[35] *T. Jud.* 24:1–6. This short chapter is "a mosaic of eschatological expectations" woven together from several messianic and end-time texts (H. C. Kee, "Testaments of the Twelve Patriarchs," *OTP* 1:801n.24a).

[36] *Tanhuma*, Genesis 38:1ff., Part VII, p. 242; *Pirqe Rabbi Eliezer*, p. 19; *Pesiqta Rabbati* 33.6; *Midr. Rabbah* Genesis, ch. 97 (NV; p. 902); *Midr.* Psalm 72.3; *b. Sanh.* 93b (p. 626); *Tg. Isa.* 11:1.

[37] *Midr.* Psalm 72.3.

[38] *Tanhuma*, Genesis 38:1ff., Part VII, p. 242.

[39] *Mekilta*, Piska, 1.156; cf. *Midr. Rabbah* Numbers 10.5 (p. 362).

[40] *Midr.* Proverbs 1.1 (p. 17).

[41] *Pesiqta Rabbati* 33.6.

at Isa 11:9 is taken to imply that the Holy Spirit has filled all the earth
with its presence.[42]

The evidence in early and late Judaism understood Isaiah 11:1–9
messianically, and clearly demonstrates that it was believed that upon
his arrival the messiah, endowed with the Spirit of wisdom and understanding, would effect judgment and fill the nations of the earth with
the knowledge of God. At this time God would also pour out this same
Spirit upon his people (see again, e.g., *T. Jud.* 24:1–3; *T. Levi* 18:11; cf.
Joel 2:28–29 ET).

New Testament Context: Isaiah 11:2, 9 in Colossians 1:9–10

Paul begins his letter to the Colossians in his customary way (1:1–2) and
then proceeds to thank God for the Colossians' faith and love (1:3–8).
God has brought the gospel even to Colossae, and it is increasing
and bearing fruit there, just as it is in "the entire world" (1:6). By this
Paul is encouraged, even as he is in chains (cf. 4:3, 18). He writes to
encourage their hearts in the gospel, so as to ward off any temptation to
succumb to a local and attractive, but heterodox, "philosophy" (2:2–4,
8). This philosophy boasts to be the way of wisdom (2:23). Therefore,
to counter this claim, Paul follows up his thanksgiving to God (1:3–8)
with a report of his prayer for the Colossians (1:9–14). He asks God
to fill them with "the knowledge of his will in all Spirit-given wisdom
and understanding" (1:9), so that they might possess true wisdom. It
is this wisdom alone that leads to a life that is pleasing to the Lord
(1:10). Later Paul will assert that through their union with Christ, the
Colossians are connected to the greatest source of wisdom they would
ever need in order to live a life fully pleasing to God (2:2–3). Thus,
the prayer report introduces the theme of (true) wisdom—and where
it is to be found—that will be elaborated upon more fully in the body
of the letter.[43]

As mentioned, Paul prays for the Colossians that God would fill
them with τὴν ἐπίγνωσιν τοῦ θελήματος αὐτοῦ (1:9; "the knowledge
of his will"), a phrase synonymous with τῇ ἐπιγνώσει τοῦ θεοῦ ("the
knowledge of God") found in 1:10b. The goal of Paul's request for

---

[42] *Mekilta*, Shirata 10.70.
[43] Peter Thomas O'Brien, *Introductory Thanksgivings in the Letters of Paul* (NovTSup 49;
Leiden: Brill, 1977), 100–1.

such knowledge is so that the Colossians might be enabled to "walk worthily of the Lord in every way that pleases" (v. 10a). He then offers with four participles the major outline of how that lifestyle should look (vv. 10b–12a).[44]

In v. 9, Paul asks God to fill the Colossians with knowledge of his will, requesting that this might be done ἐν πάσῃ σοφίᾳ καὶ συνέσει πνευματικῇ ("in all Spirit-given wisdom and understanding"). There is nothing particularly special about the hendiadys σοφία καὶ σύνεσις (or the inverse), for it does occur in Greco-Roman literature.[45] It does, however, show up there only occasionally. It occurs with some frequency in the LXX.[46] The two words also occur in close proximity elsewhere in the LXX, often in parallelism.[47] Only in the LXX, however, do σοφία and σύνεσις occur together in close connection with the word πνεῦμα out of the bulk of the extant literary texts written in Greek from Homer up to just before the NT.[48] In fact, this word cluster of three terms is found only three times in the LXX at Exod 31:3, 35:31, and Isa 11:2. Moreover, all of these share the σοφία καὶ σύνεσις hendiadys tied tightly to πνεῦμα in a genitive construction:

Exod 31:3:	πνεῦμα θεῖον	σοφίας καὶ συνέσεως
Exod 35:31:	πνεῦμα θεῖον	σοφίας καὶ συνέσεως
Isa 11:2:	πνεῦμα	σοφίας καὶ συνέσεως

Col 1:9 is the only text in the NT with this wording, though Paul employs the adjective πνευματικός instead of the noun form πνεῦμα:

Col 1:9:	σοφίᾳ καὶ συνέσει πνευματικῇ

---

[44] Grk: ἐν παντὶ ἔργῳ ἀγαθῷ <u>καρποφοροῦντες</u>... <u>αὐξανόμενοι</u> τῇ ἐπιγνώσει τοῦ θεοῦ... <u>δυναμούμενοι</u>... εἰς πᾶσαν ὑπομονὴν καὶ μακροθυμίαν... μετὰ χαρᾶς <u>εὐχαριστοῦντες</u> τῷ πατρί.

[45] See, e.g., Aristotle, *Historia animalium* 7:29–30, *Nicomachean Ethics* 1.13.20; Strabo, *Geography* 8.6.2; Diodorus Siculus, *Library of History* 9.3.3 (all LCL).

[46] Exod 31:3, 35:31, 35; Deut 4:6; 1 Chr 22:12; 2 Chr 1:10, 11, 12; Isa 11:2, Dan (Th) 2:20, 5:14.

[47] Ps 48:4 LXX; 110:10 LXX; Prov 1:7, 2:2, 3, 6, 9:10, 24:3, Job 12:13, 28:20, 39:17; Isa 10:13, 29:14; Jer 28:15 [ET 51:15]; Dan 2:21, Dan (Th) 1:17; Jdt 8:29; Sir 1:4, 14:20, 15:3, 39:6, 50:27; Bar 3:23. The only NT text is 1 Cor 1:19, which is a quotation of Isa 29:14.

[48] The three occurrences in Philo are no exception because they all arise from the explicit citation of Exod 31:3 (*Giants* 23 [twice] and 28). This was demonstrated by a *TLG* search on all relevant forms of each of the three words.

The adjective πνευματικός is commonly found in early Greek literature to denote something as of the wind, breath, or air.[49] The word is not found in either the LXX or Josephus. Philo employs it nine times, and all the occurrences are non-theological in nature except perhaps *Abr.* 113 and *QG* 1.92. These latter two usages appear to convey the meaning of something as "immaterial." The three men who visited Abraham were changed from their "spiritual and soul-like substance into the form of men"[50] to be able to visit with the patriarch. And likewise the substance (οὐσία) of the "sons of God" mentioned at Gen 6:4 is "spiritual" (Philo views them as angels), but they imitated the material form of men to be able to have intercourse with women.

In the NT, πνευματικός occurs twenty-six times, twenty-four in the Pauline literature and only twice elsewhere (both at 1 Pet 2:5). It occurs three times in Romans, fifteen times in 1 Corinthians, once in Galatians, three times in Ephesians, and twice in Colossians. The use in Rom 1:11 is slightly ambiguous, but the use in Rom 7:14 is clear. Paul writes that the Law is "spiritual," i.e., given through or inspired by the Spirit and "from God" (see vv. 22, 25b) and as such is "holy and righteous and good" (v. 14). In Rom 15:27, Paul asserts that the Gentiles' participation in the Jews' "spiritual" things obligates them to share their "material" (σαρκικοῖς) things with the Jews. It would be an error to think Paul merely has immaterial things in mind. Rather, the "spiritual things" in context is the gospel and its blessings for those embracing the message, gifts from God to humans in Christ through the Spirit. The use in 1 Cor 9:11 falls here also.

The four occurrences of πνευματικός in 1 Cor 2:13–3:1 (vv. 13 [twice], 15, 3:1) are heavily shaped by the six occurrences of God's πνεῦμα in the immediate context (2:10 [twice], 11, 12, 13, 14). Paul interprets "spiritual things" to "spiritual people," i.e., things of the Spirit to people having the Spirit. The occurrences at 1 Cor 14:37 and Gal 6:1 also belong here.[51] In 1 Cor 10:3–4, a notoriously difficult passage, the word is nevertheless consistently employed three times to convey

---

[49] LSJ, 9th ed., "πνευματικός."

[50] Grk.: πνευματικῆς καὶ ψυχοειδοῦς οὐσίας εἰς ἀνθρωπόμορφον ἰδέαν.

[51] See C. K. Barrett, *The First Epistle to the Corinthians* (BNTC; London: A&C Black, 1968; reprint, Peabody, Mass.: Hendrickson, 1996), 76; Gordon Fee, *God's Empowering Presence*, 30–31. For the use at Gal 6:1, note the frequent occurrence of πνεῦμα in the immediate context of 5:16–6:1 (eight occurrences). The NRSV rightly translates πνευματικός at Gal 6:1 as "you who have received the Spirit." Cf. TNIV: "you who live by the Spirit."

the sense of something that is from heaven or given by God. It was so with both the manna and quail (Exod 16:4–35), as well as the water from the rock (Exod 17:5–6). In 1 Cor 12:1, 14:1 the "spiritual gifts" are clearly gifts given by the Spirit (see 12:3–13). In 1 Cor 15:44, 46 [4x], Paul contrasts the σῶμα ψυχικόν ("physical body") with the σῶμα πνευματικόν ("spiritual body"). The physical body is the one that all humanity shares with Adam, a body of dust and from the earth (vv. 47–48). The spiritual body is what Christ acquired in his resurrection. It will be the body that all those who belong to him will have in the future resurrection. Christ is the man "from heaven" (v. 47). Thus, a "spiritual body" is not an immaterial body, but a resurrection body, a body fit for heaven and of heaven, "adapted to the final life of the Spirit in the eschaton."[52]

Eph 1:3 is difficult and ambiguous, while the substantive use at 6:12 clearly refers to demonic evil spirits. The use at Eph 5:19 parallels that at Col 3:16 and, taking our cue from the clear uses elsewhere in Paul, means that the believers in those churches were to instruct one another with hymns inspired by the Spirit and that have the things of God as their content.[53]

What the above demonstrates is that the typical Pauline usage of πνευματικός means that something is *of, from, given, or inspired by the Holy Spirit*.[54] Therefore, when Paul writes ἐν πάσῃ σοφίᾳ καὶ συνέσει πνευματικῇ at Col 1:9, he means "in all Spirit-given wisdom and understanding."[55] This sense is confirmed by the three parallel passages from the LXX laid out above, Exod 31:3, 35:31, and Isa 11:2, all of which

---

[52] Fee, *God's Empowering Presence*, 32.

[53] Ernest Best, *A Critical and Exegetical Commentary on Ephesians* (ICC; Edinburgh: T&T Clark, 1998), 511; Lohse, *Colossians*, 151.

[54] See also Eduard Schweizer, "πνεῦμα, πνευματικός," *TDNT* 6:436–37; J. D. G. Dunn, "Spirit, Holy Spirit," *NIDNTT* 3:706–7; Fee, *God's Empowering Presence*, 29; BDAG, "πνευματικός," definition 2; J. Kremer, "πνευματικός," *EDNT* 3:122–23.

[55] Cf. BDAG, "πνευματικός," 2.a.β.; Lohmeyer, *Kolosser*, 33, translates πνευματικός as "Spirit-given" ("geistgegeben"); cf. Charles Masson, *L'Epître de Saint Paul aux Colossiens* (CNT 10; Neuchatel: Delachaux, 1950), 94 ("reçues de l'Esprit"); Pate, *The End of the Age*, 161–62. Thomas J. Sappington, *Revelation and Redemption at Colossae* (JSNTSup 53; Sheffield: Sheffield Academic Press, 1991), 180, writes on v. 9 that Paul desired for the Colossians not some "esoteric body of information" but "a knowledge of God's will that *comes from the Spirit*" (emphasis mine); Werner Bieder, *Der Kolosserbrief* (Zürich: Zwingli-Verlag, 1943), 36: "Derselbe Geist, der die Liebe wirkt (1, 8), schafft auch die Erkenntnis"; Aletti, *Colossiens*, 71 (see also n.84); Andreas Lindemann, *Der Kolosserbrief* (ZBKNT 10; Zürich: Theologischer Verlag, 1983), 20: "'Weisheit und Einsicht' sind geistlich, d.h. sie werden von Gottes Geist gewirkt"; Furter, *Colossiens*, 90. Cf. TNIV: "through all the wisdom and understanding that the Spirit gives."

explicitly employ πνεῦμα in the sense of "Spirit of God." Moreover, the parallel passage to Col 1:9 in the letter to the Ephesians is found at 1:16–17 and reads:

> I keep mentioning you in my prayers, that the God of our Lord Jesus Christ, the Father of glory, might give to you *the Spirit of wisdom and revelation in his knowledge* [πνεῦμα σοφίας καὶ ἀποκαλύψεως ἐν ἐπιγνώσει αὐτοῦ].

Here Paul employs πνεῦμα, further confirming our reading of Col 1:9. In the side margin of NA[27] at Eph 1:17, the editors have stated that they view the phrase in Eph 1:17 to be an allusion to Isa 11:2.[56]

Paul's request is that God would fill the Colossians with "the knowledge of [God's] will" [i.e., "the knowledge of God," see v. 10] and that this would consist in "all Spirit-given wisdom and understanding." The Colossians have already begun to grasp the knowledge of God in the day they embraced the gospel (1:6, ἐπιγινώσκω), but Paul longs for them to increase in that knowledge (1:10). This knowledge is increasing, not only in Colossae, but all over the world (1:6, 10). For Paul, God was filling the world with the "knowledge of God" through the gospel. In Isa 11:2, the "Spirit of wisdom and understanding" is the enabling agent through which the promised Davidic messiah would be empowered to eradicate injustice, establish the new creation, and *fill the earth with the knowledge of God* (Isa 11:9).[57] Paul views Jesus to be this promised Davidic messiah (Χριστός = messiah, Col 1:1, 2, 3, 4, 7) and believes him to have inaugurated this promised age in the midst of the old. Isa 11:1–9 does not mention that God's people would share in the Spirit that rests upon the messiah, but this corporate participation is found elsewhere in the OT (e.g., Joel 2:28–29 [MT 3:1–2]; cf. Acts 2:17–18, 33). Indeed, Paul will say a bit later in his letter that "all the

---

[56] See also Fee, *God's Empowering Presence*, 675. Best, *Ephesians*, 163, states that if Paul was dependent upon Isa 11:2 at Eph 1:17, then the influence was probably only indirect, not direct.

[57] The verb "to fill" in LXX Isa 11:9 is ἐμπίμπλημι, a verb that has significant semantic overlap with the verb πληρόω that Paul employs at Col 1:9 (R. Schippers, "πληρόω," *NIDNTT* 1:733–41). The construction for "knowledge" at Isa 11:9 is τοῦ γνῶναι, which has a close relationship to the phrase πνεῦμα γνώσεως ("Spirit of knowledge") of Isa 11:2. In Col 1:9–10 the word for "knowledge" is ἐπίγνωσις, but it holds significant semantic overlap with γνῶσις, as seen by Paul's use of these terms in Col 2:2–3. Moreover, a comparison of their use in the LXX of Hos 4:6 and Prov 2:5–6 with their MT rendering demonstrates that there both words are merely translations of the same Hebrew term (דַּעַת). See Dunn, *Colossians*, 69n.10; E. D. Schmitz, "γινώσκω," *NIDNTT* 2:392–406.

fullness of deity" residing in messiah also fills the Colossians (1:19, 2:9–10) through their relationship to him, a phrase that is perhaps a "circumlocution for the Holy Spirit."[58] Moreover, the echoes of other new creation themes in the immediate context further supports the argument that Isa 11:1–9 is in view, for it itself is a "new creation" text (see above). All of this cumulative evidence renders the proposal that Paul has echoed Isa 11:2, 9 in Col 1:9–10 a reasonable one.

The Spirit of Wisdom in the Rest of the New Testament

The Spirit and the concept of wisdom are found closely together elsewhere in the NT (see especially Rev 1:4, 3:1, 4:5, and 5:6 for other possible allusions to Isa 11:2). In Acts 6:3, the apostles command their fellow believers to "select from among you seven men of good reputation, full of the Spirit and of wisdom" (πλήρεις πνεύματος καὶ σοφίας) to take care of the problem in the care of the Hellenistic widows (see also Acts 6:10). The parallel text to Col 1:9 in Eph 1:17 has already been noted above. In 1 Cor 12:8, one gift given through the Spirit is "the utterance of wisdom" (NASB; διὰ τοῦ πνεύματος δίδοται λόγος σοφίας). And the NA^{27} believes that Isa 11:2 has been quoted at 1 Pet 4:14 in the phrase ὅτι τὸ τῆς δόξης καὶ τὸ τοῦ θεοῦ πνεῦμα ἐφ' ὑμᾶς ἀναπαύεται. This is a possibility, but the clause lacks any mention of any of the seven virtues found in Isa 11:2 LXX. Moreover, similar language can be found elsewhere in the OT (see LXX Num 11:25, 26; 2 Kgs 2:15; cf. T. Benj. 8:2).

Isaiah 11:2 in the Early Church Fathers

It is not surprising that the early fathers saw the prophecy of Isa 11:2 fulfilled in Jesus Christ; they are in agreement on this point. In several instances, the citation of Isa 11:2 is accompanied in the near context by a citation of Joel 2:28 [MT 3:1] to support the thought that the very Spirit that rested upon the Messiah also had been poured out upon

---

[58] Clinton E. Arnold, *The Colossian Syncretism: The Interface Between Christianity and Folk Belief at Colossae* (WUNT 2/77; Tübingen: J. C. B. Mohr (Paul Siebeck), 1995; reprint, Grand Rapids: Baker, 1996), 263.

his people.[59] Among these, the one written by Tertullian holds special interest, because in his piece he is commenting upon Eph 1:12–22. He inserts his reference to Isa 11:2 at his comments upon Eph 1:17, the parallel passage to Col 1:9. The conclusion is obvious that Tertullian understood Eph 1:17 to be an allusion to Isa 11:2.

Methodius combines citations of Gen 1:28 ("be fruitful and multiply") and Isa 11:2 in a way that recalls what this present work argues Paul has done in Col 1:6, 9–10 (see chapter three of this work). God, by the sevenfold Spirit of Isa 11:2, prepares for Christ (the last Adam) his bride, the Church, enabling her to "be fruitful and multiply" numerically in both spiritual children and in grandness of her virtues.[60]

Hermeneutical and Theological Reflections

If our exegesis is correct, then Paul saw in Jesus' arrival the prophetic fulfillment of Isa 11:2. Here in Col 1:9, however, this fulfillment is merely assumed and Paul has built upon it, moving beyond what Isa 11:2 promised. In Col 1:9, it is *the Colossians* who partake of the Spirit of Isa 11:2, *via* their union with the messiah, in whom "all the fullness of deity dwells bodily." Jesus, the messiah, is the head, and they comprise part of his body (1:18, 24, 2:19); by this connection they are filled with his "fullness" (2:10).

Paul's language at Col 1:9–10 therefore presupposes that the apostle interpreted Isa 11:1–9 in accord with early (and later) Jewish interpretation of the same text (except for his identification of Jesus of Nazareth as the promised Davidic messiah). Early Jewish exegesis interpreted Isa 11:1–9 messianically and expected the messiah to fill the earth with the knowledge of God by means of the Spirit of wisdom and understanding. They also believed that, upon his arrival, the messiah would not only rule by this Spirit's power, but that he would also pour out this same Spirit on his people, enabling them to walk faithfully in accord with the covenant. Paul's thought in Col 1:9–10 is in line with these ideas and in fact appears simply to assume and build upon it.

---

[59] Justin Martyr, *Dialogue with Trypho* 87 (*ANF* 1:243); Irenaeus, *Against Heresies* 3.17.1, 3 (*ANF* 1:444–45); Novatian, *Treatise Concerning the Trinity* 29 (*ANF* 5:640–41); Tertullian, *Against Marcion* 5.17 (*ANF* 3:465).

[60] *The Banquet of the Ten Virgins* 3.8 (*ANF* 6:319–20).

Paul was convinced that the messiah promised in Scripture had come in the person of Jesus. In his thought, therefore, God had fulfilled the promises of a future messiah as found in Scripture, like Isa 11:1–9. The messianic king had arrived and thus the worldwide establishment of God's rule and the peaceful new creation had arrived also. Even in Col 1:9, however, the "already—not yet" eschatology of Paul's thought can be discerned, for the work of the Spirit as described in Isa 11:1–9 has only been inaugurated and not yet consummated. The Spirit has only begun to fill the world with the "knowledge of God." This knowledge, however, had reached even as far as Colossae from its beginning in Jerusalem, and for this Paul thanks God (1:3).

CHAPTER FIVE

THE SCRIPTURES OF ISRAEL IN COLOSSIANS 1:9–14: THE ECHO OF THE EXODUS MOTIF IN 1:12–14

Comparison of Textual Versions and Evaluation

NOTE TO THE READER: The OT texts in the chart below are offered as representative examples of the larger swath of biblical evidence; the reader should not interpret the chart below to be asserting that Col 1:12–14 is echoing these exact texts.

Deut 10:9 MT, etc.	Deut 10:9 LXX, etc.[1]	Colossians 1:12b
לֹא־הָיָה לְלֵוִי חֵלֶק וְנַחֲלָה עִם־אֶחָיו	οὐκ ἔστιν τοῖς Λευίταις μερὶς καὶ κλῆρος ἐν τοῖς ἀδελφοῖς αὐτῶν	τῷ ἱκανώσαντι ὑμᾶς εἰς τὴν μερίδα τοῦ κλήρου
Exodus 14:30 MT, etc.	Exodus 14:30 LXX, etc.[2]	Colossians 1:13a
וַיּוֹשַׁע יְהוָה בַּיּוֹם הַהוּא אֶת־יִשְׂרָאֵל מִיַּד מִצְרָיִם	ἐρρύσατο κύριος τὸν Ισραηλ ἐν τῇ ἡμέρᾳ ἐκείνῃ ἐκ χειρὸς τῶν Αἰγυπτίων	ὃς ἐρρύσατο ἡμᾶς ἐκ τῆς ἐξουσίας τοῦ σκότους

---

[1] Paul is not echoing any *specific* text, but evoking a whole OT theme or tradition, the foundational event of Israelite history. The point of offering Deut 10:9 above is not to stress what is said about the Levites, but to show that the assumption behind the statement to them is that the rest of the tribes of Israel *did* receive a portion of the inheritance of the land of Israel. Several texts employ this language to denote the promised land and its allotment. Sometimes κληρονομία is used in lieu of κλῆρος, and sometimes the thought is expressed by a verbal form instead of a noun. See Num 18:20–24, 26:53–56; Deut 10:9, 12:12, 14:27, 29, 18:1; Josh 11:23, 13:7, 18:7, 19:9, 47, Sir 44:23, 45:22; cf. 2 Sam 20:1; Ps 16:5 [LXX 15:5]; Isa 17:14, 57:6; Wis 2:9.

[2] See the use of ῥύομαι especially in the programmatic statement of Exod 6:6–8; see also Exod 5:23, 12:27; Judg 6:9; Wis 10:15, 19:7–9.

(cont.)

Deut 15:15 MT, etc.	Deut 15:15 LXX, etc.	Colossians 1:14a
עֶבֶד הָיִיתָ בְּאֶרֶץ מִצְרַיִם וַיִּפְדְּךָ יְהוָה אֱלֹהֶיךָ	οἰκέτης ἦσθα ἐν γῇ Αἰγύπτου καὶ ἐ<u>λυτρώσατό</u> σε κύριος ὁ θεός σου	ἐν ᾧ ἔχομεν τὴν ἀπο<u>λύτρωσιν</u>[3]

This proposal meets the two criteria necessary for an echo: 1) availability and 2) word agreement and rare concept similarity. Regarding *availability*, Paul was well aware of the Exodus narrative (Rom 9:17; 1 Cor 5:7, 10:1–5). Regarding *word agreement* and *rare concept similarity*, Col 1:12b–14a shares four prominent words in common with the language employed to describe the Israelite exodus from Egypt. The reader must note well that Paul did not have any one text in mind; *the texts offered above are given as typical examples of the larger swath of evidence.* Their witness is to be taken together and their evidence is cumulative. None of the words point to the exodus event on their own (e.g., not every use of the verb λυτρόω in the LXX expresses God's exodus deliverance from Egypt; larger contextual concerns must demonstrate that the exodus is in view). It is when the terms are put together in a certain way that they form the echo. In fact, this terminology is woven into Paul's description of Christians as a people whom God has chosen to deliver from a kingdom of darkness and slavery and to transfer into a kingdom of light and freedom. Paul's depiction thus also offers a striking conceptual parallel to the ancient exodus deliverance. Therefore, there is both word agreement as well as a shared rare concept between Col 1:12b–14a and the OT exodus event. Again, Paul has not echoed any one specific passage, but rather the major redemptive event of OT history.[4]

---

[3] The noun form occurs only once in the LXX (Dan. 4:34), but the cognate verb λυτρόω occurs several times to denote YHWH's redemption of Israel from Egyptian bondage: Exod 6:6, 15:13; Deut 7:8, 9:26, 13:6 [ET: 13:5], 15:15, 21:8, 24:18; 2 Sam 7:23 (twice); 1 Chr 17:21 (twice); Neh 1:10; Esth 4:17g; Isa 63:9; Pss 73:2 [74:2 ET], 76:16 [77:15], 77:42 [78:42], 105:10 [106:10]; Mic 6:4. Cf. Ps 77:35 [78:35]. The word ἀπολύτρωσις was used to signify the ransom payment made to purchase the freedom of a slave or captive (see BDAG, "ἀπολύτρωσις"; *EDNT*, "ἀπολύτρωσις," section 2; Leon Morris, *The Apostolic Preaching of the Cross* (3rd rev. ed.; Grand Rapids: Eerdmans, 1965), 16–18; see too Morris's wider discussion on pp. 11–64).

[4] Cf. Sylvia C. Keesmaat, "Exodus and the Intertextual Transformation of Tradition in Romans 8.14–30," *JSNT* 54 (1994): 29–56, who argues similarly for an echo of the exodus event (and not for a specific passage in the OT) in Rom 8.

Scholars have already detected the exodus in Col 1:12–14: Augustine, *Expositions on the Book of Psalms* (*NPNF*[1] 8:377; commenting on Ps 78:28); G. B. Caird, *Paul's Letters*

The Exodus from Egypt for the Land of Promise

The exodus from Egypt stands as the foundational event of the OT. Brevard Childs writes that it "forms the heart of Israel's earliest tradition" and its "centrality…was retained throughout the entire Old Testament and established Israel's identity."[5] Nahum Sarna also has grasped the significance of the exodus event for Israel and the Scriptures. He writes that "it is no wonder that the Exodus is the pivotal event in the Bible, and that the experiences connected with it—the slavery of the Israelites, their liberation from Egypt, the covenant between God and His people at Sinai, and the journey in the wilderness toward the Promised Land—all constitute the dominant motif of the Scriptures in one form or another."[6]

YHWH delivered the Hebrews from Egypt in order to give them the land he swore on oath to give to the seed of Abraham. This idea is encapsulated in the programmatic statement of Exod 6:6–8:

> Say therefore to the Israelites, "I am the LORD, and I will free you from the burdens of the Egyptians and *deliver* [ῥύομαι] you from slavery to them. I will *redeem* [λυτρόω] you with an outstretched arm and with mighty acts of judgment. I will take you as my people, and I will be your God.

---

from Prison (New Clarendon Bible; Oxford: Oxford University Press, 1976), 171–72; Bieder, *Der Kolosserbrief*, 48; Lohmeyer, *Kolosser*, 39, 49; Rudolf Hoppe, *Epheserbrief, Kolosserbrief* (SKKNT 10; Stuttgart: Verlag Katholisches Bibelwerk, 1987), 111; Wright, *Colossians*, 61–63; idem, *Climax of the Covenant*, 109; Robert W. Wall, *Colossians & Philemon* (IVPNTC; Downers Grove: InterVarsity, 1993), 57–59; Barth and Blanke, *Colossians*, 188, 190; Dunn, *Colossians*, 75–77, 80; MacDonald, *Colossians*, 51; Gary S. Shogren, "Presently Entering the Kingdom of Christ: The Background and Purpose of Col 1:12–14," *JETS* 31 (1988): 176–77; Yates, *Colossians*, 11–12; David M. Hay, *Colossians* (ANTC; Nashville: Abingdon, 2000), 48, who writes that "anyone familiar with Judaism would find in this imagery of deliverance and inheritance allusions to Israel's deliverance from Egypt and entrance into the promised land"; Fee, "Old Testament Intertextuality in Colossians," ad loc.; Beale, "Colossians," ad loc.

Others have detected the reference back to the promised land of Canaan in the phrase εἰς τὴν μερίδα τοῦ κλήρου, but did not mention the exodus event: Hühn, *Die alttestamentlichen Citate*, 197; Masson, *Colossiens*, 96; Francis W. Beare, "The Epistle to the Colossians" (*IB* 11; New York: Abingdon, 1955), 159; Moule, *Colossians*, 55; Norbert Hugedé, *Commentaire de L'Épître aux Colossiens* (Geneva: Labor et Fides, 1968), 44; Schweizer, *Colossians*, 50; Martin, *Colossians*, 53–54; O'Brien, *Colossians*, 26; Furter, *Colossiens*, 94–95; Richard R. Melick, Jr., *Philippians, Colossians, Philemon* (NAC; Nashville: Broadman, 1991), 205–6; Andrew T. Lincoln, "The Letter to the Colossians" (*NIB* 11; Nashville: Abingdon, 2000), 593.

[5] Brevard S. Childs, *Biblical Theology of the Old and New Testaments: Theological Reflection on the Christian Bible* (Minneapolis: Fortress, 1992), 130, 131.

[6] Nahum M. Sarna, *Exploring Exodus: The Heritage of Biblical Israel* (New York: Schocken, 1987), 1–2.

> You shall know that I am the LORD your God, who has freed you from the burdens of the Egyptians. I will bring you into the land that I swore to give to Abraham, Isaac, and Jacob; I will give it to you for a *possession* [κλῆρος]. I am the LORD." (NRSV)

In other words, God's deliverance of the Israelites out of Egypt was a *means* to an *end*. He rescued them from subjugation, not merely to free an oppressed people, but in order to fulfill his promise to Abraham that his seed would inherit the land of Canaan (Gen 15:7–8, 28:4). The land is therefore subsequently called the *inheritance*, κλῆρος or κληρονομία.[7] This inheritance was to be divided into parts or *allotments* between the tribes, in accordance with their size (Num 26:52–56).[8] The Levites, however, were not to be apportioned any μερίς or κλῆρος in the land, for the Lord himself was to be their inheritance.[9] At Josh 19:9, the two words are combined to describe the allotted inheritance of the tribes of Simeon and Judah specifically. Along with these, there are four other passages where the words μερίς and κλῆρος are explicitly combined, but do not refer to the promised land.[10]

God's foundational act of deliverance for Israel was that from Egypt. No other deliverance shaped Israel's national thought more than the exodus. With regard to this deliverance, the LXX translators selected the word ῥύομαι as one of the central terms to express this divine rescue from the power of Egypt.[11] Later in Israel's history, a prophet heralded the day when God would act once again as He did for Israel when they were in Egypt. Israel eventually found itself exiled to Babylon for flagrant covenantal disobedience, but YHWH promised a day of a magnificent "second exodus" from this oppressor that would make the first exodus appear insignificant in comparison. Here too, the LXX

---

[7] At times these words are employed in the same text as synonyms: Num 18:23–24, 27:7, 32:18–19; Josh 17:4 (both translating the Hebrew נַחֲלָה). To see this language tied explicitly to the land, see, e.g., Deut 3:18, 4:21, 5:31, 17:14, 19:10, 14, 21:23, 24:4, 25:15, 19, 26:1. See also J. Eichler, "Inheritance, Land, Portion," *NIDNTT* 2:295–98.

[8] Gk.: μερίς; Josh 18:5–7, 9, 19:9, 47; Mic 2:4; Ezek 45:7, 48:8, 21; Sir 45:22. The word can also refer to a smaller plot of land or to fields within this inheritance that have been allotted to individuals: Josh 15:13 (Caleb), 21:42 (Joshua), Ruth 2:3 (Boaz), 2 Kgs 9:25 (Naboth), etc. The cognate verb μερίζω is also employed with regard to land apportionment in Num 26:53–56; Josh 13:7, 14:5, 18:6.

[9] See Deut 10:9, 12:12, 14:27, 29, 18:1; Josh 14:3–4, where both words are closely and explicitly combined with reference to the allotment of the Levites; cf. YHWH's word to Aaron: Num 18:20; Sir 45:22.

[10] See Gen 31:14; Isa 57:6; Jer 13:25; Wis 2:9; cf. Acts 8:21.

[11] See Exod 5:23, 6:6, 12:27, 14:30; Judg 6:9; Isa 48:20–21; Wis 10:15, 19:9 (see vv. 6–12).

translators at times selected ῥύομαι to describe this great rescue in contexts that clearly intended to recall the original exodus event (Isa 51:10, 52:9; cf. 48:20–21).

The LXX translators also chose the verb λυτρόω at least twenty times to express specifically God's foundational act of deliverance of the Hebrew slaves from Egypt. In fact, it is one of the main verbs in the LXX used to describe that deliverance.[12] The verb usually has God as its subject and the basic idea is "the liberation of a prisoner or slave."[13] In the exodus narrative proper (Exod 1–15) the verb shows up at 6:6 and 15:13 to describe God's deliverance from Egypt, "the house of slavery" (Exod 13:3, 14, 20:2, etc.). The exodus narrative relates the theological history of how God delivered an enslaved people from the oppression of a harsh pharaoh of Egypt and led them out to inherit the land of Canaan in fulfillment of the promises made to the patriarchs.

The Second Exodus Theme in the Old Testament

So inscribed upon Israel's consciousness was the exodus that "each [later] generation looked to the first exodus as the archetypal expression of its own future hope."[14] Thus the original exodus provided the pattern for another crossing of a body of water: the Jordan River.[15] After forty years of wilderness wandering, God commanded Joshua and the new generation of Israelites to cross the Jordan into the promised land of Canaan. When the ark, borne by the priests, began to pass through the Jordan, the waters of that great river stood in a heap (Josh 3:13, 16) as they had at the Sea of Reeds in the first exodus (Exod 15:8; cf. Ps 78:13). The new generation crossed over the Jordan on "dry ground" (חָרָבָה; Josh 3:17) even as the first generation had at the Sea (חָרָבָה;

---

[12] Exod 6:6, 15:13; Deut 7:8, 9:26, 13:6 [ET: 13:5], 15:15, 21:8, 24:18; 2 Sam 7:23 (twice); 1 Chr 17:21 (twice); Neh 1:10; Esth 4:17g; Isa 63:9; Pss 73:2 [74:2 ET], 76:16 [77:15], 77:42 [78:42], 105:10 [106:10]; Mic 6:4. Cf. Ps 77:35 [78:35].

Another main verb describing God's activity in the exodus event—and occurring more often than either ῥύομαι or λυτρόω—is ἐξάγω ("to lead out"; e.g., Exod 6:6, 7:4, 12:51, 29:46; Lev 22:33, 26:45; Num 15:41; Deut 4:20; Isa 48:21; 2 Chr 7:22; Neh 9:18).

[13] C. Spicq, "λύτρον, λυτρόω, λύτρωσις, ἀπολύτρωσις, ἀντίλυτρον," TLNT 2:423–24; cf. C. Brown, "Redemption," NIDNTT 3:192.

[14] Michael Fishbane, "The "Exodus" Motif/The Paradigm of Historical Renewal," in Text and Texture: Close Readings of Selected Biblical Texts (New York: Schocken, 1979), 121.

[15] Fishbane, "The "Exodus" Motif," 122–25.

Exod 14:21; cf. 2 Kgs 2:8!). The new generation celebrated the Passover on the fourteenth day immediately after their exodus (Josh 5:10), even as the first generation celebrated it on the fourteenth day immediately before their exodus (Exod 12:1–28).[16]

Moreover, Joshua is patterned after Moses as a second Moses. The LORD exalts and is with Joshua (Josh 3:7) just as he was with Moses, with the result that the people feared Joshua, as they did Moses (Josh 4:14). Joshua even experienced a theophany like Moses, in that he was commanded to remove his sandals like Moses had been commanded, "for the place upon which you are standing is holy" (Josh 5:15; see Exod 3:5).

While one catches tantalizing glimpses of a promised "second" exodus after exile in Hos 2:16–17 [ET vv. 14–15] and Mic 7:15, the theme becomes explicit among other prophets: Isa 10:24–27, 11:10–16 (cf. 19:19–25); Jer 16:14–15, 23:7–8; Ezek 20:32–44 (see vv. 5–31).[17] The second exodus depicted in Isa 11:10–16 is especially significant for our purposes because it is explicitly tied to and inaugurated by the arrival of the ideal Davidic king, the "root of Jesse," interpreted in Paul's day as a reference to the messiah (Isa 11:1–9, 10).[18]

Scholars have long recognized that the exodus motif is especially concentrated in Isaiah chapters 40–55.[19] It surfaces in 43:16–21, 48:20–21, 51:9–11, and 52:11–12.[20] In Isa 43:16–21, exiled Israel is commanded

---

[16] Fishbane, "The "Exodus" Motif," 124.

[17] See Carroll Stuhlmueller, *Creative Redemption in Deutero-Isaiah* (AnBib 43; Rome: Biblical Institute, 1970), 60–66; Fishbane, "The "Exodus" Motif," 125–32.

[18] See chapter four of this study. For a description of the numerous allusions to the first exodus in Isa 11:11–16, see Sweeney, "Jesse's New Shoot in Isaiah 11," 111. Sweeney rightly observes that "Isa 11.16b makes the analogy explicit by noting that the return of the exiles will take place 'just as it was for Israel on the day of its going up from the land of Egypt'" (111).

[19] See, e.g., Roland Beaudet, "La typologie de l'Exode dans le Second-Isaïe," in *Etudes Theologiques* (ed. Roy Lorenzo; Québec: Presses de l'Université Laval, 1963), 11–21; Bernhard W. Anderson, "Exodus Typology in Second Isaiah," in *Israel's Prophetic Heritage: Essays in Honor of James Muilenburg* (eds. Bernhard W. Anderson and Walter Harrelson; New York: Harper, 1962), 177–95; Joseph Blenkinsopp, "Scope and Depth of Exodus Tradition in Deutero-Isaiah 40–55," in *The Dynamism of Biblical Tradition* (eds. Pierre Benoit, Roland E. Murphy, and Bastiaan Van Iersel; Concilium, vol. 20; New York: Paulist, 1967), 41–50.

[20] The texts listed above are those in which I confidently see a reference to a new exodus. Stuhlmueller, *Creative Redemption*, 272, Table 1, offers a helpful chart that lists not only these texts but others within Deutero-Isaiah, and the major scholars (up through the year 1970) who "recognize a reference to the exodus in these passages" (66n.212).

to recall no longer the "former things," i.e., the ancient exodus from Egypt, but rather to take thought to the "new thing," the greater exodus that the LORD was about to bring about for them (vv. 16–19a). He promises to "make a way" in the wilderness and to provide water miraculously, just as he did in the former deliverance (vv. 19b–21; see Exod 17:1–7). He will deliver them from exile in Babylon and bring them back to the land of promise. This exodus will be so magnificent that it will eclipse the former in splendor.

In Isa 48:20, the prophet commands exilic Israel to "go out" from Babylon and declare, "The LORD has *redeemed*[21] his servant Jacob!" This is immediately followed by a recollection of how God miraculously provided water from the rock in the wilderness after the deliverance from Egypt (v. 21). The implied relationship between verses 20 and 21 is that as the LORD provided in the ancient exodus, so also will he supply in the greater exodus from Babylon.

In 51:9–11 "the *creation, exodus,* and *new exodus* are fused."[22] The author pleads with the LORD to awake, fight for, and deliver his people, even as he did at the Sea of Reeds in Egypt long ago. The plea is for God to make good on the promise of a greater exodus from the Babylonian captivity.

Isa 52:11–12, which is the fourth text offering a clear second exodus reference within Isa 40–55, alludes back to at least three passages within the ancient exodus narrative. In the greater exodus, the people will *not* go out "in haste"[23] as they had done at the first exodus (Exod 12:11). God will, however, "go before them" (MT: הֹלֵךְ לִפְנֵיכֶם יְהוָה; Exod 13:21) and be both their front and rear guard, just as he was in the first (Exod 14:19–20).

Israel's Release from Babylonia as an "Already—Not Yet" Restoration

The public prayers of confession of sin found in Ezra 9 and Neh 9 show that, even after the release from Babylon and the return to the

---

[21] LXX: ἐρρύσατο; MT: גאל; See n. 2 of this chapter as well as the discussion of the Greek term above.

[22] Fishbane, "The "Exodus" Motif," 135.

[23] MT: חִפָּזוֹן, which occurs only three times in MT, all with preposition בְּ: Exod 12:11; Deut 16:3, and Isa 52:12.

promised land, Israel's restoration remained incomplete. We see this, for example, in Ezra 9:7–9:

> From the days of our ancestors *to this day* we have been deep in guilt, and for our iniquities we, our kings, and our priests have been handed over to the kings of the lands, to the sword, *to captivity*, to plundering, and to utter shame, *as is now the case*. But now for a brief moment favor has been shown by the LORD our God, who has left us a remnant, and given us a stake in his holy place, in order that he may brighten our eyes and grant us a little sustenance *in our slavery*. *For we are slaves*; yet our God has not forsaken us *in our slavery*, but has extended to us his steadfast love before the kings of Persia to give us new life to set up the house of our God, to repair its ruins, and to give us a wall in Judea and Jerusalem.[24]

---

[24] NRSV; emphases are mine and highlight phrases that seem to suggest that Ezra still considered Israel's restoration to be incomplete, even though the return from Babylonia had already taken place. Ezra is praying within the rebuilt temple precincts in Jerusalem (10:1).

N. T. Wright, *The New Testament and the People of God* (vol. 1 of *Christian Origins and the Question of God*; Minneapolis: Fortress, 1992), 268–70, argues further that an understanding of continual exile persisted up through the first century C.E. among the Jews. He states, "They believed that, in all senses which mattered, Israel's exile was still in progress. Although she had come back from Babylon, the glorious message of the prophets remained unfulfilled." Wright also states that "the present age is still part of the 'age of wrath'; until the Gentiles are put in their place and Israel, and the Temple, fully restored, the exile is not really over, and the blessings promised by the prophets are still to take place." See now the various discussions of the theme in James M. Scott, ed., *Exile: Old Testament, Jewish, and Christian Conceptions* (JSJSup 56; Leiden: Brill, 1997). See also David W. Pao, *Acts and the Isaianic New Exodus* (WUNT 2/130; Tübingen: J. C. B. Mohr [Paul Siebeck], 2000; reprint, Grand Rapids: Baker, 2002), 143–46, for his excursus on the Jewish understanding of the continuing state of the exile into the first century C.E.

Some, however, have questioned Wright's "continuing exile" paradigm on the basis that the 2nd temple literature is not monolithic on the issue. The literature seems instead to offer various perspectives on the reality of the exile, which then raises a question with regard to the accuracy of Wright's proposal. It may be more accurate to say with Steve Bryan that "the problem of Ezra-Nehemiah is not so much one of continuing exile but of incomplete restoration; for the author(s) of Ezra-Nehemiah, to equate the two, as Wright does, would have been to deny a key moment in the outworking of God's eschatological purposes" (*Jesus and Israel's Traditions of Judgement and Restoration* [SNTSMS 117; Cambridge: Cambridge University Press, 2002], 16). For others who have questioned Wright's "Israel in exile" paradigm, see, e.g., Mark A. Seifrid, *Christ, our Righteousness: Paul's Theology of Justification* (NSBT 9; Downers Grove: InterVarsity, 2000), 22–25; Bruce W. Longenecker, *The Triumph of Abraham's God: The Transformation of Identity in Galatians* (Nashville: Abingdon, 1998), 137–39; Douglas J. Moo, "Israel and the Law in Romans 5–11: Interaction with the New Perspective," in *Justification and Variegated Nomism, volume 2: the Paradoxes of Paul* (eds. D. A. Carson, Peter T. O'Brien, and Mark A. Seifrid; WUNT 2/181; Tübingen: Mohr Siebeck, 2004), 200–5.

The people were still faithless,[25] the rebuilt temple was unglamorous and inferior compared to the original,[26] and the nation still remained in slavery, under the authority of pagan kings.[27] What happened to all the glorious promises of Isa 40–55? As we will see below, it began to dawn upon at least some later Jewish interpreters that the promises of a glorious second exodus from Babylon must have been fulfilled only partially when the remnant returned under Cyrus's decree in 538 B.C.E. At least in some circles, Jewish exegetes living in the 2nd Temple period began to reread the second exodus promises in this new light, and thus to anticipate an even greater exodus. Over time, some began to connect this greater exodus to the messianic age and/or the age-to-come.

The Exodus Theme in Early and Late Judaism

The literature belonging to the second Temple period recollected God's great deliverance from Egyptian bondage often, sometimes at length.[28] The literature also recalled the release from Babylonian captivity on a frequent basis. Some took this latter subject up as a historical event of days long past (or, if written by a late author who had taken up a pseudonym of a pre-exilic patriarch, then as a certain "future historical event").[29] Other texts, affirming that the restoration from Babylonian exile had begun, as the Scripture had stated in the return under Cyrus, yet were written in such a way as to communicate that a massive restoration or exodus yet awaited the people of God. Two alternatives as to the timing of this great restoration are offered in the literature. It is either seen as a continuation and culmination of the restoration already begun from Babylon under Cyrus,[30] or as a later, distinct, and

---

[25] Ezra 9:1–7, 10–15, 10:2; Neh 13:4–29.

[26] Ezra 3:10–13; Hag 2:1–3; cf. Josephus, *Ant.* 11.80–83; Tob 14:5.

[27] Ezra 9:7–9; Neh 9:32b, 36–37.

[28] E.g., *1 En.* 89:21–28; Artap. 3.27:34–37; *Jub.* 48:12–14; 3 Macc 2:6–8, 6:4; Ps.-Philo 10:2–7; *Hel. Syn. Pr* 5:9–12, 12:66–78; Josephus, *Ant.* 2.338–46; *J.W.* 5.383; *Ag Ap.* 2.157; Philo, *Moses* 1.163–80, 2.247–57; *Heir* 203.

[29] Tob 14:4–5a; 2 Macc 1:27–29; Bar 2:29–35; CD A I, 3–12; 11Q19 LIX, 5b-13; Josephus, *J.W.* 1.70; 5.389; *Ant.* 11.1–8; *T. Mos.* 3:1–4:9; *2 Bar.* 78:5–7; *T. Naph.* 4:1–5.

[30] Tob 13:1–17; *T. Dan* 5:8–13; *T. Ash.* 7:2–7 (note that God "will save Israel and *all the nations*" [*OTP* 1:818], which probably signals here that the salvation of the nations had become viewed as an end-time event, since God had not brought it about at the time of the release from the Babylonian captivity proper).

greater work of the God of Israel.[31] Both were signs that the new age
had arrived. Concerning their description, some of these texts use
language reminiscent of the original exodus situation. Others, however, are unclear as to whether they were intended to recall the exodus
theme. *4 Ezra* 13:39–47, however, does display clear intention to bring
to mind the ancient deliverance from Egypt in order to illuminate the
great end-time deliverance. Baruch 5:5–9 alludes to the Isaianic second
exodus theme to comfort and encourage its subjugated audience with
the thought that this promised and greater exodus lay just over the
horizon for them (cf. *Pss. Sol.* 11:1–8). Philo, *Rewards*, 163–68 believed
that a great exodus awaited the Israel of his own day, if they would
"make full confession [of sin]" (163). Then Israel's scattered remnants
would come to "the one appointed place, guided in their pilgrimage
by a vision divine and superhuman unseen by others but manifest to
them as they pass from exile to their home" (165). This latter text is
an allusion to the pillar of cloud and fire that guided Israel through
the wilderness in the original exodus.[32]

The thought of an end-time exodus picked up steam within later
Judaism. Though there are some exceptions,[33] when the rabbis quote
any part of the second exodus texts mentioned above (except for Josh
chs. 3–5), they explicitly assert that the text looks to the great exodus
that God would bring about in the age-to-come and/or the messianic
age. They looked forward to a time when all Israel, scattered among
the nations, would be delivered from gentile powers and brought finally

---

[31] 2 Macc 2:17–18; Sir 36:13; 48:10 [alluding to Mal chs. 3 and 4]; *T. Benj.* 9:1–2;
T. Naph. 4:1–5; Philo, *Rewards* 163–68; *4 Ezra* 13:39–47; *Pss. Sol.* 8:28, 11:1–8; *T. Jud.*
24:1 (note the μετὰ ταῦτα ["after these things"] that begins the sentence and separates
the event of the return from exile [23:5] from that of the Messianic Age [24:1–6]);
Tob 14:5–7 (note here also at 14:5 the μετὰ ταῦτα ["after these things"] that begins the
sentence and separates the event of the return from Babylonian exile [14:5a] from the
return from exile in the New Age [14:5b–7]. Chapter 13 of Tobit, however, appears
to blur the distinction between the two returns).

[32] See also Philo, *Rewards*, p. 418, note a. (LCL).

[33] *Midr. Rabbah* Leviticus 35.8 (p. 451); *Midr.* Proverbs 14 (p.72); *Pesiqta Rabbati*, Piska
33.8.

to the land promised to the patriarchs.[34] The messiah sometimes plays a central role in this deliverance.[35]

The Exodus Theme in Colossians 1:12–14

As many other commentators have noted, the language of Col 1:12–14 echoes that used to describe God's deliverance of the Israelites out of Egypt for the promised land.[36] As God delivered Israel from the land of Egypt, so he has delivered the Colossians from the "domain"[37] of darkness (v. 13a). As God brought Israel to a new land, so God has "transferred"[38] the Colossians into the "kingdom"[39] of his Son (v. 13b).

---

[34] Let the reader keep in mind that often the rabbis quote only part of the text, expecting the reader to know the wider context:

Hosea 2:16–17 [ET: 2:14–15]: *Pesiqta Rabbati*, Piska 15.10 (pp. 319–20); *Midr. Rabbah* Ruth 5.6 (pp. 64–65); *Midr. Rabbah* Song 2.9, §3 (pp. 120–21); *Midr. Rabbah* Exodus 19.1 (p. 229); *Midr. Rabbah* Exodus 2.4 (p. 51); *b. Sanhedrin* 111a (p. 762).

Isaiah 10:24–27: *Tg. Isa.* 10:24–27.

Isaiah 11:11–16: *Tanhuma*, Genesis 25:1ff. Part IV (pp. 143–44), Genesis 30:22ff., Part V (p. 195); *Pesiqta Rabbati*, Piska 48.2 (p. 817); *Midr. Rabbah* Exodus 1.5 (p. 7); *Midr. Rabbah* Numbers 13.5 (pp. 515–16), 14.1 (p. 565), 23.14 (p. 882); *Midr.* Psalm 107.4 (pp. 197–98).

Isaiah 19:19–25: *Tanna Debe Eliyyahu*, EZ, p. 194.

Isaiah 43:16–21: *Midr. Rabbah* Numbers 23.4 (pp. 865–66); *Midr.* Psalm 149.1 (p. 378), 149.3 (p. 381).

Isaiah 52:11–12: *Pesiqta Rabbati*, Piska 15.25 (p. 341); *Midr. Rabbah* Numbers 16.25 (p. 695); *Tg. Isa.* 52:11–53:12; *Mekilta*, Piskha 7.5–20 (pp. 52–53); *Midr. Rabbah* Exodus 15.17 (p. 183); "Edom" is code for Rome, see p. 181n.4).

Micah 7:15: *Tg. Mic* 7:14–15; *Tanhuma*, Genesis 27:28ff., Part VII (p. 163); *Pesiqta Rabbati*, Piska 1.7 (p. 47); *Midr. Rabbah* Exodus 15.11 (p. 173).

Jeremiah 16:14–15, 23:7–8: *Midr. Rabbah* Ecclesiastes 1.11, §1 (p. 35); *Tanna Debe Eliyyahu*, EZ, pp. 196–97; *Tg. Jer* 23:3–8; *Mekilta*, Piskha 16.92–102 (p. 135); *b. Berakhot* 12b–13a (pp. 72–73).

Other Texts: *Pirqe Rabbi Eliezer*, p. 252; *Pesiqta Rabbati*, Piska 15.22; *Midr. Rabbah* Leviticus 27.4 (p. 347).

[35] *Tg. Isa.* 10:24–27, 52:11–53:12; *Midr. Rabbah* Ruth 5.6 (pp. 64–65); *Midr. Rabbah* Song 2.9, §3 (pp. 120–21).

[36] See again n.4 of this chapter.

[37] The term for "domain," ἐξουσία, can have several nuances, including both the ruling activity of someone in power, or the sphere, domain, or territory in which that rule is exercised (see BDAG, "ἐξουσία," 4, 6). I take the latter to be in view here, which includes the former in its definition.

[38] The Greek behind this translation is μεθίστημι + εἰς, which appears to be an idiom. It occurs also in Josephus with the sense "to remove from one place into another, to transfer": *Ant.* 4.20, 9.235, 10.144, 10.242, 18.235 (cf. 14.44, with πρός). See also 2 Macc 11:23.

[39] The term for "kingdom," βασιλεία, can refer either to reigning activity or to the realm in which that active reign is exercised (see BDAG, "βασιλεία"). I believe

As God redeemed Israel from her physical slavery, so God secured the "redemption"[40] of the Colossians from slavery to sin (v. 14).[41] As God brought his people Israel to the promised land and apportioned allotments of it to each tribe as their inheritance, so God has made the Colossians fit to share in an allotment of the inheritance of "light," together with the rest of the people of God ("the saints," 1:12).[42]

What exactly, however, did Paul mean by the mention of "light" at Col 1:12? In several places the Scriptures speak of the presence of the glory of God in terms of "light."[43] At Acts 26:12, for example, Paul begins his recollection of the meeting he experienced with the exalted Christ on the Damascus road. He declares that "I saw a *light* from heaven, brighter than the sun, shining around me and my companions" (cf. Acts 9:3, 22:6, 9, 11). On the road to Damascus, Paul encountered the glory of God in the person of Jesus Christ (cf. 2 Cor 4:6). This light, which was nothing less than the blazing glory of God and which illuminates the heavenly abode with its radiance, was unveiled briefly

---

the latter is in view here, which includes the former in its definition. I take this route largely because of the exodus imagery in the text.

[40] The word is ἀπολύτρωσις, which belongs to the λυτρόω/λύτρον word-group and which was typically used to signify the ransom payment made to purchase the freedom of a slave or captive (see BDAG, "ἀπολύτρωσις"; *EDNT*, "ἀπολύτρωσις," para. 2; Morris, *The Apostolic Preaching of the Cross*, 16–18.

[41] Cf. Eph 1:7. Paul was not the first to take the language of redemption and apply it "spiritually" to denote release from sin. The OT had already set a precedent. See Ps 130:7–8 [LXX 129:7–8] and note also Mic 7:19 with 7:15, where it appears that second exodus language may have been used to describe liberation from sin. On this see Bruce K. Waltke, "Micah," in *Obadiah, Jonah, Micah, Nahum, and Habakkuk* (ed. T. McComiskey; vol. 2 of *The Minor Prophets: An Exegetical and Expository Commentary*; Grand Rapids: Baker, 1993), 763.

[42] Commentators differ as to whether τῶν ἁγίων found at v. 12b refers to people, i.e., Christians (e.g., O'Brien, *Colossians*, 26–27) or to angels (e.g., Gnilka, *Der Kolosserbrief*, 47). P. Benoit, "Ἅγιοι en Colossiens 1.12: Hommes ou Anges?" in *Paul and Paulinism: Essays in Honour of C. K. Barrett* (eds. M. D. Hooker and S. G. Wilson; London: SPCK, 1982), 83–101, argues that *both* are probably in view in light of the evidence from Qumran (e.g., 1QS XI, 7–8) and the pseudepigraphal literature.

It is likely that ἅγιοι refers only to believers, however, because in the letter to the Colossians, Paul employs other terms to designate the angelic beings: θρόνοι, κυριότητες, ἀρχαί, ἐξουσίαι (1:16; cf. 2:8); probably στοιχεῖα τοῦ κόσμου (2:8, 20); and ἄγγελοι (2:18; cf. Eph 1:21, 3:10, 6:12). Consistently throughout the letter he employs ἅγιοι to designate the people of God in Christ (1:2, 4, 26) or to describe them (1:22, 3:12), but never to signify any kind of angelic being. See also the same use in the sister letter to the Ephesians: 1:1, 4, 15, 18 [debated], 2:19, 3:5, 8, 18, 4:12, 5:3, 27, 6:18.

[43] Hab 3:3–4; Pss 4:6 [MT 4:7], 36:9 [10], 89:15 [16], 104:2; Isa 60:1–2, 19–20; Dan 2:22; cf. Ezek 1:27–28; 1 Tim 6:16; Rev 21:11, 23, 22:5.

in Christ's commissioning of Paul as apostle to the nations.[44] This Scriptural background aids our understanding of Paul's phrase "in the light" at Col 1:12. The inheritance in which the Father has made the Colossians fit to share is stated as being "in the light." Because the stated contrast to "in the light" is the "domain of darkness" (see 1:13a), it appears that the compressed phrase can be unpacked to mean "in the [realm of] light." That is, the saints have a share in the abode where God's glory radiates and illuminates all. This realm of light is to be at least roughly equated also with the "kingdom of the Son of his love," as the parallelism in vv. 12–13 strongly suggests.

The Second Exodus Theme in the Rest of the NT

Even to attempt a decent survey here in a few paragraphs would prove woefully inadequate and would invite oversimplification. Therefore, only a few important and recent works will be pointed out to demonstrate that scholars increasingly are finding the second exodus theme to be a helpful paradigm for understanding significant parts of the NT corpus.[45] Rikki Watts has probed the second exodus theme in the Gospel of Mark,[46] and David Pao has explored its presence and influence in Acts.[47] The theme is also a sub-category of Tom Wright's program, who is the chief proponent of the interrelated "exile/restoration" paradigm as a key to understand Jesus and the New Testament.[48] The presence of the second exodus theme elsewhere in the NT corpus indicates that the presence of it in Col 1:12–14 should not be unexpected.

---

[44] So too Seyoon Kim, *The Origin of Paul's Gospel* (WUNT 2/4; Tübingen: J. C. B. Mohr [Paul Siebeck], 1981; American edition, Grand Rapids: Eerdmans, 1982), 230, who writes that "the δόξα of God which Paul saw on the Damascus road was also the δόξα of Christ because it shone in the face of Christ."

[45] Though see earlier, e.g., Harald Sahlin, "The New Exodus of Salvation According to St Paul," in *The Root of the Vine: Essays in Biblical Theology* (New York: Philosophical Library, 1953), 81–95, who wrote already in 1953 that "the typological parallel between the historical Exodus and the Messianic deliverance, which was thus anticipated by Early Judaism, is also fundamental for the New Testament, and to a far greater extent than we generally realize" (p. 82).

[46] *Isaiah's New Exodus and Mark* (WUNT 2/88; Tübingen: J. C. B. Mohr [Paul Siebeck], 1997); reprint, *Isaiah's New Exodus in Mark*. Grand Rapids: Baker, 2000.

[47] *Acts and the Isaianic New Exodus.*

[48] See his preface to *Jesus and the Victory of God* (vol. 2 of *Christian Origins and the Question of God*; Minneapolis: Fortress, 1996), xvii–xviii. See now also Scott, *Exile: Old Testament, Jewish, and Christian Conceptions*; idem, ed., *Restoration: Old Testament, Jewish, and Christian Perspectives* (JSJSup 72; Leiden: Brill, 2001).

The Exodus in the Early Church Fathers

While the early Church Fathers do often cite what I have labeled the "second exodus texts" of the OT, they offer a variety of interpretations of these passages, of which some of the more relevant and interesting ones will be offered here.

Irenaeus believed that the greater exodus promised in Jer 23:7–8 would be fulfilled at the end of the age with the general resurrection.[49] Tertullian believed that water baptism was prefigured by the water of the Red Sea that destroyed the tyrant Pharoah; in water baptism the Christian is set free from the world and leaves behind their old tyrant, the Devil, overwhelmed in the water.[50] Cyprian offered a typological view of the exodus for the Christian, writing that the Jewish people's liberation from the slavery of Pharoah and Egypt prefigured the Christians' liberation from the slavery of the devil and the world.[51]

Hermeneutical and Theological Reflections

Paul's language reveals that he presupposed that the original exodus out of Egypt provided a paradigm to portray the greater deliverance God had brought about for the Colossians in Christ from the slavery of sin. Yet the OT itself had already set a precedent of typological interpretation of this event and foresaw a greater exodus to come. Some circles within early Judaism (though not all) seemed to have understood these prophecies to depict a massive exodus of Israel that would herald the arrival of a new age. In light of this, Paul probably is echoing not only the ancient exodus, but *that initial event and its subsequent interpretive tradition.* It is likely that he saw in the gospel the prophetic fulfillment of many of the second exodus texts scattered throughout the OT prophets (cf. 2 Cor 1:20). Paul appears to depict God's deliverance of the Colossians in Christ in language that suggests a magnificent second exodus. The liberation was not from slavery in Egypt, Assyria, Babylon, or Rome, but from spiritual enslavement to the domain of darkness and sin. Therefore, while Paul's echo presupposes a typological hermeneutic at

---

[49] *Against Heresies* 5.34.1 (*ANF* 1:563–64).
[50] *On Baptism* 9 (*ANF* 3:673). Cf. Cyprian, *Epistles* 62.8 (*ANF* 5:360); *Treatises* 12.1.12 (*ANF* 5:511; Isa 43:18–21 and 48:21).
[51] *Treatises* 11.7 (*ANF* 5:500).

work, he also probably assumed that the greater exodus foreseen by the prophets had attained direct fulfillment in God's work in Christ. It is probable that both heremeneutical presuppositions are in play.

Paul wrote to the Colossian church that God had swept them up in his staggering work of deliverance. Christ, the Passover lamb, had been sacrificed for them (1 Cor 5:7; Exod 12:26–27) and had made it possible for God not to destroy them for their rebellion and idolatry, but rather to deliver them mercifully from enslavement to the domain of darkness. Paul states that this experience of the greater exodus provides the unshakeable foundation for a life of thankfulness, offered joyfully and continually to the Father, who authored this breathtaking redemption (Col 1:11b–12).

CHAPTER SIX

THE SCRIPTURES OF ISRAEL IN COLOSSIANS 1:9–14:
THE ECHO OF THE 2 SAMUEL 7 PROMISE-TO-DAVID
EXEGETICAL TRADITION IN 1:13

Comparison of Textual Versions and Evaluation

2 Sam 7:12b–14a, 18 MT	2 Sam 7:12b–14a, 18 LXX	Colossians 1:13
‏...וַהֲכִינֹתִי אֶת־מַמְלַכְתּוֹ:‏ ‏וְכֹנַנְתִּי אֶת־כִּסֵּא מַמְלַכְתּוֹ‏ ‏עַד־עוֹלָם: אֲנִי אֶהְיֶה־לּוֹ‏ ‏לְאָב וְהוּא יִהְיֶה־לִּי לְבֵן‏	καὶ ἑτοιμάσω <u>τὴν</u> <u>βασιλείαν αὐτοῦ</u>... καὶ ἀνορθώσω τὸν θρόνον αὐτοῦ ἕως εἰς τὸν αἰῶνα ἐγὼ ἔσομαι αὐτῷ εἰς <u>πατέρα</u> καὶ αὐτὸς ἔσται μοι εἰς <u>υἱόν</u>	τῷ <u>πατρὶ</u>...ὃς... μετέστησεν εἰς <u>τὴν</u> <u>βασιλείαν τοῦ υἱοῦ τῆς</u> <u>ἀγάπης αὐτοῦ</u>
‏מִי בֵיתִי כִּי‏ ‏הֲבִיאֹתַנִי עַד־הֲלֹם:‏	τίς ὁ οἶκός μου ὅτι <u>ἠγάπηκάς</u> με ἕως τούτων	

This proposal meets the two criteria necessary for an echo: 1) availability, and 2) word agreement, as well as rare concept similarity.
Regarding *availability*, Paul displays awareness of 2 Sam 7:14 because
he quotes it elsewhere in his correspondence (see 2 Cor 6:18; cf. Rom
1:3). Regarding *word agreement*, Col 1:13 shares four words in common
with the parent text (including the implied subject located in v. 12a;
see chart above). The fourth word that the two texts share is from the
ἀγάπ- word group: compare Col 1:13b with 2 Sam 7:18 LXX,[1] 12:24–25,
and 1 Chr 17:16 (on this, see below). While the four words are common in and of themselves, it is the effect within an early Jewish context
that matters when they are put together in a specific way. Therefore,
it is crucial to see also that the two texts share a *rare conceptual similarity*. One of the central pillars of OT theology is the assertion that the

---

[1] The reading ἠγάπηκάς (several MSS: -σας; "you have set [your] love") is attested
by LXX uncials B and N along with several cursives, including the Lucianic manuscripts
boc₂e₂. It is also attested in the fifth column of Origen's *Hexapla*.

God of Israel had decreed that David's lineage would reign forever over his kingdom Israel. Whenever a male ancestor of this lineage was installed as the new king, God adopted him as a "son," becoming his "father" (cf. Ps 2).

It appears that Paul did not intend his audience to recall 2 Sam 7, because nothing from the old context needs to be brought forward in order to reclaim Paul's full, *intended* communication. There is nothing in the new context whose meaning is only "unlocked" with the "key" from the old context. Therefore, the reference should be classified as an echo. Recognition of the presence of 2 Sam 7 at Col 1:13 deepens and enhances our understanding of both the letter to the Colossian church as well as Paul as biblical theologian. Other scholars have already seen 2 Sam 7 (and/or its interpretive tradition, e.g., Pss 2, 89, 132) behind Col 1:13.[2] Because 2 Sam 7 is the "fountainhead" of a specific and fundamental theme that runs throughout the OT and on into early Jewish and later Jewish and Christian interpretation, some space will be devoted to this development to offer a fuller framework for the discussion of the 2 Sam 7 echo at Col 1:13.

Old Testament Context: 2 Samuel 7:1–18

Having captured Jerusalem and having made it his capital (2 Sam 5), and having brought up the ark of God to that same city (2 Sam 6),

---

[2] Beare, "Colossians," 160; Schweizer, *Colossians*, 52; Shogren, "Presently Entering the Kingdom," 177n.14; Wall, *Colossians*, 60; Dunn, *Colossians*, 78; Wolter, *Der Brief an die Kolosser*, 67; Hübner, *An die Kolosser*, 53–54 ("...die messianische Erfüllung von 2Sam 7,16"); Fee, "Old Testament Intertextuality in Colossians," ad loc.; Beale, "Colossians," ad loc. Barth and Blanke, *Colossians*, 189–90, write that

> the closer characterization of *basileia* in Col. 1:13 through the addition of "beloved *Son*" gives impetus to interpret the proclamation of this verse also in light of the OT reference [i.e., 2 Sam 7:12ff.] since here as there, both concepts are closely connected in characteristic fashion. In 2 Sam 7:12f. it is proclaimed that the (Davidic) kingdom (LXX, *basileia*) shall last forever. We find in this passage the affirmation of YHWH concerning the inheritor of the throne, "I will be his Father, and he shall be my *Son*" [2 Sam 7:14]. The legitimization of the king as son of God was of particular significance for the Israelite kingdom, as Ps 2:7 and Ps 89:27f. make clear. Thus the king was certified by God as the legitimate ruler over God's people and his power was part of the sovereign right of God over his chosen people.
>
> Col. 1:13 refers to the confirmation of this proclamation in 2 Sam 7 and thus to the *dawn* of the kingdom of Jesus who has been legitimized by God and who is thus the true Messiah. The addition of "beloved" gives prominence to the concept that *this one* is the one who has been "chosen" by God.

David is finally established as king over Israel when the reader comes
to 2 Sam 7:1. David now rules from his centralized position at Jerusalem, from his own magnificent palace that Hiram, king of Tyre, had
built for him (2 Sam 5:11–12; 7:1). Although Hiram's motives are left
unstated, Hiram has probably built a house for David (ᾠκοδόμησαν
οἶκον τῷ Δαυιδ; MT: וַיִּבְנוּ־בַיִת לְדָוִד; 2 Sam 5:11) to secure the political
and commercial favor of the up-and-coming Israelite king.[3] In 2 Sam
7, God cuts off any possibility for David to become *his* benefactor by
rejecting David's wish to build a "house" for him. Instead, YHWH will
build a "house" for David.

2 Sam 7:1–3 provides the setting for the chapter. As the king resides
in his magnificent palace of cedar, it dawns on him that the very ark
of God himself is housed in a mere tent. The incongruity of the situation strikes David's conscience, for surely, he, the vassal, the servant,[4]
should not reside in a better house than that of his suzerain, his deity.
The king's court-prophet, Nathan, assures David to go ahead with the
plans of his heart, for God is with the king (v. 3).

That very night however, Nathan receives a word from the LORD
(v. 4). David is not to build a "house" (οἶκος; MT: בַּיִת), a temple, for
YHWH.[5] From the beginning of his involvement with Israel, God had
never dwelt in a permanent or magnificent temple, nor reprimanded
Israel's leaders for not providing him with one (vv. 5–7). God makes it
clear that YHWH works for David, not David for YHWH. The narrator
communicates this by the use of seven first common singular verbs in
the oracle of vv. 8–11, adding the pronoun "I" (אֲנִי; LXX omits it) for
emphasis at its very beginning:

I *myself* (אֲנִי) have taken you from the pasture after the sheep...
I have been with you...
I have cut off all your enemies...
I will make for you a great name...
I will set a place for my people Israel...
I will plant them [there]...
I will give rest to you from all your enemies...

---

[3] See 1 Kgs 5:1–12, esp. vv. 9–12 (MT 5:15–26).

[4] David refers to himself ten times in 2 Sam 7 as God's "servant" (δοῦλός; MT: עֶבֶד;
vv. 19, 20, 21, 25, 26 (LXX omits), 27 [twice], 28, 29 [twice]) and God himself refers
to David as "my servant" twice (vv. 5, 8).

[5] That is, a sanctuary in which the ark of God, the physical symbol of the divine
presence, may be housed (v. 2).

The point is that YHWH is the suzerain, the benefactor. David—and his kingdom, Israel—is the dependent vassal.

The list of God's beneficence climaxes in a promise to build David a "house," a word play for a royal dynasty (vv. 11b–17).[6] God promises David that he will raise up a son from David's own loins and establish his kingdom. Thrice God avers that this son's dynasty will endure ἕως/ εἰς [τὸν] αἰῶνα, "forever" (MT: עַד־עוֹלָם; vv. 13, 16). The implication is that this son's offspring will retain dominion over Israel as long as the nation endures. By this announcement, a dynastic kingship is divinely sanctioned and institutionalized for Israel. This initial son (whom we know later to be Solomon) *will* be permitted to build a "house," a temple "for [YHWH's] name" (v. 13). Moreover, this son of David will be divinely adopted by God. In what appears to be standard terminology employed to summarize a suzerain-vassal covenant relationship, God vows to be for David's son a "father," and David's son will become God's own "son."[7]

Disobedience brought Saul's dynasty down, one that would have otherwise endured "forever" (1 Sam 13:13–14). What is to say that it will not bring David's down also? It would, except that God promises to David that he will not turn aside his חֶסֶד (LXX: ἔλεός) from David's son when he sins, as he did when Saul sinned.[8] God will discipline

---

[6] The placement of the object בַיִת before the verb is a deliberate move to secure reader recognition of the play on the word: "And YHWH declares to you that *a house* YHWH will make for you." A strikingly similar play on the word "house" occurs in the Bar-Rakib Inscription (ca. 733–727 B.C.E.; see *COS* 2.38:160–61). The LXX inverts the meaning and has God telling David that *David* will build a house for *God*.

[7] The phrase reads: אֲנִי אֶהְיֶה־לּוֹ לְאָב וְהוּא יִהְיֶה־לִּי לְבֵן (= 1 Chr 17:13a; cf. 22:10, 28:6); cf. the formula at Exod 6:7: וְלָקַחְתִּי אֶתְכֶם לִי לְעָם וְהָיִיתִי לָכֶם לֵאלֹהִים. Cf. also MT Lev 26:12, Hos 1:9, 2:25b; Jer 7:23, 31:33; Ezek 36:28. And see especially in the immediate context at 2 Sam 7:24. On the formula and its ANE background, see F. Charles Fensham, "Father and Son as Terminology for Treaty and Covenant," in *Near Eastern Studies in Honor of William Foxwell Albright* (ed. Hans Goedicke; Baltimore & London: John Hopkins, 1971), 121–135. Cf. *COS* 1.102:339 (in the Kirta Epic discovered at Ras Shamra, Kirta, king of a city, is called the "son" of 'Ilu, his god and "the offspring of the Gracious and Holy One").

[8] While the term חֶסֶד is semantically flexible, as so often the term here appears to be employed to express faithfulness or loyalty. In the Hebrew Bible, the term often holds covenantal overtones ("[covenant] faithfulness") and this sense is quite possible here due to the presence of the covenant summary terminology found at v. 13a (on which, see n.7 above). Though David's son may disobey God, God promises to maintain his side of the covenant and not reject him (as he normally would be free to do once the other party broke their covenant commitment). See the summary in Katharine Doob Sakenfeld, *The Meaning of Hesed in the Hebrew Bible: A New Inquiry*

him as a father does a son, but he will not reject him outright as he rejected Saul (vv. 13b–15). The result is that the royal dynastic reign of the son of David will be established "forever," which is expressed twice at v. 16 for emphasis.

Significantly, in the first line of David's response to Nathan's oracle, the LXX in several MSS reads that David replied to God in prayer at v. 18: "Who am I...and what is my house, that you have set your love on me as far as these things [ὅτι ἠγάπηκάς (several MSS: -σας) με ἕως τούτων]?"[9] Likewise, the LXX witness at the parallel passage at 1 Chr 17:16 unanimously reads: "Who am I...and what is my house, that you have set your love on me forever [ὅτι ἠγάπησάς με ἕως αἰῶνος]?" The Chronicle's translation differs from LXX Samuel in that it offers a temporal "forever" (ἕως αἰῶνος) instead of "as far as these things [promised]" (ἕως τούτων). That is, instead of David's declaration of amazement, it reads as a strong restatement of the irrevocability of the divine election of David's lineage. David believes that God has permanently *set his love* (ἠγάπησας from ἀγαπάω) on his family. For all time, David will have a son that reigns as vicegerent over God's kingdom Israel. These LXX readings, which possibly arose out of a hearing or sight error (אהבתני from original הביאתני?),[10] probably existed in Paul's day although this cannot be proved with certainty. Instead of God "bringing" David to this point, the LXX tells of God's action of "setting his love" upon David.

It is very possible that these LXX readings, which emphasize God setting his love on David and his lineage, may have influenced the text at Col 1:13, which reads "the kingdom of the son *of his love*" [τὴν βασιλείαν τοῦ υἱοῦ τῆς ἀγάπης αὐτοῦ]. Further evidence strengthens this theory. At 2 Sam 12:24–25, the author narrates the event of Solomon's birth. In context, David's illegitimate son, begotten through his affair with Bathsheba, has recently died. To comfort Bathsheba, David goes into her with the result that she gives birth to a son, whom she names Solomon. But then significantly, God renames him:

(HSM 17; Missoula, Mont.: Scholars, 1977; reprint, Eugene, Oreg.: Wipf & Stock, 2002), 233–39 (esp. 237–39).

[9] For which manuscripts have this reading, see n.1 of this chapter.

[10] See *BHS* at 1 Chr 17:16 note a; cf. P. Kyle McCarter, *II Samuel: A New Translation with Introduction, Notes and Commentary* (AB 9; New York: Doubleday, 1984), 233.

And YHWH set his love on (אֲהֵבוֹ; ἠγάπησεν)[11] him. And he sent by the hand of Nathan the prophet and he called his name Jedidiah, on account of YHWH.

The name Jedidiah means "beloved one of YHWH." Though David committed adultery, the narrative's implications are clear. Solomon is the promised son and the initial fulfillment of Nathan's oracle to David. Solomon is the object of the divine election, and as such is "Jedidiah," the beloved of YHWH.[12] God had set his love on David and his line forever, and because of that promise, God set his love on Solomon. Such was the influence of this tradition concerning Solomon that Nehemiah recalled it centuries later: "And among the many nations there was no king like [Solomon], and he was beloved [אָהוּב; LXX: ἀγαπώμενος] by his God, and God set him as king over all Israel" (Neh 13:26).

In light of this very specific theme of God's electing love of David and his lineage as found in 2 Samuel 7:18 LXX, 12:24–25, 1 Chr 17:16 LXX, and Neh 13:26 and conveyed in the LXX with variations on the verb ἀγαπάω, it is reasonable to posit that this core element of the Promise-to-David theme has been echoed also in Col 1:13. Jesus, a son of David (see below), declared to possess the "kingdom" as the "son" of the "Father," is further described at Col 1:13 as the "son of his *love*" (τοῦ υἱοῦ τῆς ἀγάπης αὐτοῦ). According to Paul, Jesus is the object of the divine election, chosen to rule over the kingdom in accord with the promise made to David and his lineage.

2 Samuel 7:12–14 and its Interpretive Tradition in the Old Testament

2 Sam 7 and the promise to David found there is the fount from which numerous subsequent texts flow. In fact, the influence is so pervasive that our survey will be able to mention most of the texts only in passing.[13] A brief survey must and will suffice for our purposes.

2 Sam 7 is actually part of a much longer historical narrative than either the book 2 Samuel or even 1–2 Samuel. This narrative, which

---

[11] The verb אהב is translated this way because contextually it carries overtones of election. See Gerhard Wallis, "אהב," *TDOT* 1:112–13; P. J. J. S. Els, "אהב," *NIDOTTE* 1:282.

[12] So also Tomoo Ishida, "Solomon," *ABD* 6:105.

[13] For a detailed study of the Promise-to-David exegetical tradition in the Hebrew Bible, see William Schniedewind, *Society and the Promise to David: The Reception History of 2 Samuel 7:1–17* (New York: Oxford University Press, 1999).

runs from Deuteronomy– 2 Kings (typically called the Deuteronomistic History), arguably has as its climactic scene the promises given to David at 2 Sam 7.[14] It is thus no surprise that references that recall this peak in the narrative are abundant. For example, near the end of his life David recalls and exults in the "everlasting covenant" (διαθήκην αἰώνιον; MT: בְּרִית עוֹלָם) that God made with him (2 Sam 23:5). The initial fulfillment of the promises, however, arrives in the narrative at 1 Kgs 8:17–20. There Solomon, son of David, whose reign lasted approximately forty years (ca. 961–922 B.C.E.), has built the temple as God foretold. It is here in the early chapters of 1 Kings that a conditional element is introduced to the promise made to David.[15] It is also here that Solomon explicitly recalls the promise of 2 Sam 7:13 that David's son would build a house for God and believes himself to be the fulfillment of it.[16]

The Promise to David is such a prominent theme in the Deuteronomistic History that despite its harsh conclusion, its very final scene communicates a modest note of hope that assumes the promise of 2 Sam 7. Even though Jerusalem and the temple have been razed for Israel's flagrant covenant violation, King Jehoiachin of the line of David, though in exile in Babylon, lives and is well. The narrative's implication is that despite judgment and exile, the "lamp of David" had not yet been extinguished.[17]

1–2 Chronicles is largely a later revision of the account found in Samuel–Kings. At 1 Chr 17, 2 Sam 7 is carefully repeated, with two minor but significant alterations at v. 14. At v. 14a, God states that he will establish David's seed "in *my* house" and "in *my* kingdom" forever; the personal pronominal suffixes have been changed from second singular to first singular. The result is that the Chronicler has clarified that the kingdom *belongs to God*; David and his line serve only as vicegerents for YHWH, who is the true King.[18]

The promise to David at 2 Sam 7 has also influenced the Psalter. Psalms 89 and 132 directly stem from it, and many scholars would also

---

[14] Cf. A. A. Anderson, *2 Samuel* (WBC 11; Dallas: Word, 1989), 112: "2 Sam 7 is, without doubt, the theological highlight of the Books of Samuel...if not of the Deuteronomistic History as a whole."

[15] See 1 Kgs 6:12, 8:25, 9:4–5; cf. 1 Chr 28:7.

[16] See 1 Kgs 5:5 [MT 5:19], 8:19; cf. 2 Chr 6:9.

[17] 1 Kgs 11:13, 32, 36, 15:4; 2 Kgs 8:19, 19:34, 20:6; cf. 2 Chr 21:7.

[18] Cf. Jacob M. Myers, *1 Chronicles* (AB 12; Garden City, N.Y.: Doubleday, 1965), lxxxi. See 1 Chr 28:5, 29:3; 2 Chr 9:8, 13:8.

include Ps 2.[19] Psalm 89 is "an exegetical adaptation" of 2 Sam 7 by
the psalmist to address his present historical crisis.[20] The psalmist has
omitted the temple-building project, made David himself the adopted
son (not Solomon; see vv. 26–27 [MT: vv. 27–28]), and interpreted God's
relationship to David explicitly as a covenant (διαθήκη; MT: בְּרִית; vv.
3, 34, 39 [MT, LXX: vv. 4, 35, 40]).[21] Psalm 89 stresses God's uncondi-
tional commitment to David (see vv. 28–37 [MT: 29–38]). Psalm 132,
however, another psalm clearly influenced by 2 Sam 7, adds an element
of conditionality. David's sons must submit themselves to God's decrees
if they are to maintain the throne forever (v. 12).

Eighth-century prophets also display awareness of God's promises to
David. Isaiah predicted the coming of the ideal king from David's line,
who would establish justice and righteousness in the land and through
whom God would fill the earth with the knowledge of YHWH (Isa 9:2–7
[MT: 9:1–6]; 11:1–9, 10). Hosea alluded to the tradition (3:5), as did
Amos (9:11). The prophets Jeremiah and Ezekiel of the seventh to
sixth century B.C.E. promised that God would raise up another David
at the time of Israel's glorious restoration from captivity, to rule over
the renewed nation forever.[22]

In summary, the promise given to David at 2 Sam 7 is picked up
several times in the Old Testament and further developed. The exegetical tradition of 2 Sam 7 therefore begins within the Old Testament
itself.

2 Samuel 7:12–14 and Its Interpretive Tradition in Early and Late Judaism

Psalm of Solomon 17 "incorporate[s] the response of a group of devout
Jews to the capture of Jerusalem by the Romans in the first century
B.C."[23] At the same time that the author of this psalm declares that God
alone is king over Israel (vv. 1, 46), the psalmist recalls God's promise

---

[19] See also Ps 18:50 [MT 18:51] (= 2 Sam 22:51).
[20] Nahum M. Sarna, "Psalm 89: A Study in Inner Biblical Exegesis," in *Biblical and Other Studies* (ed. Alexander Altman; Studies and Texts 1; Cambridge: Harvard University Press, 1963), 39.
[21] Sarna, "Psalm 89," 37–38. Sarna argues that 2 Sam 7 originates in the time of David, and that Ps 89 was written during the crisis experienced by King Ahaz in the Aramean-Israelite invasion, ca. 735–34 B.C.E. (pp. 42–45).
[22] Ezek 37:25. See Jer 23:5, 30:8–9, 33:14–26; Ezek 34:23–24, 37:22–25.
[23] R. B. Wright, "Psalms of Solomon," *OTP* 2:639.

in 2 Sam 7 that he had sworn to David that his lineage (σπέρματος αὐτοῦ) would reign forever over Israel (v. 4).

A clear allusion to 2 Sam 7, v. 4 introduces the central purpose of the psalm. *Psalm of Solomon* 17 is a prayer for God to stay true to the promise of 2 Sam 7 by raising up for Israel the promised "Son of David" (v. 21), that is, the "Lord Messiah" (v. 32). 2 Sam 7 has clearly been given a messianic interpretation, and Ps 2 (at v. 23) and Isa 11 (at v. 37) are also alluded to in a description of the messiah and his reign that begins at v. 21 and extends to v. 43.

A manuscript from Qumran, 4QFlor (= 4Q174) I, 1–12, is a quotation from 2 Sam 7:10–14 with commentary. The author has omitted the phrase that clarifies the origin of David's seed ("which will come forth from your loins") at v. 12b and also the temple-building reference of v. 13a ("*he* will build a house for my name"). He then has written that David's promised seed, the adopted "son" of God, is in fact the "branch of David" (צמח דויד; line 11), a title adapted from Jer 23:5 and 33:15, which are passages that refer to the coming Davidic figure.[24] According to this Qumran interpreter, this personage will arise in Zion in the last days together with "the Interpreter of the Law" in fulfillment of Amos 9:11 (quoted at line 12). There is no reference to Solomon anywhere. Second Samuel 7 has been given a messianic interpretation, as has Amos 9:11 with its promise of the reestablishment of the "booth of David," here interpreted as a reference to the messiah who would arise to save Israel (line 13).

Another text from Qumran, 4Q252 V, 1–4, combines a quotation of Gen 49:10 (line 1) with allusions to Jer 33:15–17 (line 2, 3b–4a)[25] and 2 Sam 7:12–13 (line 4b). The title "branch of David" again appears (line 3b–4a), this time added as an explanatory clause to the phrase "messiah of righteousness" (משיח הצדק), a figure for whom the author still awaited. What is only implied in 2 Sam 7 is made explicit here: God made a covenant with David and his seed (לו ולזרעו), here called the "covenant of the kingdom of his people" (line 4b; ברית מלכות עמו; cf. line 2b; Sir 47:11) to endure "for everlasting generations" (עד דורות עולם). Both Gen 49:10 and 2 Sam 7:12–13 have been given a messianic interpretation.

---

[24] See DJD 5:55.
[25] See DJD 22:205–6.

While Sirach (ca. 180 B.C.E.) mentions the 2 Sam 7 promise-to-David four times, none of these are expanded upon in a messianic interpretation (45:25, 47:11, 22, 48:15). In the Hebrew text of Sirach between 51:12 and 51:13, however, a psalm of thanksgiving has been inserted. The psalm was possibly composed before 152 B.C.E. and circulated independently before being added into manuscript B of Sirach.[26] In this inserted psalm at line 8, the psalmist urges his reader to give thanks to God, "who makes a horn to sprout for the house of David" (NRSV). Skehan and Di Lella state that this language stems from Ps 132:17a (cf. Ezek 29:21), and that "the text is messianic, promising that an offspring of David will rule the people (cf. Jer 23:5; 33:15–17; Isa 11:1–5)."[27]

Yet another manuscript from Qumran, 4Q504 (4QDibHam^a) 1–2 IV, 6–7 [2nd–1st century B.C.E.], reads like a prayer to God and recounts the 2 Sam 7 promise as part of the remarkable dealings of God with Israel.[28] While the text is not explicitly messianic, in lines 8–11 mention is made of the promised future expectation when all the nations (כול הגוים; line 8b) would bring their wealth to Zion in tribute (cf. Isa 66:12, 18–20). The mention in the prayer of the covenant with David promised for "forever" (כול הימים; line 8a), then, possibly was intended to serve as a "reminder" to God of his promise to David and a plea for him to make good on it. Moreover, since the kingship had long been cut off by the time of its composition, it is reasonable to ask whether the prayer was offered in light of messianic lenses and expectations.[29]

The Eighteen Benedictions, or *Shemoneh 'Esreh*, also tap into the Davidic promise tradition. The benedictions were ordered into their final form in the final decades of the first century C.E. by Rabbi Gamaliel II, though they existed for some time before that.[30] The fourteenth and fifteenth benedictions (originally read as one) are prayers for the rebuilding of Jerusalem and for the reestablishment of Davidic rule. The fifteenth benediction "is a prayer for the rise of David's sprout, *i.e.*, the messianic king."[31] The end of the fourteenth benediction reads, "…and build [Jerusalem] speedily in our days as an everlasting structure

---

[26] Patrick W. Skehan and Alexander A. Di Lella, *The Wisdom of Ben Sira* (AB 39; New York: Doubleday, 1987), 569. Cf. *APOT* 1:277.

[27] *Wisdom of Ben Sira*, 570.

[28] I owe this text to Schniedewind, *Society and the Promise to David*, 164–65.

[29] Cf. Daniel K. Falk, *Daily, Sabbath, and Festival Prayers in the Dead Sea Scrolls* (STDJ 27; Leiden: Brill, 1998), 75–76.

[30] Emil G. Hirsch, "Shemoneh 'Esreh," *JE* 11:278a.

[31] Hirsch, "Shemoneh 'Esreh," 271b.

and soon establish there the throne of David."[32] The first part of the fifteenth benediction reads: "The sprout of David Thy servant speedily cause Thou to sprout up; and his horn do Thou uplift through Thy victorious salvation; for Thy salvation we are hoping every day."[33]

The fourteenth and fifteenth benedictions of the *Shemoneh 'Esreh* are clear evidence that the 2 Sam 7 tradition was given a widespread messianic interpretation by the first century C.E. at the latest.

The work known as *4 Ezra* (100–120 C.E.; chs. 3–14 by a non-Christian Jewish author[34]) also displays awareness of the 2 Sam 7 tradition and ties it to the coming messiah: "And as for the lion [from Gen 49:9–10] that you saw rousing up out of the forest…this is the Messiah whom the Most High has kept until the end of days, who will arise from the prosperity of David…."[35]

As noted above, the links between 2 Sam 7 and Pss 89 and 132 are quite direct, as most scholarship affirms.[36] The rabbis readily connected them as mutually interpretive.[37] As we turn our attention to the influence of the 2 Sam 7 tradition in later Judaism, we will limit our investigation to these three texts in particular.

One notable use of 2 Sam 7 in the rabbis is a passage that depicts David as having understood that God was giving him ownership over "this world…all the way into the days of the Messiah and of the world-to-come."[38]

The sections in Ps 89 pertaining to the promise to David are given various interpretations in later Judaism. The mention of the "firstborn" at v. 28 was interpreted both as a reference to David himself as well as to the coming "King Messiah."[39] The statement at v. 37 of David's throne enduring "as the sun before [God]" was variously interpreted as a reference to the Messiah or to David himself, resurrected and enjoying the Eden of the renewed heaven and earth.[40] Verses 23–26 were taken

---

[32] Hirsch, "Shemoneh 'Esreh," 271b (*italics* mine).

[33] Hirsch, "Shemoneh 'Esreh," 271b.

[34] See B. M. Metzger, "The Fourth Book of Ezra," in *The Old Testament Pseudepigrapha* (ed. James H. Charlesworth; 2 vols.; ABRL; New York: Doubleday, 1983), 1:520.

[35] Cf. *4 Ezra* 7:28–29 ("my Son the Messiah"), 13:32, 37, 52, 14:9 ("my Son").

[36] See e.g., Hans-Joachim Kraus, *Psalms 60–150* (trans. Hilton C. Oswald; CC; Minneapolis: Fortress, 1993), 476–77.

[37] *Midrash Rabbah* Ecclesiastes 3.14, §1 (p. 95).

[38] *Tanna Debe Eliyyahu*, ER 89 (p. 241). Cf. also *Kallah Rabbati* 53b.

[39] *Midrash Rabbah* Numbers 6.2 (David); *Midrash Rabbah* Exodus 19.7 (Messiah).

[40] *Midrash Rabbah* Genesis 97, new version (Messiah); *Tanna Debe Eliyyahu*, S 32 (David).

to refer to the Messiah.[41] Other texts stressed that the Psalm indicated that David's line would extend even into the world-to-come.[42]

The passages in Ps 132 pertaining to the promise to David are also variously understood. Rabbis interpreted v. 11 ("one of your own issue I will set upon your throne"; NJPS) either as a reference to Solomon or to the coming messiah.[43] The statement at v. 17, "there I will make a horn sprout for David; I have prepared a lamp for My anointed one" (NJPS) was consistently given a messianic interpretation.[44]

In several places in the rabbis the messiah is referred to as the "son of David."[45] Though there is no "son of David" language in *Tg. Isa.* 53, it is noteworthy that God's "servant," here interpreted to be the messiah, will establish his reign. He will bring about Israel's restoration from exile, intercede for her sins, rebuild the sanctuary, and overthrow the Gentiles who rule over Israel, with the result that "they shall see the kingdom of their Messiah" (v. 10).[46] The promise to David probably stands behind such a statement.

In summary, the evidence in early and later Judaism shows that the trajectory of the messianic interpretation of the 2 Sam 7 tradition begun in the Scriptures of Israel continued on before the time of the apostle Paul and endured during his day and for centuries thereafter in various circles of Judaism.

New Testament Context: 2 Samuel 7:12–14, 18 in Colossians 1:13

The echo of 2 Sam 7 in Col 1:13 surfaces near the end of Paul's prayer-report. The apostle has stated that he prays that God may enable the Colossians to walk worthily of the Lord. The fourth way that Paul offers that they can do this is by "giving thanks to the Father." In language that recalls the ancient exodus of Israel out of Egypt, Paul writes that God, the "Father," has mightily delivered the Colossians from slavery in the "domain of darkness" and transferred them into "the kingdom

---

[41] *Pesiqta Rabbati*, Piska 36.1.

[42] *Midr.* Psalms 5.4, 118.8.

[43] *Midr.* Proverbs 15:17 (Solomon); cf. *Tg Ps.* 132:10; *Midr.* Psalm 42/43.5 (Messiah).

[44] *Midrash Rabbah* Leviticus 31.11; *Tanhuma* Exodus 25:1ff., Part VI; *Tanhuma* Exodus 27:20ff., part VI ; *Midr.* Psalm 75:5.

[45] E.g., *b. Sukkah* 52a, 52b; *Midrash Rabbah* Exodus 25.12 (twice); *Pesiqta Rabbati*, Piska 36.2; *Pirqe Rabbi Eliezer*, p. 132; *Midr.* Psalm 42/43.5; *Derekh Eretz Zuta* 59a; *Kallah Rabbati* 54a.

[46] I owe this reference to Gnilka, *Der Kolosserbrief*, 49n.35.

of the Son of his love" (1:12–13). This latter phrase appears to be a Semitism, which in light of the echo of the 2 Sam 7 tradition means "the realm over which God's elect king rules." "Son" at Col 1:13b does not signify the 'second person of the Trinity' but is covenant language and a royal title for the kings of the promised Davidic lineage (2 Sam 7:14a; Pss 2:7, 89:26–27). Paul saw Jesus as the son of God *par excellence*, the messianic king; the apostle employs the title χριστός five times with reference to Jesus in Col 1:1–7 alone.

Of note is that the only other use of βασιλεία ("kingdom") in the letter to the Colossians is at 4:11, which reads "these alone are fellow-workers for the kingdom of God" (εἰς τὴν βασιλείαν τοῦ θεοῦ). Paul appears to make little distinction between the kingdom of the messianic king and his God (cf. Eph 5:5: "the kingdom of messiah and of God"). This corresponds to the Chronicler's emphasis at 1 Chr 17 that the reign of David's lineage is subsumed under the reign of God (cf. 1 Chr 17:11b with 17:14a). David's sons were vicegerents in service of the true King of Israel, YHWH, through whom God had chosen to reign. This thinking is reflected at Col 1:13b. According to Paul, Jesus Christ is the messianic and final "son of David" through whom the God of Israel was establishing his worldwide dominion (cf. Isa 11:1–9).

The 2 Samuel 7 Tradition in the Rest of the NT and in the Early Fathers

The 2 Sam 7 exegetical tradition surfaces in several places in the NT. Matthew begins his gospel with the words, "an account of the genealogy of Jesus the Messiah, *the son of God*" (1:1). In fact, the title "son of David" is one of Matthew's favorites for Jesus; it shows up also in the other synoptic gospels.[47] Luke also begins his gospel with a reference to the tradition, when he narrates that God sent the angel Gabriel to Mary, "a virgin engaged to…Joseph, *of the house of David*" (1:27; NRSV). Gabriel announces to Mary:

---

[47] Matt 9:27, 12:23, 15:22, 20:30–32 (twice; = Mark 10:47–48; Luke 18:38–39), 21:9 (= Mark 11:9b–10; cf. Luke 19:38; John 12:13), 21:15; cf. 22:42–45, in which Ps 110:1 is quoted (= Mark 12:35–37; Luke 20:41–44). In John, the one explicit reference to David further demonstrates that in the 1st century C.E. many Jews held the belief that the Messiah must be of the line of David. Some in the crowd discuss, "'Has not the scripture said that the Messiah is descended from David and comes from Bethlehem, the village where David lived?'" (John 7:42).

And now, you will... bear a son, and you will name him Jesus. He... will
be called the Son of the Most High, and the Lord God will give to him
the throne of his ancestor David. He will reign over the house of Jacob
forever, and of his kingdom there will be no end... he will be holy; he
will be called Son of God.[48]

Probably the strongest parallel to the language of Col 1:13 is to be
found at Mark 1:11//Matt 3:17//Luke 3:22, where at the baptism of
Jesus a voice from heaven states, "you are my Son, the Beloved one
(ὁ ἀγαπητός), in you I am well pleased."[49] The same language occurs
again at Jesus' transfiguration at Mark 9:7//Matt 17:5//Luke 9:35,
though Luke writes "this is my Son, *the Chosen one*" (ὁ ἐκλελεγμένος),
whereas Mark and Matthew read "this is my Son, the Beloved one (ὁ
ἀγαπητός)."[50]

In his second volume, Acts, Luke continues to stress the promise to
David and Jesus as the climactic fulfillment of it. Towards this end, Ps
132:11 (Acts 2:30), Ps 2:1–2, 7 (Acts 4:25–27, 13:33), Isa 55:3 (Acts
13:34), and Amos 9:11 (Acts 15:16) are quoted, all of which belong to
the 2 Sam 7 exegetical tradition.[51]

In the Pauline writings, reference to the tradition is uncommon. At
Rom 1:3, Paul writes that the gospel concerns "[God's] son, who came
from the seed of David [ἐκ σπέρματος Δαυὶδ]" (see also 2 Tim 2:8).[52]
At Rom 15:12, Paul quotes Isa 11:10 ("The root of Jesse shall come,
and the one who arises to rule nations...") to buttress support for his
gentile mission beyond Rome. Paul simply presupposes that his Roman
audience will make the connection that Jesus is this "root of Jesse." At
2 Cor 6:18, 2 Sam 7:14 is quoted as one in a catena of texts, but the
singular pronouns are changed to plurals, thus applying to the whole
community the promise originally made to David.[53]

---

[48] 1:31–35 (NRSV); cf. 1:69; see also Jesus' genealogical record that Luke presents,
which portrays Jesus as a descendent of David (3:23–38, see v. 31).

[49] Several textual witnesses add to the Lukan account "today I have begotten you,"
thereby creating an explicit connection to Ps 2:7, and thus to the Promise-to-David
exegetical tradition.

[50] Cf. 2 Pet 1:17.

[51] Cf. Acts 13:22–23, in which Ps 89:21 and 1 Sam 13:14 are conflated and serve
to introduce Jesus as the promised Davidic seed.

[52] Cf. again *4 Ezra* 12:32 (100–120 C.E.), where the messiah is described as one "who
shall spring *from the seed of David*" (*APOT* 2:614; emphasis mine).

[53] On this use, see James M. Scott, *Adoption as Sons of God: An Exegetical Investigation
into the Background of* ΥΙΟΘΕΣΙΑ *in the Pauline Corpus* (WUNT 2/48; Tübingen: J. C. B.
Mohr [Paul Siebeck], 1992), 187–220.

At the beginning of the letter to the Hebrews, the author argues for the supremacy of Christ, the "Son," as a mediator in comparison to the angels, and combines Ps 2:7 and 2 Sam 7:14 at 1:5 in support of his reasoning. Both passages are applied immediately to Christ to establish his unique relationship to the Father. At Heb 5:5–6, Ps 2:7 is brought together with Ps 110:4 to argue that Christ is God's chosen high priest for the new covenant people of God.

In the book of Revelation, Jesus at 5:5 is described as "the Lion of the tribe of Judah, the Root of David" in a combination of titles taken from Gen 49:9–10 and Isa 11:1, 10 (cf. Rev 22:16). In Rev 2:26–27, Christ quotes Ps 2:8–9 to the church at Thyatira and applies it to all in the covenant community who persevere. The message is that those who overcome will reign over the nations along with their messianic King. This same psalm passage is alluded to later and applied individually to Christ (Rev 12:5, 19:15). Of note is the quotation of 2 Sam 7:14 at Rev 21:7, where once again the sonship promised to David is offered to any in the community who overcomes temptation and persecution.[54]

Turning to the early church fathers, Irenaeus (2nd century C.E.) employed Ps 132:11 along with Isa 9:6 (LXX) and Ps 110:1 to argue that Jesus was truly human because he was the son of David.[55] Tertullian (d. ca. 220 C.E.) combined Ps 2:7, Isa 55:3, Ps 132:11, and 2 Sam 7:12 in his argument that Solomon could not have been the fulfillment of such prophecies.[56] Justin Martyr (d. ca. 165 C.E.), in seeking to convince the Jew Trypho that Jesus was the messiah, combined allusions to Zech 12:10, Ps 110:4, Isa 53:8, and 2 Sam 7:14 for his argument.[57] Lactantius (d. ca. 330 C.E.) argued from Isa 11 and 2 Sam 7 that the messiah must be from the house of David, and that therefore Jesus

---

The Pauline authorship of 2 Cor 6:18 is debated (as is the authenticity of the entire section of 2 Cor 6:14–7:1). For a discussion of the evidence and the arguments both for and against Pauline authorship, see Margaret E. Thrall, *A Critical and Exegetical Commentary on the Second Epistle to the Corinthians* (2 vols.; ICC; Edinburgh: T&T Clark, 1994), 1:25–36. Thrall herself concludes that "neither contextual nor theological arguments are sufficient to prove conclusively that 2 Cor 6.14–7.1 is non-Pauline" (35).

[54] For further discussion, see Beale, *The Book of Revelation*, 1058.

[55] *Against Heresies* 3.16.2–3 (*ANF* 1:440–41).

[56] *Against Marcion* 3.20 (*ANF* 3:338–39). Cf. *Against the Jews* 14 (*ANF* 3:173; combination of Ps 2:7–8 with an allusion to 2 Sam 7:13).

[57] *Dialogue with Trypho* 118 (*ANF* 1:258).

could be this messiah since he was of this lineage.[58] Cyprian (d. 258 c.e.) stated that Ps 89:27–33 spoke of Jesus Christ.[59]

In summary, the evidence demonstrates that the 2 Sam 7 tradition has influenced every major block of the NT, strengthening the case that the presence of 2 Sam 7 at Col 1:13 is likely. This trajectory continued on into the early church fathers along the lines developed in the NT.

Hermeneutical and Theological Reflections

Paul's language at Col 1:13 reveals the presupposition that Christ was the final fulfillment of 2 Sam 7:12–16. Because it is a prophetic promise, Paul probably echoed the tradition (whether consciously or unconsciously) out of the conviction that God had not merely promised a son, Solomon (who certainly was the initial fulfillment of the promise), but an entire line of "sons," i.e., an enduring lineage. As we have seen, this is a fairly straightforward reading of the text. Paul therefore would have believed that the promise had come to an ultimate fulfillment, since Jesus, a true descendent of David, had been resurrected for installation as God's messianic king forever.

That Paul has echoed 2 Sam 7 at Col 1:13 contributes to our understanding of Paul's Christology. According to Paul, the Colossian Christians had been transferred into a realm, into the sphere where the active reign of the God of Israel was executed through his elect vicegerent, the messianic son of God. In Paul's thinking, this reign had spilled over beyond the traditional theocratic boundaries of Israel, making its way as far as the town of Colossae in Asia Minor. According to Paul, God's dominion had been given an eschatological, worldwide escalation in the coming of Jesus his messiah, the son of David, the son of God.

---

[58] *The Divine Institutes* 4.13 (*ANF* 7:113); cf. Cyprian, *The Treatises of Cyprian* ("*To Quirinius*") 12.2.11 (*ANF* 5:520).
[59] *The Treatises of Cyprian* ("*To Quirinius*") 12.2.1 (*ANF* 5:516).

CHAPTER SEVEN

THE SCRIPTURES OF ISRAEL IN COLOSSIANS 1:15–20: THE ALLUSION TO THE PROVERBS 8:22–31 INTERPRETIVE DEVELOPMENT IN 1:15–20

Comparison of Textual Versions and Evaluation

Prov 8:22–31 MT	Prov 8:22–31 LXX	Colossians 1:15–20
יְהוָה קָנָנִי רֵאשִׁית דַּרְכּוֹ	κύριος ἔκτισέν με	ὅς ἐστιν εἰκὼν τοῦ
קֶדֶם מִפְעָלָיו מֵאָז׃	<u>ἀρχὴν</u> ὁδῶν αὐτοῦ εἰς	θεοῦ τοῦ ἀοράτου,
מֵעוֹלָם נִסַּכְתִּי	ἔργα αὐτοῦ	<u>πρωτότοκος</u> πάσης
מֵרֹאשׁ מִקַּדְמֵי־אָרֶץ׃	<u>πρὸ</u> τοῦ αἰῶνος	κτίσεως, ὅτι ἐν αὐτῷ
בְּאֵין־תְּהֹמוֹת חוֹלָלְתִּי	ἐθεμελίωσέν με ἐν ἀρχῇ	ἐκτίσθη τὰ πάντα ἐν
בְּאֵין מַעְיָנוֹת נִכְבַּדֵּי־	<u>πρὸ</u> τοῦ τὴν γῆν ποιῆσαι	τοῖς οὐρανοῖς καὶ ἐπὶ
מָיִם׃	καὶ	τῆς γῆς...τὰ πάντα δι᾿
בְּטֶרֶם הָרִים הָטְבָּעוּ	<u>πρὸ</u> τοῦ τὰς ἀβύσσους	αὐτοῦ καὶ εἰς αὐτὸν
לִפְנֵי גְבָעוֹת חוֹלָלְתִּי...	ποιῆσαι	ἔκτισται· καὶ αὐτός
בַּהֲכִינוֹ שָׁמַיִם שָׁם אָנִי...	<u>πρὸ</u> τοῦ προελθεῖν τὰς	ἐστιν <u>πρὸ πάντων</u> καὶ
וָאֶהְיֶה אֶצְלוֹ אָמוֹן	πηγὰς τῶν ὑδάτων	τὰ πάντα ἐν αὐτῷ
	<u>πρὸ</u> τοῦ ὄρη ἑδρασθῆναι	συνέστηκεν, καὶ αὐτός
	<u>πρὸ</u> δὲ πάντων βουνῶν	ἐστιν ἡ κεφαλὴ τοῦ
	<u>γεννᾷ με</u>...ἡνίκα	σώματος τῆς ἐκκλησίας·
	ἡτοίμαζεν τὸν	ὅς ἐστιν <u>ἀρχή</u>...
	οὐρανόν συμπαρήμην	
	αὐτῷ...ἤμην παρ᾿ αὐτῷ	
	ἁρμόζουσα	

Paul has not alluded to Prov 8:22–31 in a strict sense, but rather to it *in its first century C.E. interpretive development*, which was "in the air" of his day.[1] The underlining in the chart above shows where Prov 8:22–31 and Col 1:15–20 intersect directly with regard to word agreement (the two texts also directly share conceptual similarities); as we will see, there are numerous other links between the two texts *via* the interpretive development of Prov 8:22–31 as found in early Jewish literature

---

[1] See again Evans, "Listening for Echoes of Interpreted Scripture," 49–50.

(on which, see below). Paul has not alluded to any one text that had already developed Prov 8 (e.g., Wis 7 or Sir 24).

This proposal meets our three criteria necessary for an allusion: 1) availability, 2) word agreement, as well as rare concept similarity, and 3) essential interpretive link.[2] Regarding *availability*, Paul displays awareness of the book of Proverbs. He quotes from it at Rom 2:6 (Prov 24:12; Ps 61:13 LXX), 12:20 (Prov 25:21), and 2 Cor 9:7 (Prov 22:8a). Regarding *word agreement* and *rare concept similarity*, Col 1:15–20 holds numerous words and concepts in common with the Prov 8:22–31 interpretive development (see again chart above, but especially discussion below). Regarding *essential interpretive link*, the reader must recognize the allusion to this parent text (in its 1st century C.E. development), realize that it is deliberate, remember aspects of this text in its development, and connect one or more of these aspects to get the point that Paul is depicting Christ in language typically used in regard to Wisdom, the figure present at God's side before and during his work of creation at the dawn of time.[3] If the first readers had failed to make this connection, they probably would not have picked up Paul's intention to link Wisdom to Christ (Paul also, however, moves beyond what was typically said about Wisdom). They would, of course, still have comprehended the surface-level meaning or "un-allusive sense" of the passage (see p. 30n.73 of this study).[4]

---

[2] See chapter two of this study and the first tier of evidence given there for the validation of a proposed allusion (pp. 28–32).

[3] See again the discussion on p. 19 of this study.

[4] Numerous other scholars have already seen the connection between the Prov 8 tradition and Col 1:15ff. In fact, Dunn, *Colossians*, 86n.8, wrote in 1996 that "the Wisdom character of the hymn is a matter of broad consensus." Many mention Prov 8 explicitly in this regard; others refer to the personified Wisdom theme generally (which ultimately stems from Prov 8): see Hühn, *Die alttestamentlichen Citate*, 197; C. F. Burney, "Christ as the APXH of Creation (Prov. viii 22, Col. i 15–18, Rev. iii 14)," *JTS* 27 (1925–6): 160–77; Moule, *Colossians*, 59; A. Feuillet, *Le Christ Sagesse de Dieu d'après les Épîtres Pauliniennes* (ÉB; Paris: Gabalda, 1966), 269–72; Lohse, *Colossians*, 46–50; Martin, *Colossians*, 58; Gnilka, *Der Kolosserbrief*, 60; W. D. Davies, *Paul and Rabbinic Judaism: Some Elements in Pauline Theology* (4th ed.; Philadelphia: Fortress, 1980), 150–52; O'Brien, *Colossians*, 40ff.; Lindemann, *Der Kolosserbrief*, 25; Bruce, *Colossians*, 60, 62; Wright, *Colossians*, 67–68; idem, *Climax of the Covenant*, 107–13; Eckhard J. Schnabel, *Law and Wisdom from Ben Sira to Paul* (WUNT 2/16; Tübingen: J. C. B. Mohr [Paul Siebeck], 1985), 255–58 (and see 255n.151 for other scholars not listed here); Aletti, *Colossiens*, 116 (with qualifications); J. D. G. Dunn, *Christology in the Making: A New Testament Inquiry into the Origins of the Doctrine of the Incarnation* (2nd ed.; Grand Rapids: Eerdmans, 1996), 163–96; Wolter, *Der Brief an die Kolosser*, 76f.; Hay, *Colossians*, 53–55; Hübner, *Vetus Testamentum in Novo*, 518–20; MacDonald, *Colossians*, 66; Lincoln, *Colossians*, 605; NA[27] outer margin apparatus ("Prv 8, 23–27"). Fee, "Old Testament Intertextuality

Old Testament Context: Proverbs 8:22–31

In Prov 1:20–33 and 8:1–9:12 (cf. 2:2–6), the reader encounters the fascinating but mysterious "literary personification,"[5] lady Wisdom. Her function in these passages is to stir up a passionate pursuit of wisdom within the reader by appeal to the universal desire for the good life. Those who hearken to noble Wisdom's instruction find life and prosperity, wealth and honor (8:18, 21, 35, 9:11). On the other hand, those who heed dame Folly will find themselves in the grave (9:13–18; cf. 7:6–27).

The aim of the two complementary sections of Prov 8, vv. 1–21 and 22–31, is to "magnify the authority of Wisdom"[6] so that readers will attune their lives to her ways. According to Wisdom, life and death are at stake. Therefore, she appeals to the reader with an urgent call of decision immediately following these two sections (vv. 32–36). In the first section of vv. 1–21, Wisdom takes her place at the city gates and earnestly cries out to all who will listen. She insists that her instruction is worth more than any other desirable thing (vv. 6–11). She is aligned with YHWH (v. 13) and promises greatness to those who love her (vv. 12–21). In the second section of vv. 22–31, the reader encounters a piece that has no counterpart in all the rest of the Old Testament. Here Wisdom is exalted as the preexistent beginning of God's creative activity and as God's delight. Wisdom celebrates in his presence in the world he has made and she herself delights in the human race.

The first verse of this section, however, immediately confronts us with an interpretive problem (v. 22). Does the verb קנה mean to "acquire" or "create"? The versions differ: the LXX (ἔκτισεν), Syriac, and Targum (ברא) support the latter,[7] while Philo (*Drunkenness* 31), Aquila, Symmachus,

---

in Colossians," ad loc., argues vigorously *against* this allusion; Beale, "Colossians," ad loc., ponders it as a possibility.

[5] Roland E. Murphy, *Proverbs* (WBC 22; Nashville: Thomas Nelson, 1998), 278. Murphy also notes that, while the search for the appropriate ANE background for the lady Wisdom figure continues [and should continue], "there is great uncertainty on this score [i.e., on the origins of the personification of Wisdom]....the biblical presentation itself is independent enough to be heard largely on its own as something new and unique" (279). For an introduction to the discussion of ANE backgrounds for personified Wisdom, see B. Lang, "Wisdom," *DDD* (1999 rev. ed.), 900–5.

[6] William McKane, *Proverbs* (OTL; Philadelphia: Westminster, 1970), 351; so too Bruce K. Waltke, *Proverbs: Chapters 1–15* (2 vols.; NICOT; Grand Rapids: Eerdmans, 2004), 392, 407.

[7] Sirach 1:4, 9 and 24:8, 9 also lend evidence in support of this reading.

Theodotion (all reading ἐκτήσατο) and the Vulgate (*possedit*) support the former. Significantly, קנה occurs thirteen other times in the book of Proverbs, and all without exception in their respective contexts carry the meaning "to acquire, obtain, get" (or even "buy," as in to purchase something).[8] This reading at Prov 8:22 is also the more theologically difficult: Wisdom is so exalted and desirable that even YHWH "acquired" her. The LXX produces a reading that fits more comfortably theologically within a strict monotheism by putting Wisdom in her place. She is explicitly made a creation of God and thus subordinate to him.

In the context of the book of Proverbs, the reason the author wrote that YHWH himself "acquired" Wisdom is in line with the purpose of Prov 8 as a whole, namely, to "magnify the authority of Wisdom" so that the readers pursue her and attune their life to her ways. YHWH thus becomes the model for his people.[9] Though he prefers the meaning "to create" for the verb קנה, Michael Fox also perceives that this is why the term was selected. Fox writes that "the verb *qanah* is chosen to designate divine acquisition of wisdom to show that this is the prototype of human acquisition of wisdom, even though they gain wisdom in quite different ways."[10]

The text goes on in 8:22 to state that God acquired Wisdom, "(at) the beginning of his way" (יְהוָה קָנָנִי רֵאשִׁית דַּרְכּוֹ). While several modern translations add the word "as" or "at" to clarify what they believe to be the sense of the phrase,[11] no preposition is attached to the word in

---

[8] See Prov 1:5, 4:5 [twice], 7 [twice], 15:32, 16:16, 17:16, 18:15, 19:8, 20:14, 23:23. LXX translates four of these with κτάομαι (1:5, 17:16, 18:15, 19:8), none with κτίζω, and for four occurrences offers no translation at all (4:7 [2x], 20:14, 23:23). I have subsequently found that Bruce Vawter, "Prov 8:22: Wisdom and Creation," *JBL* 99 (1980): 205–16, likewise offers a very strong argument for the meaning "to acquire" based upon both the other uses in Proverbs as well as those found in the rest of the HB. His balanced consideration of versional evidence and extra-biblical material rounds out and strengthens his argument.

[9] While I would retain the translation "acquire" to maintain the connection with the other occurrences of קנה in Proverbs, context clearly demonstrates that YHWH did not acquire something that was already in existence, but that he acquired Wisdom when she was given birth (see vv. 24–25; cf. Gen 4:1). Waltke, *Proverbs 1–15*, 408–9, prefers to emphasize the birthing imagery and sees the "acquisition" imagery as present but secondary ("As Procreator the LORD also acquired Wisdom, but this is a derivative thought" [409]). He translates קנה as "to beget," "to bring forth." Therefore, Waltke and I both understand the word to have two nuances, but we differ as to which is being emphasized.

[10] Michael V. Fox, *Proverbs 1–9* (AB 18A; New York: Doubleday, 2000), 280.

[11] E.g., NRSV, NJPS, NIV, NASB.

the Hebrew. A preposition was explicitly added in later versions like the Syriac, Targum, and Vulgate (cf. *BHS* note a). The Greek translations, however, retained the syntax of the Hebrew, translating רֵאשִׁית without adding an article or preposition.[12] The syntactical construction may be a double accusative construction of "narrow" apposition, where the two substantives are put "in the same case in order to define more exactly (or to complete) the one by the other, and, as a rule...the former by the latter."[13] Therefore, while a linking word such as "as" or "at" may seem attractive for good English, it is not necessary in Hebrew, and may not accurately capture what the Hebrew is doing. "Narrow" Hebrew apposition commonly implies a "that is" or "who/which is" statement of identification or definition between the two items in apposition, not an "as" statement of comparison.[14] On another reading, however, רֵאשִׁית could be an adverbial accusative of time, "(at) the beginning of his way," signifying when the acquisition took place.[15] GKC labels this type of apposition as one possibility of the "wider" use (see GKC §131 p.). This "wider" appositional reading is also supported by the immediate context of vv. 22–26, the point of which is to highlight Wisdom's temporal preexistence before all the rest of creation.[16] Some within later Jewish interpretation took the latter part of the apposition as a sort of title ("Beginning"; on which, see below).

The entire point of vv. 22–26 is to stress Wisdom's status as temporally first in existence before anything else of creation. The intent of vv. 27–29 is similar and stresses that at the time of God's creating work, Wisdom was present (שָׁם אָנִי; LXX: συμπαρήμην αὐτῷ; v. 27). The main point of vv. 22–29 is that both before and during the construction of the world, Wisdom existed and was present.

---

[12] LXX, Symmachus, Theodotion: ἀρχήν ("beginning"); Aquila: κεφάλαιον ("head, principle"; see LSJ, "κεφάλαιον"); Philo (*Drunkenness* 31): πρωτίστην ("first"); cf. NAB, NJB. Vawter, "Prov 8:22: Wisdom and Creation," 214–15, argues that רֵאשִׁית means "principle" or "model"; see Jean de Savignac, "Note sur le sens du Verset viii 22 des Proverbes," *VT* 4 (1954): 429–32, upon whose argument Vawter appears to build. Jean B. Bauer, "Encore une fois Proverbes viii 22," *VT* 8 (1958): 91–92, replies to Savignac's article and insists that רֵאשִׁית carries a temporal idea.

[13] GKC §131 a.1.

[14] See GKC §131 for its numerous examples.

[15] GKC §118 i.

[16] Fox, *Proverbs 1–9*, 280; Murphy, *Proverbs*, 48 note "22.a.," offers this as one of the two most likely options, with his first option being the narrow appositional interpretation noted above.

In the final section of vv. 30–31, yet another interpretive problem arises, this time with the term אָמוֹן. Does the word mean "(1) artisan, (2) constant(ly), [or] (3) ward/nursling?"[17] The versions offer various understandings, perhaps arising out of an uncertainty of the vocalization of the consonants of the Hebrew. The Vulgate (*conponens*), Syriac,[18] and evidence in Wis 7:21, 8:6 (Wisdom as τεχνῖτις, "artisan, craftsman, architect") support the first interpretation.[19] The Greek versions Symmachus and Theodotion, as well as the Aramaic Targum, support the second,[20] while Aquila supports the third.[21] The LXX is vague enough to support either interpretation (1) or (2), or neither of these.[22] According to Fox, many scholars have argued that the closest parallel is the Akkadian *ummānu*, meaning "scribe, scholar, master craftsman, officer."[23] Fox points out, however, that the attested Hebrew cognate to that word is actually אָמָּן, and not אָמוֹן.[24] Fox believes it is better to understand אָמוֹן as deriving from the verbal root אמן II ("to nurse, look after"; passive: "one who is looked after").[25] He retains the Masoretic vocalization and reads it as a qal infinitive absolute, employed as an adverbial complement.[26] Fox's route avoids emendations and appeal to cognates in other languages, making good sense of the word as it stands in the MT. Fox offers the translation, "And I was near him, growing up."[27] Waltke likewise takes it as a qal inifinitive absolute, but of the verbal root אמן I ("to be reliable, faithful"), not אמן II, which he

---

[17] Fox, *Proverbs 1–9*, 285. Fox offers a concise summary of the various proposals offered (285–87).

[18] I am indebted to R. B. Y. Scott, "Wisdom in Creation: The ʾĀmôn of Proverbs VIII 30," *VT* 10 (1960): 219, for this understanding of the Syriac. Scott states that the Syriac is an active participle and translates it as "fashioning" (cf. Lamsa: "establishing").

[19] Evidence in the LXX at v. 22 also supports this interpretation. God created Wisdom "for his works" (εἰς ἔργα αὐτοῦ), a phrase that expresses the *purpose* of his creation of Wisdom; contrast MT's temporal "before [קֶדֶם] his works."

[20] Symmachus and Theodotion read ἐστηριγμένη, from στηρίζω, "to establish."

[21] Aquila reads τιθηνουμένη, from τιθηνέω, "to bring up, nurse."

[22] The LXX reads ἁρμόζουσα, from ἁρμόζω, meaning "to closely associate with, to fit in with, to be in harmony with"; see BDAG, "ἁρμόζω," def. 1 intransitive; LSJ, "ἁρμόζω," def. II intransitive; and Lust, "ἁρμόζω."

[23] *Proverbs 1–9*, 286.

[24] *Proverbs 1–9*, 286. Note also the lack of the doubled consonant in אָמוֹן.

[25] See *HALOT*, "אמן II."

[26] Fox, *Proverbs 1–9*, 286–87. The use of the infinitive absolute as an adverbial complement is well attested; Fox offers good examples and points to Bruce K. Waltke and M. O'Connor, *An Introduction to Biblical Hebrew Syntax* (Winona Lake, Ind.: Eisenbrauns, 1990), §35.3.2, who offer others.

[27] Fox, *Proverbs 1–9*, 285, 287.

argues—convincingly in my view—"best satisfies the parallels according to the MT accents:

And I was	beside him	faithfully;
And I was	delighting	daily
	celebrating before him	at all times"[28]

Moreover, while Fox's interpretation is attractive because it does justice to the form as found in the MT (as does that of Waltke, however), his interpretation seems to run counter to the purpose of Prov 8 (whereas Waltke's accords with it). He understands Wisdom to be as a child *playing* before YHWH, growing up beside him. A more likely interpretation is that Wisdom is depicted as a mature daughter *celebrating* before YHWH.[29] This latter understanding accords better with the aim of Prov 8, which is to "magnify the authority of Wisdom" so as to stir up the confidence of the reader in her admonitions. The imagery of a carefree child undermines this purpose, whereas that of a noble and mature woman of great antiquity, who possesses an unsurpassed understanding of the created order, strengthens it.[30] In Israel, the elders of the community, those who had lived many years, were believed to have acquired invaluable experience, and thus to be sources of wisdom. This illuminates why the unmatched antiquity of lady Wisdom is stressed. The conventional thought was that the oldest members of the community were the wisest (cf. Job 8:8–10, 12:12, 15:7–10). The effect would be to leave the reader with the impression that Lady Wisdom, with her origins stretching back before creation itself, embodied all the sagacity that a lasting right relationship with YHWH and an unsurpassed experiential knowledge of the created order could give. She would be completely worthy of the reader's trust, and should be heeded.[31]

---

[28] Waltke, *Proverbs 1–15*, 420.

[29] The verb שׂחק can be used to convey either meaning and context determines which is in view (e.g., "playing": Zech 8:5; "celebrating": 1 Sam 18:7; 2 Sam 6:5, 21).

[30] So also Cleon L. Rogers III, "The Meaning and Significance of the Hebrew Word אמון in Proverbs 8,30," *ZAW* 109 (1997): 217; Scott, "Wisdom in Creation," 218–19, who writes that "for this high claim to grave authority the imagery of gay, thoughtless childhood is inappropriate." Cf. Waltke, *Proverbs 1–15*, 419: "Whatever the text or form [of the word אָמוֹן], Wisdom's [supposed] claim that while she was a little child she rejoiced delightfully in the LORD's creative work does not make her claim to grave authority very credible."

[31] Gale A. Yee, "An Analysis of Prov 8 22–31 According to Style and Structure," *ZAW* 94 (1982): 58–66, upon conclusion of her structural analysis, argues that the point of Prov 8:22–31 is "to portray Wisdom as the ultimate mediator between God

Proverbs 8:22–31 and Its Interpretive Development in Early and Late Judaism

Our survey will offer the early Jewish evidence in rough chronological order. We therefore begin our investigation with a look at the Wisdom of Ben Sira (or Sirach; 2nd century B.C.E.).

Lady Wisdom shows up here at 1:4–10, 4:11–19, 6:18–31, 14:20–15:8, 51:13–21 [= 11Q5 XXI, 11–18][32] and especially 24:1–22. In this last section, Wisdom explains her divine origin (vv. 3–4), her preexistent creation (v. 9;[33] cf. 1:4, 9), her everlasting existence (v. 9b) and her search for a place to dwell in creation (vv. 5–7). God finally commanded her to abide in the temple at Jerusalem among Israel, which she did (vv. 8–12). She bids all to come to her to eat and drink their fill; those who obey her do not sin (vv. 19–22).

The author proceeds to identify Wisdom with the Law, or Torah "that Moses commanded us," which overflows with wisdom, like one of the great rivers (Sir 24:23–29). Wisdom is also identified as the Torah in the book of Baruch (see 3:9–4:4 [esp. 4:1]).[34]

In a direct allusion to Prov 8, Aristob. 5.10–11a (mid-second century B.C.E.) clearly affirms Wisdom's preexistence. She is described as a "lantern," from which "all light" originates; those who follow her have "calm."

Personified Wisdom appears again heavily in the Wisdom of Solomon

---

and humanity" (66). If Yee is on the right track with her analysis, then her conclusion would only further strengthen the argument that the point of Prov 8:22–31 is to magnify the authority of Wisdom so that the reader will heed her admonitions. She is the divinely ordained "bridge" between YHWH and humanity, and consequently to reject her is to cut oneself off from YHWH and the blessed life he offers. Cf. Waltke, *Proverbs 1–15*, 85: "Woman Wisdom is a one-of-a-kind heavenly mediatrix who mediates God's wisdom to humanity. . . . she rubs shoulders with the masses in the rough-and-tumble of the city gate, and, in an amazing display of grace, invites the unresponsive youths to repent at her rebuke before eternal death overtakes them."

[32] Lady Wisdom perhaps also appears in the DSS at 1QH^a IX, 13b–14 and 11Q5 XXVI, 13b–14. Lady Wisdom's competition, Dame Folly, shows up at 4Q184.

[33] The statement reads πρὸ τοῦ αἰῶνος ἀπ᾽ ἀρχῆς ἔκτισέν με and is a direct allusion to Prov 8:22–23 LXX.

[34] The stimulus for such a connection between the Law and wisdom already sits latent in earlier passages like Deut 4:5–6 and Jer 8:8–9 (cf. Isa 33:6 LXX). That Torah was considered to be the supreme source of wisdom can be seen in Sir 1:26, 15:1, 19:20; 38:34b–39:10; Wis 6:17–20; *4 Ezra* 8:12, 13:53–55; *2 Bar.* 38:1–4, 44:14, 46:4–5a, 48:24, 51:3–4, 7, 54:13–14, 77:15–16a; *T. Levi* 13:1–8; *4 Macc* 1:15–17; 1QM X, 9b–10; 4Q525 2 II, 3b–4. For an excellent in-depth analysis of the relation between the Law and wisdom in the 2nd temple literature, see Schnabel, *Law and Wisdom*; on p. 162nn.364–72 he offers numerous other texts not listed here as further evidence for this connection.

(1st century B.C.E.) at 1:4–7 and 6:12–11:1. She was present when God made the world (9:9), and was the "artificer" or "craftsman" of all that exists (NAB; 7:22, 8:6; cf. 14:2; Greek: τεχνῖτις). By his Word and with his Wisdom, God formed humanity to have dominion over his entire world (9:1).[35] Here "Word" and "Wisdom" are interchangeable synonyms (more on this below).[36] Her dwelling is with God in the "holy heavens," "on the throne of [God's] glory" (9:10; cf. 8:3, 9:4, 18:15; see Col 3:1).

The author of Wisdom heavily employs πᾶς ("all") to describe the extent of Wisdom's nature and activity. She is "all-powerful" (παντοδύναμον)[37] and "oversees all" (πανεπίσκοπον; 7:23). She penetrates and pervades "all things" (πάντων; 7:24), is able to do "all things" (πάντα; 7:27), and knows and understands "all things" (πάντα; 9:11). Wisdom is the artificer of "all things" (πάντων; 7:22 [7:21 LXX]), renews "all things" (τὰ πάντα; 7:27), extends over all the earth and excellently orders or manages "all things" (τὰ πάντα; 8:1), and is the active cause of "all things" (τὰ πάντα; 8:5; NRSV). God remains the ultimate source of creation, but did by means of his Word/Wisdom make "all things" (τὰ πάντα; 9:1). It is therefore worthy to note in light of this evidence the fact that in Col 1:15–20 the author has employed πᾶς eight times in five verses to describe the extent of Christ's nature and activity.

At Wis 7:26, Wisdom is called the "image" of God's goodness. The oft-quoted text reads:

> For she is a breath of the power of God, and a pure emanation of the glory of the Almighty; therefore nothing defiled gains entrance into her. For she is a reflection of eternal light, a spotless mirror of the working of God, and an image [εἰκών] of his goodness.   (NRSV)

Philo of Alexandria, however, is the author whose work is most laden with the Word/Wisdom theme. A Hellenistic Jew, Philo was a philosopher

---

[35] This is an allusion to Gen 1:26–28 and is more evidence that Wisdom was often connected with Gen 1 (on which, see below).

[36] Against Gordon D. Fee, "Wisdom Christology in Paul: A Dissenting View," in *The Way of Wisdom: Essays in Honor of Bruce K. Waltke* (eds. J. I. Packer and Sven K. Soderlund; Grand Rapids: Zondervan, 2000), 259, who does not think that personified Wisdom is in view at Wis 9:1–2. This is a stretch, however, in light of the previous three chapters of the book that are laden with personified Wisdom. How would the author expect the reader *not* to read personified Wisdom into the text after the previous three chapters' focus upon her? Moreover, personified Wisdom is in the immediate context at vv. 4 and vv. 9–10.

[37] Cf. 18:15–16 and God's "all-powerful Word" (ὁ παντοδύναμός σου λόγος).

and contemporary of Jesus and Paul (d. ca. 50 C.E.). For Philo, the
Word is a central concept.[38] It is God's reason, or his "mental activity"
employed in the act of creation.[39]

For Philo, the Word is related conceptually to Wisdom, and the two
are closely intertwined and at times appear virtually identical, although
perhaps they are not fully interchangeable. This relation can be seen
first of all in the fact that Philo labels both Word and Wisdom with the
same rare titles of "Beginning" and "Image" (the reader at this point
is urged to read the explicit quotations of *Alleg. Interp.* 3.96, *Confusion*
146–47, and *Alleg. Interp.* 1.43 below). Second, this relationship can be
observed in discourses of Philo, as seen, for example, in the text below.
In it Philo is commenting allegorically upon Gen 2:10. Here, Wisdom
and Word are virtually identical:

> But let us look also at the words. "And a river," it says, "issues forth from
> Eden to water the garden." "River" is generic virtue, goodness; this issues
> forth from Eden, the Wisdom of God, which is the Word of God [ἐξ
> Ἐδὲμ, τῆς τοῦ θεοῦ σοφίας· ἡ δέ ἐστιν ὁ θεοῦ λόγος]; for in accordance
> with the Word of God generic virtue has been made."[40]

Already in 1888, J. Drummond had investigated the relation between
the Word and Wisdom in Philo. He concluded that they were virtually interchangeable figures, and that the preference in Philo's writing
for the Word arose in part out of the gender issue: the "Word" is a
masculine term in Greek, whereas Wisdom is a feminine.[41] Time and
again, Drummond was struck by the interrelational fluidity of the two
figures:

> We have observed before that Philo's allegorical interpretations follow a
> pretty regular system. We are accordingly told elsewhere that Scripture
> "calls the Wisdom of the Self-existent Eden" [*Dreams* 2.242]; and yet we
> are informed in another passage that "Eden is, symbolically, right and
> divine Reason" [*Posterity* 32]. Further on in the same treatise, Wisdom
> and the Logos seem to be used as interchangeable terms. The soul is
> "watered by the stream of Wisdom" [*Posterity* 125]. "The Logos of God
> gives drink to the virtues; for it is the beginning and fountain of beautiful

---

[38] So also Jacob Jervell, *Imago Dei: Gen 1, 26f. im Spätjudentum, in der Gnosis und in den
paulinischen Briefen* (FRLANT 76; Göttingen: Vandenhoeck & Ruprecht, 1960), 53; see
n.108 for bibliography.

[39] Peder Borgen, "Philo of Alexandria," *ABD* 5:339; see *Creation* 17–20, 24f.

[40] *Alleg. Interp.* 1.65 (translation mine). Cf. *Dreams* 2.242.

[41] Differences also appear to have arisen when the figures were pressed into service
in an allegorical interpretation.

deeds." The virtues "have grown from the divine Logos, as from one root" [*Posterity* 127–29]. "Whence is it likely that the understanding, thirsting for prudence, should be filled except from the Wisdom of God, the unfailing fountain?" Presently we hear again of "Wisdom," the divine fountain," and then of "the stream of Wisdom" [*Posterity* 136–38]; and farther on, "the sacred Logos which waters the sciences is itself the stream" [*Posterity* 153].... Wisdom and the Logos appear alike under the figures of Eden, of a fountain, of a stream. The words are similarly interchanged when it is said that "in those by whom the life of the soul has been honoured the divine Logos dwells and walks"; and a few lines farther on, "they have a secure and unshaken power, being fattened by the Wisdom which nourishes virtue-loving souls" [*Posterity* 122].[42]

Drummond's study continues on at some length to discuss numerous texts that attribute the most striking characteristics of the Word to Wisdom.[43] Both, for example, are represented as the highest of divine powers.[44] Both are identified as the miraculous rock, fountain, and manna as narrated in the exodus wilderness account (cf. 1 Cor 10:4).[45] Both are understood as preexistent and as agents in the creating process.[46] Both have the same titles or names applied to them (e.g., "Beginning"; "Image"; "Seeing Israel" = "the vision of God").[47] Both serve as archetypes for earthly wisdom and virtue.[48] In sum, though there are "apparent inconsistencies in Philo's language," these "may be explained without violating the ultimate identity of the Logos and Wisdom."[49]

Numerous other scholars also have observed this fluid relationship in Philo between Word and Wisdom. While Philo speaks of the Word much more than of Wisdom, scholars who discuss the subject nevertheless recognize the significant interrelatedness in Philo of the two figures. Wolfson speaks for many when he concluded his brief study on the relation between Word and Wisdom in Philo with the statement that "Wisdom, then, is only another word for Logos, and it is used in

---

[42] James Drummond, *Philo Judaeus; or, The Jewish-Alexandrian Philosophy in its Development and Completion* (2 vols.; London: Williams and Norgate, 1888), 2:202–3. His investigation on the relation between Word and Wisdom is found on pp. 201–13.

[43] Drummond, *Philo Judaeus*, 203–207.

[44] Drummond, *Philo Judaeus*, 203.

[45] Drummond, *Philo Judaeus*, 203–4. See *Worse* 115–18.

[46] Drummond, *Philo Judaeus*, 204–6.

[47] Drummond, *Philo Judaeus*, 206–7.

[48] Drummond, *Philo Judaeus*, 207.

[49] Drummond, *Philo Judaeus*, 211.

all the senses of the term Logos."[50] Sometimes scholars discuss them as one concept, coining terms like 'the Wisdom-Word' to capture their interrelationship.[51] Erwin R. Goodenough, the author of a respected introduction to Philo, states with regard to the Word [or, the Logos] that

> [Philo] was not even committed to the term Logos: Sophia or Virtue would do just as well. The fact that in one place he says that Sophia is the source of the Logos, in another that the Logos is the source of Sophia, need not bother us any more than it bothered him, when we come to recognize with him that any description of the Stream has only relative value, value for us; that is, in helping us to visualize the richness of a conception through its varied figurative presentations, not in being a literal statement of metaphysical fact in the way that the doctrine of the Trinity was later presented.[52]

This interrelationship and overlap between the two figures of Wisdom and Word can also be observed outside of the works of Philo at Wis 9:1–2:

---

[50] Harry Austryn Wolfson, *Philo: Foundations of Religious Philosophy in Judaism, Christianity, and Islam* (2 vols.; rev. ed.; Cambridge: Harvard University Press, 1948), 1:258 (see 253–61). Likewise Gregory E. Sterling, "Prepositional Metaphysics in Jewish Wisdom Speculation and Early Christian Liturgical Texts" in *Wisdom and Logos: Studies in Jewish Thought in Honor of David Winston* (ed. David T. Runia; Studia Philonica Annual 9; Atlanta: Scholars Press, 1997), 229, who writes that "[Philo] does not, however, speak exclusively of the Logos as the instrument of creation: he uses some of the same expressions for Wisdom (σοφία). This is not terribly surprising since he can equate the Logos with Wisdom"; C. H. Dodd, *The Interpretation of the Fourth Gospel* (Cambridge: University Press, 1968), 263–85 (esp. 273–78), writes that "with Wisdom we are already half-way to Philo's Logos, which is in many places almost a doublet of Wisdom, as it certainly has the Wisdom-concept for one of its ancestors" (276); Craig S. Keener, *The Gospel of John: A Commentary* (2 vols.; Peabody, Mass.: Hendrickson, 2003), 1:345, states that "Philo's Logos blends naturally into divine Wisdom.... Philo also utilizes the image of divine Wisdom, which he identifies with the Logos"; Martin Scott, *Sophia and the Johannine Jesus* (JSNTSup 71; Sheffield: JSOT Press, 1992), 93, writes that "for Philo, Logos and Sophia are virtually synonymous in meaning and function, while at the same time retaining some individual characteristics"; F. W. Burnett, "Wisdom," *DJG* 876, comments that "Logos and Wisdom were virtually interchangeable concepts in both Philo...and The Wisdom of Solomon (9:1–2; 18:15)." Cf. Raymond E. Brown, *The Gospel According to John* (2 vols.; AB 29; Garden City: Doubleday, 1966), 1:521–23; Samuel Sandmel, *Philo of Alexandria: An Introduction* (New York: Oxford University Press, 1979), 98–99; Borgen, "Philo of Alexandria," *ABD* 5:339; Hay, *Colossians*, 54.

[51] See, e.g., Waltke, *Proverbs 1–15*, 128 ("Logos-Wisdom"); Sterling, "Prepositional Metaphysics in Jewish Wisdom Speculation," 238 ("Wisdom/Logos"); Burnett, "Wisdom," *DJG* 876 ("Wisdom-Word of God"), who is describing part of Jesus' portrait in the Gospel of John.

[52] Erwin R. Goodenough, *An Introduction to Philo Judaeus* (2nd ed.; Oxford: Basil Blackwell, 1962), 102–3.

O God of the fathers and Lord of mercy, who made all things *by your Word*, and *by your Wisdom* created humanity to rule over all the creatures that you have made...give to me *the Wisdom that sits by your throne*....[53]

In light of the above evidence, because the two concepts of Wisdom and Word overlap and were often interrelated in early Judaism, this study will at times refer to this phenomenon as the "Wisdom/Word" complex. The two concepts were not kept apart in separate compartments in early Jewish thought, but their identities and activities were often merged.

As mentioned previously, for Philo the Word is God's "image" (cf. Col 1:15a). This language stems from Gen 1:26–27, as can be seen at *Alleg. Interp.* 3.96:

But God's shadow is His Word, which he made use of like an instrument, and so made the world. But this shadow...is the archetype for further creations. For just as God is the Pattern of the Image, to which the title of Shadow has just been given, even so the Image becomes the pattern of other beings, as the prophet made clear at the very outset of the Law-giving by saying, "And God made the man after the Image of God" (Gen i. 27), implying that the Image had been made such as representing God, but that the man was made after the Image when it had acquired the force of a pattern.[54]

In fact, in Philo "image" is one of the chief titles for the Word:

But if there be any as yet unfit to be called a [s]on of God, let him press to take his place under God's First-born, the Word, who holds the eldership among the angels, their ruler as it were. And many names are his, for he is called, "the Beginning," and the Name of God, and His Word, and the Man after His image....For if we have not yet become fit to be thought sons of God yet we may be sons of His invisible image, the most holy Word. For the Word is the eldest-born image of God.[55]

Philo bestows the same title upon Wisdom at *Alleg. Interp.* 1.43:

By using many words for it Moses has already made it manifest that the sublime and heavenly [W]isdom is of many names; for he calls it "beginning" and "image" and "vision of God"; and now by the planting of the

---

[53] Translation mine.
[54] Colson, Whitaker, and Marcus, LCL.
[55] *Confusion* 146–47 (Colson, Whitaker, and Marcus, LCL).

[garden of Eden] he brings out the fact that earthly wisdom is a copy of this as of an archetype.[56]

It should be noted also that Philo calls the Word and Wisdom figures by the title "Beginning" in the two citations offered above (cf. Col 1:18b).[57] This title of "beginning," like that of "image," stems from Gen 1 (see Gen 1:1), as well as Prov 8:22.

Philo elsewhere also bestows the title "Firstborn" upon the Word (cf. Col 1:15b):

> But if there be any as yet unfit to be called a Son of God, let him press to take his place under God's First-born [πρωτόγονος],[58] the Word, who holds the eldership among the angels, their ruler as it were.... For if we have not yet become fit to be thought sons of God yet we may be sons of his invisible image, the most holy Word. For the Word is the eldest-born image of God.[59]

> For there are, as is evident, two temples of God: one of them this universe, in which there is also as High Priest His First-born [πρωτόγονος], the divine Word, and the other the rational soul, whose Priest is the real Man.[60]

> This hallowed flock [i.e., the universe] He leads in accordance with right and law, setting over it His true Word and Firstborn Son [πρωτόγονον υἱόν] Who shall take upon Him its government like some viceroy of a great king...[61]

---

[56] Colson, Whitaker, and Marcus, LCL. See also *Creation* 25: man is "an image of an image," i.e., an image of the Word; *Alleg. Interp.* 2.4; *Creation* 31, 146; *Planting* 19–20; *Confusion* 97; *Flight* 12–13, 101; *Names* 223; *Dreams* 1.239, 2.45; *Moses* 1.66; *Spec. Laws* 1.81, 1.171, 3.83, 3.207; *Heir* 231; *QG* 2.62. In light of these references, as well as the three quoted explicitly up above (i.e., *Alleg. Interp.* 1.43, 3.96; *Confusion* 146–47), there are therefore twenty-two extant texts, including Wis 7:26, that call Wisdom/Word the "image" of God in early Hellenistic Judaism. I have subsequently found that Friedrich-Wilhelm Eltester, *Eikon im Neuen Testament* (BZNW 23; Berlin: Töpelmann, 1958), 34–38 (see especially 35n.1), had already noticed most of these texts in Philo.

[57] Cf. also *Alleg. Interp.* 1.19; *Posterity* 127 (both use ἀρχή, though not as formal titles).

[58] Wilhelm Michaelis, "πρωτότοκος," *TDNT* 6:871, states that this word is a synonym of πρωτότοκος (see Col 1:15, 18), but whose occurrence is much more frequent in extra-biblical Greek writings than πρωτότοκος.

[59] *Confusion* 146–47 [Colson, Whitaker, and Marcus, LCL]. Cf. *Confusion* 62–63.

[60] *Dreams* 1.215 (Colson, Whitaker, and Marcus, LCL).

[61] *Agriculture* 51 (Colson, Whitaker, and Marcus, LCL). See also *Heir* 117–19, where Philo uses πρωτότοκος to describe "the divine Word," which is the exact same word Paul employs at Col 1:15, 18 to describe Christ. This last text in Philo should be carefully read. This ample evidence (given here and above) that the Word was titled "firstborn" in Philo, coupled with the fact that Wisdom and Word significantly overlap in Philo

The word is clearly connected to the ideas of primacy in rank and authority to rule. The reason for the title stems in part also from the idea that the Word or Wisdom existed before the rest of creation,[62] as the firstborn of a family would exist before other siblings. This latter concept of temporal priority, as we observed, was the central concern of Prov 8:22–31.

According to Philo, the Word/Wisdom is the agent "through whom the universe came into existence."[63] It is "antecedent to all that has come into existence," the "rudder" by which God "guides all things on their course," and the "instrument" that "God employed" "when He was fashioning the world" (cf. Col 1:16–17a).[64]

At the same time, the Word is also the mediator and peace-maker between God and humanity. It serves as the "harbinger of peace to creation from that God whose will it is to bring wars to an end, who is ever the guardian of peace."[65] Indeed, "The divine Logos...becomes a mediator and arbitrator for the two sides [i.e., God and humanity] which seem to be divided from each other, bringing about friendship and concord, for it is always the cause of community and the artisan of peace" (cf. Col 1:20).[66]

(and elsewhere) at least raises a question with regard to Fee's second argument against the identification of Christ with Wisdom ("Wisdom Christology in Paul: A Dissenting View," 259). On 275n.41 Fee (rightly) questions the two texts in Philo that Dunn offers as "firstborn" parallels (and Fee is responding to Dunn's arguments in particular). But Fee then shows no awareness of the texts in Philo adduced here. He is correct to argue that Wisdom is not named "firstborn" explicitly, and so linguistically his argument stands (although Prov 8:22–25 comes pretty close). Given, however, that Wisdom and Word are often virtually identical in Philo's thought (as argued above), the *concept* of being "firstborn" is present (that is, for Wisdom; for the Word it is linguistically explicit) and consequently Fee needs to reckon with it before dispatching such a hasty dismissal. Fee writes on p. 260 that "there are no certain linguistic ties in the Colossian passage with the Wisdom literature at all, certainly not of a kind to allow the use of the term as Wisdom Christology." Fee does not see a "Wisdom motif at all in the Pauline texts," especially 1 Cor 8:6 and Col 1:15–20 (276n.45).

[62] For Philo, this includes angelic beings (see again the first cited text above); cf. Col 1:15–17.

[63] *Flight* 109. See also *Spec. Laws* 1.81; *Heir* 199; *Migration* 6; *Sacrifices* 8; *Alleg. Interp.* 3.96; *Drunkenness* 30–31; *Worse* 54 reads "If you accord a father's honour to Him who created the world, and a mother's honour to Wisdom, by whose agency the universe was brought to completion, you will yourself be the gainer" (Colson, Whitaker, and Marcus, LCL).

[64] *Migration* 6. See also *Virtues* 62; *Dreams* 1.241.

[65] *Heir* 205–06.

[66] *QE* 2.68 (Colson, Whitaker, and Marcus, LCL).

Furthermore for Philo, the Word is that which "contained all [God's] fullness" (cf. Col 1:19),[67] and who, as "a glue and bond," gives coherence to everything, "filling up all things with His being," itself needing nothing.[68] It is the "bond of all existence" and "holds and knits together all the parts, preventing them from being dissolved and separated" (cf. Col 1:17b).[69] The Divine Word is "the fountain of Wisdom" from which one may drink and "gain life eternal as a prize."[70] Wisdom for Philo is the undefiled "daughter of God," but can also be thought of in masculine terms as one who sows and begets virtues in the souls of men.[71] The Word is God's temple (or "house"; cf. Col 1:19).[72] Wisdom/ Word is an ever-flowing, unbounded fountain of all kinds of knowledge and virtue, especially able to slake the thirst of those that long for God.[73] She is the instrument by which God "draws the perfect man from things earthly to Himself" (cf. Col 3:1–4).[74]

Personified Wisdom also appears in *1 En.* 42:1–2. The passage is found in "The Book of the Similitudes" (chs. 37–71). The date of this section is disputed; Isaac offers a date of the first century C.E.[75] Here Wisdom is described as seeking for a place to dwell among humanity, and, finding no suitable home, returns to heaven to settle permanently among the angels (cf. Sir 24:8–12; Bar 3:37; *4 Ezra* 5:9–10; John 1:14).

The work entitled *2 Enoch*, which is dated to the late first century C.E.,[76] states at 30:8 that "on the sixth day I [God] commanded my wisdom to create man...." The decision to use lowercase for the word "wisdom" is an interpretation that is inadequate in light of the evidence adduced here in the present chapter. This text provides further evidence that Wisdom was thought to take an active role in the creating

---

[67] *Dreams* 1.75.

[68] *Heir* 187–88.

[69] *Flight* 112.

[70] *Flight* 97.

[71] *Flight* 50–52.

[72] *Migration* 4–6, with Gen 28:17 in the background. See chapter eight of this study on the use of Ps 68:16 [67:17 LXX] in Col 1:19, which is an echo that depicts Christ as the temple of God.

[73] *Posterity* 136, 151–52; *Flight* 195–96; *Alleg. Interp.* 2.86; *Creation* 158; cf. *Worse* 115–18.

[74] *Sacrifices* 8.

[75] See E. Isaac, "1 (Ethiopic Apocalypse of) Enoch," *OTP* 1:7.

[76] F. I. Anderson, "2 (Slavonic Apocalypse of) Enoch," in *The Old Testament Pseudepigrapha* (ed. James H. Charlesworth; 2 vols.; ABRL; New York: Doubleday, 1983), 1:91.

process. Here she is actually commanded to create man, the climax of creation. The text is also further evidence that demonstrates that Gen 1 and Prov 8 were often connected in early Judaism.

This development of personified Wisdom continues on into later Judaism. In the *Hellenistic Synagogal Prayers* (2nd–3rd century C.E.), Wisdom is the agent of creation and especially of humanity made in the image of God (3:16–19, 12:36).[77] God is her "Father," and she is a "Mediator" (4:38), created by God (5:3). The passage at 12:9–15, however, though tantalizingly rich with Wisdom theology, has been heavily edited by a later Christian hand, and it is difficult to know what of the section was original.[78] *Targum Neofiti* Genesis 1:1 is probably more evidence that Gen 1 and Prov 8 were often connected, adding that "with wisdom" the Lord created and perfected heaven and earth. This connection between Gen 1 and Prov 8 is found elsewhere in later Judaism.[79]

Consistently throughout the rabbinic literature, the personified Wisdom of Prov 8:22–31 is identified as the Torah, beginning with *m. Avot* 6:10 (ca. 200 C.E.).[80] The main emphasis in these passages is that Torah was one of a select few things that preexisted creation. Elsewhere the rabbis play on the word רֹאשׁ ("head") and the word רֵאשִׁית ("beginning") that is found at Prov 8:22, to signify that Torah (= Wisdom) is the "Head" of God's ways (cf. again Aquila's κεφάλαιον ["head, principle"] at Prov 8:22).[81] Like contemporary scholarship, the rabbis appear to have had difficulty with the word אָמוֹן of Prov 8:30, offering at one point the possible meanings 1) "nursling," 2) "tutor," 3)

---

[77] Gen 1:26 is explicitly cited at 3:19. The text at 3:18–19 reads: "And the goal of the creative work—the rational living creature, the world citizen—having given order by your Wisdom, you created, saying, *Let us make man according to our image and likeness*" (D. A. Fiensy and D. R. Darnell, "Hellenistic Synagogal Prayers," in *The Old Testament Pseudepigrapha* [ed. James H. Charlesworth; 2 vols.; ABRL; New York: Doubleday, 1983], 2:679).

[78] Fiensy and Darnell, "Hellenistic Synagogal Prayers," *OTP* 2:690 note a.

[79] *Midr. Rabbah* Genesis 1.1, 4; *Tanhuma* Genesis 1:1ff., Part V.

[80] See *b. Avot* 6:10; *b. Pesahim* 54a, 87b; *b. Nedarim* 39b; *Midr.* Psalm 5:2, 90.12, 93.3; *Pirqe Rabbi Eliezer*, p. 10; *Mekilta*, Shirata 9.123; *Kallah Rabbati* 8:10; *Avot of Rabbi Nathan* 31:3; *Midr. Rabbah* Genesis 1.1, 4, 8, 8.2, 85.9; *Midr. Rabbah* Exodus 30.9; *Midr. Rabbah* Leviticus 11.3, 19.1; *Midr.* Proverbs ch. 8; *Midr. Rabbah* Song of Songs 5.11, §1; *Pesiqta Rabbati*, Piska 53.2; *Tanhuma* Genesis 1:1ff., Part V; *Sifre* Deuteronomy, Piska 37; *Tanna Debe Eliyyahu*, ER 71, 112, 160, EZ 171, S 20.

[81] *Midr. Rabbah* Song of Songs 5.11, §1; *Midr. Rabbah* Leviticus 19.1.

"covered," 4) "hidden," 5) "great," 6) and "workman."[82] It is the last suggestion that receives the most attention in the passage.

In summary, Wisdom/Word is consistently depicted as existing before creation. The figure frequently plays an instrumental role in the creating process. The extent of Wisdom's activity and nature were portrayed in the broadest and most comprehensive terms ("all"; "all things"). The figure was known by several titles, especially "image," "firstborn," "beginning," and occasionally "head." Wisdom was often identified with Torah in early Judaism, and this became the fixed interpretation in the later rabbinic writings.

New Testament Context: The Use of the Proverbs 8:22–31 Interpretive Development in Colossians 1:15–20

This study will not offer a full exegesis of Col 1:15–20. The aim of this section is much more specific and limited in that it seeks to show that Prov 8:22–31 has been alluded to at Col 1:15–20 *via its interpretive development in early Judaism*. The striking parallels will be presented in an orderly fashion. The cumulative weight of evidence validates the allusion to this development as virtually certain.

For our purpose, there is no need to discuss the questions surrounding the possible redaction of an earlier hymn; the concern here is with the hymn's final form. Most of NT scholarship regards Col 1:15–20 as a self-contained unit, a probable hymn, confession, or creed of some kind. At the very least, "the structure indicates that we have here something more elevated and carefully thought-out than straightforward prose. It is some kind of poem."[83] As to structure, this study largely follows Tom Wright's outline:[84]

---

[82] *Midr. Rabbah* Genesis 1.1 (cf. *Midr. Rabbah* Exodus 30.9). The last meaning of "workman" is taken ultimately in the passage to mean that Torah served at creation as the diagram that an architect would use to build a palace; on this see also *Tanna Debe Eliyyahu*, ER 160.

[83] Wright, *Climax of the Covenant*, 103.

[84] *Climax of the Covenant*, 101–2, 104. See Aletti, *Colossiens*, 89–93 for a summary of the various structural analyses of the hymn offered and the scholars who hold to them.

Christ Preeminent in Creation [1:15–17]

A ὅς ἐστιν...πρωτότοκος...ὅτι ἐν αὐτῷ...τὰ πάντα δι' αὐτοῦ καὶ εἰς αὐτὸν [vv. 15–16]

    B καὶ αὐτός ἐστιν...[v. 17]

Christ Preeminent in the Renewed Creation[85] [1:18–20]

    B¹ καὶ αὐτός ἐστιν...[v. 18a]

A¹ ὅς ἐστιν...πρωτότοκος...ὅτι ἐν αὐτῷ...δι' αὐτοῦ...τὰ πάντα εἰς αὐτόν [vv. 18c–20]

Lohse observes that the entire unit begins with a relative pronoun clause, just like other hymnic or confessional material embedded in the NT. This strengthens the argument that the composition is independent material that has been inserted at this point in the letter (cf. Phil 2:6; 1 Tim 3:16; 1 Pet 2:22; Heb 1:3).[86] This observation is also helpful, because in the context the relative pronoun is both unexpected and awkward (though not grammatically impossible). The antecedent is somewhat difficult to trace, but can be pinned to τοῦ υἱοῦ τῆς ἀγάπης αὐτοῦ, "the Son of his love," back in 1:13. We have argued in chapter six of this study that this phrase is part of an echo of 2 Sam 7:13–14, 18. Christ is the ultimate fulfillment of God's promise to David that he would have a son on the throne forever.

At Col 1:15, Christ is designated the "image of the invisible God" and the "firstborn of all creation" (cf. 2 Cor 4:4; Rom 8:29). One may be initially tempted to think that a direct allusion to Gen 1:26–27 has been made, for there the first human couple is declared to have been made "in the image of God."[87] The "image" (εἰκών) language here does ultimately derive from Gen 1:26–27, as the strong evidence in Philo has shown (see above).[88] Moreover, the only other use of the word εἰκών in Colossians occurs at 3:10 and there Paul makes direct

---

[85] Cf. Dunn, *Christology in the Making*, 188, who writes for many when he states that "the basic movement of thought [of the hymn] also seems clear enough—from Christ's (pre-existent) role in creation (first strophe) to his role in redemption (second strophe), from his relationship with the old creation (protology) to his relationship with the new (eschatology)."

[86] Lohse, *Colossians*, 41n.65.

[87] So also Gnilka, *Der Kolosserbrief*, 59.

[88] Against Schweizer, *Colossians*, 66n.27, who writes "Where wisdom appears as the image of God. [*sic*] Gen. 1:26 is not involved, and vice-versa...."

allusion to Gen 1:26–27 (on which, see chapter thirteen). This evidence
further "confirms that in 1.15 the christological title *eikōn tou theou* is
drawn from Gen. 1 and has not been independently formulated."[89]
The language, nevertheless, is not *first* an allusion to Gen 1:26–27, as
if the writer were developing a last Adam Christology.[90] Rather, the
title is first of all a designation for the divine Wisdom/Word that was
current in Hellenistic-Jewish circles of Paul's day, and the use of the
language here is intended to recall first of all this figure as it is found
together with the rest of the language of Col 1:15–20. Granted this
priority of the language of "image" as it serves in an overall allusion
to the Wisdom/Word figure of the Prov 8 development, we could subsequently speak of a secondary echo of Gen 1:26–27 here at Col 1:15.
This is especially the case in light of how we have observed how early
Judaism often connected Gen 1 with Prov 8 and how the language of
Gen 1 had informed it.[91] It is not a case of "either/or," but "both/and,"
although with the priority and stress upon the Wisdom/Word allusion,
and not Gen 1 (see chapter 13 for discussion of the Gen 1:26–27 allusion at Col 3:10). The allusion is to the Wisdom/Word development,
with Gen 1 echoing within this larger cavern of tradition.

That Wisdom/Word is being alluded to at 1:15 and not primarily
Gen 1:26–27 is confirmed by the ground given in v. 16, stating *why*
these titles may be appropriately attributed to Christ. It is *because* (ὅτι)
"in," "through," and "for" him all things were created. Since Adam
was not the mediator of all God's creating activity, nor was this ever
claimed for him in any of the early Jewish literature, it is improbable
that Christ is here depicted as a final Adam figure. Those who argue for
a direct allusion to Gen 1:26–27 at Col 1:15 seem to focus on the word
"image" but neglect the rest of the context and especially the immediate
logical argument. Moreover, this language of agency in the establishment of creation in v. 16 finds remarkable and numerous parallels in
early Jewish literature with regard to personified Wisdom/Word, which
provides the necessary evidence for an alternate background for the

---

[89] Francis Watson, *Text and Truth: Redefining Biblical Theology* (Grand Rapids: Eerdmans, 1997), 282.

[90] So also Aletti, *Colossiens*, 116. Against Jervell, *Imago Dei*, 200–1, who appears to
fail to pick up the Wisdom allusion. I disagree with Aletti, however, who states that
Gen 1:27 is not in the picture at all ("le titre ne renvoie donc pas à Gen 1,27"). And
of course Paul *does* describe Christ as the last Adam in Rom 5:12–21.

[91] We also saw how later Judaism continued this trajectory of interpretation (see
above).

allusion (see above). Furthermore, as in the early Jewish literature that speaks of the Wisdom/Word figure, God is carefully upheld as Creator and as the ultimate source of creation here in the poem. The verb ἐκτίσθη at v. 16a ("all things were created") is a divine passive: *God* is the one who created "all things."

This is also the case with the title "firstborn" (πρωτότοκος), a title here in apposition to "image," even though Adam was literally the first of his race. The evidence in Philo should be recalled at this point (*Confusion* 146–47; *Dreams* 1.215; *Agriculture* 51; *Heir* 117–19). The language of "firstborn" ultimately derives from Prov 8:22–25, where the author has employed birthing imagery to describe God's acquisition of Wisdom ("I was brought forth"; LXX: γεννᾷ με, "he begat me").

In the LXX, the term πρωτότοκος ("firstborn") most often refers to that offspring (whether human or animal) that first opened a womb (Exod 13:2). Thus the word typically carried a temporal significance. Moreover, a human male πρωτότοκος held a privileged place in the family and possessed unique authority over all the other siblings. So primacy in rank was also conveyed with the use of the term.[92] Both the people of Israel and King David were called God's πρωτότοκος, though neither of these are in mind here at Col 1:15.[93] The main rationale for not seeing an allusion to Ps 89:27 here, as some do, is once again because of the clear logical relation between v. 15 and v. 16. Verse 16 gives the reason why Christ is the "firstborn of all creation": it is not because he is the ultimate son of David (though he indeed is that, as the echo of 2 Sam 7 at Col 1:13 implies; see chapter six), but because "in him," "through him," and even "for him" all things were created. The title πρωτότοκος at Col 1:15b (and 18c) articulates both Christ's rank *as well as* his temporal preeminence in relation to any being within the created order who may have been considered to be a legitimate contender for his authority. The term functions as a part of the magisterial allusion

---

[92] See e.g., Gen 27 (esp. vv. 19, 29, 32), 48:12–20 [esp. v. 18]; Deut 21:15–17; 1 Chr 5:1–2, 26:10; 2 Chr 21:3.

[93] For Israel, see Exod 4:22; Jer 38:9 (ET 31:9); cf. Sir 36:11 [36:17 NRSV]; *4 Ezra* 6:58; *Jub.* 2:20; *Pss. Sol.* 18:4. For David, see Ps 88:28 (ET 89:27). So also Dunn, *Colossians*, 90n.18; cf. Wright, *Colossians*, 67n.1; Burney, "Christ as the ΑΡΧΗ," 173–74; against Hühn, *Citate*, 197; Beare, "Colossians," 164. Lightfoot, *Colossians*, 146, O'Brien, *Colossians*, 44, and Bruce, *Colossians*, 59–60 see both Ps 89:27 and the Logos/Wisdom idea behind the use of the term "firstborn" at Col 1:15. Fee, "Old Testament Intertextuality in Colossians," ad loc., sees only an allusion to Ps 89:27 and argues against any Wisdom influence.

to Prov 8:22–31 as viewed in the light of its first-century interpretive development in early Judaism.

The confession continues and at v. 18 attributes the titles "head," "beginning," and, once again "firstborn" to Christ. As we have seen, there exists some evidence in the literature that "head" may have also served as a title for Wisdom.[94] The title "beginning" was ascribed both to the Word and to Wisdom in Philo, as shown above (Word: *Confusion* 146–47; Wisdom: *Alleg. Interp.* 1.43). This last title arises from Prov 8:22, where Wisdom is said to be the "beginning" of God's creative activity. These creational overtones are retained yet transformed in the new context of Col 1:18. Christ is the "beginning," though not here merely as the beginning of God's initial work of creation, but now the "beginning" of the renewed creation, as the first to experience the resurrection from the dead ("firstborn from the dead").[95]

In accord with the early Jewish tradition stemming from Prov 8:22–31, Christ is πρὸ πάντων, "before all things" (v. 17a). Six times in LXX Prov 8:23–25 the preposition πρό is used to stress Wisdom's existence *temporally* before all other created things (see again the chart at the beginning of this chapter). This thought is condensed and picked up here at v. 17a in one concise phrase.[96]

As we saw earlier in this chapter, the author of Wisdom of Solomon heavily employed πᾶς ("all") to describe the extent of Wisdom's nature and activity. It is therefore worth noting that the hymn employs the word πᾶς ("all") eight times to describe the extent of Christ's activity and nature. He is firstborn of "all" creation (1:15b), and "all things" (τὰ πάντα; twice) have been created in, through, and for him (1:16). He existed before "all things" (πάντων; 1:17a), and "all things" (τὰ πάντα) hold together in him (1:17b). He has attained preeminence in

---

[94] See Aquila's κεφάλαιον at Prov 8:22 (LSJ, "κεφάλαιον," states that the word can be merely an equivalent for κεφαλή); *Midr. Rabbah* Song of Songs 5.11, §1; *Midr. Rabbah* Leviticus 19.1.

[95] Burney, "Christ as the ΑΡΧΗ," 174, argues that the mention of "beginning" (רֵאשִׁית) at Prov 8:22 "immediately suggested to the Apostle" the use of "beginning" (בְּרֵאשִׁית) at Gen 1:1. Our investigation in both early and later Judaism confirms that Prov 8:22–31 and Gen 1 were often connected with regard to discussions on Wisdom, and both texts have certainly influenced Col 1:15–20. I am less confident of Burney's hypothesis, however, that Paul has offered a rabbinic midrash upon all the meanings of רֵאשִׁית, since the data can be explained better in light of the overall Jewish Wisdom tradition that Paul has inherited. In this light, Burney's interpretation appears forced; cf. Jervell, *Imago Dei*, 200n.107.

[96] Against Dunn, *Christology in the Making*, 191.

"all things" (πᾶσιν; 1:18d), and "all" the fullness of deity was pleased both to dwell in him (πᾶν; 1:19) as well as to reconcile "all things" (τὰ πάντα) through him and for him (1:20a).

Christ is both the agent of creation as well as its sustainer (v. 16, 17b). Moreover, like Philo's Word, all the divine "fullness" was pleased to dwell in Christ, which in Col 1:19 is language taken from Ps 67:17 LXX (cf. again Philo, *Dreams* 1.75; *Migration* 4–6). Also like Philo's Word, Christ is the mediator of peace between God and humanity (1:20; see again *Heir* 205–06; *QE* 2.68).

It may be helpful at this point to summarize the parallels between Col 1:15–20 and the first-century interpretive development of Prov 8:22–31 in a chart:

First century C.E. development of the Proverbs 8:22–31 Wisdom figure	Colossians 1:15–20
Wisdom/Word is the "image" of God:	Christ is the "image" of God (v. 15a)
Wis 7:25–26; Philo, *Alleg. Interp.* 1.43, 2.4, 3.96; *Confusion* 97, 146–47; *Creation* 25, 31, 146; *Planting* 19–20; *Flight* 12–13, 101; *Names* 223; *Dreams* 1.239, 2.45; *Moses* 1.66; *Spec. Laws* 1.81, 1.171, 3.83, 3.207; *Heir* 231; *QG* 2.62.	
Wisdom/Word is the "firstborn" (of all creation):	Christ is the "firstborn" of all creation (v. 15b)
Philo, *Confusion* 146–47; *Dreams* 1.215; *Agriculture* 51; *Heir* 117–19; cf. Prov 8:25.	
Wisdom/Word is the "beginning" (of creation):	Christ is the "beginning" of the renewed creation (1:18b)
Philo, *Confusion* 146–47; *Alleg. Interp.* 1.43. Cf. Prov 8:22.	
Wisdom/Word preexisted creation:	Christ preexisted creation (v. 17a):
Prov 8:23–25 LXX (πρό [6x]); Sir 24:9; Wis 9:9; Aristob. 5.10–11a; Philo, *Migration* 6; cf. John 1:1–3.	αὐτός ἐστιν πρὸ πάντων

Table *(cont.)*

First century C.E. development of the Proverbs 8:22–31 Wisdom figure	Colossians 1:15–20
Wisdom/Word was the agent of creation: Prov 8:22 LXX (εἰς ἔργα αὐτοῦ); Wis 7:22, 8:6, 9:1; Philo, *Flight* 12, 109; *Spec. Laws* 1.81; *Unchangeable* 57; *Heir* 199; *Migration* 6; *Worse* 54, 115–16; *Sacrifices* 8; *Alleg. Interp.* 1.65, 3.96; *Drunkenness* 30–31; *Virtues* 62; *Dreams* 1.241, 2.45; *2 En.* 30:8; cf. *Alleg. Interp.* 2.49; *Heir* 53; John 1:1–3	Christ was the agent of creation (v. 16f): τὰ πάντα δι' αὐτοῦ...ἔκτισται
Word/Wisdom sustains the created order: Philo, *Flight* 112; *Heir* 187–88; cf. Wis 1:6–7 ("Wisdom" and "Spirit of the Lord" are interchangeable in this last text)	Christ sustains the created order (v. 17b): τὰ πάντα ἐν αὐτῷ συνέστηκεν
Wisdom is the "Head": N.B.: The evidence here is from *after* the first century C.E.; it may nevertheless reflect a tradition that goes back to the time of the apostle Paul. Aquila's κεφάλαιον at Prov 8:22 (ca. 140 C.E.); see *Midr. Rabbah* Song of Songs 5.11, §1; *Midr. Rabbah* Leviticus 19.1.	Christ is the "Head" of the Church, his Body (v. 18a).
Heavy employment of πᾶς ("all") to describe the extent of Wisdom/Word's nature and activity: Wis 7:22, 23, 24, 27, 8:1, 5, 9:1; Philo, *Flight* 112.	Heavy employment of πᾶς ("all") to describe the extent of Christ's nature and activity: Col 1:15, 16a, 16f, 17a, 17b, 18d, 19, 20
a) The Word "contains all [God's] fullness" [LCL]: Philo, *Dreams* 1.75	In Christ "all the fullness" of God was pleased to dwell (v. 19)
b) Wisdom/Word is the "house" (temple) of God: Philo, *Migration* 4–6; cf. *Alleg. Interp.* 3.46	N.B. Col 1:19 is an echo of Ps 67:17 LXX (see chapter eight), a reference to the presence of God in the temple on Zion. In light of the strong temple overtones of 1:19, these other references in Philo are included here as significant parallels.
Wisdom is agent of reconciliation and peace between God and humanity: Philo, *Heir* 205–6; *QE* 2.68.	Christ is the agent of reconciliation and peace between God and humanity (v. 20)

The ten parallels between what was being said about Wisdom/Word before and in the first century C.E. and what is said about Christ at Col 1:15–20 are striking.

> To sum up, the author of the hymn attributed the sapiential functions of creational and salvational mediation to Jesus Christ thus portraying the pre-existent, incarnate, and exalted Christ in the light of the Jewish divine wisdom.[97]

The composer of the hymn or poem, however, has taken his description of Christ in the language of Wisdom/Word an astonishing step beyond anything said about the Wisdom/Word figure in the early Jewish literature. At v. 16, the hymn states that all things were not created merely through Christ but adds that it was created εἰς αὐτὸν, "for him."[98] That is, Christ is both the *agent* by which creation came into existence as well as the *purpose* and goal for which all of it exists. This is language that elsewhere in the NT is reserved for God alone (see Rom 11:36; 1 Cor 8:6; Heb 2:10).

That Wisdom was identified with Torah in the Judaism of Paul's day may be significant for why the apostle inserted a hymn that identified Christ as Wisdom (and which went beyond what was typically written about it). There are significant Jewish elements to the philosophy Paul was combating, and it seems likely that the Colossians were being tempted to adopt 1) Jewish holy days like the festivals, Sabbath, and new moon celebrations (2:16b), 2) Jewish dietary laws (2:16a), and 3) circumcision (2:11, 13, 3:11). In light of this, Paul may well be launching an offensive against the claim of the sufficiency of Torah as God's revelation to Israel by identifying *Christ*, not Torah, as the divine Wisdom.

Proverbs 8:22–31 and Its Exegesis in the Rest of the NT
and in the Early Church Fathers

The passages that possibly appear to have been most influenced by the Prov 8:22–31 personified Wisdom exegetical tradition include John 1:1–3 and Heb 1:2b–3 (perhaps also 1 Cor 8:6, 10:4; Rev 3:14?).[99]

---

[97] Schnabel, *Law and Wisdom from Ben Sira to Paul*, 258.
[98] Cf. O'Brien, *Colossians*, 47; Dunn, *Colossians*, 92.
[99] For an investigation of the Wisdom theme elsewhere in Paul, see Feuillet, *Le Christ Sagesse de Dieu d'après les Épitres Pauliniennes*. See also Schnabel, *Law and Wisdom*,

Christ, the Word, existed "in the beginning" (John 1:1a, in an allusion to Gen 1:1 LXX), was with God at this time (1:1b), and served as the agent through which God created all things (1:3). He became flesh and made his dwelling in Israel (1:14; cf. Sir 24:8–12; *4 Ezra* 5:9–10; *1 En.* 42:1–2).[100] At Heb 1:2b, Christ is the one through whom God made the "world" (RSV, ESV; TNIV: "universe"), and at 1:3 is described as the "reflection" (ἀπαύγασμα) of God's glory and the "exact imprint" of God's nature (NRSV; cf. Wis 7:25–26). Christ upholds "all things" (τὰ πάντα) by his powerful word (1:3b).

Several early Church fathers quote a portion of Prov 8:22–31 and understand it as a description of Jesus Christ.[101] Some also quote from Col 1:15–20 in close proximity to a quotation from Prov 8:22–31 for the same purpose.[102] Methodius combines Gen 1:1, Prov 8:22, and John 1:1–2,[103] and displays awareness of "Beginning" as a title for Christ,[104] as does Theophilus of Antioch (d. after 180 C.E.) minus the explicit reference to John.[105] Cyprian (d. 258 C.E.) quotes Prov 8:22–31 in its entirety and combines it with Sir 24:3–7, Ps 89:27–33, John 17:3–5, Col 1:15, 18 and 1 Cor 1:22–24 ("Christ the power and the wisdom of God") to defend that Christ is the firstborn Wisdom of God.[106] Tertullian quotes from Prov 8:22–30 (several times), Gen 1:3, Pss 2:7, 45:1, John

---

236–64. For a discussion of the possibility of influence at Rev 3:14, see Beale, *Book of Revelation*, 297–301.

[100] For an extensive treatment of the Wisdom motif in John, see Scott, *Sophia and the Johannine Jesus*. For an investigation of the theme in the Synoptics, see Felix Christ, *Jesus Sophia: Die Sophia-Christologie bei den Synoptikern* (ATANT 57; Zürich: Zwingli-Verlag, 1970).

[101] Justin Martyr (d. ca. 165 C.E.), *Dialogue with Trypho* 61 (*ANF* 1:227–28), 129 (*ANF* 1:264); cf. 126 (*ANF* 1:262); Athenagoras (d. 177 C.E.), *A Plea for the Christians* 10 (*ANF* 2:133); Clement of Alexandria (d. before 215 C.E.), *Miscellanies* 7.2 (*ANF* 2:525); Dionysius of Alexandria (d. 264/5 C.E.), *Extant Fragments* 4.3 (*ANF* 6:92); Lactantius (d. 330 C.E.), *The Divine Institutes* 4.6 (*ANF* 7:105).

[102] Irenaeus (d. 202 C.E.), *Against Heresies* 4.20.2–3 (*ANF* 1:488; here also Irenaeus argues that Christ is the Word and the Spirit is Wisdom); Alexander of Alexandria (d. 328 C.E.), *Epistles on the Arian Heresy* 1.6–7 (*ANF* 6:293); Dionysius of Rome (d. 259–69 C.E.), *Against the Sabellians* 2 (*ANF* 7:365); Origen (d. 253/4 C.E.), *First Principles* 1.2.1 (*ANF* 4:245–46; also 1 Cor 1:24). In *First Principles* 1.2.5 (*ANF* 4:247), Origen combines Col 1:15, Heb 1:3, and Wis 7:25; see his full argument in *First Principles* 1.2.1–13 (*ANF* 4:245–51).

[103] So also Tertullian (d. after 220 C.E.), *Against Hermogenes* 20 (*ANF* 3:488–89); see also *Against Hermogenes* 18 (*ANF* 3:487–88), where Tertullian quotes Prov 8:27–31 and ties it to John 1:1 and 10:30; cf. *Against Hermogenes* 32 (*ANF* 3:495–96) and 45 (*ANF* 3:502).

[104] *Fragments* 8 (*ANF* 6:381).

[105] *To Autolycus* 2.10 (*ANF* 2:97–98).

[106] *The Treatises of Cyprian* ("*To Quirinius*") 12.2.1 (*ANF* 5:515–16).

1:1, 3, and Phil 2:6, and alludes to Col 1:15, to argue that Christ was a distinct person from the Father.[107]

The interpretation of Col 1:15 and Prov 8:22 came under intense scrutiny when Arius (d. 335/6 C.E.) used them to promulgate the teaching that Christ, while perfect, was a created being, and therefore "there was a time when he was not."[108] He and his doctrines were eventually condemned at the Council of Nicaea (325 C.E.). The council hammered out a statement that asserted that Christ was "of the same substance as the Father," "true God from true God," "begotten not made," and "of one substance with the Father."[109] From the time of this pivotal council up until today, the Nicene Creed has provided a foundation upon which subsequent Christological study has been built.

Hermeneutical Reflections

With Paul's allusion to Prov 8:22–31 as it was interpretively developed in his own first century C.E. historical context, the figure of Wisdom has undergone a significant development. Beginning as a literary personification, the Wisdom figure has been connected to the crucified and resurrected Jesus Christ, an actual historical figure. This interpretation stood in strong contrast to the Judaism of the apostle's day, which identified Wisdom with their Scriptures, the Torah.

Paul's move in connecting the Word/Wisdom development to Christ does not indicate that the apostle saw a direct fulfillment of a predictive prophecy, because Prov 8 is not a prophecy. Raymond Van Leeuwen writes that

> Christian tradition has thus in various ways identified Wisdom in Proverbs 8 and Christ as one. A better move, perhaps, would be to understand Christ as the hidden reality underlying and fulfilling the cosmic and personal imagery of Wisdom in Proverbs 8, without positing a direct one-to-one correspondence in all particulars.[110]

---

[107] *Against Praxeas* 6–7 (*ANF* 3:601–2). Cf. *Against Praxeas* 11 (*ANF* 3:605–6) and 19 (*ANF* 3:614).

[108] J. N. D. Kelly, *Early Christian Creeds* (2nd ed.; London: Longman's, 1960), 232–33.

[109] See Kelly, *Early Christian Creeds*, 234–42.

[110] "The Book of Proverbs: Introduction, Commentary, and Reflections," (NIB 5; Nashville: Abingdon, 1997), 99.

Van Leeuwen's comments perhaps best accord with what is known as *sensus plenior* (Van Leeuwen himself does not mention this expression). *Sensus plenior* ("fuller sense") is the hermeneutical term used to describe the phenomenon of a text acquiring a fuller meaning in the light of further revelation.[111] Liable to abuse, those who have written on the subject maintain that the key control must be that the meaning of the original context forms the essence and foundation of the fuller sense, and may not be contradicted or set aside.[112] *Sensus plenior* assumes that to varying degrees the human author was unaware of all of the meaning of what he or she was writing. It also may assume that God superintended the entire writing process even while the human author freely wrote in accord with his own language, style, thought, and historical horizon.[113]

It is probably more accurate, however, to classify Paul's use of the Prov 8 interpretive tradition along the lines of a typological interpretation.[114] Paul seeks to make a bold statement about Jesus Christ by strategically picking up language that typically had circled around discussions of the enigmatic Wisdom/Word figure in his day. By borrowing language used to depict this figure, Paul portrays Christ as the embodiment of the wisdom and revelation of God and the mediator between God and humanity *par excellance*. Paul does not state that Christ *is* Wisdom or equate the two, but rather appropriates the language typically employed to depict Wisdom/Word to highlight that all that this familiar but shadowy figure represented had found its ultimate and concrete expression in the reality of Jesus Christ. The antitype, however, goes beyond what was ever said about the type (which was merely a literary personification in the first place). No extant writing had said

---

[111] Raymond Brown, *The "Sensus Plenior" of Sacred Scripture* (Baltimore: St. Mary's University, 1955), 92, defines *sensus plenior* as "that additional deeper meaning, intended by God but not clearly intended by the human author, which is seen to exist in the words of a biblical text (or group of texts, or even a whole book) when they are studied in the light of further revelation or development in the understanding of revelation."

[112] Douglas J. Moo, "The Problem of *Sensus Plenior*," in *Hermeneutics, Authority, and Canon* (eds. D. A. Carson and John D. Woodbridge; Grand Rapids: Baker, 1995), 201, 210; G. K. Beale, "Did Jesus and his Followers Preach the Right Doctrine from the Wrong Texts? An Examination of the Presuppositions of Jesus' and the Apostles' Exegetical Method," *Them* 14 (April 1989), 90–91; see also bibliography in Beale on p. 95n.20 for other scholars who insist on this control.

[113] Moo, "*Sensus Plenior*," 201–4.

[114] My decision to view Paul's use here as a typological interpretation was strengthened and confirmed by the comments of Waltke, *Proverbs 1–15*, 127–33, although I disagree with him in particulars of his argument.

previously that all of creation existed "for" Wisdom or the Word, but Paul declares that this is true of Jesus Christ. A typological framework also offers a satisfactory explanation for what is otherwise an obvious difficulty with regard to gender: personified Wisdom of Prov 8 is female, while Jesus of Nazareth is male. The type and antitype, however, do not require one-to-one correspondence in all matters; almost invariably in the use of typological interpretation similarities and differences exist between the two items being compared. The agreement comes at the fundamental levels of deep structure.[115] The fact that both Wisdom and Christ are portrayed as existing before creation, that both were agents in the creating process, that both sustain creation, that both serve as intermediaries between God and humanity as vehicles of revelation and wisdom, etc.; these are the deep structural correspondences that are to be recognized and grasped by Paul's audience in the use of the allusion, even as Paul's description goes well beyond what was ever said about Wisdom or the Word.

The heterodox "philosophy" may have taught that Torah was God's sufficient wisdom and revelation, and that its precepts—especially the keeping of the Mosaic covenant's festivals, holy days, and food laws (Col 2:16–17), and quite possibly circumcision (Col 2:11–13)—needed to be kept to be pleasing to God. The rhetorical effect of the hymn serves to strengthen the Colossian church's confidence in Christ as the sufficient source of wisdom for right living before God. The hymn or confession leaves little reason for the Colossians to think they need anyone or anything but Christ, who holds preeminence in the old creation as well as the in-breaking new by virtue of his resurrection from the dead.

---

[115] Baker, "Typology and the Christian Use of the Old Testament," 327.

CHAPTER EIGHT

THE SCRIPTURES OF ISRAEL IN COLOSSIANS 1:15–20: THE ECHO OF PSALM 68:16 (67:17 LXX) IN 1:19

Comparison of Textual Versions and Evaluation

Psalm 68:17 MT	Psalm 67:17 LXX	Colossians 1:19
לָמָּה תְּרַצְּדוּן הָרִים גַּבְנֻנִּים	ἵνα τί ὑπολαμβάνετε	ὅτι ἐν αὐτῷ εὐδόκησεν
הָהָר חָמַד אֱלֹהִים לְשִׁבְתּוֹ	ὄρη τετυρωμένα τὸ	πᾶν τὸ πλήρωμα
אַף־יְהוָה יִשְׁכֹּן לָנֶצַח׃	ὄρος ὃ εὐδόκησεν	κατοικῆσαι
	ὁ θεὸς κατοικεῖν ἐν	
	αὐτῷ καὶ γὰρ ὁ κύριος	
	κατασκηνώσει εἰς τέλος	

This proposal meets our two criteria necessary for an echo: 1) availability, and 2) word agreement.[1] Regarding *availability*, Paul often quoted from the Psalms (twenty-four times, according to the count by Silva)[2] and thus demonstrates that the Psalter was well known by him. Significantly, Ps 68:18 is quoted in Ephesians 4:8, though the Pauline authorship of the letter is disputed. Regarding *word agreement*, the texts

---

[1] Other scholars have seen Ps 67:17 LXX behind Col 1:19. Wright, *Colossians*, 78n.1; idem, *Climax of the Covenant*, 117, states that it is an "allusion"; T. K. Abbott, *A Critical and Exegetical Commentary on the Epistles to the Ephesians and to the Colossians* (ICC; Edinburgh: T&T Clark, 1897), 219 ("the words seem to be an echo of Ps lxviii.17, ὁ Θεὸς εὐδόκησε κατοικεῖν ἐν αὐτῷ"); Paul Beasley-Murray, "Colossians 1:15–20: An Early Christian Hymn Celebrating the Lordship of Christ," in *Pauline Studies: Essays Presented to Professor F. F. Bruce on his 70th Birthday* (eds. by Donald A. Hagner and Murray J. Harris; Grand Rapids: Eerdmans, 1980), 177; Hay, *Colossians*, 62, proposes it as a possible allusion ("Perhaps the phrasing is based on Ps 68:16 (LXX 67:17)"); Beale, "Colossians," ad loc., argues for its validity as an allusion.

Others have noted that Ps 67:17 LXX is the strongest or one of the strongest parallels in the OT, but leave the question of actual dependence up for the reader to decide. So Lohmeyer, *Kolosser*, 65n.1; Gnilka, *Der Kolosserbrief*, 71; Aletti, *Colossiens*, 110n.81; Lohse, *Colossians*, 58; Schweizer, *Colossians*, 77; P. W. Comfort, "Temple," *DPL* 925; Wolter, *Der Brief an die Kolosser*, 85; Barth and Blanke, *Colossians*, 212; Arnold, *Colossian Syncretism*, 262; O'Brien, *Colossians*, 52; Dunn, *Colossians*, 101; MacDonald, *Colossians*, 63.

[2] M. Silva, "Old Testament in Paul," *DPL* 631. His count includes the quotation of Ps 68:18 in Eph 4:8.

share four words in common, with a fifth (ὁ θεός, "God") paraphrased in a circumlocution, possibly for poetic heightening (πᾶν τὸ πλήρωμα, "all the fullness").

Old Testament Context: Psalm 68(67): 16–19 [15–18 ET]

"There is hardly another song in the Psalter which in its corrupt text and its lack of coherence precipitates such serious problems for the interpreter as Psalm 68."[3] With these words Kraus begins his comments on Psalm 68, and they serve both to warn and to restrain any would-be exegete of overconfidence in its interpretation. Textual difficulties abound, the *Sitz im Leben* is hotly disputed,[4] and the form appears to be conglomerate, containing elements of the song of trust (vv. 2–4), the hymn (vv. 5–7, 33–36), the recital of God's past saving actions (vv. 8–15), the Zion psalm (vv. 16–19), and the enthronement psalm (vv. 25–28).[5] It also includes petition (as in a lament, vv. 29–32). The section of interest for this study, vv. 16–19, contains as its central theme one that corresponds broadly with that found in other Zion psalms (see Pss 46, 48, 76, 84, 87, 122).[6] "Zion psalms" are so named because they extol Zion's (i.e., Jerusalem's) special status as the "city of God" due to the divine election. This is the fundamental theme of Ps 68:16–19 (see also vv. 29–35). An exegesis of these verses is given below, with connection to the larger context following.

At v. 16 [v. 15 ET], the phrase "mountain of God" is in apposition to "mountain of Bashan." Of significance is that the phrase "mountain of God" is found four times elsewhere in the OT as a designation for Mt. Horeb, i.e., Sinai (Exod 3:1, 18:5, 24:13; 1 Kgs 19:8).[7] Sinai was the mount upon which God revealed himself to Israel in a terrifying theophany

---

[3] Kraus, *Psalms 60–150*, 47.

[4] See Kraus, *Psalms 60–150*, 49.

[5] Cf. also Kraus's analysis, *Psalms 60–150*, 48.

[6] These are the psalms classified as "songs of Zion" by Bernhard W. Anderson, *Out of the Depths: The Psalms Speak for Us Today* (3rd ed.; Louisville: Westminster John Knox, 2000), 219–24. Anderson tentatively classifies Ps 68 as a "Zion liturgy" but immediately adds that the psalm is "almost impossible to classify" (221).

[7] At Num 10:33, Sinai is called the "mountain of *YHWH*" (הַר־יְהוָה; LXX: τό ὄρος κυρίου; cf. *Jubilees* 1:2). At Isa 2:3 (= Mic 4:2), Ps 24:3, Isa 30:29, and Zech 8:3 (which adds, "of hosts"), Zion is also called the "mountain of YHWH." Cf. also Gen 22:14 (which at *Jub.* 18:13 is interpreted to be Mt. Zion).

of thunder, lightning, thick cloud, fire, smoke, blasts of trumpets, and violent quaking (Exod 19:16–19). Upon it Moses alone was allowed to ascend, receiving the two stone tablets of the ten commandments (Exod 19:20–20:21, 31:18). For "the mountain of Bashan" to be so designated indicated that it was a place of considerable religious importance. It means that it was where God or the gods were thought to visit and reside—a sort of lightning rod for the divine activity and presence. The implied assertion, perhaps, was that this mountain's importance rivaled that of Sinai. This interpretation is strengthened by the explicit mention of Sinai at v. 18 (v. 17 ET; "the Lord among them, Sinai in the holy place").

The phrase "mountain of Bashan" is found nowhere else in the Hebrew Bible. Bashan was a fertile plateau east of the Sea of Galilee, north of the Yarmuk River, and south of Mt. Hermon.[8] The ascription "mountain of Bashan" is probably another way of referring to the majestic and rugged Mt. Hermon that towers and overlooks the entire region of Bashan from the north.[9] The title may refer to the entire Hermon range, which is 50km long and extends along a NE-SW axis 25km wide,[10] or especially to the southern spur, the highest peak in the range (2814 meters or roughly 9200 feet).[11] Hermon is the highest mountain in Israel or its near environs.[12]

In the ANE, high hills and mountains were considered to be spots frequented by the gods, possibly because the summits were closer to the heavens than the rest of the outlying land (the heavens were believed to be the permanent dwelling of the gods).[13] Therefore Hermon, the tallest and most formidable range in Israel's immediate vicinity, would have naturally acquired fame as a habitation of the gods. This typical viewpoint is represented at Ps 68:16, but is parodied. The psalmist

---

[8] Joel C. Slayton, "Bashan," *ABD* 1:623.

[9] Cf. Kraus, *Psalms 60–150*, 50, who, however, states it with more caution that "it could be that originally Mount Hermon in the Canaan area was considered to be the 'mountain of Bashan.'"

[10] Rami Arav, "Hermon, Mount," *ABD* 3:159.

[11] Arav, "Hermon," 159.

[12] For incredible, high-resolution satellite photographs that display the majesty and prominence of Mt. Hermon as it is situated in Bashan and near Galilee, go to www .bible.org/products/maps.htm#samples. Scroll down and click on maps #1 and #2. The photographs are part of the larger NET Bible internet project of the Biblical Studies Foundation.

[13] Cf. Arav, "Hermon," 158.

does not believe that Hermon, the "mountain of Bashan," though the tallest and most majestic mountain, is the abode of YHWH—the deity that matters for the psalmist—at all.

This is made clear at v. 17 [v. 16 ET]. Here, the psalmist turns to address directly these mountains of "many peaks" (he switches to the plural, perhaps to address the entire Hermon range, or to include Mt. Zalmon that was mentioned at v. 15). The psalmist asks them why they "look with envy"[14] at the mountain God has desired for his dwelling. This is none other than Mt. Zion, the broad ridge in Jerusalem upon which Solomon had built the temple of the LORD.[15] The permanence of the divine choice is especially highlighted (εἰς τέλος; MT: לָנֶצַח; "forever"). The LORD in his sovereignty has chosen the little outcropping of Zion, snubbing her larger competitor in the north, the intimidating "mountain of Bashan," Mt. Hermon.[16]

The imagery of the LORD as a warrior, who had to fight his way to victory in order to claim Zion for his dwelling, is depicted in vv. 18–19 MT. In the first line of v. 18, God is portrayed as riding on his chariot amidst myriad thousands of others that belong to his (heavenly?) retinue. The word רֶכֶב (LXX: τὸ ἅρμα) is probably a collective.[17] God and his vast army are storming Zion. The second line requires no emendation (against BHS note b-b). The line literally reads, "The Lord among them, Sinai in the sanctuary." The first half explains that the Lord is among his army of chariots, himself a charioteer (see vv. 5, 34 MT, רכב). The second half states that "Sinai" is now "in the sanctuary" or holy place of the Temple on Zion. The phrase בְּקֹדֶשׁ; (LXX: ἐν τῷ ἁγίῳ) occurs twenty times in the MT, at least seventeen of which are used to express a special and specific location within the tabernacle or temple precinct;

---

[14] So NRSV, NAB, NIV, NASB; the Hebrew verb is a *hapax legomenon* and its meaning is uncertain. The LXX's ὑπολαμβάνετε, "to take up," is somewhat ambiguous (to consider? to fight? to reply? See lexicons for possibilities). Aquila reads ἐρίζετε, "to challenge, contend with, strive"; Symmachus offers περισπουδάζετε, "to desire, yearn after"; Theodotion gives δικάζεσθε, "to go to law with."

[15] See v. 30; cf. Pss 9:12 [ET: v. 11], 132:13–14. So also Marvin E. Tate, *Psalms 51–100* (WBC 20; Dallas: Word, 1990), 181.

[16] So also A. A. Anderson, *The Book of Psalms* (2 vols.; NCB; Grand Rapids: Eerdmans, 1972), 1.490: "...the Mount (or 'mountain-range') of Bashan is rebuked for its jealousy of Mount Zion, which YHWH had chosen as his dwelling place instead of his old abode, Sinai."

[17] The singular of this word is commonly used to express a collective idea; see *HALOT*, "רֶכֶב," and the numerous examples of this offered there.

thus the rendering "in the sanctuary/holy place."[18] Possibly the use of this phrase at v. 18b is used more generally, like at Exod 15:11 and Ps 77:14, to mean "in holiness." The use of the phrase later at v. 25 of our psalm in the former sense, however, strengthens our argument that the holy place within the temple at Zion is in view here at v. 18b.[19]

"Sinai" is in parallelism with "the Lord" in the first half of the line, and is shorthand for "the theophanic presence of Yhwh that had come to reside upon Mt. Sinai."[20] The second half of the line therefore states that this divine presence had transferred to Zion.[21] "Sinai" here is thus an apt and succinct metonymy for yhwh. "Sinai is wherever the God of Sinai is."[22]

In v. 19, the psalmist describes three things that yhwh accomplished as the Divine Warrior *in order that* "he might dwell [in Zion]" (לִשְׁכֹּן; LXX: τοῦ κατασκηνῶσαι; see again the use of this verb at v. 17c).[23] First, he ascended "the height" (לַמָּרוֹם; LXX: εἰς ὕψος), which here is shorthand for "the height of the mountain."[24] In context, this refers to the temple mount, Zion. Second, the Lord "took captives,"[25] probably enemy warriors. Third, God took gifts בָּאָדָם (LXX: ἐν ἀνθρώπῳ), meaning probably either "from men," "among men," or "gifts [comprised of] men."[26] The second line of v. 19 picks up "men" from the first line, more clearly defining the "men" from whom God received tribute. These are the "rebels," those who fought against the Lord to prevent him from obtaining Zion. The last phrase in the line has caused interpreters trouble, but also requires no emendation (against *BHS* note b-b). The phrase יָהּ אֱלֹהִים is probably another vocative, "O

---

[18] See Exod 28:43, 29:30, 35:19, 39:1, 41; Lev 6:23, 10:18, 16:17, 27; Num 4:12, 28:7; 2 Chr 29:7, 35:5; Ps 63:3, 68:25, 74:3; Ezek 44:27 (cf. Num 4:16).

[19] Cf. *Pesiqta Rabbati*, Piska 47.2 (though on Sinai, not Zion), RSV, NKJV, NAB, NIV, TNIV, NRSV, NJB, ESV.

[20] Cf. Tate, *Psalms 51–100*, 181.

[21] Tate, *Psalms 51–100*, 181.

[22] Tate, *Psalms 51–100*, 181.

[23] Taking the preposition לְ to denote purpose, as it commonly does with an infinitive construct; see Ronald J. Williams, *Hebrew Syntax: An Outline* (2nd ed.; Toronto: University of Toronto, 1976), §277. Cf. the LXX construction.

[24] Cf. 2 Kgs 19:23: עָלִיתִי מְרוֹם הָרִים, "I ascended to the height of the mountains." See *HALOT*, "מָרוֹם," definition 1.

[25] The idiom שָׁבָה שֶׁבִי occurs elsewhere and consistently expresses such a meaning (Num 21:1; Deut 21:10; Judg 5:12; 2 Chr 28:17).

[26] Cf. Tate, *Psalms 51–100*, 166 [19.a.]; Anderson, *Psalms*, 1.492. See *HALOT*, "בְּ" for interpretive options on the preposition.

Yah, God," a phenomenon common in the psalm (vv. 8, 11, 25, 29; cf. v. 17; but see LXX).

In vv. 16–19, it is very possible that the psalmist is poetically depicting the movement of the ark from the foot of Sinai to Zion, a journey that in reality spanned centuries and according to the tradition included a forty-year wilderness wandering and a holy war against the inhabitants of the land of Canaan. There are other indications within Ps 68 that may point in this direction, for vv. 8–11 is a portrayal of Israel in the Sinai wilderness (where they were on the march to take possession of Canaan by "holy war"), and vv. 25–28 is a processional [of the ark?] into the Jerusalem temple precincts. David brought up the ark from the house of Obed-edom to Jerusalem in the early tenth-century B.C.E. amidst a great processional and celebration (2 Sam 6:12–19). His son Solomon later transferred it from its tent to the innermost room of the temple he had built for YHWH (1 Kgs 8:1–12). Upon the completion of this ceremony, the priests could not stand to minister because "the glory of the LORD *filled* [LXX: ἔπλησεν from πίμπλημι] the house of the LORD" (v. 11, NRSV).

The strongest reason to interpret the section as a poetical portrayal of the movement of the ark from Sinai to Zion is found at the first line of the psalm proper, at 68:2 [LXX: 67:2]. There, the war-cry that Moses would call out whenever the ark would set out before the people Israel in the Sinai wilderness is quoted in full:[27]

Num 10:34: ἐξεγέρθητι κύριε διασκορπισθήτωσαν οἱ ἐχθροί σου
            φυγέτωσαν πάντες οἱ μισοῦντές σε
Num 10:35: קוּמָה יְהוָה וְיָפֻצוּ אֹיְבֶיךָ וְיָנֻסוּ מְשַׂנְאֶיךָ מִפָּנֶיךָ:
Num 10:35: Rise up, O LORD! And let Your enemies be scattered, and
            let those who hate You flee before You.   (NASB)

Ps 67:2:   ἀναστήτω ὁ θεός καὶ διασκορπισθήτωσαν οἱ ἐχθροὶ αὐτοῦ
            καὶ φυγέτωσαν οἱ μισοῦντες αὐτὸν
Ps 68:2:   יָקוּם אֱלֹהִים יָפוּצוּ אוֹיְבָיו וְיָנוּסוּ מְשַׂנְאָיו מִפָּנָיו:
Ps 68:1:   Let God arise, let His enemies be scattered, and let those
            who hate Him flee before Him.   (NASB)

---

[27] So also Anderson, *Psalms*, 1.482: "This verse reproduces, with slight variations, Num 10:35…by which the Ark of the Covenant was greeted on its going out and return." Cf. Kraus, *Psalms 60–150*, 51.

Awareness of the unmarked quotation and its original context significantly shapes how the rest of the psalm is to be read. The Mosaic war
cry of Ps 68:2 [67:2] signals that once again the ark is setting out in
movement before Israel (see Num 10:33–36). The ark was both a war
palladium and a symbol of YHWH's presence among Israel.[28] Moses
would also call out a second war-cry whenever the ark came to a halt,
having found rest: "Return, O LORD of the ten thousand thousands
of Israel" (NRSV). In light of the fact that Num 10:35 [10:34] is quoted
in Ps 68:2 [67:2], this second cry may also have an echo at Ps 68:18
[67:18]:

Num 10:35: ἐπίστρεφε κύριε χιλιάδας μυριάδας ἐν τῷ Ισραηλ
Num 10:36: שׁוּבָה יְהוָה רִבְבוֹת אַלְפֵי יִשְׂרָאֵל
Num 10:36: Return, O LORD, to the myriad thousands of Israel.

(NASB)

Ps 67:18: τὸ ἅρμα τοῦ θεοῦ μυριοπλάσιον χιλιάδες
Ps 68:18: רֶכֶב אֱלֹהִים רִבֹּתַיִם אַלְפֵי שִׁנְאָן
Ps 68:17: The chariots of God are myriads, thousands upon thousands.

(NASB)

Seen in the light of the influence of Num 10:35–36, the "chariots of
God" of 68:18 could possibly include a reference to the ark as God's
own chariot, since God rides "among" the chariots, himself a charioteer (see again vv. 5, 34 MT; רכב). The rhetorical effect would be to
strengthen the idea that YHWH had come to "rest" and reside victori-
ously in the sanctuary at Zion after the battle.

In sum, the section depicts YHWH's resolve to move his earthly
dwelling from Mt. Sinai to Mt. Zion. In this decision, Mt. Bashan, the
natural choice for God's dwelling in or near Israel, is snubbed. Zion is
the chosen and desired destination and abode. Zion, however, would
not be taken without a fight. Rebels existed who did not want God to
dwell and to establish his rule upon Zion. Therefore YHWH rode his
war-chariot among his vast army of heavenly host and stormed the
height. He took captives, received tribute, and subdued the rebels, all
in order to dwell on top of Zion, the desired abode, in the temple.
The language of the entire section is poetic, and the time element has
been telescoped.

---

[28] C.L. Seow, "Ark of the Covenant," *ABD* 1:388.

Psalm 68:17 and its Exegetical Tradition in Early and Late Judaism

If we are correct that Ps 68:17 [67:17 LXX] is echoed in Col 1:19, then Col 1:19 appears to be the earliest extant reference back to this particular statement of Scripture. The text is not quoted in Josephus, Philo, or the Apocrypha. A possible echo may be found in *Sib. Or.* 5.420, which is a product of Egyptian Judaism (late first–early second century C.E.).[29] Here a messianic figure is depicted as coming "from the expanses of heaven" (v. 414) to bring worldwide judgment on "evildoers" (v. 419) and to make "brilliant" "the city which God desired" (i.e., Jerusalem). This latter phrase is language reminiscent of Ps 68:17.[30] This messianic figure will make a "holy temple, exceedingly beautiful," having a tower that touches the clouds so that the glory of God can be seen by all peoples (vv. 422–27). The time that this oracle is to find fulfillment is in the "last time of holy people," i.e., the end-time (v. 432).

Curiously, the later Jewish literature offered different identifications of the mountain mentioned at Ps 68:17. A couple of times it is identified as Zion,[31] though more often it is understood to be Sinai, the place of God's revelation of his will to Israel as embodied in the Torah.[32] *Midrash Rabbah* Genesis 99.1 cites both, first offering Sinai and subsequently Zion as the identification of the mountain in question at Ps 68:17.

The rabbis often interpreted the mention of the "twice ten thousand, thousands upon thousands" (NRSV) at 68:18 to be a reference to the angels of God's host.[33] Some of these interpreted the myriad of angels to be the host that accompanied God when he descended upon Sinai

---

[29] See J. J. Collins, "Sibylline Oracles," in *The Old Testament Pseudepigrapha* (ed. James H. Charlesworth; 2 vols.; ABRL; New York: Doubleday, 1983), 1:390–91.

[30] Greek: καὶ πόλιν ἥν ἐπόθησε θεός; cf. especially with Symmachus of Ps 67:17: τὸ ὄρος ὅπερ ἐποθησεν ὁ θεός. The obvious difference between the two is the switch from "mountain" to "city," which, when speaking about Jerusalem, a city that sits upon a mountainous ridge, may connote very little difference in meaning.

[31] *Midr. Rabbah* Exodus 32.2; *Midr. Rabbah* Genesis 99:1.

[32] *Tg. Ps.* 68:17; *b. Megillah* 29a (p. 176); *Mekilta de Rabbi Ishmael*, Bahodesh, 4:24–25; *Midr. Psalms* 68.9, 92.2; *Midr. Rabbah* Genesis 99:1; *Midr. Rabbah* Exodus 2.4; *Midr. Rabbah* Numbers 1.8; *Pirqe Rabbi Eliezer*, p. 140.

[33] *Midr. Rabbah* Genesis 75.10; *Midr. Rabbah* Exodus 29.2, 8, 32.6; *Midr. Rabbah* Numbers 2.3; *Midr. Psalms* 17.3, 18.17; *Tg. Ps.* 68:18; *Midr. Tanhuma*, Exodus 20:2ff., Part 1; *Pesiqta de Rab Kahana*, Piska 12.22, 21.7–8, 10; *Tanna Debe Eliyyahu*, ER 119, S 55; *Midr. Psalm* 68.10; cf. *Hel. Syn. Pr.* 4:15 (ca. 150–300 C.E.); *3 En.* 24:6 (5th–6th century C.E.).

to give Moses the Torah.[34] In fact, at 68:19 the consistent rabbinic interpretation is that *Moses* is addressed by the psalmist as the one who ascended the height (of Sinai) and "took captive" the Torah from God.[35] The straightforward reading, as we have seen, is that the psalmist addresses YHWH. It is God, not Moses, who ascends the mountain and takes captives from the opposing rebel force.

Some within early Judaism believed that at the end-time and new creation, a new and glorious temple of God would be (re)built on Mt. Zion.[36] This eschatological expectation was probably fueled by such texts as Isa 2:1–4 (cf. Mic 4:1–4), 4:2–6, 66:18–23, and Ezekiel 40–48. The author of *Jubilees* believed that through this glorious temple all the earth would be "sanctified from all sin and from pollution throughout eternal generations" (4:26). He also wrote that the LORD had four sacred places upon earth, the "mountain of the East" (identification uncertain), the garden of Eden, Mount Sinai, and Mount Zion, with the latter three facing each other (4:26; 8:19). The author of *1 Enoch* believed worldwide final judgment would begin when God once again descended upon Sinai from heaven (1:1–9).

In sum, both early and late Judaism offered various interpretations of Ps 68:17. Some identified the mountain on which "God was pleased to dwell" as Zion, others as Sinai. In late Judaism, it is usually more often identified as the latter. In the rabbinic tradition, the text was then connected further with Moses and the reception of Torah as the embodiment of the revelation of God. In the eschatological age, it was thought by some that a new and magnificent temple would be built upon Zion, through which the entire world would be purified from sin.

---

[34] *Midr. Rabbah* Exodus 29.2, 8, 43.8; *Midr. Rabbah* Numbers 2.3; *Tg. Ps.* 68:17–18; *Pesiqta de Rab Kahana*, Piska 12.22, 21.7–8, 10; *Midr. Tanhuma*, Exodus 20:2ff., Part 1; *Tanna Debe Eliyyahu*, ER 119, S 55; cf. *Midr.* Psalms 18.17, 68.10; *Tanna Debe Eliyyahu*, EZ 193.

[35] *b. Shabbat* 89a; *Pesiqta Rabbati*, Piska 20.4, 47.4; *Pirqe Rabbi Eliezer*, p. 362; *Midr. Rabbah* Exodus 28.1, 30.5, 33.2; *Midr. Rabbah* Song of Songs 8.11 §2; *Midr. Rabbah* Ruth 2.3; *Avot of Rabbi Nathan*, ch. 2, sec. 3; *Midr.* Psalm 22.19, 68.11 (cf. *Soferim*, ch. 16, rule 10); *Tg. Ps.* 68:19; cf. *Sifre on Deuteronomy*, Piska 49.

[36] *Jub.* 1:27–29, 4:26; Tob 14:5; *Sib. Or.* 5:414–33; *1 En.* 90:28–29, 91:13; 11Q19 XXIX, 8–10; cf. Sir 36:18–20.

New Testament Context: Psalm 68:16 (67:17 LXX) in Colossians 1:19

The echo of Ps 67:17 LXX appears in the letter to the Colossians at 1:19, embedded in the Christ-Hymn found at vv. 15–20. As mentioned previously in chapter seven, this hymn breaks down into two basic parts: Christ preeminent in creation (vv. 15–17), and Christ preeminent in the renewed creation (vv. 18–20). The echo of Ps 67:17 LXX therefore informs especially how Christ is preeminent in the renewed creation, since it occurs at v. 19. In fact, v. 19 serves as the first ground (ὅτι) that answers *why* Christ had come to attain preeminence over all created beings, both in the old and new creation. It is because "in him all the fullness was pleased to dwell."

Yet what does the phrase "all the fullness" mean? If Paul was not the author of the Christ-Hymn of vv. 15–20, then we have little context to go on to figure out what was meant. We do, however, have a clear indication of how *Paul* understood the phrase, for at 2:9 he refers back to 1:19 of the hymn, adding to the phrase [ἐν αὐτῷ κατοικεῖ] πᾶν τὸ πλήρωμα the word τῆς θεότητος, "of divinity."[37] All the fullness of divinity, of God himself, had taken up residence in Christ, according to Paul. Paul further adds that this fullness dwells in Christ σωματικῶς, "bodily." Not merely before the incarnation but also as a human, who died on a cross (1:20, 22), "all the fullness" of God was (and "is")[38] pleased to dwell in Christ.

Where does the "fullness" language come from? While some have pointed to a predominantly Hellenistic origin,[39] an OT background is close at hand and also informs the "fullness" language of v. 19. Indeed, in light of the echo of Psalm 67:17 LXX, it would seem that the possibility of an OT-Jewish background can and should at least be raised as a feasible possibility.[40] While the word πλήρωμα does occur in the LXX (fifteen times), it is never used there to denote the divine

---

[37] Cf. the phrase πᾶν τὸ πλήρωμα τοῦ θεοῦ at Eph 3:19.

[38] Note the change of tense of the verb κατοικέω from aorist to present tense at 2:9, denoting ongoing action.

[39] E.g., Lohse, *Colossians*, 58. Martin Dibelius and D. Heinrich Greeven, *An die Kolosser, Epheser, an Philemon* (3rd ed.; HNT 12; Tübingen: J. C. B. Mohr [Paul Siebeck], 1953), 18, believes it is a Gnostic term ("dürfen wir wohl schließen, daß πλήρωμα ein Terminus der kolossischen Gnostiker ist"); cf. Lindemann, *Der Kolosserbrief*, 28. Against the understanding that the word has been taken from Gnosticism, see P. D. Overfield, "Pleroma: A Study in Content and Context," *NTS* 25 (1979): 384–96.

[40] Against Hugedé, *Colossiens*, 70n.224 ("Ces [Old Testament] préoccupations ne sont pas celles de l'Epître aux Colossiens").

presence as found here. The term does, however, belong to a family of words—the verbs πληρόω, πίμπλημι, and ἐμπίμπλημι ("to fill"), and the adjective πλήρης ("full")—that *are* employed in the LXX with regard to the divine presence, its location, or its activity. The words convey the idea that God's presence had come to dwell or was dwelling in specific locales, including the tabernacle or temple,[41] the whole earth,[42] or even individuals by means of the Spirit.[43] Not that the OT believed that any place could hold all of the omnipresent divine glory.[44] In a genuine and special way, however, the divine presence could yet reside in such specific locales. In light of such evidence, "fullness" appears to be a circumlocution for the divine presence, with the accompanying qualifier "all" permitting no understanding other than the totality of this presence. Nothing of any aspect lacked—all of God was pleased to dwell bodily in Christ.

This interpretation is further confirmed when one detects the echo of Ps 67:17 LXX, wherein ὁ θεός is the explicit subject and which at Col 1:19 has been paraphrased as πᾶν τὸ πλήρωμα, possibly for poetic heightening.[45] As we have observed, the reference is to the divine presence that had been pleased to take up residence on Mt. Zion at the temple (and which had been upon Mt. Sinai) to dwell among the people Israel. With this language at Col 1:19, the implication appears to be that the temple presence of God has taken up residence in Jesus Christ. The text gives little help as to when this indwelling occurred. Christ is here depicted as a "temple": he is the locus of the divine presence among the people of God in the renewed creation. Christ holds the

---

O'Brien, *Colossians*, 52, asserts that "there is no need to look beyond the OT for the source of Paul's ideas," citing others in support. Cf. Dunn, *Colossians*, 100: "The theme, then, is traditionally Jewish and is wholly of a piece with the Wisdom tradition, which was so powerfully influential in the first strophe." Arnold, who is especially sensitive to Hellenistic backgrounds in his *Colossian Syncretism*, yet concludes that at 1:19 "'fullness' is thus an appropriate expression... *derived from the LXX*" (264, emphasis mine).

[41] Exod 40:34–35; 1 Kgs 8:10–11; 2 Chr 5:13–14, 7:1–2; Isa 6:3–4; Ezek 10:3–4, 43:5, 44:4; Sir 36:13 [ET 36:19].

[42] Num 14:21; Ps 71:19 [ET: 72:19]; Isa 6:3; Jer 23:24; Sir 42:16; Wis 1:7; cf. Isa 11:9; Hab 2:14; Pss 32[33]:5, 118[119]:64.

[43] Exod 28:3 (see NASB, NET), 31:3, 35:31; Deut 34:9; Mic 3:8; Sir 39:6, 48:12. This language carries over to the NT: Luke 1:15, 41, 67, 4:1; Acts 2:4, 4:8, 31, 6:3, 5, 7:55, 9:17, 11:24, 13:9, 52.

[44] 1 Kgs 8:27; Isa 66:1–2a.

[45] Poetic heightening or stylistic alterations are quite appropriate in a poem or hymn. Aletti observes that the activity of God proper has been intentionally subdued in the hymn in order to set in relief the excellencies of Christ (*Colossiens*, 109).

unequaled position of preeminence that he does because the fullness of the divine presence was pleased to dwell in him.

The echo of Ps 67:17 LXX at Col 1:19 also informs the interpretation of Col 2:9–10a. This is because Paul explicitly picks up the language from the hymn at 1:19 again at 2:9 and makes a point with it at 2:10a with regard to the Colossians. Paul here adds that the Colossians "are filled in him," a phrase which is a periphrastic participial construction that emphasizes the completed action. The Colossian church, the Body, *via their organic union with their Head*, Christ, is also full of the divine presence (1:18, 24, 2:19).[46] The implication is that they, in a derivative fashion, have become a locus of the presence of God, a temple.

The thought that Christ is a temple, or the locus of the divine presence among the people of God, is found elsewhere in the NT. At John 2:19–21, Christ is misunderstood to have said that he could, if the Jerusalem temple were razed, rebuild it in three days. But the narrator corrects the misunderstanding with the aside "but [Jesus] was speaking of the temple of his body." Jesus had referred instead to his upcoming resurrection (cf. Mark 14:58). At Rev 21, John the seer wrote that at the end of time after the final judgment, God would establish the new heavens and earth and make his home among redeemed humanity (vv. 1, 3). Here no temple exists "for its temple is the Lord God the Almighty and the Lamb" (v. 22; NRSV). Here again Christ, the aforementioned "Lamb," is depicted as a temple. In the letter to the Ephesians, Christ is portrayed as the "cornerstone" (NRSV, NIV, NASB) of the new temple, upon whom disciples are being "built" as a temple for God (2:19–22). Elsewhere Paul teaches that the church, both in its individual members as well as a corporate entity, is a temple of the Holy Spirit.[47]

It appears that only once did the early church fathers cite Ps 68:16. The text first crops up in the *Apostolic Constitutions* 6.2.5 (*ANF* 7:451). According to this text, God has rejected the Jerusalem temple due to Israel's wickedness (quoting Jer 12:7 and Isa 5:6 in support). The Church is now the house or temple in which God is pleased to dwell forever.

It appears that the hymn-writer has picked up Ps 67:17 LXX at Col 1:19 with a typological approach. As God resided in the temple on Mt. Zion in the old age, so now he has been pleased in the new age

---

[46] Cf. Eph 1:22b–23, 3:19, 4:13.
[47] 1 Cor 3:9c–17, 6:15–19; 2 Cor 6:16; cf. 1 Pet 2:4–8.

to take up residence in Christ. The eschatological heightening of the second strophe of the Christ-Hymn (vv. 18–20) shapes the meaning of the echo. Christ is portrayed as the locus of the divine presence in the inaugurated new creation. Has, therefore, the temple in Jerusalem thus been replaced? The rest of the NT points in this direction, but the Christ-Hymn of Col 1:15–20 offers little help. If any other ripples from Ps 68 were meant to be heard in the echo at v. 19, it may be significant that one of the psalm's central purposes is to portray the transferral of God's presence from one abode to another, from Sinai to Zion. This ripple of theme possibly could be present in our text at Col 1:19, but it is difficult to prove. If this is the case, God has once again transferred his presence from one abode to another, from Zion to Christ. The systematic difficulty with this, however, is that then one is implying that there was a time when the divine presence had *not* dwelt in Christ. Perhaps, then, the answer is the incarnation. Though God was eternally always in the Son, yet on earth the divine presence had come to dwell in a real way at specific locales at high points in redemptive history. These included Sinai, the tabernacle, and Solomon's temple upon Zion. According to Col 1:19, this list must now include a human, Jesus Christ.[48]

Summary: The Proverbs 8 Wisdom Development and Ps 67:17 LXX in Col 1:15–20

In the hymn of Col 1:15–20, Christ has been depicted as personified Wisdom, a tradition that ultimately stems from Prov 8:22–31. It is within this framework that the hymn echoes Ps 67:17 LXX at Col 1:19, with language that appears to fit what is said about Wisdom/Word elsewhere. Philo wrote about the Word that it was "the model or pattern" that "contained all [God's] *fullness.*"[49] Philo also wrote at one point that the Word was God's "house" or temple.[50] This is language that parallels what is said about Christ as Wisdom at 1:19.

The final editor of the hymn has employed language to portray Christ in some of the most exalted language found in the NT concerning

---

[48] Recall the added emphasis σωματικῶς, "bodily" at Col 2:9.
[49] *Dreams* 1.75 (emphasis mine); Greek: πληρέστατος, the superlative form of πλήρης.
[50] *Migration* 4–6, with Gen 28:17 as background. See also *Alleg. Interp.* 3.46.

him. The rhetorical aim of this exalted portrayal was to strengthen the confidence of the Colossians in Christ's sufficiency as God's revelation, in his preeminence over the spirit world, and in his superiority over anything the false "philosophy" could offer, so that they would entrust themselves to him alone.

CHAPTER NINE

THE SCRIPTURES OF ISRAEL IN COLOSSIANS 2:8–15:
THE ECHO OF DEUTERONOMY 30:6 IN 2:11

Comparison of Textual Versions and Evaluation

In whom also you were circumcised with a circumcision without hands, (consisting) in the removal of the body of flesh, in the circumcision of Christ

Deut 30:6 MT	Deut 30:6 LXX	Deut 30:6 Aquila	Colossians 2:11
וּמָל יהוה אֱלֹהֶיךָ אֶת־לְבָבְךָ	καὶ περικαθαριεῖ κύριος τὴν καρδίαν σου	καὶ περιτεμεῖται κύριος τὴν καρδίαν σου	περιετμήθητε περιτομῇ ἀχειροποιήτῳ

Paul's thought is more in line with the MT than the LXX, which freely interprets the divine circumcision as a "cleansing." Aquila (ca. 130 C.E.) has rendered his Greek version so as to literally reflect the Hebrew, as is his custom, and his translation further confirms that Paul's echo is closer to the MT.

This proposal meets the two criteria necessary for an echo: 1) availability and 2) rare concept similarity. Regarding *availability*, the book of Deuteronomy was certainly known and read by Paul (see Gal 3:10, 13; Rom 10:6–8). Regarding *rare concept similarity*, the two texts share the otherwise unique theme of a divinely accomplished circumcision. While several texts of Scripture speak of a circumcision (or uncircumcision) of the heart (e.g., Deut 10:16; Jer 4:4, 9:25–26; Ezek 44:7, 9), only one ever speaks of *God* circumcising the heart. That text is Deut 30:6.[1]

---

[1] Some scholars do mention Deut 30:6 in their discussions on Col 2:11. However, none argue that Deut 30:6 is specifically (or only) in mind; most mention Deut 30:6 along with several other of the OT "heart-circumcision" texts (such as Deut 10:16; Jer 4:4, etc.) and offer it simply as background material. All miss that Deut 30:6 is the only text that speaks of God circumcising anything.

The above-mentioned scholars include: Hühn, *Die alttestamentlichen Citate*, 197; Lohmeyer, *Kolosser*, 108n.3; Bruce, *Colossians*, 103; Melick, *Philippians, Colossians, Philemon*,

It appears that Paul did not intend his audience to recall Deut 30:6, because nothing from Deut 30:1–10 needs to be brought forward in order to reclaim Paul's full, intended communication at 2:11. That is, there is nothing in the new context whose meaning is only "unlocked" with the "key" from the original context of Deut 30:1–10. Therefore, because Paul's intended communication is grasped apart from any reader awareness of Deut 30:6, the reference should be classified as an echo. Moreover, because the reference stems from the proto-MT text-type, which was probably unavailable to the church of Colossae because it would not have had access to the Hebrew Bible (or been able to read it if it did), Paul probably did not expect his gentile audience to overhear without help the biblical text that had almost certainly influenced his thought at Col 2:11. Nevertheless, recognition of Deut 30:6 deepens and enhances the meaning of Col 2:11 and enlarges our understanding of Paul as a biblical theologian.

Old Testament Context: Deuteronomy 30:1–10

Deut 30:1–10 immediately precedes what is arguably the rhetorical climax of the entire book of Deuteronomy, the call to decision at 30:11–20. The combination of the location of the passage together with its unprecedented promise of a divinely wrought circumcision and a national restoration, despite Israel's covenant infidelity, exalts the text to prominence within Deuteronomy. Indeed, Deut 30:1–10 stands as a towering mountain-peak in the vast range of the Pentateuch as a whole. Note the section's place of prominence in Deuteronomy in the structural analysis given below:

1. Introductory Superscription: Preamble   (1:1–5)
2. Moses' First Speech: Historical Prologue   (1:6–4:43)
3. Moses' Second Speech: Covenant   (4:44–28:68)
   Stipulations
   A. Covenant Stipulations, Summation: (5:6–21)
      Decalogue

257; Furter, *Colossiens*, 137; Wolter, *Der Brief an die Kolosser*, 129–130; Barth and Blanke, *Colossians*, 319; Hübner, *An die Kolosser*, 81 (indirectly, *via* Rom 2:28f.). See now, however, Beale, "Colossians," ad loc.

B. Preamble to Law-Code: Exhortation to   (5:22–11:32)
   Loyalty
C. Covenant Stipulations, Specifics: The   (12:1–26:15)
   Law-Code
D. Covenant Blessings and Curses   (26:16–28:68)
4. Moses' Third Speech   (29–30)
   A. Exhortation to Keep the Covenant   (29:1–29)
   B. Restoration Clause   **(30:1–10)**
   C. Call to Decision and Summons of   (30:11–20)
      Heaven and Earth as Witnesses to the
      Covenant
5. Moses Prepares Israel for his Death   (31)
   A. Moses Appoints Joshua as Successor   (31:1–8)
   B. Provision for Regular Public Reading of (31:9–13)
      Stipulations
   C. YHWH's Prediction of Israel's   (31:14–30)
      Unfaithfulness and the Securing of
      further Covenant-Witnesses
6. The Song of Moses: Covenant-Witness   (32)
   against Israel
7. The Blessing of Moses: Prayer for Israel's   (33)
   Faithfulness and Ultimate Prosperity
8. The Account of the Death of Moses   (34)

Deuteronomy consists of the speeches Moses addressed to the Israelites in the plains of Moab just outside the promised land of Canaan. The first generation of Israelites had finally perished in the wilderness after forty years of wandering in it, the consequence of refusal to obey the LORD when he commanded them to enter and possess Canaan (Deut 1:3, 2:14–18). Moses has received permission to lead the second generation to the brink of Canaan. Before they may cross over the Jordan, however, the new generation must embrace for themselves their parents' great deliverance from Egypt by God and swear exclusive allegiance to him (Deut 5:3–6).

The "restoration clause" of Deut 30:1–10 simply assumes that Israel has willfully disobeyed the covenant that they had ratified with YHWH and that because of this, God has enacted all the covenant curses threatened in 27:15–28:68, including forced removal into a land far from that of Canaan (Deut 28:63–65; cf. 29:27–28). The tenor of the text is prophetic: Moses foresees Israel's certain future faithlessness. In the land of their exile, however, Israel will come to their senses. They will recall their former blessed state in the land of Canaan even as they waste away in exile. Moses predicts that this heart-searching will lead Israel to "return," that is, repent (שׁוּב).[2] They will turn away from their idolatry and embrace YHWH alone as their God.

This repentance will lead to full compliance to the Mosaic covenant stipulations, an obedience that will in turn initiate a remarkable turn of events (30:3–7). Because of their renewed obedience, the Lord in mercy will bring about a full restoration for the people Israel (וְשָׁב יְהוָה אֱלֹהֶיךָ אֶת־שְׁבוּתְךָ;[3] NRSV, TNIV: "restore your fortunes"; NET: "reverse your captivity"; NASB: "restore your captivity").

Deuteronomy 30:3b–7 explains what is involved in this restoration. God will have compassion and reverse his stance towards Israel. No longer will he stand against her in wrath, enacting covenant curses, but will delight in her, heaping covenant blessing. First, he will gather his people from all the nations to which he had dispersed them and resettle them back into the land of promise (vv. 3b–5a). By this act, God returns Abraham's offspring to the land that he had promised to the patriarch as a perpetual possession.[4] Second, in this restoration from exile God also promises to multiply Israel's population until they are an innumerable multitude (v. 5b; see Deut 1:10). Behind the divine activity of increasing the nation stands the promise made to Abraham that his seed would be "multiplied" until they were as the stars of the heavens in number (Gen 22:17).[5] Third, God promises to circumcise Israel's heart at the time of the restoration ("Moreover, the LORD your God will circumcise your heart and the heart of your descendents"; 30:6 NRSV). What God previously demanded in 10:16 ("Circumcise then

---

[2] See HALOT, "שׁוּב," qal, 2.

[3] This idiom is frequently used as "a technical term for the eschatological restoration of the nation to its primal glory" (William L. Holladay, The Root šûbh in the Old Testament: with Particular Reference to its Usages in Covenantal Contexts [Leiden: Brill, 1958], 113. See Holladay's full discussion on pp. 110–115. See also HALOT, "שׁוּב," qal, 3.c.). For this usage, see also Jer 29:14, 30:3, 18, 31:23, 32:44, 33:7, 11, 26; Ezek 16:53 (along with Sodom [!] and Samaria), 39:25; Hos 6:11; Joel 4:1 [ET: 3:1]; Amos 9:14; Zeph 2:7, 3:20; Pss 14:7, 53:7 [ET: 53:6], 85:2 [ET: 85:1], 126:1, 4; and Lam 2:14. There are a few usages of the idiom that do not refer to the eschatological restoration of Israel: the man Job: Job 42:10; Moab: Jer 48:47; Ammon: Jer 49:6; Elam: Jer 49:39; Egypt: Ezek 29:14.

The LXX at Deut 30:3 freely renders this technical term with καὶ ἰάσεται κύριος τὰς ἁμαρτίας σου, "and the Lord will heal your sins." Tg. Onq., Syr., and Vulg. support the MT, while Tg. Neof. has "will receive your repentance" and Tg. Ps.-J. reads "will accept with pleasure your repentance."

[4] Gen 17:7–8; see Deut 4:31b, 9:5, 27 and 29:13b.

[5] See chapter three of this study.

your heart, and stiffen your neck no more"), God himself will grant in the return from exile.[6]

Circumcision is the practice of removing the foreskin from the head of the male sexual organ. The ANE peoples in general practiced the custom, but it was especially practiced among the western Semitic groups. The evidence suggests that from earliest times the practice was a puberty or marriage rite that prepared a boy for manhood, marriage, and fruitful reproduction.[7] Deut 30:6 employs the concept of circumcision metaphorically to signify a divine action on the heart that enables Israel to keep the Mosaic covenant stipulations. The text implies that the heart of the people was *uncircumcised* and therefore flawed, unable to keep the obligations imposed upon them by Moses.[8] As a result, the covenant curses, including exile, have come upon them. In the restoration, however, the LORD promises to circumcise Israel's heart so that she will "love the LORD your God with all your heart and

---

[6] The versions differ widely in how they translate the phrase "circumcise your heart," offering a couple of noteworthy interpretations. The LXX renders the verb מול with περικαθαρίζω, "to cleanse." While Syr. and *Tg. Neof.* give a literal translation of the MT, both *Tg. Onq.* and *Tg. Ps.-J.* render it as "to remove the obduracy of" the heart. The Vulg. appears to follow the LXX. Aquila, as is characteristic of his work, has brought the LXX closer to the Hebrew, rendering מול with περιτεμεῖται, the same verb the apostle Paul employs at Col 2:11.

[7] Jack M. Sasson, "Circumcision in the Ancient Near East," *JBL* 85 (1966): 473–76; Robert G. Hall, "Circumcision," *ABD* 1:1025; G. Mayer, "מול," *TDOT* 8:159–60. Cf. Jer 9:24–25 [ET: 9:25–26].

[8] This interpretation is supported by the evidence elsewhere in the OT. Moses is "uncircumcised of lips" (עֲרַל שְׂפָתָיִם), i.e., his speaking skills are poor or flawed and he is unable to deliver YHWH's message effectually to Pharoah (Exod 6:12, 30). Likewise, Israel's "ear" is uncircumcised (עֲרֵלָה אָזְנָם), that is, the people are unable to "hear" the word of God (Jer 6:10). Their "ear" has an impediment; it is flawed, unable to do what it was created to do. And strikingly similar to our passage in thought, Lev 26:41 asserts that Israel's heart in exile is "uncircumcised." If, however, Israel humbles itself and make amends for its sins, YHWH will remember the covenant made with the patriarchs (see 26:42–45). Along these lines, God through the prophet Jeremiah commands Israel

> to circumcise yourselves to the LORD, remove the foreskin of your hearts, O people of Judah and inhabitants of Jerusalem, or else my wrath will go forth like fire, and burn with no one to quench it, because of the evil of your doings.
> (Jer 4:4 NRSV)

Elsewhere in Jeremiah God declares by the prophet that

> The days are surely coming, says the LORD, when I will attend to all those who are circumcised only in the foreskin: Egypt, Judah, Edom, the Ammonites, Moab, and all those with shaven temples who live in the desert. For all these nations are uncircumcised, and all the house of Israel is uncircumcised in heart.
> (Jer 9:25–26 NRSV)

with all your soul" (Deut 30:6b), a phrase that is nearly verbatim with the covenant stipulation of Deut 6:5:[9]

Deut 6:5: וְאָהַבְתָּ אֵת יְהוָה אֱלֹהֶיךָ בְּכָל־לְבָבְךָ וּבְכָל־נַפְשְׁךָ וּבְכָל־מְאֹדֶךָ:
Deut 6:5: You shall love the LORD your God with all your heart,
and with all your soul, and with all your might. (NRSV)

Deut 30:6b: לְאַהֲבָה אֶת־יְהוָה אֱלֹהֶיךָ בְּכָל־לְבָבְךָ וּבְכָל־נַפְשְׁךָ לְמַעַן חַיֶּיךָ:
Deut 30:6b: ...so that you will love the LORD your God with all your heart
and with all your soul, in order that you may live. (NRSV)

The echo of the previous text is unmistakable. The exclusive allegiance demanded by God from his people will be granted by him. He will enable Israel through an inner heart circumcision to fulfill the covenant's demand for full and glad compliance to its stipulations.

The answer for why Israel is in desperate need of a heart circumcision is woven throughout Deuteronomy and surfaces at several points. What becomes evident is that the commands are not too difficult or that the stipulations erect an unachievable ideal that no human could possibly attain. The problem is with the *people*, not the covenant (cf. Rom 7:12). The bulk of chapter nine of Deuteronomy is devoted to recalling the persistent rebellion of Israel. They are a people "stiff of neck":

> Know, then, that the LORD your God is not giving you this good land to occupy because of your righteousness; for you are a stubborn people. Remember and do not forget how you provoked the LORD your God to wrath in the wilderness; you have been rebellious against the LORD from the day you came out of the land of Egypt until you came to this place.
> (Deut 9:6–7 NRSV)

From the very first Israel had persisted in rebellion (cf. 9:24). The apostasy climaxed with the incident of the golden calf while Moses was on Mt. Sinai receiving the two tablets (see Exod 32). God's wrath nearly broke out and destroyed the people (9:8), but Moses' prayer averted the disaster (9:19). God only continues with the people on account of the covenant with Abraham, as well as because of how the Egyptians would

---

[9] The verb "to love" in this covenantal context, while not devoid of emotional affection, means "to be loyal to, to give full allegiance." See William J. Moran, "The Ancient Near Eastern Background of the Love of God in Deuteronomy," *CBQ* (1963): 77–87; Dennis J. McCarthy, "Notes on the Love of God in Deuteronomy and the Father-Son Relationship between YHWH and Israel," *CBQ* 27 (1965): 144–47; Jeffrey H. Tigay, *Deuteronomy* (JPS Torah Commentary; Philadelphia: Jewish Publication Society, 1996), 77.

misinterpret his slaying of Israel in the wilderness (9:27–28). Hardness of heart and wickedness comprise the character of the people (9:27).

The second half of Deut 31 is likewise blunt in its evaluation of Israel's heart. Moses is taught a song that he is to write down and place beside the book of the Law and the Ark of the Covenant (31:26). The song exists to serve as a (covenant) witness against Israel when (not if) she acts corruptly and turns away from YHWH into all kinds of idolatry, evil, and apostasy (vv. 16, 18, 20, 21, 27–29). Even on the very day Moses is mediating the covenant in the plains of Moab, the people's intent was already bent toward corruption (v. 21). The situation is bleak. Already at Sinai at the initial covenant ceremony, God said:

> Oh that they had such a heart in them, that they would fear Me, and keep all My commandments always, that it may be well with them and with their sons forever! (Deut 5:29 NASB)

The people, however, do not have such a heart, and the only one who can give them such a heart is God himself. At the time of Moses, God had not yet been pleased to grant it:

> And Moses summoned all Israel and said to them, "You have seen all that the LORD did before your eyes in the land of Egypt to Pharaoh and all his servants and all his land; the great trials which your eyes have seen, those great signs and wonders. Yet to this day the LORD has not given you a heart to know, nor eyes to see, nor ears to hear." (Deut 29:2–4 NASB)

Israel has seen but does not "see." They do not have a heart "to know." Israel, "stiff of neck," does not get such a heart until the promised restoration from exilic captivity.

At vv. 8–10, the thought of the previous seven verses is reiterated and the restoration clause of 30:1–10 is concluded. God will renew the covenant blessings, reversing his stance toward Israel. The basis for this reversal is repeated in v. 10a. Israel will obey all the covenant stipulations written in the Mosaic legislation, having returned wholly to God in exile. The tenor of the text is prophetic. In spite of Israel's corrupt heart, the restoration *from* exile will take place as certainly as the banishment *to* exile. Israel will repent, obey the Mosaic covenant, and thus be returned to her land. Glad and full obedience will flow from a circumcised heart and consequently God will heap covenant blessing, including causing Israel to multiply and prosper in the land promised to Abraham.

Old Testament Parallels to Deuteronomy 30:6

Does Deut 30:6 show up in other OT materials? Several scholars highlight the similarities that the text has with Jer 31:33 and Ezek 36:26–27
(cf. 11:19–20).

Jeremiah 31:33 and Deuteronomy 30:6

We turn first to discuss the relevant text in Jeremiah as it stands in its
wider context:

> [31] The days are surely coming, says the LORD, when I will make a new
> covenant with the house of Israel and the house of Judah. [32] It will not
> be like the covenant that I made with their ancestors when I took them
> by the hand to bring them out of the land of Egyp—a covenant that
> they broke, though I was their husband, says the LORD. **[33] But this is the
> covenant that I will make with the house of Israel after those
> days, says the LORD: I will put my law within them, and I will
> write it on their hearts; and I will be their God, and they shall
> be my people.** [34] No longer shall they teach one another, or say to each
> other, "Know the LORD," for they shall all know me, from the least of
> them to the greatest, says the LORD; for I will forgive their iniquity, and
> remember their sin no more.   (Jer 31:31–34 NRSV; emphasis mine)

Difficulties arise, however, once this text is compared with Deut 30:1–10.
First, if there is a vector of literary dependence, which direction does
it move? Source-criticism dates Deut 30:1–10 to around the era of the
exile,[10] and the prophet Jeremiah ministered both before the exile and for
a short time after.[11] Thus, according to a wide consensus of scholarship,
the two texts are from the same period. From this perspective, dating
issues therefore complicate the question of literary dependence. Second,
several scholars are hesitant to speak of a direct literary dependence

---

[10] The actual destruction of Jerusalem took place in 587 B.C.E. See Otto Eissfeldt,
The Old Testament: An Introduction (trans. Peter R. Ackroyd; New York: Harper and Row,
1965), 219–33, for the dating of various sections of Deuteronomy. It should be noted
that a conservative minority regard Moses to be the essential author of Deuteronomy,
including 30:1–10 (see, e.g., Peter Craigie, *The Book of Deuteronomy* [NICOT; Grand
Rapid: Eerdmans, 1976], 24–29). The apostle Paul would have regarded Moses as the
author of Deuteronomy and as a work that existed for centuries prior to the time of
Jeremiah and Ezekiel.
[11] William L. Holladay, *Jeremiah 2* (Hermeneia; Minneapolis: Fortress, 1989), 25–35.

on other grounds, for there are significant differences between the texts. For example, Deut 30:1–10 does not mention a "new covenant," while Jer 31:31–34 omits any mention of "circumcision." Many scholars nevertheless still acknowledge that striking similarities exist. One of the most notable is the interior renovation that enables Israel to fulfill her covenant obligations.[12]

Jer 31:31–34 is lodged within chapters 30–33, the section in Jeremiah traditionally entitled the "book of consolation." The section's major concern is the restoration of Israel from exile. According to 31:31–34, the LORD promises to make a new covenant with the house of Israel and Judah at the time of the restoration (v. 31). This new covenant will not be like the one ratified at Sinai. The latter covenant the people repeatedly broke (v. 32). In contrast, the new will *not* be broken, for YHWH will write his *torah* (תּוֹרָתִי) upon Israel's heart (v. 33). Here *torah* refers to that body of stipulations within the Mosaic covenant to which Israel was to comply. This is due to the mention of that covenant in the preceding verse, as well as to the consistent use of the term throughout Jeremiah.[13] Thus בְּרִית and תּוֹרָה in this passage are to be distinguished. The term בְּרִית refers to the whole of the treaty relationship between suzerain and vassal, YHWH and Israel. On the other hand, תּוֹרָה denotes a specific part of that covenant, namely, the *stipulations* that Israel needed to observe in order to please the suzerain YHWH and stay within the sphere of covenant blessing.[14]

The problem with Israel in the book of Jeremiah is her heart.[15] It is evil, rebellious, and sick with sin. The problem is, once again, with the *people*, not the covenant. For it is not God's *torah* but "sin" that is engraved upon Israel's heart:

> The sin of Judah is written down with an iron stylus; with a diamond point it is engraved upon the tablet [לוּחַ] of their heart.   (Jer 17:1 NASB)

---

[12] William McKane, *Jeremiah* (2 vols.; ICC; Edinburgh: T&T Clark, 1996), 823, 827; Robert P. Carroll, *The Book of Jeremiah* (OTL; Philadelphia: Westminster, 1986), 613–14; Pierre Buis, "La Nouvelle Alliance," *VT* 18 (1968): 1–15.

[13] The Hebrew noun תּוֹרָה occurs eleven times in the book: 2:8, 6:19, 8:8, 9:13, 16:11, 18:18, 26:4, 32:23, 44:10, and 44:23.

[14] See Dennis J. McCarthy, *Treaty and Covenant: A Study in the Ancient Oriental Documents and in the Old Testament* (AnBib 21A; Rome: Biblical Institute, 1978), 9–13.

[15] See Jer 4:4, 5:23–24, 6:28, 7:22–26, 9:25–26, 11:6–8, 16:11–12, 17:1, 9, and 18:12.

With the "new covenant," however, YHWH will address and resolve this dilemma. God will supernaturally weave into Israel's heart the covenant legislation in such a way that Israel will gladly and fully obey the covenant stipulations. The two parties will again be in right covenant relationship: "I will be their God, and they shall be my people" of v. 33 is a covenant formula and indicates such.[16] Unlike the old covenant, this new covenant will not be written on tablets of stone, but on the tablet of the heart. And unlike the old covenant, the new will never be broken. The whole covenant community will "know YHWH" (v. 34a), and the basis upon which the new covenant will rest will be his forgiveness of Israel's rebellion (v. 34b).

Ezekiel 36:26–27 and Deuteronomy 30:6

The parallel in Ezek 36:26–27 with Deut 30:6 likewise yields thorny dating issues. We therefore opt not to argue for a direct dependence. Nevertheless, Ezek 36:26–27 contains a striking resemblance both to Jer 31:33 and to Deut 30:6 and therefore warrants further examination:

> [24] For I will take you from the nations, gather you from all the lands and bring you into your own land. [25] Then I will sprinkle clean water on you, and you will be clean; I will cleanse you from all your filthiness and from all your idols.
> **[26] Moreover, I will give you a new heart and put a new spirit within you; and I will remove the heart of stone from your flesh and give you a heart of flesh. [27] I will put My Spirit within you and cause you to walk in My statutes, and you will be careful to observe My ordinances.** [28] [Then] you will live in the land that I gave to your forefathers; so you will be My people, and I will be your God.
> (Ezek 36:24–28 NASB)

Once again, the text is embedded in a longer section concerned with the restoration of Israel from exile (chs. 36–39). At this time YHWH will cleanse[17] his people from their moral filth and idols (v. 25). Israel's idolatry has flowed from a "heart of stone."[18] God, however, will accomplish an interior renovation, resolving the dilemma by enabling the people to

---

[16] On the formula, see W. Holladay, *Jeremiah 1* (Hermeneia; Philadelphia: Fortress Press, 1986), 262.

[17] Hebrew: טהר; LXX: καθαρίζω; cf. Deut 30:6 LXX περικαθαρίζω.

[18] לֵב הָאֶבֶן; cf. 2:4, 3:7, 11:19, 21, 18:31, 20:16, and 33:31.

fulfill the Sinaitic covenant stipulations.[19] He will implant within them a new "heart of flesh" (לֵב בָּשָׂר) and put his Spirit within them, resulting in full obedience that gladly flows from the heart. The result of this new obedience will be that God will bring Israel back to live in the land of their ancestors (vv. 24, 28a). Israel will then enjoy a restored covenant relationship with God (note again the covenant formulary "you will be my people, and I will be your God" at v. 28b).

The following diagram lines up the three texts under discussion to highlight the remarkable similarities:

Deuteronomy 30:1–10	Jeremiah 31:31–34	Ezekiel 36:22–32
Restoration clause of Mosaic Covenant	Located within the "Book of Consolation" (chs. 30–33), which is concerned with the Restoration of Israel	Located within a climactic section concerned with the Restoration of Israel (chs. 36–39)
Circumcision of the Heart (v. 6)	Law Engraved Upon the Heart (v. 33)	New Heart of Flesh; God's Spirit (vv. 26–27)[20]
Full Covenant Obedience Flowing from New Heart	Full Covenant Obedience Flowing from New Heart	Full Covenant Obedience Flowing from New Heart
Return to Land (vv. 3–5a)	Return to Land (30:3; 31:1–14)	Return to Land (vv. 24, 28)
Curses Upon Enemies (v. 7)	Destruction of Enemies (30:11	Destruction of Enemies (38:1ff.)
Population Increase (v. 5b)	Population Increase (30:19)	Population Increase (36:37)

---

[19] See v. 27; the phrases "my statutes" and "my ordinances" occur together fourteen times in Ezekiel and refer to the Mosaic covenant obligations. See 5:6, 7, 11:12, 20, 18:9, 17, 20:9–24 (six times), 36:27, and 37:24. That the Sinaitic legislation is in view is especially clear from the occurrences in 20:9–24 and from 44:24.

[20] *Targum Ezekiel* renders vv. 26–27: "And I will give you a *faithful* heart, and I will put a *faithful* spirit *deep* inside of you; and I will *demolish the wicked heart, which is as hard* as stone, from your flesh; and I will give you a heart *that is faithful before Me, to do My will*. And My *holy* spirit will I put *deep* inside of you and I will act so that you shall walk in My statutes and keep My laws and observe them" (Samson H. Levey, *The Targum of Ezekiel: Translated, with a Critical Introduction, Apparatus, and Notes* [eds. Kevin Cathcart, Michael Maher, and Martin McNamara; ArBib 13; Wilmington, Del.: Michael Glazier, 1987], 102).

Table (*cont.*)

Deuteronomy 30:1–10	Jeremiah 31:31–34	Ezekiel 36:22–32
Abundant Crops/ Herds (v. 9)	Abundance Crops/ Herds (31:12)	Abundance Crop/Herds (vv. 29–30)
Cleansing (LXX, v. 6)	Forgiveness of Sin (v. 34b)	Cleansing (v. 25)[21]
—	Davidic King (30:9)	Davidic King (34:23–4; 37:24)

In summary, the Scriptures of Israel foresee a day when God will decisively act to remedy the defective component within his Sinaitic covenant relationship with Israel. The defect exists neither with YHWH nor with the stipulations. Instead, the heart of the people is diseased with sin, rendering them unwilling (and thus ultimately unable) to comply. Therefore God will make a "new covenant," within which Israel will gladly and fully observe the original Sinai covenant stipulations.[22] God can then heap covenant blessing upon them for this obedience. The prophets Jeremiah and Ezekiel add that at the time of Israel's restoration, YHWH will install his Davidic King, the Messiah.

Deuteronomy 30:6, Jeremiah 31:31–34, and Ezekiel 36:26–27 in Early and Late Judaism

A few texts of the DSS suggest that the Qumran community believed they were Jeremiah's "new covenant" community and the true remnant of Israel.[23] Several texts likewise indicate that the Qumran community

---

[21] *Targum Ezekiel* adds "And *I will forgive your sins, as though you had been* purified by the waters of sprinkling and *by the ashes of the heifer sin-offering*" (Levey, *Targum of Ezekiel*, 101–2).

[22] McCarthy, *Treaty and Covenant*, 69n.64, has observed that the OT is not the first place to show evidence where the same provisions from a former treaty are brought forward into the new. The Hittites practiced this with at least two peoples, the Amurru and the Kizzuwatna.

[23] 4Q266 VI, 19; VIII, 21; 4Q267 XX, 12. See also James C. VanderKam, "Covenant," in *Encyclopedia of the Dead Sea Scrolls* (Oxford: Oxford University Press, 2000), 1:151–55.

believed that the Deut 30:6/Jer 31:33/Ezek 36:26–27 tradition had begun to take place in their own day, in their own community.[24]

Both Bar 2:30–3:7 (second to first-century B.C.E.) and *Jub.* 1:22–25 (second-century B.C.E.) pick up this tradition. Israel has rebelled against the Lord and for this God has sent them into exile. But God "will give them a heart that obeys and ears that hear" (Bar 2:31). The author of *Jubilees* combines Deut 30:6 and Ezek 36:25–27 from the tradition, declaring that God will "cut off the foreskin of their heart," "create for them a holy spirit," and "purify them" so that Israel will never again disobey (1:23). This evidence demonstrates that at least within some circles of Jewish thought that existed over a century before Paul believed that the promised restoration and interior renovation of Israel still had not been fulfilled, even though Israel had been back in the land for over three centuries.

Philo was also influenced by the heart-circumcision tradition. The Alexandrian philosopher argued that a true proselyte to Judaism was one who circumcises, not his physical foreskin, but his soul (ψυχή) with all its desires and passions (cf. Rom 2:25–29).[25] He asserted that Israel was uncircumcised in heart in his own day.[26] Significantly, Philo explicitly connected the heart-circumcision tradition with the circumcision mandate that God gave to Abraham and his offspring at Gen 17:11:

> What is the meaning of the words, "There shall be circumcised every male of you, and you shall be circumcised in the flesh of your foreskin"?
>
> I see two circumcisions, one of the male, and the other of the flesh; that of the flesh is by way of the genitals, while that of the male, it seems to me, is by way of the reason. For that which is, one might say, naturally male in us is the mind, whose superfluous growths it is necessary to cut off and throw away in order that it may become pure and naked of every evil and passion, and be a priest of God.

---

[24] See 1QpHab XI, 12–14a; 1QS V, 4b–6a; 1QH^a XXI, 4–5, 9, 10b, 11b–13a; 4QCatena A II, 14b–16a; 4Q504 4 III, 7–13a; 4Q434 1 I, 3–4, 10b–11a; 4Q435 I, 1–5; 4Q504 1–2 II, 13–16; 4Q177 9 II, 15b–16. This last reference R. Le Déaut believes to be "un amalgame des formulas" from Deut 10:16, Jer 4:4, and Gen 17 ["Le Thème de la Circoncision du Coeur (Dt. XXX 6; Jér. IV 4) dans les Versions Anciennes (LXX et Targum) et à Qumrân," in *Congress Volume* (Vienna 1980; VTSup 32; Leiden: Brill, 1981), 194n.66].

[25] *QE* 2.2.

[26] *Spec. Laws* 1.304–6.

Now this is what He indicated by the second circumcision, stating (in) the Law that "you shall circumcise your hardness of heart," which means your hard and rebellious and refractory thoughts, and by cutting off and removing arrogance, you shall make the sovereign part free and unbound.[27]

The rabbis of late Judaism taught that circumcision for Israel was foundational for the nation's relationship to God. So important was its implementation that its completion for the male infant overrode the prohibition of work on the Sabbath.[28] They believed that no male who remained uncircumcised—Jew or Gentile—would be allowed to dwell in the world-to-come.[29] Any Jew found to be uncircumcised was liable to the punishment of "extirpation," that is, to being cut off from Israel by execution.[30] An uncircumcised male was considered more unclean than even a dead carcass, for "the foreskin is more unclean than all unclean things" and a "blemish above all blemishes."[31] Thus a Gentile was regarded as abominably unclean. Nevertheless, a Gentile could enter the Mosaic covenant and become a full member of the Jewish commonwealth as a proselyte through the three rites of circumcision, immersion, and sacrificial atonement (cf. Col 2:11–13).[32]

While Gentiles were unclean, the rabbis conceded that Israel was "uncircumcised in heart."[33] The near unanimous opinion of the rabbis was that the promised renewed heart of the Deut 30:6/Jer 31:33/Ezek 36:26–27 tradition would only be brought about in the world to come.[34]

---

[27] Philo, *QG* 3.46 (Colson, Whitaker, and Marcus, LCL), quoting Deut 10:16; see also *Pirqe Rabbi Eliezer*, p. 206 (Ezek 36:26).

[28] *m. Nedarim* 3:11.

[29] *Tanna Debe Eliyyahu*, ER, p. 121.

[30] *m. Kerithot* 1:1. Cf. *Sifre on Numbers*, §112, p. 100: "R. El'azar [1st cent. C.E.] of Modi'im says: "He who profanes the holy things (*the Sanctuary*), and despises the *festivals*, and breaks the covenant of Abraham our father (*circumcision*), even if he has in his hands many good deeds, is worthy to be thrust out of the world" (*i.e.* of the world to come)." See also Philo, *QG* 3.52.

[31] *Pirqe Rabbi Eliezer*, p. 203.

[32] *Sifre on Numbers*, §108, p. 92: "Rabbi says: 'As Israel entered the covenant by three rites: circumcision, immersion (prob. founded on Ex. xix.10), and sacrificial atonement (Ex. xxiv.5–8), so also do the proselytes [enter by the same rites].'"

[33] *Pirqe Rabbi Eliezer*, p. 206.

[34] *Midr. Rabbah* Exodus 41.7 (p. 479); *Midr. Rabbah* Numbers 15.16, 17.6, 23.14; *Midr. Rabbah* Deuteronomy 6.14 (p. 131); *Midr. Rabbah* Song of Songs 1.2, §4 (p. 26); *Midr. Rabbah* Ecclesiastes 2.1 (p. 51); *Midr.* Psalms 14.6, 73.4; *Pirqe Rabbi Eliezer*, p. 206; *Tanna Debe Eliyyahu*, ER, p. 19; *Tanhuma*, Exodus 19:1ff., Part VII (p. 106), *Tanhuma*, Exodus 31:18ff., Part V (p. 157); *Tanhuma*, Leviticus 4:1ff., Part V (p. 196).

Jeremiah 31:33 and Ezek 36:26 are explicitly connected in this regard.[35] The promised inner renewal is also connected with the eschatological outpouring of the Spirit found in Joel 3:1 [MT].[36]

Like Philo earlier, *Pirqe Rabbi Eliezer* explicitly connects the heart-circumcision tradition with the circumcision mandate given to Abraham and his offspring at Gen 17:11:

> The uncircumcision of the heart does not suffer Israel to do the will of their Creator. And in the future the Holy One, blessed be He, will take away from Israel the uncircumcision of the heart, and they will not harden their stubborn (heart) any more before their Creator, as it is said, "And I will take away the stony heart out of your flesh, and I will give you an heart of flesh" (Ezek xxxvi. 26); and it is said, "And ye shall be circumcised in the flesh of your foreskin" (Gen xvii. 11).[37]

The text implies that only when God circumcises the heart of Israel in the future will the physical circumcision of Gen 17:11 find its true fulfillment.

In summary, the heart-circumcision promises were variously interpreted with regard to the time of their fulfillment. The evidence suggests that the Qumran community believed that the promised heart circumcision had arrived and taken place among their community, setting them apart as the true remnant within Israel. Other streams of early Judaism reveal the conviction that the promise yet awaited a future fulfillment. Israel, although back in the promised land, still remained uncircumcised in heart. The nation awaited God's intervention into history to bring about her glorious restoration and the heart-cirucmcision that would accompany it and finally secure full and glad covenant obedience. Physical circumcision needed to be accompanied by heart circumcision for one to be a true Jew.

New Testament Context: Deuteronomy 30:6 in Colossians 2:11

After greeting the Colossians (1:1–2) and offering thanks to God for their faith in Christ (1:3–8), Paul reports that he prays unceasingly for them that they might be filled with the knowledge of God. He prays

---

[35] *Midr. Rabbah* Song of Songs 1.2, §4.
[36] *Midr. Rabbah* Deuteronomy 6.14 (p. 131); *Midr.* Psalm 14.6; *Tanna Debe Eliyyahu,* ER, p. 19.
[37] *Pirqe Rabbi Eliezer,* p. 206 (Ezek 36:26); Philo, *QG* 3.46 (Deut 10:16).

for this so that they might walk worthily of the Lord, who delivered them in a second exodus from the authority of darkness (1:9–14; see chapter five). Paul then writes out a hymn that exalts Christ, stockpiling his theological ammunition in order to unload it in the coming paragraphs against the heretical "philosophy" (1:15–20). After Paul asserts his divine commission to bring the proclamation of Christ to the nations (1:24–29), he assures the Colossians of his concern and struggle for them as well, especially that they might know that Christ is the storehouse of wisdom they seek and need so that they will not be deceived to look elsewhere (2:1–4). All the fullness of deity dwells in Christ; they have all they need in him. They must keep walking by faith in him just as they began (2:6–15). They must neither look to the philosophy's teaching about angelic powers nor to superseded Mosaic covenant regulations for help or wisdom for full Christian living (2:16–23).

In 2:8–15 Paul engages the heresy directly, warning the Colossian church to watch out for those who want to take them captive with a "philosophy" that is an "empty deception" because it has a merely human origin and is not in accordance with the apostolic tradition they had received (2:8). Paul argues that the church should not fall prey to this deception, and gives a lengthy basis for why they should not capitulate.[38] Paul's list is impressive, first stating that "all the fullness of deity dwells bodily"[39] in Christ and that in their union with him the Colossians are filled with this fullness (2:9–10a). Moreover, Christ has authority over every angelic ruler and authority (2:10b); they need not fear them (if they are evil) nor must they look to them for divine aid (if they are good). They are inferior beings who cannot compare to the preeminent Christ (1:18b).

At 2:11 Paul gives another reason why the Colossian believers should not succumb to the philosophy. In their union with Messiah Jesus, they have undergone a circumcision accomplished "without hands." The word translated "without hands," ἀχειροποιήτῳ, distinguishes this circumcision from the physical circumcision practiced by Jews and required of any Gentile who desired to identify fully with the

---

[38] The ground or basis Paul gives is quite long, extending from 2:9 to 2:15 and driven by seven main verbs (κατοικεῖ, ἐστὲ... πεπληρωμένοι, περιετμήθητε, συνηγέρθητε, συνεζωοποίησεν, ἦρκεν, and ἐδειγμάτισεν) that are accompanied by several participles.

[39] The phrase is an allusion back to the Christ-hymn at 1:19, which is itself an echo of Ps 67:17 LXX. See chapter eight of this study.

Jewish people and their faith.[40] This physical circumcision was accomplished upon the flesh "with hands"[41] and served as the initiation rite that brought one into the Jewish covenant community.[42] The word ἀχειροποίητος is rare,[43] though it is found in Mark 14:58 and 2 Cor 5:1. In Mark 14:58, the gospel writer reports that some Jews, in their attempt to indict Jesus, offered false testimony that Jesus had asserted he was going to tear down the temple of Jerusalem "made with hands" (χειροποίητον)[44] and construct another after three days "without hands" (ἀχειροποίητον). The emphasis on the (merely) human origin of the Jerusalem temple is contrasted with the divine origin of the one Jesus claims he will build.[45] Likewise in 2 Cor 5:1, the synonym for a "building from God (οἰκοδομὴν ἐκ θεοῦ) is "a house not made with hands" (οἰκίαν ἀχειροποίητον), demonstrating here that ἀχειροποίητον = ἐκ θεοῦ, or something that originates or is accomplished by God. The passive form of the verb at Col 2:11 (περιετμήθητε) should be considered a *divine passive*, further supporting that this circumcision is not of human origin but is accomplished by God.[46]

The OT speaks in several places of an inner circumcision of the heart,[47] but only in one place does it speak of God circumcising anything. That text is Deut 30:6: "And YHWH your God will circumcise your heart and the heart of your offspring." The best reason contextually for the echo of this text at Col 2:11 is that some within the church embracing the philosophy were insisting on observing Mosaic covenant-specific stipulations, especially the food laws, the festivals, the Sabbath, and probably also circumcision, although this last item is debated (2:11–13, 16).[48] Paul asserts, however, that these were merely "shadows of the

---

[40] See e.g., Jdt 14:10.

[41] Cf. Eph 2:11b: περιτομῆς ἐν σαρκὶ χειροποιήτου.

[42] See Le Déaut, "Le Thème de la Circoncision du Coeur," 183.

[43] That is, rare in the extant literature before and contemporaneous with the NT. After the NT, the word occurs often in the Church Fathers, who were influenced to a significant degree by the NT use of the term. The word does not occur in the LXX, Josephus, Philo, or the extant Greek portions of the pseudepigraphal literature.

[44] This word occurs fifteen times in the LXX, all in a pejorative sense. It consistently denotes an idolatrous object of worship, something merely made by human hands. I owe this insight to G. K. Beale, personal communication.

[45] Cf. the synonymous ἄνευ χειρῶν of Dan 2:34, 45 LXX with regard to the establishment of the kingdom of God.

[46] Cf. Masson, *Colossiens*, 125n.5.

[47] See e.g., Deut 10:16; Jer 4:4, 9:25–26; Ezek 44:7, 9.

[48] So, e.g., Schweizer, *Colossians*, 142, states that "it is very doubtful that what we have here is a polemic against a practice introduced by the Colossian philosophy." It

coming things" (σκιὰ τῶν μελλόντων); the "reality" (σῶμα) had arrived in Christ (2:17). Therefore, perhaps against those insisting that the believers must be physically circumcised to obtain the spiritual "full-ness" desired, Paul asserted in 2:11 that God had performed the greater circumcision upon the Colossian Christians, the divine circumcision, to which the "shadow" of physical circumcision had pointed. Because the reality had arrived on the scene of salvation-history in the coming of Messiah Jesus, the shadow that served as a pointer was unnecessary and had been rendered obsolete.[49]

In light of this, though the context of Deut 30:6 speaks of God's circumcision of the heart taking place in the restoration of Israel from exile, Israel's restoration is not the point at Col 2:11.[50] The emphasis in context is on the fact that the greater circumcision has arrived, leaving the lesser "shadow" behind as part of the old, fallen age (2:14, 17, 20, 3:1–3). The Colossian believers need not be physically circumcised to secure participation in the fullness of the Messiah.

It should be pointed out that Paul does not mention a circumcision of the *heart* but rather a circumcision "(consisting) in the removal of the body of flesh" (ἐν τῇ ἀπεκδύσει τοῦ σώματος τῆς σαρκός).[51] The jump should not be made too quickly to interpret "flesh" (σαρκός) here in the special moral Pauline sense.[52] First, the word has already been used four times in the letter neutrally (1:22, 24, 2:1, 5). Secondly, Paul has already used the phrase σῶμα τῆς σαρκός at 1:22 to describe Christ's physical body, in which Christ reconciled the Colossian believers to himself through death. There the phrase certainly lacks a pejorative tone. In fact, the phrase σῶμα τῆς σαρκός or its Hebrew equivalent occurs elsewhere in Jewish literature, all without a negative nuance

---

seems clear, however, that the adherents of the philosophy *did* insist on other elements prescribed by the Mosaic covenant, such as its dietary regulations and its sacred days, including the Sabbath (2:16; see the detailed discussion in chapter eleven of this work). In light of this, it seems at least reasonable to infer that circumcision also probably played a role in the philosophy. The central argument of this chapter, however, is unaffected whether circumcision was actually prescribed by the philosophy or not.

[49] Cf. Clinton E. Arnold, "The σκιά/σῶμα contrast is...best explained as a reference to the turning of the ages with the coming of Christ" (*The Colossian Syncretism: The Interface between Christianity and Folk Belief at Colossae* [Grand Rapids: Baker, 1996], 221).

[50] It is nevertheless possible that those who detected Paul's echo might have wondered whether this was the unexpressed implication of the apostle's thought. The fact that Paul has echoed this text points in the direction that the apostle held to the presup-position that the restoration of Israel had begun in Messiah's arrival.

[51] Wolter, *Der Brief an die Kolosser*, 129–30.

[52] As e.g., the NIV ("the sinful nature"), NAB ("the carnal body"), and NKJV ("the body of the sins of the flesh") have done.

in and of itself (Sir 23:17; *1 En.* 15:9 [recension B], 102:5; 1QpHab IX, 2). Nevertheless, the addition of "flesh" to "body" in all of these texts does appear to be used to emphasize the susceptibility of the body to various ills, whether maladies (1QpHab IX, 2), inhabitation by evil spirits (*1 En.* 15:9 [B]), sinners, curse, and plague (*1 En.* 102:5), sensuality (Sir 23:17) or death (*1 En.* 102:5; Col 1:22).[53]

For the two occurrences of the phrase in Colossians, we can tighten the intended meaning even further. The occurrences at Col 1:22 and 2:11 are references to the body inherited from Adam, the mortal body of the old, fallen age.[54] For the Colossians (though not for Christ), this fallen existence led to estrangement as "enemies in the mind," consisting "in evil works" (Col 1:21); they were "dead" in trangressions (2:13). This is further supported by the observation that the phrase "(consisting) in the removal of the body of flesh" at 2:11 is reiterated with a synonymous phrase at 3:9, "having removed the old man":

Col 2:11: ἐν τῇ ἀπεκδύσει   τοῦ σώματος τῆς σαρκός
Col 3:9: ἀπεκδυσάμενοι   τὸν παλαιὸν ἄνθρωπον

This "old man" at 3:9 is then contrasted with the "new man" that the Colossians have "put on" (3:11).[55] This old humanity is characterized by all the vices mentioned in Col 3:5–9. In contrast, the new humanity that the Colossians have donned is in process of renewal "according to the image" of God (3:10b). This language is an allusion to Gen 1:26–27 and a clear indication that the new humanity is being recreated after the pattern of the pre-fall Adam/humanity.[56] Therefore, what is removed in the divine circumcision of Col 2:11 is the fallen, mortal body inherited from Adam, of which Christ himself partook (Col 1:22; though Christ was without sin: Rom 8:3; Heb 4:15).[57] Not merely a part of the body, as in physical circumcision, but the whole body of

---

[53] Cf. Lohse, *Colossians*, 102: "The phrase 'body of flesh'…characterizes the human body in its earthly frailty wherein it is subject to suffering, death, and dissolution (cf. on 1:22)."

[54] Cf. Dunn, *Colossians*, 158, "If there is a moral note in 'flesh' here [at 2:11], it probably reflects a variation of Paul's Adam christology at this point. It was not simply 'his' flesh that Christ stripped off, but the flesh of the first Adam…." See also Arnold, *The Colossian Syncretism*, 296.

[55] See Rom 5:12–6:6, especially 6:6; cf. Eph 4:22–24.

[56] See chapter thirteen of this study.

[57] Against, e.g., MacDonald, *Colossians*, 99, 106, who states that what was circumcised was the "sinful nature." This inner corruption is certainly included in the phrase, but Paul goes much further than this, stating that the whole, fallen, physical body was "cut off."

flesh had been "stripped off."[58] This is a metaphor for physical death
(cf. 2:12a, 20, 3:1–3). Paul states that the Colossians had actually died
bodily (not merely "spiritually") with Christ. This raises a theological
problem, however, because obviously the Colossian believers had not
yet experienced physical death. The reference must be understood in
the light of Paul's "already" and "not yet" eschatological tension.[59] Here
Paul has stressed the "already" aspect, describing the Colossians' salvation as if it had been consummated in order to accentuate that they
had been completely removed from the domination of the old, dying
epoch and the angelic powers that pervaded it (cf. 3:1–3).

The final phrase of 2:11, "in the circumcision of Christ" (ἐν τῇ
περιτομῇ τοῦ Χριστοῦ) may either be a subjective genitive ("the circumcision which Christ performs") and thus a restatement of the previously
mentioned "circumcision accomplished without hands,"[60] an objective
genitive ("the circumcision that Christ underwent"), understood as a
metaphor for his violent death by crucifixion,[61] or a genitive of quality
("Christian circumcision").[62] The argument cannot be rehashed in
detail here (for an extended discussion on the subjective and objective
genitive possibilities, see Bruce, *Colossians*, 104; O'Brien, *Colossians*, 117;

---

[58] Note the same language of Theodotus, *On the Jews*, frag. 5, in comments upon
the circumcision recorded in Gen 17: "Once (God) himself, when he led the noble
Abraham out of his native land, from heaven called upon the man and all his family
to strip off the flesh [σάρκ' ἀποσυλῆσαι]...and therefore he accomplished it." (See
F. Fallon, "Theodotus," *OTP* 2:792). For the Greek text of the fragment, see Albert-
Marie Denis, *Concordance Grecque Des Pseudépigraphes D'Ancien Testament* (Louvain-la-Neuve:
Université Catholique De Louvain, 1987), p. 920; 9.22.7.

[59] On which see, among others, C. Marvin Pate, *The End of the Age Has Come: The
Theology of Paul* (Grand Rapids: Zondervan, 1995).

[60] John Calvin, *The Epistles of Paul the Apostle to the Galatians, Ephesians, Philippians, and
Colossians* (trans. T. H. L. Parker; Calvin's New Testament Commentaries 11; Grand
Rapids: Eerdmans, 1965), 332; Lightfoot, *Colossians*, 183; Schweizer, *Colossians*, 143;
Lindemann, *Der Kolosserbrief*, 41; Wall, *Colossians*, 114–15; Bruce, *Colossians*, 104; Hugedé,
Colossiens, 128 and n.94; cf. NIV. Masson, *Colossiens*, 126n.2, argues *against* this interpre-
tation ("Mais d'après le contexte, les Colossiens ont été circoncis en Christ par Dieu
lui-même") and believes the genitive to be a possessive genitive, which is "indiquant
que cette circoncision est propre à Christ et à ceux qui la subissent en Lui."

[61] Moule, *Colossians*, 96; Lohmeyer, *Kolosser*, 111; Barth and Blanke, *Colossians*, 364–65;
Martin, *Colossians*, 82–83; O'Brien, *Colossians*, 117; Dunn, *Colossians*, 158; Yates, *Colossians*, 42; so also Meredith G. Kline, *By Oath Consigned: A Reinterpretation of the Covenant
Signs of Circumcision and Baptism* (Grand Rapids: Eerdmans, 1968), 45–46, on account
of OT background (see his argument on pp. 39–49).

[62] Abbott, *Colossians*, 251; Wright, *Colossians*, 105; Gnilka, *Der Kolosserbrief*, 132n.70;
Wolter, *Der Brief an die Kolosser*, 128–29; Aletti, *Colossiens*, 171–72; Pokorný, *Colossians*,
125; Hübner, *An die Kolosser*, 82, offers both the subjective genitive as well as the genitive of quality as strong possibilities. For a discussion of the genitive of quality, see
BDF §165.

on the genitive of quality, Hübner, *An die Kolosser*, 82, and Wolter, *Der Brief an die Kolosser*, 128–29). This study prefers the objective genitive; the verb "you were circumcised" is in the passive tense and should be taken as a divine passive: God himself, not Christ, is the one who has accomplished this spiritual circumcision upon those "in Christ" (ἐν ᾧ).[63] In support of this interpretation is the completely overlooked fact that in every case of the use of περιτομή + the genitive in the surrounding Jewish literature, the person or thing in the genitive is who or what has undergone the act of circumcision.[64]

Therefore, according to Col 2:11, *two* circumcisions have been performed. The first occurred when Christ was violently crucified on the cross, an event which secured a cosmic redemption (Col 1:20–22). The second God performed upon the Colossian believers when they came into union with Christ and his "circumcision." All of this is another way of declaring that the believers at Colossae died with Christ when they became united to him by faith (Col 2:12; see Rom 6:1–11). Paul has thus argued that the circumcision of the heart prophesied by Moses in Deut 30:6 has arrived in Messiah Jesus and is to be equated with "the removal of the body of flesh." By this Paul meant the death and removal of the mortal, fallen, Adamic body that belonged to the old age, which took place when the Colossians were united with Messiah's death. This death and burial with Christ was publicly portrayed (and realized) in the initiation rite of baptism (2:12a). The promised circumcision of the heart of Deut 30:6 had arrived in Messiah Jesus and Paul has recast its shape into a cruciform mold. He also develops this reality later with creation-new creation language in Col 3:9–10.[65]

Deuteronomy 30:6, Jeremiah 31:33, and Ezekiel 36:26–27
in the Rest of the NT and in the Early Fathers

The Deut 30:6/Jer 31:31–34/Ezek 36:26–28 tradition surfaces several times in the NT: Luke 22:20, Rom 2:28–29,[66] 1 Cor 11:25, 2 Cor 3:3

---

[63] Cf. Masson, *Colossiens*, 126n.2. I do not, however, follow Masson in opting for the construction as a possessive genitive.

[64] See LXX Exod 4:25–26 (twice); Jer 11:16; Rom 2:25, 29; Josephus, *Ant.* 1.192, 8.262, 12.241, 13.319; *Ag Ap.* 2.137–38; Philo, *Spec. Laws* 1.2.

[65] See chapter thirteen of this study.

[66] For defense of this allusion, see now Timothy W. Berkley, *From a Broken Covenant to Circumcision of the Heart: Pauline Intertextual Exegesis in Romans 2:17–29* (SBLDS 175; Atlanta: SBL, 2000), 98–107.

and 6,[67] Heb 7:22, 8:6–13, 9:15, and 10:16–17.[68] Space prohibits development of these texts.

The author of *Barnabas* (70–138 C.E.) devotes a full section to the circumcision of the heart (chapter nine). Combining allusions and quotations of Jer 4:4, 9:25 (LXX), and Deut 10:16, he argues that Christians have received the true circumcision (which enables them to hear and obey), whereas Jews still trust in a circumcision that "has been abolished, for [God] declared that circumcision is not a matter of the flesh" (9:4). The author connects Gen 17 with the "circumcision of the heart" tradition, arguing that those who embrace Jesus as Messiah have partaken of the circumcision that matters before God (9:4–8).

The author also ties the "circumcision of the heart" tradition to the inaugurated new creation. Christians are created anew, partakers of the second creation of the last days, because the promised interior renovation of Ezek 36:26 (= Ezek 11:19) has been wrought within them. God has removed their "heart of stone" and given them a "heart of flesh," which has made them fit to be the holy temple of the Lord and partakers of the new creation.[69]

The eleventh hymn of the *Odes of Solomon* (ca. 100 C.E.) likewise mentions the divine circumcision in connection with new creation or paradisal language. The author writes that his "heart was pruned," that the Most High "circumcised me by his Holy Spirit" (vv. 1–2).[70] The result is that his heart "produced fruits for the Lord" (v. 1): he became like a land or tree of Paradise, planted with the rest of the Lord's fruit-bearing, flourishing people (vv. 12–24). This fruit is later interpreted as "good works" (v. 20; cf. Col 1:10; Gal 5:22–23). In this circumcision the author has "stripped off" the "folly cast upon the earth" (v. 10; cf. Col 2:11).

Much of this resembles Paul's thought in Col 2:11–13, 3:9–10. What emerges in embryonic form in Colossians, *Barn.* and *Odes Sol.* draw out in some detail along similar lines.

---

[67] See Scott J. Hafemann, *Paul, Moses, and the History of Israel: The Letter/Spirit Contrast and the Argument from Scripture in 2 Corinthians 3* (WUNT 81; Tübingen: J. C. B. Mohr [Paul Siebeck], 1995), chapter 2 passim.

[68] See also Acts 7:51; Phil 3:3. Cf. Rom 6:15–23, 8:1–4; Phil 2:12–13; Heb 13:20–21.

[69] *Barn.* 6:13–16.

[70] Le Déaut writes on this that "Comme c'est Dieu lui-même qui circoncit, Dt. xxx 6 semble être encore à l'arrière-plan" ("Le Thème de la Circoncision du Coeur," 197–98).

Hermeneutical Reflections

Paul has echoed Deut 30:6 in Col 2:11, revealing that he believed Moses' promise of a circumcision of the heart of Israel had begun to be realized in the death and resurrection of Messiah Jesus. Paul appears to have the context of Deut 30:6 only generally in mind, capitalizing on the fact that it promised a "greater" circumcision, which implied that physical circumcision in and of itself was inadequate before God. The presupposition that appears to lie behind Paul's echo is that in the Messiah's arrival upon the scene of history, a significant OT prophecy promised *to Israel* had been realized—and this among Gentiles, as the proclamation of Messiah reached them in the insignificant town of Colossae in Asia Minor.

CHAPTER TEN

THE SCRIPTURES OF ISRAEL IN COLOSSIANS 2:8–15: THE ECHO OF GENESIS 17 IN 2:13

Comparison of Textual Versions and Evaluation

And you, being dead in transgressions and your foreskin of flesh, [God] made alive together with him, canceling for us all transgressions.

Genesis 17:11, 14, 23, 24, 25 MT	Genesis 17:11, 14, [23], 24, 25 LXX	Colossians 2:13
v. 11: וּנְמַלְתֶּם אֵת בְּשַׂר עָרְלַתְכֶם	v. 11: καὶ <u>περιτμηθήσεσθε τὴν σάρκα τῆς ἀκροβυστίας ὑμῶν</u>	[<u>περιετμήθητε</u>; 2:11] <u>τῇ ἀκροβυστίᾳ τῆς σαρκὸς ὑμῶν</u>
v. 14: יִמּוֹל אֶת־בְּשַׂר עָרְלָתוֹ	v. 14: <u>περιτμηθήσεται τὴν σάρκα τῆς ἀκροβυστίας αὐτοῦ</u>	
v. 23: וַיָּמָל אֶת־בְּשַׂר עָרְלָתָם	v. 23: <u>περιέτεμεν τὴν σάρκα τῆς ἀκροβυστίας αὐτῶν</u>[1]	
v. 24: בְּהִמֹּלוֹ בְּשַׂר עָרְלָתוֹ	v. 24: <u>περιέτεμεν τὴν σάρκα τῆς ἀκροβυστίας αὐτοῦ</u>	
v. 25: בְּהִמֹּלוֹ אֵת בְּשַׂר עָרְלָתוֹ	v. 25: <u>περιετμήθη τὴν σάρκα τῆς ἀκροβυστίας αὐτοῦ</u>	

This proposal meets the three criteria necessary for an echo: 1) availability, and 2) word agreement. Regarding *availability*, Paul certainly knew the Abraham account found in the book of Genesis, and had almost certainly read it himself (see Rom 4). Regarding *word agreement*, Col 2:13 shares a rare word-combination with the source text, with both

---

[1] Although Alexandrinus (MS "A," which serves as the base text of Brooke, McLean, and Thackeray for Genesis 17, as well as for Rahlfs) reads περιέτεμεν τὰς ἀκροβυστίας αὐτῶν at v. 23, numerous Greek MSS read the above. This reading at v. 23 is further supported by the MT, Syriac Peshitta, Vulgate, *Tg Ps.-J.*, *Tg Neof.*, Ethiopic, Armenian, and Cyril (d. 444 C.E.).

texts discussing circumcision in the immediate context. While not a rare topic within Judaism, the concept of circumcision is specific enough to further justify our investigation. The two texts thus also share a concept similarity. It appears that Paul has intentionally played on the two key words of the phrase by switching their word order, and the intended rhetorical effect of this play produces a transformation in meaning (on which, see below). Though the play on words appears to have been intentional, the reference is still classified as an echo because nothing from the original context of Gen 17 needs to be brought forward to understand adequately Paul's statement in the new context.[2]

Old Testament Context: Genesis Chapter 17

The interaction in Gen 17 between God and Abraham took place when Abraham was ninety-nine years old (17:1), twenty-four years after he departed from Haran (12:4) and thirteen years after Ishmael had been born to him through Hagar, his wife's servant girl (Gen 16:16). God's appearance to Abraham possibly took place near Hebron, by the "oaks of Mamre," where Abraham had settled in tents with his household (13:18, 14:13, 18:1).

Genesis seventeen relates the fifth appearance of God to Abraham within a narrative that began at 11:27. In each of the previous four appearances, God has made promises to Abraham, with the fourth culminating explicitly in a covenant with him (15:18). The promises involve innumerable descendents and the land of Canaan for them to live in, as well as blessing for all the families of the earth through him (12:3).

---

[2] A few recent scholars have come close to observing this echo: Wolter, *Der Brief an die Kolosser*, 128; Hübner, *An die Kolosser*, 82, but their comments are for 2:11 and not 2:13 and it is not clear that they make the full connection with regard to the phrase τῇ ἀκροβυστίᾳ τῆς σαρκὸς ὑμῶν in 2:13. Dunn, *Colossians*, 155 (although his comments come under his section on 2:11 and not 2:13), writes that 'the disparaging note of 2:13—"the uncircumcision of your flesh"—should not be taken as 'the uncircumcision which is your flesh," with "flesh" understood as a moral category.... Rather, it *echoes the classic description of circumcision as marking God's covenant with Israel* (*Gen. 17:11–14*: "So shall my covenant be in your flesh an everlasting covenant")...' (emphasis mine). This study will disagree with Dunn's interpretation of the phrase, but it is in full agreement with him that Paul here at Col 2:13 "echoes" Gen 17. See now also Beale, "Colossians," ad loc.; see too BDAG, "ἀκροβυστία," def. 2, which invites the reader to compare Col 2:13 with Gen 17:11.

In light of these astonishing promises, Sarai, who is barren, persuades her husband Abraham to obtain a descendent through her servant-girl Hagar, a move which appears to be culturally acceptable. Even more, however, the move is a humanly obtainable means of securing the promise that God had made to Abraham with regard to descendents. The result is a son, Ishmael (16:15). Nevertheless, in spite of Sarai's striving, God declares that he will bless Sarai and give Abraham a son through *her*, the barren woman, and this in spite of the patriarch's disbelief (17:15–17). Moreover, the covenant God has made with Abraham will be established with this promised son, to be named Isaac, and not with Ishmael (17:18–21). It shall be through Isaac that all the families of the earth will be blessed (22:18, 26:4).

Chapter seventeen opens with an appearance of God, who addresses the patriarch with a succinct summary of the covenant relationship between them (17:1b–2). Abraham's response is one of homage (v. 3), whereupon God reviews and expands his side of the covenant obligations initially made to Abraham (v. 4).[3] First, God increases the number of nations that will come from Abraham. Not only does God promise to make from Abraham a great nation (12:2); he will also make him the father of a "multitude of nations" (17:4, 5b, 6a). He will make Abraham "fruitful" and "multiply" him exceedingly (17:2, 6).[4] God commits himself to be the deity of both Abraham and his offspring in what shall be a perpetual covenant—generation after generation (17:7, 8b).

After reviewing and expanding his own covenant obligations to Abraham his vassal, God turns to expand Abraham's covenant obligations.[5] Not only must Abraham be "blameless" in his relationship with God (v. 1),[6] but now God adds the stipulation that Abraham and his descendents are to circumcise every male among them (v. 10). They are to cut off the "flesh of your foreskin" (MT: בְּשַׂר עָרְלַתְכֶם), the prepuce or fold of skin that covers the head of the male genital organ.

The LXX renders this genitive construction with τὴν σάρκα τῆς ἀκροβυστίας, a phrase that appears in the LXX a total of seven times,

---

[3] Note the "As for me"; so NRSV, NIV, NASB (MT: אֲנִי הִנֵּה; LXX: ἐγὼ ἰδού).

[4] In the literary context, this language is used intentionally to connect Abraham to the original creation mandate of Gen 1:28, "be fruitful and multiply," and which was first reiterated to Noah and his sons at Gen 9:1. See chapter three of this study (especially pp. 44–48).

[5] Note the "As for you"; see NRSV, NIV, NASB (MT: וְאַתָּה; LXX: σὺ δέ).

[6] Kline, *By Oath Consigned*, 40, interprets this as Abraham's obligation to live before God in "true loyalty" (not sinless perfection, but wholehearted fidelity).

four of which occur here in Gen 17 (vv. 11, 14, 24, 25). Numerous Greek MSS and versions, including the MT, have the phrase at v. 23 also, raising the total to five occurrences of the phrase concentrated in Gen 17 in the MT (see chart at the beginning of this chapter and footnote 1). In all the occurrences in the LXX, the phrase takes the exact word order, with the word σάρξ first, followed by the article and then ἀκροβυστία, demonstrating that the construction was probably fixed.[7] It always follows the verb περιτέμνω as the direct object. The other three texts in which the phrase occurs in the LXX outside of Gen 17—Gen 34:24, Lev 12:3, and Jdt 14:10—mention the phrase incidentally and do not highlight it or the circumcision rite in the prominent way that Gen 17 does. Moreover, the occurrence at LXX Gen 34:24 is lacking in the MT, where the LXX nevertheless has added it as an interpretive gloss due to its influential and pervasive use in Gen 17. Furthermore, while at first glance Lev 12:3 may appear to hold a place of some importance due to the fact that it is the only expression of the command to circumcise in the Sinaitic legislation, a closer look at the larger context reveals that the entire section is concerned with 'clean' and 'unclean' regulations. Women who have recently given birth require elaboration in this regard, and circumcision is mentioned merely in passing in the midst of this larger concern. The appearance of the fixed phrase at Jdt 14:10 almost certainly stems from its biblical use at Gen 17 and is hardly the source for Paul's phraseology. In light of this, it is virtually certain that Paul's language at Col 2:13 stems from the foundational circumcision text of the OT, Gen 17.

The result of such a circumcision of the "flesh of the foreskin"[8] is that the exposed head of the male organ will serve as a "sign" (σημεῖον; MT: אוֹת) of the covenant that God has initiated with Abraham and his descendants. "Signs" serve in a few different functions in the OT, but Michael Fox has argued that circumcision in Gen 17 serves, not as an identity marker of the people of God, but as a "reminder" sign, which stirs God to recall his covenant obligations to Abraham and to fulfill

---

[7] The phrase in the LXX consistently renders the Hebrew in a literal manner in all six places where the phrase appears in the MT.

[8] The major English translations all translate the phrase this way (though some have "foreskins" instead of "foreskin"): KJV, ASV, NAB, NASB, NET, NJB, NLT, RSV, NKJV, NRSV, NJPS; the NIV/TNIV is the lone exception, providing a paraphrase instead.

them.[9] We concur with Fox's findings but would further argue that the sign of circumcision was intended to remind *both* parties of the covenant of their respective obligations.[10] The sign of circumcision thus serves to remind Abraham's posterity of the covenant God made with their forefather and thus of their obligation to circumcise their male infants generation after generation.

Having established the covenant obligation of circumcision, God further explains who is to be circumcised: "every male" (πᾶν ἀρσενικόν; MT: כָּל־זָכָר) on the eighth day after birth of every generation (v. 12a). This includes those not directly descended from Abraham, including slaves born in the household or those purchased from foreigners. The sign of the covenant is to be upon all who belong to Abraham's household. A male refusing to undergo the rite is to be "cut off" from the people; he willfully has broken God's covenant and will consequently experience the covenant curse for his disobedience (v. 14c).[11] The language of being "cut off" suggests that the offender will be put to death.[12]

The Gen 17 Old Testament Interpretive Tradition

While Gen 17 is not taken up explicitly in any other OT text, the phrase σάρκα τῆς ἀκροβυστίας (see vv. 11, 14, [23], 24, 25) occurs at Gen 34:24 LXX. It appears that at Gen 34:24, the LXX translator was almost certainly influenced by Gen 17 and the pervasive and repeated use of the phrase there. The Hebrew equivalent of the phrase, however, is not present in the MT at 34:24, nor is the phrase found in the early Greek versions of Symmachus, Aquila, and Theodotion, nor does its equivalent occur in the Syriac Peshitta, Vulgate, *Tg. Neof.* or *Tg. Ps.-J.*

The fixed phrase also occurs at Lev 12:3, but to posit a particular direction of literary dependence (if any) between the two texts would be speculative due to dating issues.[13]

---

[9] Michael Fox, "The Sign of the Covenant: Circumcision in the Light of the Priestly *ōt* Etiologies," *RB* 81 (1974): 595.

[10] See also Gordon J. Wenham, *Genesis 16–50* (WBC 2; Dallas: Word, 1994), 23–24.

[11] So too Kline, *By Oath Consigned*, 40: "Curse sanction appears too, appended to the stipulation regarding circumcision (v. 14)."

[12] Cf. Gen 9:11; Exod 31:14; Josh 11:21; Judg 4:24; 1 Sam 2:33; so also Wenham, *Genesis 16–50*, 25; cf. Kline, *By Oath Consigned*, 41–43.

[13] The apostle Paul would have held that Moses wrote both Gen 17 and Lev 12:3.

Genesis 17 in Early and Late Judaism

The phrase σάρκα τῆς ἀκροβυστίας also shows up in Jdt 14:10. Achior, an Ammonite, puts his faith in "the God of Israel" and is circumcised after seeing the deliverance God had accomplished through Judith. By this act Achior "joined the house of Israel."

The construction appears also in 1Q21 3, 18–23 ar (Aramaic):

> Jacob my father, and Re[uben my brother...] and we said to them [...]...[...] they desire our daughters, and we will all be br[others] and friends. Circumcise the *foreskin of your flesh* [עורלת בשרכון] and you shall look li[k]e [us], and you shall be sealed like us with the circumcision of [...] and we shall be to y[ou]

The fragment is a paraphrase of Gen 34:14–16. The phrase does not occur either in the MT or LXX of Gen 34:14–16, but it does occur at Gen 34:24 LXX just a few verses later. Genesis 34:24 narrates the compliance of Hamor, Shechem, and all the men of their city to the demand of circumcision by the sons of Jacob. It appears that the repeated and pervasive use of the phrase at Gen 17 has influenced this text from Qumran, as it did Gen 34:24 LXX.

Like Col 2:13, the word order of the phrase in this text from Qumran is reversed in the genitive construction in relation to how it appears in Gen 17:11, 14, 23, 24, 25, and Lev 12:3. The switch does not appear intentional; the sense is unaffected and no play on the words seems to have been intended. The author, perhaps dependent upon memory, wrote the phrase out in reverse order without producing a change in meaning.

In another text from Qumran, the angel Mastema turned from pursuing Abraham after he was finally circumcised, and also turns away from any who return to the Law of Moses to observe it.[14]

After faithfully narrating the text of Gen 17, the author of *Jubilees* says that Israel was given circumcision so that her people might enjoy the presence of God and of his (circumcised) angels in heaven.[15]

Philo argues that two circumcisions can be seen in Gen 17:10–11, that of the flesh and the "second circumcision" of the reason or heart. He explicitly quotes Deut 10:16 ("circumcise, then, the foreskin of your heart") to support this, thus combining Gen 17 with the "circumcision

---

[14] 4Q271 frag. 4, col. II.6–7a. Note that circumcision serves to ward off an evil angel.
[15] *Jub.* 15:26–27. Cf. the emphasis on angelic powers in Col 1:13, 16, 2:8, 15, 18, 20.

of the heart" tradition (as Paul has done; see below).[16] According to Philo, without this second circumcision, one's soul cannot be saved from destruction.[17]

Circumcision was considered so important by the rabbis that its observance overrode the obligation to abstain from work on the Sabbath when such a conflicting circumstance arose.[18] Failure to circumcise a Jewish male infant was punishable by extirpation ("cutting off").[19] Even Abraham was not considered "whole" until he had been circumcised.[20] Yet by virtue of Abraham's merit of obedience, God promised to save all Israel from Gehenna.[21] Other rabbis agreed that because of circumcision Israel would be saved from Gehenna. The nations, however, were destined for Gehenna due to their uncircumcised state.[22] The uncircumcised were separated from God and were not to eat of the paschal offering or come near the sanctuary; their state rendered them unclean and as dead.[23] The rabbis also believed that in the future, God would circumcise Israel in the heart, fulfilling both Ezek 36:26 as well as Gen 17.[24] This last text explicitly connects Gen 17 with the "circumcision of the heart" tradition, as Paul has done (see below).

New Testament Context: Genesis 17's
τὴν σάρκα τῆς ἀκροβυστίας in Colossians 2:13

Having stated that the Colossian believers experienced the death and burial of their Adamic body, Paul asserts that they also have participated in Messiah's resurrection due to their union with him (ἐν ᾧ; 2:12a). Though not yet consummately resurrected as Jesus was, they nevertheless have experienced the inauguration of the end-time resurrection. The end-time "day of the LORD" had dawned in Messiah Jesus and, quite unexpectedly, been extended into a period of time that was to culminate in consummate resurrection for believers and a universal divine judgment. Paul states that the Colossians had been resurrected together with

---

[16] *QG* 3.46.
[17] *QG* 3.52.
[18] *m. Shabbat* 18:3, 19:2; *m. Nedarim* 3:11; cf. John 7:22.
[19] *m. Kerithot* 1:1.
[20] *Tanhuma* Gen 17:1ff., Part VI (p. 84); *Midr. Rabbah* Genesis 46.5.
[21] *Tanna Debe Eliyyahu*, EZ, p. 522.
[22] *m. Nedarim* 3:11; *Tanhuma* Genesis 17:1ff., Part VIII (p. 85); *Midr.* Psalm 6:1.
[23] *Pirqe Rabbi Eliezer*, pp. 205, 208–9.
[24] *Pirqe Rabbi Eliezer*, p. 206.

Christ by God, who had raised Jesus from the dead (νεκρῶν; 2:12b). The mention of the physically dead (νεκρῶν) at the end of 2:12b triggers a new metaphor for Paul, which he develops in 2:13. Paul declares in a word play that the Colossians also had once been "dead" (νεκρούς), living an existence characterized by willful violation of divine moral standards. They had been morally unclean, excluded from the covenant community of God. They had been spiritually dead.

The phrase ἀκροβυστίᾳ τῆς σαρκός found here at 2:13 is an echo of the phrase as found several times in Gen 17, the classic and foundational circumcision text of the ot. A comprehensive *TLG* search demonstrated that before Paul's use at Col 2:13, this combination of words had only ever occurred earlier in the Greek translation of the ot. Moreover, the search revealed that all later usages of the word-combination occur only in the Church Fathers, who use it under the influence of the Scriptures.[25] Therefore Paul, saturated with the Scriptures of Israel, in a context where circumcision has already played a prominent role in the argument at 2:11, has almost certainly penned a phrase whose language derives from Gen 17. The combination of words occurs in the lxx in a fixed form. The word σάρξ is followed by ἀκροβυστία with the article in a genitive construction. Each occurrence is also followed by a personal pronoun in the genitive ("your," "his," "their"). Moreover, each occurrence is used as the direct object of the verb περιτέμνω ("to circumcise"). The phrase in each case should be translated "the foreskin of the flesh" and is an appositional genitive: "the flesh *that is* the foreskin."[26] The fixed phrase occurs several times in the classic circumcision text of Gen 17. A list of these as well as the three occurrences outside Gen 17 in the lxx is given below:

Genesis 17:
Gen 17:11: περιτμηθήσεσθε   τὴν σάρκα τῆς ἀκροβυστίας ὑμῶν
Gen 17:14: περιτμηθήσεται   τὴν σάρκα τῆς ἀκροβυστίας αὐτοῦ
[Gen 17:23: περιέτεμεν   τὴν σάρκα τῆς ἀκροβυστίας αὐτῶν][27]

---

[25] That is, except for one occurrence of the phrase penned by Flavius Claudius Julianus, the pagan Roman emperor of the 4th century c.e. In his work *Against the Galileans*, he quotes Gen 17:10–11 to marshal evidence against Christians that their faith had departed from the ot (See LCL, *Julian*, III.421). Therefore, every occurrence without exception that the *TLG* located stems from the Scriptures, including this instance penned by Flavius Claudius Julianus.

[26] On the appositional genitive, see BDF §167.

[27] For the evidence for the reading of the phrase at v. 23, see the first footnote of this chapter.

Gen 17:24: περιέτεμεν   τὴν σάρκα τῆς ἀκροβυστίας αὐτοῦ
Gen 17:25: περιετμήθη   τὴν σάρκα τῆς ἀκροβυστίας αὐτοῦ

Others:
Gen 34:24: περιετέμοντο   τὴν σάρκα τῆς ἀκροβυστίας αὐτῶν[28]
Lev 12:3: περιτεμεῖ   τὴν σάρκα τῆς ἀκροβυστίας αὐτοῦ
Jdt 14:10: περιετέμετο   τὴν σάρκα τῆς ἀκροβυστίας αὐτοῦ

In Col 2:13, however, Paul has reversed the order of the words. Instead, the word ἀκροβυστία is followed by σάρξ in the genitive construction. Is the change in word-order accidental or intentional? The context suggests that the word reversal is intentional. The phrase is still an appositional genitive, "the foreskin *that is* the flesh,"[29] though now a quite different meaning has been produced from the original.[30] In a subtle play on words, Paul refers not primarily to the Colossians' physical uncircumcision, but to their previous *spiritual* uncircumcision—their state of deadness in trespasses and exclusion from God's (new) covenant people.[31] Paul asserts, perhaps against the Jewish element of the "philosophy,"[32] that the Colossians' deepest dilemma was not that they were physically uncircumcised but that they had been existing in a *spiritually* uncircumcised state. This gravest of problems God had

---

[28] As noted earlier in the study, this phrase or its equivalent at Gen 34:24 is not found in the MT, Peshitta, Vulgate, Targums, Symmachus, Aquila, or Theodotion. It appears to be a scribal addition due to the pervasive use of the phrase in the foundational text on circumcision, Gen 17.

[29] Against Dunn, *Colossians*, 155.

[30] I translate ἀκροβυστία with "foreskin" instead of "uncircumcision" to retain a sense of continuity with the nigh unanimous decision of the major English translations to translate the phrase in Gen 17 consistently as "flesh of the foreskin" (not "flesh of the uncircumcision"). See n.8 of this chapter. The meaning "foreskin" for ἀκροβυστία is the first definition BDAG gives for the term; see also LSJ; Lust.

[31] Another example of such a play on words may help to illuminate what Paul has done. In a discussion on Thomas Carew's erotic poem, *The Rapture*, John Hollander (*The Figure of Echo: A Mode of Allusion in Milton and After* [Berkeley: University of California Press, 1981], 84–85) keenly observes that Carew has alluded to the biblical book *Song of Songs* with his mention of a "vale of lilies." Carew's line reads:

> taste the ripened cherry,
> The warm, firm apple, tipped with coral berry;
> Then will I visit with a wandering kiss
> The vale of lilies, and the bower of bliss.

Hollander remarks:

> The echoic reversal of the "lily of the valley" from the Song of Songs substitutes place on a person for the biblical trope of person in a place. (Indeed, this flickering back and forth between body in garden and garden in body is one of the complex strategies of Carew's whole masterpiece.).

[32] For a discussion of the question as to whether the opponents were advocating physical circumcision in the church at Colossae, see Wolter, *Der Brief an die Kolosser*, 157.

remedied with a spiritual circumcision, one "not made with hands" (2:11). That both circumcision and death have been spiritualized in the immediate context strongly supports the interpretation of the phrase as an uncircumcision that is spiritual. The word σάρξ ("flesh") looks back to its use at 2:11 and is shorthand for the "body of flesh," the Adamic, fallen existence that belongs to the old and dying age. The Colossians were not in need of the circumcision given to Abraham, which would have only introduced them into the (now defunct and superseded) Mosaic covenant. They needed the circumcision that would usher them into God's new covenant community, into union with the resurrected Christ, the head of the "new humanity" and last Adam, and into the age of the new creation (2:11–13, 3:1–4, 9–11).

Other *NT* Passages and the Early Church Fathers

Gen 17 shows up elsewhere in the NT at Rom 4:10–11, John 7:22, and Acts 7:8 (cf. Luke 1:59). None of these directly cite Gen 17, but rather are based upon it. Irenaeus explicitly connects Gen 17:9–11 with Col 2:11 and Deut 10:16, stating that Abraham's circumcision typified the circumcision of the Spirit.[33] Tertullian connects Gen 17:9–14 with Jer 4:3–4 and 31:31–32 and argues likewise.[34] They therefore develop the themes in line with what Paul has done in Col 2:11–13 (see discussion below).

Hermeneutical and Theological Reflections

It is possible that Paul saw physical uncircumcision as a marker (or type) that pointed to the deeper dilemma of spiritual uncircumcision. It is probable moreover that Paul alluded to the language of Gen 17 in an intentional rhetorical play on words to stress that the Colossians were not in need of physical circumcision, which merely removed the foreskin of the male organ. Rather, they were in need of spiritual cir-cumcision that removed the mortal body of flesh inherited from Adam. This circumcision they received by faith, which united them with the circumcised (i.e., crucified) Christ.

---

[33] *Against Heresies* 4.16.1 (*ANF* 1:480–81).
[34] *Against the Jews* 3 (*ANF* 3:153–55).

Since their fall in Paradise (Gen 3), Adam and Eve's progeny, the human race, has inherited "bodies of flesh": bodies that succumbed to disease and death, to temptation and sin. This was God's judgment upon their rebellion. Humanity's heart also became characterized by corruption at this time: "The LORD saw that the wickedness of human-kind was great in the earth and that every inclination of the thoughts of their hearts was only evil continually" (Gen 6:5 NRSV). This inner corruption was not stamped out by the Flood (see Gen 8:21, which alludes back to 6:5), and while God did elect Israel to be his special people, only sin churned out of the heart of the vast majority of them (Deut 9:6–7; Jer 17:1). *All* of humanity had inherited the fallen, mortal body from Adam, including Israel. But in the fullness of time (Gal 4:4), God's Messiah came upon the scene of history to die, or, as Col 2:11 puts it, to undergo "circumcision." He himself partook of the body inherited from Adam to do so (Col 1:22). According to the apostle Paul, those who identified with this last Adam by faith are also "circumcised" with him, that is, they died with him, having stripped off forever the body of flesh, i.e., the old, fallen, Adamic, sin-enslaved humanity. Made alive again, believers are clothed with the "new man," via their union with Christ (Col 3:9–11). They now await the comple-tion of this renewed existence in the resurrection in the consummated new creational age at the end of time, where Adam's fall and its effects will be fully reversed. At that time this humanity, both inwardly and outwardly, will be completely renewed. Obedience will fully, gladly, and eternally flow from circumcised hearts, even as they began to do so in the midst of the old age.

Summary: Deuteronomy 30:6 and Genesis 17 in Colossians 2:11, 13

In Col 2:11–13, Paul has made reference to the thought and language of the two great circumcision texts of the Scriptures of his people, Gen 17 and Deut 30:6. According to Paul, the promised circumcision of the heart that God himself would perform in the glorious restoration of his people Israel had arrived in the coming of Messiah Jesus. Moreover, it had been wrought among pagan gentiles in western Asia Minor in the obscure town of Colossae. In this circumcision God had removed, not a part of the flesh, but the *whole*, the fallen bodily existence inherited from Adam. By this the Colossians participated in the circumcision that Christ underwent: they died and were buried in his death and burial.

In this act they were permanently removed from the domination of the old fallen age with all its malevolent angelic powers.

The Colossians desperately needed this spiritual circumcision because they, along with all the rest of unredeemed humanity, abided in a state of spiritual *un*circumcision—a spiritually dead existence characterized by rebellion against divine standards. They were morally unclean and thus excluded from God's new covenant community. To remedy this, God had circumcised them and then brought them to life. With this language, Paul stresses the "already" of his already/not yet inaugurated eschatology to emphasize that the Colossians presently enjoyed all the "fullness" of God in Christ. They neither needed to look to angelic powers nor to defunct and superseded Mosaic covenant stipulations for the wisdom, life, aid, and protection that they sought.

CHAPTER ELEVEN

THE SCRIPTURES OF ISRAEL IN COLOSSIANS 2:16–23:
THE ECHO OF ISAIAH 29:13 IN 2:22

Comparison of Textual Versions and Evaluation

Isaiah 29:13 MT	Isaiah 29:13 LXX	Colossians 2:22
וַיֹּאמֶר אֲדֹנָי יַעַן כִּי	καὶ εἶπεν κύριος	ἅ ἐστιν πάντα
נִגַּשׁ הָעָם הַזֶּה בְּפִיו	ἐγγίζει μοι ὁ λαὸς	εἰς φθορὰν τῇ
וּבִשְׂפָתָיו כִּבְּדוּנִי וְלִבּוֹ רִחַק	οὗτος τοῖς χείλεσιν	ἀποχρήσει, κατὰ
מִמֶּנִּי וַתְּהִי יִרְאָתָם אֹתִי	αὐτῶν τιμῶσίν με	τὰ <u>ἐντάλματα</u>
מִצְוַת אֲנָשִׁים מְלֻמָּדָה:	ἡ δὲ καρδία αὐτῶν	<u>καὶ</u> <u>διδασκαλίας</u>
	πόρρω ἀπέχει ἀπ' ἐμοῦ	<u>τῶν</u> <u>ἀνθρώπων</u>
	μάτην δὲ σέβονταί	
	με διδάσκοντες	
	<u>ἐντάλματα</u> <u>ἀνθρώπων</u>	
	<u>καὶ</u> <u>διδασκαλίας</u>	

This proposal meets our two criteria necessary for an echo: 1) availability and 2) word agreement. Regarding *availability*, Paul quotes from Isa 29:14 at 1 Cor 1:19, Isa 29:16 at Rom 9:20, and Isa 29:10 at Rom 11:8 (with Deut 29:3[4]), demonstrating Paul's familiarity with Isa 29. Regarding *word agreement*, the two texts share four words that are in syntactical agreement, though Paul has altered the somewhat awkward word order of the LXX to make for better Greek. Numerous other scholars have already detected Isa 29:13 in Col 2:22.[1]

---

[1] Hühn, *Citate*, 198; Lightfoot, *Colossians*, 204; Abbott, *Colossians*, 275; Beare, "Colossians," 207; Masson, *Colossiens*, 137n.3 ("citation de Es. 29.13"); Ellis, *Paul's Use of the Old Testament*, 154; Lohmeyer, *Kolosser*, 128n.5; Moule, *Colossians*, 108; Lohse, *Colossians*, 124; Lindemann, *Der Kolosserbrief*, 51; Hugedé, *Colossiens*, 156; Caird, *Paul's Letters from Prison*, 201; Fred O. Francis, "A Re-examination of the Colossian Controversy," 164; Martin, *Colossians*, 97; Ernst, *Kolosser*, 213; Schweizer, *Colossians*, 167 (who mistakenly states that the quotation is from LXX *Jeremiah* 29:13 and not Isaiah); Gnilka, *Der Kolosserbrief*, 158; O'Brien, *Colossians*, 151; Bratcher, *Old Testament Quotations in the New Testament*, 58; Bruce, *Colossians*, 127; Wright, *Colossians*, 126; Hoppe, *Kolosserbrief*, 137; Furter, *Colossiens*, 156–57; Pokorný, *Colossians*, 153; Aletti, *Colossiens*, 203; Barth and Blanke, *Colossians*, 64, 357; Wolter, *Der Brief an die Kolosser*, 152–53; Dunn, *Colossians*, 193; Arnold, *Colossian*

Old Testament Context: Isaiah 29:13–14

The oracle of Isa 29:13–14, in the form of an announcement of judgment,[2] is found within the literary block of Isa 28–33, which is concerned with the imminent Assyrian threat to Jerusalem of 705–701 B.C.E.[3] In this section, Isaiah denounces Jerusalem's leaders, both civil (29:14) and religious (29:10; cf. 28:7) for their faithlessness to YHWH. The civil leaders have turned to Egypt for aid against the Assyrian juggernaut instead of God (30:1–7, 31:1–3), while the religious leaders, the prophets and seers (and priests?), are spiritually blind and incapacitated like drunkards (29:9–10). The people they were to shepherd worship idols of silver and gold (30:22, 31:6–7) and do not want to hear any instruction from YHWH (30:9–11). For their rebellion and faithlessness God threatens Jerusalem and the surrounding region of Judah with devastation by the hand of Assyria (28:22, 29:1–8, 30:12–17).

The unit of 29:13–14 fits into this context as a further continuation of the denunciation of the religious leaders and the people they lead. Because the people's YHWH worship is mere lip service (their true loyalties are with their idols and with Egypt) and follows instruction that originates merely in men, God is soon to bring an astonishing work of judgment upon the religious leaders in that any remnants of true wisdom that they may yet possess will be removed from them. Such leaders are the "wise" and the "understanding" of the people, but because they have forsaken the LORD and have failed to lead the people, true wisdom and understanding will vanish from Jerusalem.

The unit of 29:13–14 begins with an indictment of accusation (v. 13).[4] The indictment consists of two parts. First, the people do not offer true worship from the heart to God.[5] Their loyalties are elsewhere, with their idols and with Egypt (30:1–7, 22, 31:1–3, 6–7). They offer

---

Syncretism, 223; Hübner, *An die Kolosser*, 91; Hay, *Colossians*, 111; MacDonald, *Colossians*, 116; Lincoln, "Colossians," 634 (via the Jesus tradition found at Mark 7); Fee, "Old Testament Intertextuality in Colossians," ad loc.; Beale, "Colossians," ad loc.; cf. Hübner, *Vetus Testamentum in Novo*, 538–39; NA[27] side margin; UBS[4] bottom note.

[2] Sweeney, *Isaiah 1–39*, 380.
[3] Sweeney, *Isaiah 1–39*, 353.
[4] Sweeney, *Isaiah 1–39*, 380.
[5] The verb נָגַשׁ ("to draw near, approach"; LXX: ἐγγίζω) here likely carries cultic overtones, as it often does in the Hebrew Bible (e.g., Exod 19:22, 20:21, 24:2, 28:43, 30:20; Lev 2:8, 8:14, 21:21 [twice], 23; Num 4:19, 8:19; Amos 5:25; Mal 1:7, 8, 3:3). Behind its use may be the thought of when the people are actually in the temple

God lip service all the while their heart belongs to another god, to what they believe will offer security from the imminent Assyrian threat. Second, the worship or devotion they do offer to God is to a god made in the image of their religious leaders' fanciful imagination. These have prescribed instruction that has its origin merely in man, and not in accord with divine revelation. The people therefore go astray from God even as they think they please him.

Because of this, an announcement of punishment in v. 14 follows the indictment of v. 13.[6] God through his prophet announces in the first line of v. 14 that he is about to deal in an astonishing manner with his rebellious people.[7] The second line either interprets what the punishment of the first line is or is the result that flows out of that punishment. The second line announces that the wisdom and discernment of Judah's "wise" and "discerning" men will perish and be hidden. The identification of these "wise" and "discerning" of Judah is not certain, but based on the context of chs. 28–33, they are probably to be understood as the religious leaders of the people (see esp. 29:9–10).[8] As judgment for the ineptitude of their spiritual leadership, YHWH is removing any remnants of true wisdom that the religious leaders of Jerusalem and of Judah may have otherwise possessed. Seers will no longer have access to visions, nor the prophets to the oracles that give understanding of events from God's point of view (cf. 29:11–12). The religious leaders will be left with their own corrupt wisdom and devices. Their judgment consists in being cut off from access to God and to his instruction and wisdom. This "deep sleep," this spiritual blindness, is directly from God (29:9–10; cf. Isa 6:9–10).

---

precincts presenting their sacrifices to the priests, or it may be more metaphorical and general in its scope. See H. Ringgren, "נגשׁ," *TDOT* 9:216–17.

[6] Sweeney, *Isaiah 1–39*, 380.

[7] The LXX reads instead that God will proceed to "remove" (possibly an allusion to the exile) or "change" the people, possibly in a look forward to the positive word of renewal at 29:17–24 (the verb μετατίθημι can be used to connote either meaning; see entry in Lust, LSJ, BDAG).

[8] Hans Wildberger, *Isaiah 28–39* (trans. Thomas H. Trapp; CC; Minneapolis: Fortress, 2002), 91–92, interprets the "wise" and "intelligent" as "those who serve as the king's advisers" and "politicians."

Isaiah 29:13–14 in Early and Late Judaism

The extant writings of early Judaism do not quote Isa 29:13–14. Neither the apocryphal nor the pseudepigraphical literature, nor the DSS exhibit any overt reference back to it. Neither Josephus nor Philo cite it. It does show up in later Judaism, but only rarely, and there is no citation of it in the Mishnah, Tosefta, or Talmud (Babylonian or Palestinian). At *Midr. Rabbah* Exodus 5.14, the text of Isa 19:11 ("the princes of Zoan are utterly foolish; the wise counselors of Pharaoh give stupid counsel"; NRSV) is further interpreted by Isa 29:14. The Pharaoh's counselors offer "wisdom" that is actually foolishness, because they do not know the God of Israel.[9] Thus the text is applied to *Egyptian* court counselors. Elsewhere it is applied to the righteous of Israel: the righteous are the genuinely "wise" and "understanding" whose demise grieves God.[10] Elsewhere, Isa 29:13–14 is cited to warn those who claim to put God first but do not honor father and mother (Exod 20:12).[11] This text has a remarkable similarity to the argument of Jesus in Mark 7:6–13// Matt 15:1–9, which quotes both Isa 29:13 as well as Exod 20:12 // Deut 5:16 ("Honor your father and your mother"). Such worship is mere lip-service and is liable to harsh punishment.

New Testament Context: Isaiah 29:13 in Colossians 2:22

The exegetical difficulties of the section of text within which the allusion to Isa 29:13 is embedded are numerous and infamous (2:16–23). Space does not allow a detailed study of every jot and tittle. What follows below nevertheless is to a large degree an exegetical investigation, with the study concentrating upon the major issues. We will look especially at how the presence of LXX Isa 29:13 affects the passage.

Colossians 2:16

At 2:16 Paul adduces an inference from his argument in vv. 9–15. Because the salvific benefits described in vv. 9–15 apply to those in Christ, therefore the Colossian faithful are not to let their opponents

---

[9] Cf. *Midr.* Proverbs, chapter 27 (pp. 111–12).
[10] *Midr. Rabbah* Lamentations 1.9 §37.
[11] *Tanna Debe Eliyyahu*, ER 134.

condemn them because they do not observe the dietary food laws or the sacred days of the Jews as prescribed in the Scriptures of Israel. That Paul has in mind the Mosaic Law is made clear in the second half of the verse with the mention of ἑορτῆς ἢ νεομηνίας ἢ σαββάτων ("feast or new moon observance or Sabbaths"). This tripartite phrase stems directly from the Greek Old Testament and is found in several places there (though the word sequence varies among these). The phrase serves as a sort of summary statement of all the festivals and sacred days that the Torah of Moses required the Jews to observe (1 Chr 23:31; 2 Chr 2:3, 31:3; Ezek 45:17; Hos 2:13; Neh 10:34; 1 Esd 5:51; Jdt 8:6; 1 Macc 10:34; cf. Isa 1:13–14; *Jub.* 1:14).

In light of this, the mention of "food" and "drink" (ἐν βρώσει καὶ ἐν πόσει) in the first half of v. 16 is also to be understood as a reference to laws prescribed by the Mosaic covenant, namely, the dietary regulations as found in Lev 11, 17:10–14, and Deut 14:3–21. Some have argued that drinks were not included among the dietary regulations of the Mosaic covenant, except in the special case of the Nazirites (see Num 6:1–4) or in the case of the priests serving at the tabernacle (Lev 10:9).[12] But this is to overlook the prescription found at Lev 11:32–34 that covers drink in a comprehensive way. It is true that no drinks were unclean in themselves, as was the case for some foods, such as the pig (Lev 11:7). But any drinkable liquid could easily become unclean by virtue of being contained in a vessel that came into contact with a dead specimen of any of the eight swarming creatures (Lev 11:29–34). The text reads at Lev 11:32–34 that

> anything upon which any of [the eight swarming creatures] falls when they are dead shall be unclean, whether an article of wood or cloth or skin or sacking, any article that is used for any purpose....And if any of them falls into any earthen vessel, all that is in it shall be unclean....Any food that could be eaten shall be unclean if water from any such vessel comes upon it; *and any liquid that could be drunk shall be unclean if it was in any such vessel.*   (NRSV; emphasis mine)

Two things can be observed from this passage. First, drinkable liquids (or at least "water") can serve as a transmitter of uncleanness. Second, any drinkable liquid becomes unclean if found to be in a vessel that had become unclean. The least that can be said is that drink was in

---

[12] E.g., O'Brien, *Colossians*, 138 (who nevertheless shows awareness of Lev 11:34, 36); Lincoln, *Colossians*, 631.

fact within the realm regulated by the Mosaic covenant and almost
certainly would have been a dietary concern for conscientious Jews
seeking to be faithful to Torah in first-century Colossae and its environs.
Unclean swarming creatures, like the mouse and lizard, would have
posed a continual problem for Jews seeking to maintain a "clean" status
because of their ubiquity in the ancient world.

That Jewish dietary regulations are in view at Col 2:16a is further
confirmed by the striking parallel in Rom 14.[13] The problem in view
at Rom 14 is that some Jewish Christians, as well as perhaps some
Gentiles, "could not with a clear conscience give up the observance
of such requirements of the law as the distinction between clean and
unclean foods, the avoidance of blood, the keeping of the Sabbath and
other [Jewish] special days."[14]

This minority was "passing judgment" or "condemning"—the Greek
word is κρίνω, the same word as in Col 2:16a—the majority for their
failure to observe such regulations of the Mosaic covenant. Paul employs
the word κρίνω five times in this way in the context (Rom 14:3, 4, 10,
13, 22). The apostle sides with the strong, declaring all foods to be clean
(Rom 14:14, 20; 15:1), but urges that love dictate the disagreement so
that there may be peace (vv. 15, 19). Paul buttresses his argument with
the assertion that "the kingdom of God is not food and drink [βρῶσις
καὶ πόσις] but righteousness and peace and joy in the Holy Spirit"
(v. 17 NRSV), indicating that there were scruples over both food and drink.
Significantly, the word for "drink," πόσις, occurs only three times in
the NT: here at Rom 14:17, once at John 6:55, and finally at Col 2:16,
the passage currently under investigation.[15] In Rom 14, a "drink" is
specifically mentioned in the context, that of "wine" (οἶνος; v. 21). As

---

[13] Cf. also Dunn, *Colossians*, 173–74.

[14] C. E. B. Cranfield, *The Epistle to the Romans* (2 vols.; ICC; Edinburgh: T&T Clark,
1979), 2:695; see also D. Moo, *The Epistle to the Romans* (NICNT; Grand Rapids: Eerdmans, 1996), 829–32; J. D. G. Dunn, *Romans 9–16* (WBC 38B; Dallas: Word, 1988),
799–802. Peter J. Tomson, *Paul and the Jewish Law: Halakha in the Letters of the Apostle to
the Gentiles* (CRINT 3/1; Assen/Maastricht: Van Gorcum, 1990), 244, focuses especially
on the dietary aspect and writes, "Thus it seems that the food problem in Rom 14 was
complex. At one level Paul's plea appears to have been for willingness on the part of
gentile Christians to make allowances for basic Jewish food laws. On another level, he
argued that gentile Christians should also bear with [Jewish] "hyper-halakhic" anxieties
regarding gentile wine and meat. As we have seen the details are not quite decisive
and we have to leave both possibilities open."

[15] Even the use at John 6:55 (also used with βρῶσις) has Jewish dietary regulations
as the crucial backdrop to Jesus' offensive statement found there.

mentioned previously, wine was only off limits to some Jews, namely, those who took a nazirite vow (Num 6:2–4; cf. v. 20). Daniel, however, also abstained from wine that came from the royal rations of Babylon, lest he become "defiled" (גאל II; Dan 1:8). The language suggests that the concern is with Torah-prescribed dietary regulations.[16] At Dan 10:3, however, the text does not make sense apart from the presupposition that at other times, Daniel did drink wine.[17] The problem at Dan 1:8 then, is that the food and wine come from the "royal rations," i.e., from pagan food-preparers in the king's service who knew and cared nothing for Jewish dietary regulations. Thus Daniel had no way of knowing whether the food and wine given him to eat was unclean or not. His action therefore probably "can be understood as an attempt to safeguard the observance of the Levitical laws."[18] Collins also cites LXX Esth 4:17, Tob 1:10–11, Jdt 12:1–4, 1 Macc 1:61–62 [see vv. 62–63], and *Jub.* 22:16 as texts that show similar Jewish concern with unclean foods.[19] To these texts that Collins adduces could be added 3 Macc 3:4 and 3:7, 2 Macc 6:18–31, and 4 Macc 5:1–6:30. Collins adds further that "there is, moreover, a general assumption in the Prophets that the food eaten in exile would be unclean (Hos 9:3–4; Ezek 4:13)."[20]

On p. 143 in n. 140, Collins mentions also *Let. Aris.* §§128–171 and §181 as further evidence. Collins does, however, appear to have overlooked the explicit mention at §128 of *drink* as a category of food covered by the Levitical purity laws: "It is my opinion that mankind as a whole shows a certain amount of concern for the parts of [the Jews'] legislation concerning meats *and drink* and beasts considered to be unclean."[21] This concern is also found at §§180b–82. The king of Egypt addresses the delegation of Jews who have embarked from Israel and arrived at Alexandria in order to translate the Hebrew Bible into Greek:

> "It will therefore be my wish to dine with you this day. Everything of which you partake," he said, "will be served in compliance with your habits; it

---

[16] So John J. Collins, *Daniel* (Hermeneia; Minneapolis: Fortress, 1993), 142.

[17] Collins, *Daniel,* 143.

[18] Collins, *Daniel,* 142.

[19] Collins, *Daniel,* 142–43.

[20] Collins, *Daniel,* 143.

[21] R. J. H. Shutt, "Letter of Aristeas," in *The Old Testament Pseudepigrapha* (ed. James H. Charlesworth; 2 vols.; ABRL; New York: Doubleday, 1983), 2:21. So also §142: "So, to prevent our being perverted by contact with others or by mixing with bad influences, he hedged us in on all sides with strict observances connected with meat and *drink* and touch and hearing and sight, after the manner of the Law" (emphases mine).

will be served to me as well as to you." [The delegation of Jews] expressed
their pleasure and the king ordered...the preparations for the banquet to
be made.... The number of prominent [Jewish] delegates corresponds to
the number of cities, all having the same customs in matters *of drink* and
food and bedding. All preparations were made in accordance with these
[Jewish] customs, so that when they came in the presence of the kings
they would have a happy visit, with no cause for complaint.[22]

All the above is offered to demonstrate that the mention of "drink" at
Col 2:16a (as well as Rom 14:21) lies well within the scope of Jewish
concerns for maintaining Torah-prescribed dietary regulations in the
first-century C.E. and to establish the validity of the interpretation that
the mention of "drink" at Col 2:16a probably refers to such Jewish
concerns.[23]

Colossians 2:17

At v. 17 Paul gives the reason why the Colossians should not let anyone
pass judgment on them over Torah-prescribed dietary regulations or
sacred days. All of these things are a "shadow" (σκιά) of the coming
things, but the "reality" (σῶμα) belongs to Christ. The "shadow—
reality" language appears to be an idiom to describe the relation of
something that is merely an outline of a thing and that thing in concrete reality. Philo uses this idiom at least twice, once to compare the
mere beauty of a phrase to the real beauty of the matter expressed
in the phrase:

> Again, quit speech also, "thy father's house," as Moses calls it, for fear
> thou shouldst be beguiled *by beauties of mere phrasing*, and be cut off from *the*

---

[22] Shutt, "Letter of Aristeas," *OTP* 2:24–25 (emphasis mine).

[23] In his discussion on the problem of Jewish and Gentile table fellowship, Philip
F. Esler, *Galatians* (London: Routledge, 1998), 93–116, argues that the issue at Gal
2:11–14 (and elsewhere, like Acts) is not due to Torah-prescribed dietary regulations
per se, but rather to a Jewish prohibition against table fellowship with Gentiles *when the
guests at table would be sharing food, drink, and vessels*. The fear was that, by this intimate
association, a Jew would unwittingly commit idolatry in light of the common practice
of the gentiles to offer wine libations to their gods at such meals. According to Esler,
the prohibition stems from the Pentateuchal commands against idolatry.

With regard to Col 2:16 (which Esler does not treat), the evidence in the letter to
the Colossians seems to be too sparse to discern whether this was part of the issue at
Colossae. My point with the evidence I adduce above is simply to highlight that the
mention of "drink" at 2:16 fell well within the scope of orthodox first-century Jewish
concerns, in order to legitimate my reading of 2:16 to be dealing in its entirety with
wholly Jewish concerns, and not with a syncretism of Jewish ("Sabbath") *and* pagan
religious scruples ("food and drink").

real beauty, which lies in the matter expressed. Monstrous it is that *shadow* [σκιάν] should be preferred to *substance* [σωμάτων] or a *copy* to *originals*. And verbal expression is like a *shadow* [σκιᾷ] or *copy*, while the *essential bearing* of the matters conveyed by words resembles *substance* [σώμασι] and *originals*; and it behooves the man, whose aim it is *to be* rather than *to seem*, to dissociate himself from the former and hold fast to the latter.[24]

In the second use, Philo employs the idiom to explain the relationship between the "outward and obvious" interpretation of the Babel incident (Gen 11) and the deeper, "allegorical" interpretation:

> Still I would exhort them not to halt there, but to press on to allegorical interpretations and to recognize that the letter is to the oracle but as the *shadow* [σκιάς] to the *substance* [σωμάτων] and that the higher values therein revealed are what really and truly exist.[25]

The idiom is also found in Josephus in his account of Antipater's oration against Archelaus, who had made himself the successor of his father King Herod upon the latter's death. Archelaus asked for the right to rule from Caesar only well after he had begun to act as king, which was considered a grave offence: "And after all this [Archelaus] had now come to beg from [Caesar] for the *shadow* [σκιάν] of royalty, of which he had already appropriated the *substance* [σῶμα], thus making Caesar a dispenser not of realities, but of mere titles!"[26]

The idiom crops up also in Lucian the satirist (ca. 120–190 C.E.). Lycinus is discussing with one Hermotimus, who is enthralled with a certain philosophy. Lycinus argues that Hermotimus and his fellow philosophers have neglected the "fruit" of philosophy, "acting justly and wisely and bravely," and traded them for the "husk," that is, incessant studying "to find and compose your wretched texts and syllogisms and problems." After Hermotimus concedes the truth of the accusation, Lycinus continues, "Then wouldn't it be right to say that you forget the *substance* [σῶμα] and hunt the *shadow* [σκιάν], or ignore the crawling serpent and hunt the slough?"[27]

Paul has made use of this σκιά—σῶμα idiom, and has set it in a carefully crafted statement. Unlike Philo's use of it to support his allegorical method, Paul sets the idiom within a redemptive-historical framework by his use of the substantival participle τῶν μελλόντων ("the

---

[24] Philo, *Migration* 12 (Colson, Whitaker, and Marcus, LCL; emphasis mine).
[25] Philo, *Confusion* 190 (Colson, Whitaker, and Marcus, LCL; emphasis mine).
[26] Josephus, *J.W.* 2.28 (Thackeray, LCL; emphasis mine).
[27] Lucian, *Hermotimus* 79 (Harmon, Kilburn, MacLeod, LCL; emphasis mine).

coming things").[28] Paul carefully selects his argument because Torah-prescribed sacred days and dietary regulations were *from God* and were in force for Israel, the people of God, for an appointed age in history. But in Paul's understanding, these were "shadows" that served in this old age to point forward to the "reality" of the coming age, to the Messiah (τοῦ Χριστοῦ; v. 17b; cf. Heb 10:1). The rhetorical effect of the use of the "shadow-reality" idiom is to persuade the reader that these Mosaic covenant stipulations are no longer in force now that Messiah has arrived and ushered in the "age-to-come."

Colossians 2:18–19

Paul attacks the philosophy on several fronts, and in vv. 18–19 he takes aim at the arrogance bred by the visionary heavenly ascent element of the heterodox teaching. The exegetical difficulties of 2:18a–b are infamous, and much ink has been spilled in trying to make sense of the pieces. We will take these difficulties up one at a time.

The Colossians are to let no one "rule against" (καταβραβευέτω) them (v. 18a). The word in context likely carries semantic overlap with the word κρινέτω in v. 16a.[29] The metaphor is probably from a judicial or legal, and not an athletic, contest (see below on ἐμβατεύω). The word καταβραβεύω is rare. It occurs in the NT only here at Col 2:18 and is not found in the LXX, Josephus, Philo, the pseudepigraphical literature, or the Apostolic Fathers. The two extant occurrences of the word[30] that temporally precede Paul's use occur in a legal or judicial context. In Demosthenes (384–322 B.C.E.), *Against Meidias*, a wealthy and ruthless man named Meidias, having been condemned lawfully in a suit through the legal arbitrator Strato, takes his vengeance on the unassuming Strato. Through trickery, Meidias is able to appeal against Strato in court in the latter's absence and have him stripped of all his Athenian civic rights. The text states that in this legal action, Meidias was able to have Strato "ruled against" or "condemned" (καταβραβευθέντα) by an unsuspecting arbitrator or judge.[31]

---

[28] Cf. Matt 12:32; Eph 1:21; 1 Cor 3:22; Heb 2:5, 6:5; 1 Tim 4:8.

[29] So also Hay, *Colossians*, 105.

[30] BDAG mentions a third occurrence in the works of Didymus the grammarian (1st century B.C.E.–1st century C.E.), but I was unable to locate it in his works either manually or by a *TLG* search.

[31] Demosthenes, *Against Medias*, 93 (J. H. Vince, LCL, renders the verb as "victimized," but this translation fails to catch the judicial verdict of the law-court in the action being taken against Strato).

The second extant use of the verb temporally prior to Paul's use in Col 2:18 is found in inscription 4512[B.57], dated between 167–134 B.C.E.[32] The inscription deals with "a Ptolemaic dispute regarding succession."[33] While the MM quotation of the Greek from the inscription is not lengthy, what is offered bears striking resemblance to petitions to ruling or court authorities for legal redress in situations of illegal acquisition or use of another's property or inheritance.[34]

A third extant use of the term καταβραβεύω dates to the second century C.E. The verb is used by the astrologer Vettius Valens, who writes that "the earth appears... to rule over [καταβραβεύειν] the rest, herself holding in all things as a parent."[35] The word is used generally with no legal overtones. Chrysostom (died ca. 407 C.E.) preached in a homily on Colossians 2:16–19 that the verb καταβραβεύω "is employed when the victory is with one party, and the prize with another, when though a victor thou art thwarted."[36] This general definition would fit well in a context of either a legal or athletic contest. The upshot for all of this for Col 2:18 is that the verb καταβραβεύω is probably synonymous with κρίνω, has a judicial ring to it, and can be translated as "to rule against, to condemn."

At 2:18b–c, the heterodox proponents "rule against" or "condemn" the Colossian faithful by their "delighting in" (θέλων ἐν)[37] the "humility and worship of the angels, which things they had seen upon entering." But what does all of that mean? 2:18b–c has given commentators fits, yet the clause is also primarily responsible for why scholars understand the philosophy that Paul combats in the letter to be syncretistic in nature.

The first question that must be answered is whether the phrase τῶν ἀγγέλων as attached to θρησκείᾳ is an objective ("worship directed toward the angels") or subjective genitive ("worship the angels offer [to God]"). Either is a genuine grammatical possibility, and both uses

---

[32] MM, "καταβραβεύω," 324.

[33] MM, 324.

[34] See S. R. Llewelyn, ed., *New Documents Illustrating Early Christianity* (9 vols.; Sydney, Australia: Macquarie University, 1994), 7:130–49.

[35] MM, "καταβραβεύω," 324. Translation mine.

[36] Chrysostom, "Homily VII: Colossians ii.16–19," *NPNF*[1] 13:288.

[37] There is good evidence in the LXX that this is an idiom meaning "to delight in." See 1 Sam 18:22; 2 Sam 15:26; 1 Kgs 10:9; 1 Chr 28:4; LXX Pss 111:1, 146:10; *T. Ash.* 1:6; see BDAG, "θέλω," 3.b; cf. O'Brien, *Colossians*, 142; Dunn, *Colossians*, 178; Wolter, *Der Brief an die Kolosser*, 145.

are attested in contemporaneous literature.[38] The question cannot be answered apart from the context, and in this case, the following phrase ἃ ἑόρακεν ἐμβατεύων provides crucial information for the correct answer. The relative pronoun ἃ is the object of the verb ἑόρακεν.[39] Significantly, the relative pronoun is neuter plural, yet there is no antecedent that is neuter and plural. This is because the relative pronoun is being employed to signal that the antecedent includes the totality of the things just mentioned, irrespective of the gender of the individual antecedents. In this case the antecedent is ἐν ταπεινοφροσύνῃ καὶ θρησκείᾳ τῶν ἀγγέλων.[40] This use of a neuter plural relative to refer back to the totality of a plural antecedent actually occurs several times in the immediate context (ἃ: 2:17, 18, 22, 3:6; ἅτινα: 2:23). This means that what the person has "seen," upon "entering" (ἐμβατεύων, which is in a temporal relationship to the main verb ἑόρακεν) is the "humility and worship of angels." This is the content of what has been seen by the heterodox opponent, and what he "delights in."

Until the seminal work of F. Francis, most scholars interpreted the genitive τῶν ἀγγέλων as attached to θρησκείᾳ as an objective genitive ("worship directed toward the angels").[41] Many scholars have accepted Francis's proposal and built upon it.[42] These scholars take

---

[38] For examples of both the subjective as well as the objective use, see Arnold, *Colossian Syncretism*, 90–92. Arnold opts for the objective genitive after adducing strong evidence for it (92–95).

[39] For the interpretation that the relative ἃ introduces the direct object of the participle ἐμβατεύων and not of the main verb ἑόρακεν, see Arnold, *Colossian Syncretism*, 121–23, who then has to translate the phrase as "invoking angels because he 'entered the things he had seen'" (123). The subjective genitive interpretation is crucial to Arnold's overall argument, and this interpretation leads him to have to take the relative pronoun in this way. This decision with the relative, however, is very awkward syntactically and much less probable than taking the relative naturally as the object of ἑόρακεν.

[40] So also Lohse, *Colossians*, 120n.50; Fred O. Francis, "Humility and Angel Worship in Col 2:18," in *Conflict At Colossae: A Problem in the Interpretation of Early Christianity Illustrated by Selected Modern Studies* (eds. and trans. Fred O. Francis and Wayne A. Meeks; rev. ed.; Missoula, Mont.: Scholars Press and SBL, 1975), 167; Christopher Rowland, "Apocalyptic Visions and the Exaltation of Christ in the Letter to the Colossians," in *The Pauline Writings: A Sheffield Reader* (eds. Stanley E. Porter and Craig A. Evans; Sheffield: Sheffield Academic Press, 1995; repr. from *JSNT* 19 [1983]: 73–83), 225–26; Sappington, *Revelation and Redemption*, 160; cf. Dunn, *Colossians*, 182 (body and also n.29).

[41] Francis, "Humility," 164. He notes, however, that others before him had taken the genitive as a subjective (e.g., "Ephraem, Luther, Melanchthon, Wolf, Dalmer, Hofmann, Zahn, Ewald").

[42] E.g., O'Brien, *Colossians*, xxxvi–xxxviii, 142–45; Craig A. Evans, "The Colossian Mystics," *Biblica* 63 (1982): 188–205; Rowland, "Apocalyptic Visions," 220–28; Roy Yates, "'The Worship of Angels' (Col 2:18)," *ExpTim* 97 (1985): 12–15; Sappington, *Revelation and Redemption*, 17–20 and throughout; Dunn, *Colossians*, 180–84.

the construction as a subjective genitive ("worship the angels offer [to God]"). Francis argued that the most likely background was not the mystery religions and initiation into such cults, as the standard hypothesis begun in 1917 by Martin Dibelius proposed.[43] Francis proposed instead that the closest background lay in "ascetic and mystic trends of piety" wherein one partook of rigorous asceticism in order to obtain visionary entrance into the heavenly realm.[44] Thomas J. Sappington has built upon Francis's work (in my opinion, in a generally successful way) narrowing the background even further to this type of piety as found within Jewish apocalypticism.[45] If Sappington is correct, then the heterodox teaching is fundamentally Jewish (whether stemming from Jews or Christian Jews, or Gentiles proselytized by these). The background material adduced by Francis and those building upon him demonstrates the deep-seated influence of the "heavenly vision" stream in Jewish apocalyptic piety and makes for an attractive background for understanding Col 2:16–23.[46]

---

[43] Martin Dibelius, "The Isis Initiation in Apuleius and Related Initiatory Rites," in *Conflict At Colossae: A Problem in the Interpretation of Early Christianity Illustrated by Selected Modern Studies* (eds. and trans. Fred O. Francis and Wayne A. Meeks; rev. ed.; Missoula, Mont.: Scholars Press and SBL, 1975), 61–121.

[44] Francis, "Humility," 166 and throughout.

[45] Sappington, *Revelation and Redemption*, 21.

[46] See again n.42 above for some scholars who have built upon Francis and who offer a wealth of Jewish background. Cf. James M. Scott, "Heavenly Ascent in Jewish and Pagan Traditions," *DNTB* 447–52. Other recent proposals for the background of the Colossian "philosophy" includes Richard E. DeMaris's proposal that the heterodox teaching "appears to be a distinctive blend of popular Middle Platonic, Jewish, and Christian elements that cohere around the pursuit of wisdom" (*The Colossian Controversy: Wisdom in Dispute at Colossae* [JSNTSup 96; Sheffield: JSOT Press, 1994], 17), Troy W. Martin's proposal that the opponents were "Cynic philosophers" (*By Philosophy and Empty Deceit: Colossians as Response to a Cynic Critique* [JSNTSup 118; Sheffield: Sheffield Academic Press, 1996], 15), and Clinton E. Arnold's hypothesis that the background is a syncretistic Phrygian folk belief (*The Colossian Syncretism: The Interface Between Christianity and Folk Belief at Colossae* [WUNT 2/77; Tübingen: J. C. B. Mohr (Paul Siebeck), 1995; reprint, Grand Rapids: Baker, 1996]).

I find Arnold's hypothesis especially attractive, but because his work unjustifiably downplays the strong Jewish element of the philosophy, nor explains how the philosophy's emphasis on the local angelic powers explains the letter's emphasis on wisdom, I am forced to conclude that Arnold's hypothesis does not capture fully the background situation of the problem at Colossae that made it necessary for the apostle to write his letter. I cannot help but wonder whether the solution is found in a combination of the hypotheses of Arnold and Sappington, though I am convinced that the philosophy is fundamentally a Hellenistic Judaism possibly influenced by surrounding pagan ideas of the spirit world, and not fundamentally pagan folk belief sprinkled with a few elements of Jewish religion.

A working hypothesis of what the philosophy may have taught will now be given at this point to provide a working framework so that the reader doesn't get lost in the rest of this section's detailed exegetical arguments. Cautiously putting the pieces together, it appears that the adherents of the philosophy were advocating ascetic rigor, with conformity to standards of the Mosaic covenant as a foundational prerequisite (especially circumcision, Sabbath and festival observance, and dietary regulations), in order to attain visionary heavenly ascent, wherein one could enter the heavenly inheritance and "see" (and join with?) the angels of heaven in their worship of God. Those who had experienced such amazing spiritual experiences had become arrogant and insinuated that Christians who had not experienced heaven in this way were disqualified from the heavenly inheritance.

Returning to the exegesis proper, the reader will recall that the verb καταβραβεύω found at 2:18, though rare, was found in legal contexts with the case presented before an arbitrator. Significantly, the verb ἐμβατεύω, also found at Col 2:18, occurs several times in the papyri in legal contexts of property or inheritance rights.[47] In these instances, the verb may be translated "to take possession of [a property or inheritance]."[48] Whether this is lawfully or unlawfully done depends upon the context. Noteworthy is the lexicographer Pausanias's use of the verb (2nd century C.E.) in his lexical entry for the ἐξούλης δίκη, a legal suit that prosecuted the accused for any use of immovable property (like a piece of land) without the consent of the lawful owner.[49] He wrote that a ἐξούλης δίκη was a lawsuit taken up when

> those who won a lawsuit so as to recover a piece of land or home, upon taking possession [ἐμβατεύειν] are being prevented, or after taking possession [ἐμβατεύσαντες] are being driven out, are entering into lawsuit with those driving them out or not permitting them to take possession [ἐμβατεύειν]. And this ἐξούλης δίκη is being named from [the verb] ἐξίλλειν ["to keep forcibly from"].[50]

---

[47] See the abundant evidence in MM, "ἐμβατεύω," p. 205; Fred O. Francis, "The Background of EMBATEUEIN (Col 2:18) in Legal Papyri and Oracle Inscriptions," in *Conflict At Colossae: A Problem in the Interpretation of Early Christianity Illustrated by Selected Modern Studies* (eds. and trans. Fred O. Francis and Wayne A. Meeks; rev. ed.; Missoula, Mont.: Scholars Press and SBL, 1975), 198–99.

[48] Cf. Francis, "The Background of EMBATEUEIN," 197, who writes that the most common meaning of the verb is "entry into possession of property"; MM, "ἐμβατεύω," p. 205; cf. BDAG, "ἐμβατεύω," def. 2.

[49] Llewelyn, *New Documents*, 148.

[50] Translation mine, based upon the Greek text found on the *TLG*.

Note the three uses of ἐμβατεύω in the definition of a lawsuit over property and its meaning "to take possession [of property]." Nevertheless, a lawsuit background need not be present for the word to have this meaning. Compare the use in Euripides's *Children of Heracles* (fifth-century B.C.E.):

> Children, now at last you will be free from trouble, free from the accursed Eurystheus! You will see your father's city and take possession of [ἐμβατεύσετε] your estates [κλήρους...χθονός] and sacrifice to the gods of your ancestors, from whom you have been cut off as you lived the life of wandering strangers.[51]

There are three things to observe here. First, note the use of ἐμβατεύω with its common meaning "to enter into possession of an inheritance or property." Second, note the explicit mention of the property as κλήρους...χθονός, literally, "inheritances of land." Third, note that the children are taking possession of property that is rightfully theirs, but from which they were barred wrongfully (or illegally) until the time of the speech.

Another use of the verb ἐμβατεύω in this way is found in the LXX at Joshua 19:49 and 51. Note the use at v. 49: "And they proceeded *to take possession of* [ἐμβατεῦσαι] the land according to their boundaries. And the sons of Israel gave an *inheritance* [κλῆρον] to Joshua, son of Nun among them." The context is the conquest of the Promised Land under the leadership of Joshua, Moses' successor. Israel has experienced the exodus out of Egypt and is now fighting to take over land that is now rightfully theirs: God had given it to them as their "inheritance."

In light of all of the evidence above, it is highly significant that Paul discusses the Colossians' salvation in language taken from the biblical exodus account, calling their hope of heaven a μερίδα τοῦ κλήρου, "a share of the inheritance" (1:12) and a κληρονομία, "inheritance" (3:24). We investigated this echo of the exodus in chapter five. Then Paul here in 2:18a employs καταβραβεύω, a term found elsewhere within the context of legal disputes, and subsequently the term ἐμβατεύω at 2:18c, which connotes entry, yet frequently with the nuance of entry into possession of an inheritance or property.[52] Add the references

---

[51] Euripides, *Children of Heracles* 876 (Kovacs, LCL).
[52] Cf. Calvin, *Colossians*, 340, who writes that "the common signification of the word ἐμβατεύειν is 'to enter upon an inheritance', or 'to take possession', or 'to set foot anywhere'."

together, and suddenly one has the real possibility that the Colossian faithful were being harangued by those that made it clear to them that, in their opinion, they had no right to obtain any share in the heavenly inheritance.

The opponents were therefore condemning the Colossian faithful because of their lack of experience or refusal to join in entering heaven through visions, which were brought on in part by rigorous preparatory asceticism. This rigorous preparatory asceticism included full observance of Mosaic covenant regulations as its necessary prerequisite, because it was believed that one needed to be righteous for visionary heavenly entrance.[53] The visionary experiences bred a spiritual elitism within the Christian community, causing some of those who had experienced a vision to pass judgment upon those who had not had such visions and to regard them as "second-class Christians,"[54] even insinuating that they were unworthy of any share in the heavenly inheritance. This makes the statement in Col 1:12 that God had made *all* the Colossian Christians sufficient or worthy of a share of the heavenly inheritance that much more poignant, and supports that this line of interpretation is on the right track.

The Meaning of ταπεινοφροσύνη at 2:18 and 2:23

Francis is probably correct to see in the use of the word ταπεινοφροσύνη ("humility"), at least in the use at 2:23, a reference to ascetic practices including fasting, yet "bound up with regulations of much broader effect than fasting."[55] In the LXX, the idiom "to humble the soul" (ταπεινοῦν τὴν ἑαυτοῦ ψυχήν) could denote forms of self-denial that at times included fasting, bowing of the head, ashes and sackcloth (Lev 16:29, 31, 23:27, 29, 32; Ps 34:13 LXX; Isa 58:3, 5).[56] In Sir 34:26 [ET v. 31], similar language of humbling oneself at minimum embraces fasting: "So if one fasts for his sins, and goes again and does the same things, who will listen to his prayer? And what has he gained by humbling himself [ἐν τῷ ταπεινωθῆναι αὐτόν]?" (NRSV).

---

[53] On this see Sappington, *Revelation and Redemption*, 63–65.
[54] Yates, "Worship of Angels," 14.
[55] Francis, "Humility," 168.
[56] See BDAG, "ταπεινόω," def. 4; on the idiom in Leviticus, see Jacob Milgrom, *Leviticus 1–16* (AB 3; New York: Doubleday, 1991), 1054. Milgrom offers 2 Sam 12:16–20 as an illustration of the activity without the actual use of the idiom.

In LXX Dan 10:12 the text reads that Daniel set his mind *to humble himself*.[57] In context this humiliation includes Daniel's mourning (10:2), his abstention from "rich food," "meat," and "wine" (10:3a NRSV), and the decision not to anoint himself (10:3b), all for a full three weeks (10:2, 3b). His humiliation especially encompasses his lengthy and contrite prayer of confession for Israel and himself due to covenant infidelity (9:4–19), undertaken with "fasting and sackcloth and ashes" (9:3b NRSV). It is because of this humiliation that a heavenly messenger comes to grant understanding to Daniel in a vision that Daniel alone saw (10:1, 7, 12, and 14).

In *Jos. Asen.* chapters 10–13, Aseneth's "humiliation"[58] includes weeping and brooding (10:2), beating of the breast (10:2), fasting for seven days, even from bread and water (10:2, 17; 13:9), wearing a black tunic and the removal of all ornamentation (10:9–11), girding on of sackcloth (10:14), lying in ashes (10:15), and sighing and screaming (10:15c). She grounds her idols down to pieces (10:12), throws her royal dinner to the dogs (10:13), pulls hair from her head (11:1), and engages in two, long, mournful soliloquies (11:3–18). Her time of humiliation climaxes with a lengthy prayer of confession to God (12:1–13:15). As a result of such abject humiliation, no less than the "chief of the house of the Lord and commander of the whole host of the Most High" (14:8) visits her and announces her acceptance with God (see chs. 14–17). Significantly, as with Daniel, Aseneth's self-imposed "humiliation" results in a visitation from heaven.

What then, of the mention of ταπεινοφροσύνη at 2:18, which we have suggested is part of what the philosophy's adherents delight in and have seen upon entering heaven by visionary experience? This humility mentioned at 2:18 would be part of the worship that the angels offered to God and would include demonstrations of deference and submission, prostration, covering of the face and feet, and liturgical confession, as seen in Isa 6:2–3 and Rev 4:8–11. The adherents to the philosophy, then, are possibly emulating the humility that they have seen the angels render before God in heaven (cf. 2:18 with 2:23).

---

[57] The verb is ταπεινόω, which is closely related to ταπεινοφροσύνη.

[58] Greek: ταπείνωσις; see 10:17; 11:2, 6, 10, 12, 17; 13:1; 15:3; cf. the use of the same word at *T. Jos.* 10:2.

All of these examples well illustrate some practices that were possibly included in the use of the term at Col 2:18 and 23.[59] It is noteworthy that at Col 2:23 the phrase ἀφειδίᾳ σώματος, "severe treatment of the body," is in apposition to ταπεινοφροσύνῃ; the καί between the two words is in brackets in the NA[27]/UBS[4] to show its highly uncertain status as the original reading. It should, in fact, be omitted.[60] The phrase ἀφειδίᾳ σώματος ("severe treatment of the body") then further explains what is meant by ταπεινοφροσύνῃ ("humility") and confirms Francis's interpretation of the word. It encompasses ascetic rigors done to express devotion to God and which probably serve to prepare the practitioner for entrance into heaven by means of visionary experience. In the immediate context of Colossians, such rigors certainly included, at the least, regulations about certain foods and drinks (2:16, 21–22).

Colossians 2:20–23

In vv. 20–23 Paul offers four reasons why the Colossian faithful should not embrace the "philosophy." First, the Colossians have died with Christ, a momentous event that had taken them out from under the pervasive influence of the τὰ στοιχεῖα τοῦ κόσμου. This phrase probably refers to spirits, angels, or demons, possibly those believed to be behind and over the stars, planets, moon, and four elements (air, earth, fire, water).[61] According to Arnold, these στοιχεῖα "were an integral

---

[59] References written *after* Paul's letter to the Colossians include: *Pss. Sol.* 3:8; *1 Clem.* 53:2, 55:6; Herm. *Vis.* 3.10.6 and Herm. *Sim.* 5.3.5–7, both of which explicitly employ ταπεινοφροσύνη in context of fasting (the latter also has the verb ταπεινοφρονέω).

[60] This is because both external and internal evidence point toward the omission as the original reading. Externally, the evidence slightly favors the omission with witnesses 𝔭[46] and B attesting its reading, while internally the evidence strongly favors the omission. It is both the shorter as well as the more difficult reading and it better explains the existence of the other variant rather than the other way around. A scribe added the καί to smooth out the reading. Cf. Dunn, *Colossians*, 188n.2; Troy Martin, *By Philosophy and Empty Deceit*, 50–51; Lincoln, "Colossians," 634.

[61] For an excellent history of interpretation of the phrase, as well as an elaboration of the three different interpretations of it defended in scholarship, see A. J. Bandstra, *The Law and the Elements of the World: An Exegetical Study in Aspects of Paul's Teaching* (Kampen: Kok, 1964), 5–30. My position is in line with what Bandstra calls the "Personalized-Cosmological" interpretation, which he defines as "spiritual beings, conceived to be personal, active in and through the physical and heavenly elements" (25). See also Arnold, *Colossian Syncretism*, 158–194, who adduces strong evidence that the στοιχεῖα were in fact defined along these lines in the first century c.e.; cf. Dunn, *Colossians*, 148–51.
It is not so much that the interpretation of the phrase as the physical elements of "earth, water, air, and fire" is wrong, for there is ample evidence for this meaning, as Schweizer, "Slaves of the Elements and Worshippers of Angels: Gal 4:3, 9

part of the present evil age. They function as masters and overlords of unredeemed humanity working through various means—including the Jewish law and pagan religions—to hold their subjects in bondage."[62] The Colossians, in dying with Christ, were removed from the sphere of the present evil age, from the κόσμος, and consequently from the tyranny and control of the στοιχεῖα. These στοιχεῖα, though the philosophy is mediated through humans (κατὰ τὴν παράδοσιν τῶν ἀνθρώπων; 2:8), are in fact the ultimate source or power behind the opponents' religious system (κατὰ τὰ στοιχεῖα τοῦ κόσμου; 2:8).[63] The Colossians were freed from oppressive systems these spirits instituted to capture humanity into bondage. They were not, therefore, to submit to decrees that belonged to the sphere of the κόσμος ("world") and that originated in the demonic, such as those taught by the "philosophy" that was encroaching upon the Colossian church.

Paul in v. 21 quotes some of the opponents' own regulations and he does so in a way that summarizes the gist of their prescriptions: "You may not touch, nor taste, nor handle." The first prohibition is from ἅπτω ("to touch") and is also found as a prohibition several times in Lev 11 (the chapter on dietary regulations) in association with the carcasses of unclean animals.[64] The second prohibition is from γεύομαι ("to taste"), a verb used also at 2 Macc 6:18–20 in the narration of the execution of a Jewish scribe named Eleazar, who refused to eat swine's flesh, a meat prohibited by the Mosaic covenant.[65] It is also frequently found in the early Jewish literature in contexts of voluntary fasting for special purposes.[66] The third verb, θιγγάνω ("to handle, touch"),

---

and Col 2:8, 18, 20," *JBL* 107 (1988): 455–68, has demonstrated. This interpretation simply doesn't extend far enough off of this well-established foundation to embrace the *divinization* of these physical elements, for which there is 1st century C.E. evidence (e.g., Philo, *Decalogue*, 52–54; *Contempl. Life* 3–5). This interpretation makes the best sense of the evidence as found in the immediate context of Col 1–2, with its mention of the "authorities" and "rulers" at 1:16, 2:10, and 2:15 (cf. 2:18). Cf. Lohse, *Colossians*, 96–99; Masson, *Colossiens*, 122–23; Martin, *Colossians*, 10–14; Wright, *Colossians*, 101–2; O'Brien, *Colossians*, 129–132; Furter, *Colossiens*, 133; Hay, *Colossians*, 87–88. For a different opinion, see Aletti, *Colossiens*, 164–67; Barth and Blanke, *Colossians*, 373–78; Yates, *Colossians*, 40; Wolter, *Der Brief an die Kolosser*, 122–24.

[62] *Colossian Syncretism*, 194.

[63] Arnold, *Colossian Syncretism*, 188.

[64] LXX Lev 11:8, 24, 26, 27, 31, 36, 39; see also Lev 5:2, 7:19, 21; Deut 14:8.

[65] See also the attempt to force Jewesses to eat swine's flesh at the instigation of Flaccus (Philo, *Flaccus*, 96); see too 4 Macc 5:2, 6; 6:15; 10:1. The verb employed in these texts is ἀπογεύω ("to taste"), which is synonymous with γεύομαι.

[66] 1 Sam 14:24; 2 Sam 3:35; 1 Esd 9:2; Jonah 3:7; Acts 23:14; *Jos. Asen.* 10:20; *T. Reu.* 1:10; *T. Zeb.* 4:2; Josephus, *Ant.*, 6.119, 377; 7.42; 11.147; Tob 7:12 [v. 11 ET]. Cf. Herm. *Sim.* 5.3.7.

overlaps semantically with ἅπτω (cf. Exod 19:12), and occurs rarely in early Jewish literature. When it does occur it is sometimes the word of choice for touching with regard to forbidden or sacred objects.[67] One should probably not read specific practices into any one of these three verbal prohibitions; they overlap and probably pertain to dietary prohibitions based upon Torah-prescribed dietary regulations, but that probably also have gone beyond such regulations for preparation for visionary experiences in heaven (for more on this, see below).

The second reason Paul gives to the Colossians in vv. 20–23 to persuade them not to embrace the philosophy is that "these are all things" (ἅ ἐστιν πάντα) that are "destined for" or "lead to" (the Greek word is εἰς) "dissolution" or "corruption" (φθορά) by their "use" (ἀπόχρησις). Others have rightly asked whether the antecedent of the relative pronoun ἅ is the prohibitions themselves or the objects to which they refer (see v. 21). Some commentators, whether knowingly or unknowingly, assume it to be the latter. A good case can be made for the former, however, because the very next two clauses refer *to the prohibitions* and not to the objects themselves. It is the *prohibitions* of the opponents that are "according to the commandments of men" (v. 22b) and "have the appearance of wisdom" (v. 23), not the foodstuffs. If this is the case, the relative ἅ of v. 22 may well also refer to the prohibitions,[68] thus maintaining a consistency in what the following clauses of vv. 22–23 lambaste. Consequently, the mention of εἰς φθοράν may not be a mention to what is the end of the prohibited objects ("they perish with the use") but to what is the end for *those who submit to such decrees*. The meaning would then be that submission to decrees that ultimately stem from the στοιχεῖα τοῦ κόσμου lead the unsuspecting *practitioner* to (spiritual) corruption.[69] The preposition εἰς would then connote result and not

---

[67] Exod 19:12 (cf. Heb 12:20); Philo, *Hypothetica*, 7.3; *Let. Aris.* §106. It is also used without such a connotation; see e.g., Ezek. Trag. 186; Heb 11:28; cf. MM, "θιγγάνω."

[68] Aletti, *Colossiens*, 204, opts for this interpretation: "La solution proposée ici essaie de respecter autant que possible la syntaxe; voilà pourquoi il a paru nécessaire de rattacher directement la relative (au moins le v. 22a) aux trois impératifs du v. 21." So also Barth and Blanke, *Colossians*, 357; Francis, "Re-examination," 160–61, 163.

[69] I have subsequently found that Barth and Blanke, *Colossians*, 356–57, have a good discussion (especially on ἀπόχρησις) and opt for this interpretation, as does Hugedé, *Colossiens*, 155–56, and Francis, "Re-examination," 160. Aletti, *Colossiens*, 203, also considers this as a possible interpretation, though he does not in the end go with it. Francis has a thorough discussion on ἀπόχρησις showing how it can just mean "use," but then somewhat surprisingly opts for the rarer meaning "abuse," a meaning that

purpose.[70] Such a concept in Paul has a remarkable parallel in Gal 6:8 (employing the same word, φθορά): "If you sow to your own flesh, you will reap corruption [φθοράν] from the flesh; but if you sow to the Spirit, you will reap eternal life from the Spirit" (NRSV).[71] Noteworthy is that in the larger context in Galatians Paul polemicizes against the works of the Law like circumcision and Mosaic dietary regulations, which were under the στοιχεῖα τοῦ κόσμου (Gal 4:3, 9). It is difficult, nevertheless, to decide between the two interpretations for Col 2:22a; the traditional sense has much to commend it.[72]

The third reason Paul gives to the Colossians in vv. 20–23 to persuade them not to embrace the philosophy is that the opponents' prohibitions "originated with men, and have not God as their Author" (see v. 22b).[73] Commentators are nigh unanimous that Paul has taken up language from LXX Isa 29:13 and here employed it against the adherents of the philosophy. As mentioned above, the adherents of the philosophy have gone beyond Mosaic dietary regulations and have prescribed other prohibitions, in a way possibly analogous to that found in Mark 7// Matt 15.[74] They have done so to secure visionary experiences in heaven. Striking, then, are the whispered correspondences between the immediate context of Isa 29:13 and Col 2:16–23. The philosophy's adherents claim to have the path of wisdom (v. 23; "having an appearance of wisdom [σοφίας]"), but God in judgment is making the "wisdom" of the "wise" (τὴν σοφίαν τῶν σοφῶν), who also happen to be religious leaders, perish and be hidden (Isa 29:14).[75] The opponents desire to have visions into heaven (2:18), but God is shutting the eyes of the seers and closing up visions like a sealed scroll; there will be no more revelation for those whose hearts are far from him (Isa 29:9–11).[76] The Colossian opponents are convinced their way pleases God, but as we have seen above, there is a strong undertone of the condemnation of idolatry in

---

seems unlikely at Col 2:22 ("Re-examination," 161–62, n.50); see also Furter, *Colossiens*, 157: "Il faut donc traduire ici *apochrèsis* par « usage » et non par « abus », sens que le terme prend parfois."

[70] See BDAG, "εἰς," 4.e; Francis, "Re-examination," 160. The preposition is also commonly employed to denote purpose, however; see BDAG 4.d.

[71] So also Francis, "Re-examination," 163n.52.

[72] See e.g., Lohse, *Colossians*, 124, O'Brien, *Colossians*, 150, and Dunn, *Colossians*, 193, for the traditional interpretation.

[73] Calvin, *Colossians*, 201.

[74] Gnilka, *Der Kolosserbrief*, 159.

[75] So also Francis, "Re-examination," 164.

[76] Cf. Francis, "Re-examination," 167.

the Isa 29 passage. If this correspondence is to be carried over into the new context of Col 2, Paul's critique could not be more caustic.

Finally, Paul gives a fourth reason in vv. 20–23 for why the Colossians should not embrace the heterodox teaching. "Although indeed"[77] it has the appearance of wisdom, the regulations of the opponents are of no value to anyone for the satisfaction or the "filling" of the flesh (v. 23). At first glance, the point seems obvious: of course abstaining from foods would not satisfy bodily appetites. But there are a couple of reasons to think that Paul had something else in mind. First, the use of σάρξ ("flesh") here at v. 23 recalls the use at v. 18, which clearly has taken on a negative connotation. Earlier in the letter, Paul had used σάρξ with reference to Christ's "body of flesh," and this use held no negative moral connotation (1:22), though such a body did belong to the fallen age and was therefore mortal and susceptible to various ills (cf. 2:11). It is clear, however, that Paul's use of the word σάρξ in the letter gradually takes on a negative nuance (see 2:13 and especially 2:18). Here at 2:23, the mention of σάρξ should be seen as describing fallen human nature estranged from God and belonging to the present evil age.[78]

The word πλησμονή at v. 23 shows up several times in the LXX with the common meaning "satisfaction" and is often associated with food.[79] It can be used to signify spiritual satisfaction, as seen in Isa 56:11, and this offers a parallel to what is going on at Col 2:23. The word could also be translated as "filling."[80] The opponents were attempting to find that which would fill their spiritual cravings, but in adhering to

---

[77] Following in part the exegesis of Troy Martin, *By Philosophy and Empty Deceit*, 47–48. A key to v. 23, according to Martin, is not taking ἐστιν...ἔχοντα as a periphrastic participial construction, but respecting the disruptive force of the postpositive μέν and observing that ἔχοντα is functioning "as a circumstantial participle in its own phrase." This seems correct to me. I do not, however, follow Martin when he argues that the imbedded participial clause runs all the way to include τινι, but believe it ends sooner than that, concluding with σώματος. The main clause resumes after σώματος.

My translation of v. 23 thus runs as follows: "these prohibitions—although indeed having an air of wisdom in self-chosen worship and humility, that is, harsh treatment of the body—are not of value to anyone for the satisfaction of the flesh."

[78] Cf. O'Brien, *Colossians*, 154, who writes that the term refers to "the old Adam-nature in its rebellion against God." Cf. Paul's use of the term at Gal 5:13, 16, 17 (twice), 19, 24, 6:8 (twice); Rom 7:5, 18, 25, 8:3 (three times), 4, 5 (twice), 6, 7, 8, 9, 12 (twice), 13; cf. Eph 2:3 (twice).

[79] E.g., Exod 16:3, 8; Lev 25:19, 26:5; LXX Ps 77:25 [78:25]; Prov 27:7; Isa 55:2; Ezek 39:19.

[80] Cf. e.g., the NRSV's translation of the word at Sir 1:16 ("fullness of wisdom"). BDAG twice mentions the verb πίμπλημι, "to fill," in its lexical entry for the word, indicating that the noun is related to that verb. LSJ, "πλησμονή," for its first entry

a religion of merely human origin they had cut themselves off from Christ the Head (2:19), through whom alone one could experience the divine filling or "fullness" (Col 2:9–10).[81]

The error that Paul combats in 2:16–23 is a unified whole; Paul does not have two different opponents at Colossae.[82] While the error that Paul works against is a unified whole, he *does* separate components of the teaching and deals with them in different ways. As stated previously, Paul's attack against the philosophy is leveled on several fronts. With regard to the first component that stems directly from the Mosaic covenant and that regulates diet and the observance of sacred days, Paul carefully handles by appeal to the larger redemptive-historical schema of the divine economy (2:16–17). With regard to the second component that advocated visionary heavenly ascent, Paul strikes—not at the experience himself—but at the arrogance and exclusivism that it bred (2:18–19).[83] With regard to the third component that insisted upon ascetic rigors and prohibitions thought to facilitate visionary ascent, Paul undercuts it by pointing out the merely human origin of such religion as well as its inability to "fill" or satisfy the flesh (vv. 20–23). The proponents probably did go beyond Torah-prescribed dietary regulations and prescribed additional dietary prohibitions for ascetic purposes (such as fasting), which were not divine but merely human in origin. This accounts for Paul's scathing reference to Isa 29:13 LXX at Col 2:23, which denounces the prohibitions of the opponents as merely "commandments and teachings of men" (cf. Col 2:8: "traditions of men"). The opponents were certainly prescribing ascetic rigors and traditions that went beyond anything written in the Mosaic Law (2:23).[84] It is difficult to see how Paul could ever call any Mosaic covenant regulation, however much he believed it to be no longer in force, as originating

---

offers "a being filled, satiety," and offers "filling" as the definition for the closely related adjective πλησμονώδης.

[81] Cf. Dunn, *Colossians*, 196n.16; Lohse, *Colossians*, 127; O'Brien, *Colossians*, 155.

[82] Francis, "Humility," 182 (though I do not agree entirely with how Francis puts it together as a unified whole). Cf. Arnold, *Colossian Syncretism*, 228: "It is sufficiently clear in the language of the letter that there is only one opposing front and that it has surfaced from within the church."

[83] Cf. Yates, "Worship of Angels," 13: "The visionary ascent is not condemned as such, only boasting about it afterwards."

[84] Cf. Jesus' quotation of Isa 29:13 LXX against the Jewish religious leaders in the Synoptic tradition (Mark 7:6–7//Matt 15:8–9). Jesus' indictment is not leveled at the Pharisees' attempts to keep explicit commands of the Mosaic covenant, but rather at their elevation of the merely human traditions that had developed over time, making them as binding as the commands themselves and even overruling them.

in men. Paul vigorously maintained, even after becoming a Christian, his stance that the Torah was of divine origin. Elsewhere the apostle had stated that the Law "is holy, and the commandment is holy and righteous and good" (Rom 7:12) and that it was "spiritual," that is, of and from the Spirit of God himself (Rom 7:14).

It has to remain a possibility, however, that Paul in fact may have done just this very thing, including Mosaic covenant stipulations in his denunciation of the opponents' rules as "of man." On this reading, if a divinely mandated stipulation of the now defunct Mosaic covenant was being foisted upon members of the new covenant community in Christ, when that stipulation had been divinely abrogated along with the covenant of which it was a part, then the stipulation is no longer of divine origin but merely of man, and need not be heeded. Colossians 2:16–17 seems to offer several such Mosaic covenant stipulations that had been abrogated in the light of the arrival of Messiah. (On this reading, the implied regulations with regard to diet at 2:16 find their equivalent, at least in part, in the explicit prohibitions of 2:21.) The rhetorical effect of Paul's echo of Isa 29:13 could not be more blistering or infuriating for the opponents. If this reading is correct, then abrogated Mosaic covenant stipulations are now merely "of man" if foisted upon the new covenant members of Messiah, and must not be heeded. At the least, Paul's Colossian audience certainly must not let their opponents browbeat them with these now merely human rules (2:16, 18a).

In the context of Isa 29, the "commandments and traditions of men" that the Jewish leadership espoused and to which the people conformed stemmed from their idolatrous hearts and was an expression of their idolatry. If Paul is carrying this theme into Col 2, then he may well view the Colossian heterodox teaching as idolatry, a worship that leads away from authentic worship of the true God. The proponents were turning the exalted visionary experiences and the rigorous asceticism needed for such experiences into a god. The visionary experiences of such an exalted nature made them arrogant, "puffed up in their mind of flesh" (2:18d). A striking parallel that sheds light on this situation is 2 Cor 12:1–7. Paul himself had visited the third heaven, had witnessed "visions and revelations of the Lord" and seen and heard inexpressible, sacred things (vv. 1–4). Such a visionary experience may well have given Paul opportunity to "boast" (vv. 5–6), but God gave him a "thorn" "to keep me from exalting myself" (v. 7 NASB). The overlap with Col 2:18 is remarkably close if the thesis of Francis is correct. Heavenly visionary experiences into the presence of God and his countless, worshipping, angelic host proved to be an almost irresistible basis for adopting a superior attitude with those who had not been given opportunity for such an amazing spiritual experience. Nevertheless, in their arrogance the opponents were no longer "holding fast to the Head (2:19a)," to Messiah. Consequently, they were cutting themselves off from the source of both wisdom, "fullness," and life itself (2:3, 9–10, 19b, 3:4), possibly the very things they had hoped to obtain through their visionary experiences. The reference implies that the opponents *were* at one time holding fast to Christ, and thus were presumed to be "brothers" and fellow Christians.[85]

Isaiah 29:13 in the Rest of the NT and in the Early Fathers

As already noted above, LXX Isa 29:13 is also quoted in the NT (in full) at Mark 7:6–7//Matt 15:8–9. The chart is offered below for convenience of comparison:

LXX Isa 29:13:   διδάσκοντες ἐντάλματα ἀνθρώπων καὶ
                              διδασκαλίας
Mark 7:7//Matt 15:9: διδάσκοντες διδασκαλίας ἐντάλματα ἀνθρώπων
Colossians 2:22:   κατὰ τὰ ἐντάλματα καὶ διδασκαλίας τῶν ἀνθρώπων

At Mark 7//Matt 15, some Pharisees from Jerusalem had come to Jesus and observed that his disciples were eating their food with unwashed hands. According to the tradition of the elders, the disciples were "unclean" or "defiled" because of their neglect. But Jesus denounced the Pharisees as hypocrites, quoted Isa 29:13 to them, and accused them of forsaking the commandment from God to hold fast to the tradition of the elders, which was merely τὴν παράδοσιν τῶν ἀνθρώπων ("tradition of men." It is worth noting that Paul brands the false philosophy with the same exact statement at 2:8: τὴν παράδοσιν τῶν ἀνθρώπων). Jesus was of the opinion that at least some of the Jewish leaders had made an idol out of their man-made religion, and he denounces them in the prophetic spirit of Isaiah.

The early church fathers often quoted Isa 29:13, probably due to the memorable use of it by Jesus in the gospel accounts. The mention of Isa 29:13a in *1 Clem.* 15:2 is the earliest reference in the fathers

---

[85] So also Lincoln, "Colossians," 632; O'Brien, *Colossians*, 146; Dunn, *Colossians*, 185.

(ca. 95 C.E.).[86] It also occurs in the homily known as *2 Clem.* (before 150 C.E.) and is cited to admonish Christians to acknowledge Christ by doing righteousness and not merely by offering him honor with their lips (3:5). The quotation is sometimes employed against what is perceived as false Jewish teaching[87] or against unbelieving Jews generally.[88] Clement of Alexandria (d. before 215 C.E.) quoted it to demonstrate that God is concerned with what is done in the heart.[89] Cyprian (d. 258 C.E.) leveled Isa 29:13 at other church leaders who were teaching differently than accepted practice with regard to the Lord's Supper[90] or of baptism.[91] Elsewhere he cited it against two bishops who had committed idolatry and other crimes.[92]

Hermeneutical Reflections

It appears that in echoing LXX Isaiah 29:13 in Colossians 2:22, the apostle reveals that he presupposed that the "philosophy" threatening the Colossians was analogous enough to the idolatry that had snared Israel in Isaiah's day that it stirred him to apply the language of the prophet's denunciation against it. Paul thus viewed the proponents of the Colossian philosophy as those, as in Isaiah 29, from God's own people who claimed to have the path of wisdom, yet as those who added man-made regulations to the divine revelation they had already received. We noted above other possible correspondences between the two texts, such as the fact that in Isa 29 the man-made doctrines stemmed from idolatrous hearts, and that in judgment God was blinding spiritually such seers who had claimed grand visionary experiences. All these themes were already present and connected in Isa 29, and so Paul's heart and mind, saturated as it was with Scripture, applied it to an analogous situation in his own day.

---

[86] Cf. Clement of Alexandria, *Miscellanies* 4.6 (*ANF* 2:414).

[87] Justin, *Dialogue with Trypho* 78 (*ANF* 1:238), 140 (*ANF* 1:269); Irenaeus, *Against Heresies* 4.12.4 (*ANF* 1:476).

[88] Tertullian, *Against Marcion* 5.11 (*ANF* 3:453), 5.14 (*ANF* 3:460).

[89] *Miscellanies* 2.14 (*ANF* 2:361).

[90] *Epistles of Cyprian* 62.14 (*ANF* 5:362).

[91] *Epistles of Cyprian* 73.3 (*ANF* 5:387).

[92] *Epistles of Cyprian* 67.2 (*ANF* 5:370).

CHAPTER TWELVE

THE SCRIPTURES OF ISRAEL IN COLOSSIANS 3:1–4: THE ECHO OF PSALM 110:1 IN 3:1

Comparison of Textual Versions and Evaluation

Psalm 110:1 MT	Psalm 109:1 LXX	Colossians 3:1
נְאֻם יְהוָה לַאדֹנִי שֵׁב לִימִינִי עַד־אָשִׁית אֹיְבֶיךָ הֲדֹם לְרַגְלֶיךָ:	εἶπεν ὁ κύριος τῷ κυρίῳ μου <u>κάθου ἐκ δεξιῶν μου</u> ἕως ἂν θῶ τοὺς ἐχθρούς σου ὑποπόδιον τῶν ποδῶν σου	ὁ Χριστός ἐστιν <u>ἐν δεξιᾷ τοῦ θεοῦ καθήμενος</u>·

This proposal meets our two criteria for an echo: 1) availability, and 2) word agreement. Regarding *availability*, Paul often quoted from the Psalms; according to the count by Silva, he did so at least 24 times.[1] Moreover, Paul definitely alludes to Psalm 110:1 at 1 Cor 15:25 and probably echoes it at Romans 8:34. It is also echoed at Eph 1:20, the sister letter to Colossians. Therefore, Paul was acquainted with Psalm 110 and this knowledge further supports that Paul may have echoed Psalm 110:1 at Col 3:1.

Regarding *word agreement*, the two texts share three words in common, since the identity of the person behind the possessive pronoun μου at LXX Psalm 109:1 is God. For Paul to have carried over the pronoun at Col 3:1 would have been awkward, and he replaces the pronoun with its clear referent, ὁ θεός. Numerous other scholars also see Psalm 110:1 behind Col 3:1.[2] Moreover, Psalm 110:1 has the honor of being

---

[1] M. Silva, "Old Testament in Paul," *DPL*, 631. Silva's count includes the quotation of Ps 68:18 in Eph 4:8.

[2] Hühn, *Citate*, 198; Masson, *Colossiens*, 139n.3; Ellis, *Paul's Use of the Old Testament*, 154; Hugedé, *L'Épître aux Colossiens*, 160n.4; Lohse, *Colossians*, 133; Caird, *Paul's Letters from Prison*, 202; Ernst, *Kolosser*, 221; R. Martin, *Colossians*, 101; Schweizer, *Colossians*, 174; Gnilka, *Der Kolosserbrief*, 172; O'Brien, *Colossians*, 162; Lindemann, *Der Kolosserbrief*, 53–54; Bruce, *Colossians*, 132; Wright, *Colossians*, 131–32; Pokorný, *Colossians*, 159; Furter, *Colossiens*, 161; Melick, *Colossians*, 280–81; Wall, *Colossians*, 133; Aletti, *Colossiens*, 218n.4

the most oft-quoted OT reference in the NT. This adds further support to the thesis that Paul has echoed Psalm 110:1 at Col 3:1.

Old Testament Context: Psalm 110

Psalm 110 is widely classified as a royal psalm,[3] and it does share some affinities with other royal psalms (see Pss 2, 20, 21, 45, 72, 89, and 132).[4] In terms of structure, Psalm 110 breaks down naturally into two strophes, vv. 1–3 and vv. 4–7. Both strophes are introduced by an oracle of YHWH addressed to a ruler and mediated by a subordinate. The identification of both the ruler and the subordinate mediating the oracle is not given; that the subordinate is a court prophet addressing his Davidic king is currently the prevailing interpretation among OT scholars.[5] In the NT, however, Jesus explicitly identifies the subordinate mediating the oracle of Ps 110 as King David *himself*, and the addressed ruler as the Messiah. David himself thus addresses the Messiah as his own "Lord"; see Mark 12:36//Mt 22:44//Luke 20:42–43 (cf. Acts 2:34–35).

The ruler addressed is almost certainly of David's lineage, because Zion is mentioned as the locus from which YHWH extends the unnamed ruler's dominion (see 110:2). In the background stands YHWH's promise to David of an enduring dynasty, after David had captured Jerusalem/Zion and established it as his capital (2 Sam 5–7). Also in the background stands the tradition of the divine election of Zion, a tradition closely woven together with the Davidic dynasty (see e.g., Ps 132).

That the subordinate is acting as a prophet as he addresses his Davidic "lord" is clear from the use of the phrase נְאֻם יְהוָה at v. 1 (the

---

("L'allusion au Ps 109–110,1 est obvie."); Yates, *Colossians*, 72; Barth and Blanke, *Colossians*, 64n.98, 394; Wolter, *Der Brief an die Kolosser*, 167; Dunn, *Colossians*, 203; Arnold, *Colossian Syncretism*, 306; Hübner, *An die Kolosser*, 98; MacDonald, *Colossians*, 127, 129; Lincoln, *Colossians*, 638; Hay, *Colossians*, 116; Fee, "Old Testament Intertextuality in Colossians," ad loc.; Beale, "Colossians," ad loc.; cf. Hübner, *Vetus Testamentum in Novo*, 538–39; see side margin of NA[27] and bottom note of UBS[4] at Col 3:1.

[3] Anderson, *Out of the Depths*, 223; Mitchell Dahood, *Psalms 101–150* (AB 17A; Garden City, N.Y.: Doubleday, 1970), 112; Leslie C. Allen, *Psalms 101–150* (WBC 21; Waco, Tex.: Word, 1983), 83; Kraus, *Psalms 60–150*, 345–46.

[4] See the Appendix in Anderson, *Out of the Depths*, 219–24.

[5] Nathan (2 Sam 7:2–17) and Gad (2 Sam 24:11) both served as court prophets to David and it is likely that David's lineage was also attended by such prophets. Psalm 45, likewise a royal psalm, serves as an approximate example in that it consists of a court poet's direct address to the king.

LXX lacks the phrase). The phrase is a fixed technical expression for a formal divine oracle mediated through YHWH's prophet.[6] The word נְאֻם occurs over 360 times in the Hebrew Bible, but significantly only in the Psalms here at 110:1.

Through the oracle, God commands the Davidic ruler to "sit at his right" until God subdues all of the ruler's enemies and subjects them as a "footstool" for the ruler's feet. To "sit at the right" of a king was to be offered the place of highest honor in the presence of that king (cf. 1 Kgs 2:19). The Davidic ruler is thus highly exalted. He is commanded to sit at the right hand of YHWH himself. He rules, however, as YHWH's vicegerent, and it is God himself who grants the victory. Elsewhere in the Bible and the ANE generally, to be "put under the foot" or made a "footstool" was a sign of defeat and forced submission to a greater king and warrior.[7]

The oracle proper ends at v. 1, and in vv. 2–3 the prophet interprets and expands upon it. The psalmist declares that YHWH is going to enlarge the Davidic king's dominion from Zion outward until it extends into the nations surrounding Zion and beyond (the purview of the psalm is universal, see v. 6). In v. 3a, the psalmist announces that the king's people (i.e., Israel) are as "free-will offerings" in the day that God strengthens the king for universal dominion. The word נְדָבָה ("free-will offering"; probably misunderstood by the LXX translator at v. 3a) consistently refers to a voluntary offering within a cultic context,[8] though rarely it is used as an adverb to mean "freely" (Hos 14:5). The former meaning should be understood here. The description of the people as free-will offerings begins a cultic theme that anticipates the stunning declaration of the king as a permanent priest patterned after the Melchizedek figure of Gen 14. The mention in v. 3b that the people are arrayed in holy splendor or attire (הָדָר; LXX: λαμπρότης) may well contribute to this theme,[9] for elsewhere such apparel is mentioned in

---

[6] Cf. *HALOT*, "נאם."

[7] Josh 10:22–25; *COS* 2.22 (line 29b), 2.125 (line §22), 2.149 (lines 1.13–15). *COS* 2.149n.18 cites an inscription in which the Assyrian king Tukulti-Ninurta I (1234–1197 B.C.E.) asserts of the Babylonian king that "I trod with my feet upon his lordly neck as though it were a footstool. Bound I brought him as a captive into the presence of Aššur, my lord" (taken from RIMA 1:245).

[8] In the singular: Exod 35:29, 36:3; Lev 7:16, 22:21, 22:23; Num 15:3; Deut 16:10, 23:24; Ezek 46:12 [twice]; Ps 54:8; Ezra 1:4, 3:5, 8:28; 2 Chr 35:8. In the plural: Lev 22:18, 23:38; Num 29:39; Deut 12:6, 17; 2 Chr 31:14; Amos 4:5; cf. Ps 119:108.

[9] Or is it *the king* that is arrayed in the holy attire? The reference is obscure.

connection with worshippers who are bidden to come to God's temple courts to bring offerings and praise to God.[10]

The account at 2 Chr 20:20–24 provides a parallel that may shed some light on Ps 110. A Davidic king, Jehoshaphat, faces an imminent threat from Ammon, Moab, and Edom. He humbly calls upon YHWH (2 Chr 20:5–12), who promises to fight for Judah and his vicegerent (20:13–19; cf. Psalm 110:1–2, 5–7). In faith, the people go forth to fight, with worshippers going forward in praise before the army in "holy attire" (20:20–21; cf. Psalm 110:3). God subsequently routs these enemy nations, strewing corpses everywhere on the earth (20:22–24; cf. Psalm 110:5–7).

The second strophe commences at v. 4 with the second oracle pronouncement. The subordinate prophet again addresses his "lord," mediating another oracle from YHWH. The prophet announces that God has irrevocably sworn that his "lord" will serve forever as priest for YHWH "on account of" Melchizedek. Yet what does "on account of" Melchizedek mean? The phrase עַל־דָּבַר/דִּבְרָה occurs about twenty times in the HB and nearly always serves as an idiom meaning "because of" or "on account of," or sometimes "concerning" or "with regard to."[11] There is little evidence that it means "after the order of," though the LXX translated it this way (κατὰ τὴν τάξιν). The point of the HB is clear enough: God has appointed his Davidic king a priest because of Melchizedek.

Melchizedek appears in Gen 14:18–20 and disappears as suddenly as he arrives. His name probably means "king of righteousness."[12] The text informs the reader that Melchizedek is both king of Salem, which is probably a shortened form of Jerusalem (see Ps 76:2), and a priest of "God Most High." The two offices of king and priest are combined in the one person. Melchizedek declares that God Most High has blessed Abram and delivered the enemies into his hand. The narrator does not portray Melchizedek as a pagan priest. Moreover,

---

[10] The Hebrew is בְּהַדְרַת־קֹדֶשׁ; see Ps 96:8–9; 1 Chr 16:29; 2 Chr 20:21 and the NAB, NASB, NET, RSV translations of these texts; cf. Ps 29:2.

[11] The rare דִּבְרָה is the feminine form of דָּבָר; see HALOT, "דִּבְרָה." The references that demonstrate such a meaning are: Gen 12:17, 20:11, 18, 43:18; Exod 8:8; Num 17:14, 25:18 [twice], 31:16; Deut 22:24 [twice], 23:5; 2 Sam 13:22, 18:5; Ps 45:5, 79:9; Eccl 3:18, (7:14??), and 8:2. Note that the LXX translation of several of these usages begins with either ἕνεκα ("because of, account of"), διά + the accusative (= "on account of"), or περί + the genitive ("concerning, with regard to").

[12] Michael C. Astour, "Melchizedek," ABD 4:684.

Abram affirms that "God Most High," Melchizedek's god, the "maker of heaven and earth," is his God also (cf. v. 19 with v. 22!).[13] Abram offers a tithe to Melchizedek, which further confirms that Melchizedek is God's legitimate priest at Jerusalem in the time of Abraham. Bruce Waltke writes: "Melchizedek celebrates Abraham as God's warrior and blesses him. Abraham recognizes Melchizedek as the legitimate priest and king of his God."[14]

The upshot for Ps 110:4 is that the exalted Davidic king, who now rules from "Salem," like his legitimate ancient forerunner Melchizedek, has been appointed "priest" because of Melchizedek. Melchizedek is viewed as the ideal model of what God's vicegerent over Jerusalem should look like, and thus Melchizedek provides the pattern for his future Davidic heir. Observed in this light, the LXX's translation of the Hebrew idiom עַל־דִּבְרָתִי with κατὰ τὴν τάξιν at v. 4 is interpretive but adequately conveys the Hebrew's intention.

Elsewhere in the OT, David performs some priestly functions at exceptional religious occasions, but the OT never asserts that he was appointed an "eternal priest" such as Ps 110:4 claims for the ideal Davidic figure.[15] It is true that at 2 Sam 8:18, David's sons are explicitly described as "priests," כֹּהֲנִים (but LXX reads αὐλάρχαι, "chiefs of the court"). The parallel passage at 1 Chr 18:17, however, changes David's sons to הָרִאשֹׁנִים, "chief officials" (LXX: οἱ πρῶτοι διάδοχοι, "chief court officials"). David, in the special religious occasion of the bringing up of the ark to Jerusalem, did wear a linen ephod[16] and offer sacrifices.[17] It is noteworthy, however, that David's predecessor Saul is condemned for overstepping his bounds and playing the part of a priest (1 Sam

---

[13] The presence of the word יהוה in the MT at v. 22 is probably an addition added by a scribe to clear Abraham of any accusation of possible syncretism. The word or its equivalent is not in most of the MSS of the LXX, and is not in the Syriac or 1Qap Gen XXII, 21.

[14] Bruce K. Waltke and Cathi J. Fredricks, *Genesis: A Commentary* (Grand Rapids: Zondervan, 2001), 235.

[15] In the surrounding nations of David's time, the vocations of priest and king were often combined in one person. The pharaohs of Egypt and the kings of Assyria were considered to be both kings and priests; see Henri Cazelles, "Sacral Kingship," *ABD* 5:863–64 and Jeremy Black, "Ashur (god)," *Dictionary of the Ancient Near East*, 36, who writes that "the Assyrian *king* was [Ashur's] chief *priest* and lieutenant on earth" (emphasis mine). Ashur was the supreme god of Assyria.

[16] 2 Sam 6:14; cf. 1 Sam 2:18, 28, 14:3, 22:18; 1 Chr 15:27.

[17] 2 Sam 6:13, 17; cf. 24:25.

13:8–14), as was Uzziah (2 Chr 26:16–21). After weighing the evidence, Roland de Vaux offered this statement on the issue:

> Anointing did not confer on the king a priestly character, since, as we have seen, priests were not anointed in the days of the monarchy; but it did make him a sacred person, with a special relationship to Yʜᴡʜ, and in solemn circumstances he could act as the religious head of the people. But he was not a priest in the strict sense.[18]

Psalm 110:4 thus offers something altogether different than what typically held in the Davidic monarchy. Psalm 110 portrays a Davidic priest-king through whom Yʜᴡʜ will extend from Zion his dominion over all nations. The imagery corresponds to none of the depictions of David or to any of his sons in the ᴏᴛ's historical books; the psalm's original intention encompasses an ideal and universal scope.[19]

Instead of expanding upon and interpreting v. 4 further, the psalmist in vv. 5–7 returns to the primary theme of vv. 1–3. *God* is now said to be *at the right hand* of his *vicegerent*, although this time the scene is not a throne room but a battlefield (cf. with v. 1). It is still Yʜᴡʜ who subdues the enemies. God is the warrior and God secures the victory. The vicegerent reigns with a derived authority and only wins battles because Yʜᴡʜ fights them through and for him. Yʜᴡʜ crushes kings (v. 5b) and executes judgment upon the enemy nations (v. 6a), filling the land with their corpses and smashed heads (v. 6b) in the day of his righteous wrath (v. 5b).

Psalm 110:1 in Early and Late Judaism

There are no quotations of Ps 110:1 in the writings of early Judaism. Neither does Psalm 110:1 appear in some of the major writings of later Judaism, including the Mishnah and Tosefta. It does finally crop up in the Talmud and other rabbinic works, and is understood by the rabbis to have been addressed to at least four different figures. On several

---

[18] Roland de Vaux, *Ancient Israel: Its Life and Institutions* (trans. John McHugh; New York: McGraw-Hill, 1961), 114.

[19] See Derek Kidner, *Psalms 73–150* (TOTC; London: Inter-Varsity, 1975), 391–92; Edward J. Kissane, *The Book of Psalms* (Dublin: Browne and Nolan, 1964), 509; C. A. Briggs, *A Critical and Exegetical Commentary on the Book of Psalms* (2 vols.; ICC; Edinburgh: T&T Clark, 1907), 2:376; R. T. France, *Jesus and the Old Testament: His Application of Old Testament Passages to Himself and His Mission* (Downers Grove: InterVarsity, 1971; reprint, Vancouver, British Columbia: Regent College Publishing, 1998), 163–69.

occasions, the oracle is interpreted to have been given to Abraham.[20] On one occasion it is applied to corporate Israel as the "son" of God.[21] In a few instances, David is understood as the one addressed.[22] On a few occasions it is understood as a reference to the coming Messiah.[23] *Targum Psalm* 110 combines these latter two interpretations, claiming that David himself will arise and stand as prince in the world to come (as the promised Messianic ruler) on account of his righteous merit as a king in this world. It is apparent from the gospel accounts that Jesus presupposed that his messianic interpretation of the psalm would be a premise held in common with his Jewish audience (see Mark 12:36// Matt 22:44//Luke 20:42–43). Jesus' presupposition serves as strong evidence that in the early first century at least some Jews understood the psalm to refer to the coming Messiah.

New Testament Context: Psalm 110:1 in Colossians 3:1–4

Two distinct yet related ideas govern this section of Colossians. First, Colossians 3:1–4 is a classic text for observing the Pauline "already— not yet" eschatological framework at work. Though the Colossians had already experienced "resurrection" with Christ (2:12, 13, 3:1), their full resurrection yet awaits the time of the revelation of Christ, as hinted at in 3:4 ("Whenever Christ is revealed...then you also together with him will be revealed in glory").[24] This horizontal timeline, however, is also turned upward to encompass a vertical and spatial understanding, as we will elaborate upon more in a moment.

The second idea that pervades 3:1–4 is the concept of the Colossian church's union with Christ. Because of this real and spiritual union, what is true of Christ is true—in a derivative manner—of those who belong to him through baptism (2:11).[25] The Colossian faithful were circumcised in Christ's circumcision (i.e., his death; 2:11). They had died

---

[20] *b. Nedarim* 32b; *b. Sanhedrin* 108b; *Midr. Rabbah* Leviticus 25.6; *Midr. Psalm* 110.1, 4; *Mekilta*, Shirata 6.35–41; *Midr. Tanhuma*, Genesis 15:1ff., Part V; Genesis 18:1ff., Part IV.

Ps 110:4 is likewise applied occasionally to Abraham; see *Pirqe Rabbi Eliezer*, pp. 53–54; *Midr. Rabbah* Genesis 46.5, 55.6, and 55.7.

[21] *Midr. Psalm* 2.9.

[22] *Midr. Psalms* 18.32, 110.5; *Tanna Debe Eliyyahu* ER 90 (cf. ER 94 [Psalm 110:4]).

[23] *Midr. Psalms* 2.9, 18.29; *Avot of Rabbi Nathan* 34.4 (with Zech 4:14).

[24] See also Arnold, *Colossian Syncretism*, 307–8.

[25] So also Wolter, *Der Brief an die Kolosser*, 167.

with him (2:20, 3:3), had been buried with him (2:12a), were raised up
in resurrection with him (2:12b, 3:1), made alive with him (2:13b), and
hidden away in heaven with him in God (3:3b). When he is revealed
in his second coming, then they too will be revealed along with him,
clothed in glory (3:4). He is the firstborn from the dead and the beginning of the new age, the new creation (1:18b–c); in their union with
him they too have entered the new creational age as part of the new
humanity wherein Christ pervades as prototype, source, and sovereign
(3:9–11; 1:18).

This organic relationship between Christ and those who belong to
him is captured also in the head-body imagery (1:18, 2:19). He is the
spring and source of their (resurrection) life (3:4). The relationship of
union also surfaces when Christ is spoken of as having "all the fullness" of deity dwell in him and consequently his people likewise are
derivatively "filled" with God's presence in him (2:9–10).

The vertical, spatial understanding of the "already—not yet" eschatological framework mentioned above is seen in the exhortations to the
Colossians to "seek" and "think on" the things above, where Christ is
seated at the right hand of God (3:1–2). The exhortations flow out of
the indicative reality of resurrection with Christ. The assumption, of
course, is that "the things above" are in heaven; this was where the
throne of God was believed to reside.[26] Indeed, at Col 4:1 Christ as
"Lord" is affirmed to reside "in heaven." Col 3:1 makes this explicit
by explaining that the things above are located "where Christ is at
the right hand of God, seated." The language echoes that of lxx Ps
109:1 (et: 110:1). The resurrected Christ is therefore affirmed to be
the coming and ideal Davidic vicegerent through whom God would
extend his worldwide dominion and for whom he would destroy all
enemy rulers. In this respect, the striking language of God defeating
the enemy "rulers and authorities" at 2:15 through Christ and his cross
should be noted. Clinton Arnold writes that

> Although [Paul] does not explicitly cite the portion of the Psalm that
> speaks of the defeat of the enemies, the familiarity of this passage to
> the Christian readers would have prompted a recollection of the rest of
> the text. Early Christians typically identified the enemies of the Psalm
> with the hostile demonic powers that Christ subjugated by his death and

---

[26] See, e.g., Isa 6:1, 66:1; Pss 11:4, 103:19; 2 Chr 18:18; Dan 7:9.

exaltation. This allusion to Ps 110:1 is especially appropriate following the dramatic depiction in 2:15 of Christ's defeat of the principalities and powers on the cross.[27]

Because of both this victorious exaltation to the right hand of God in heaven as well as to the union theology discussed above, the Colossians are also hidden away in heaven with Christ "in God" (3:3–4; cf. Eph 3:9). The new age, however, is not yet fully consummated: the "philosophy" remains a real and present danger, perpetuated as it is by the στοιχεῖα τοῦ κόσμου (2:8, 20). Paul still labors to present every member of the community "complete" (τέλειος) before God (1:28–29),[28] the faithful still await their manifestation with Christ in glory (3:4; cf. 3:24), and final judgment is held out as an impending yet unaccomplished future reality (3:6; cf. 4:5). Therefore, while the "already" pole of the "already—not yet" spectrum is stressed, an eschatological reserve remains in the text.[29] The Colossians, as part of the new humanity of the new creational age, are yet on earth in the midst of the old age, and the heavenly glory of their new nature awaits Christ's second coming for its manifestation (3:4).

In exhorting the Colossians to seek the things above, Paul admonishes them to find the wisdom they seek in heaven, in Christ, "in whom all the treasures of wisdom and knowledge are hidden" (2:3). Because of their participation with Christ, they are not to succumb to the philosophy's claims to wisdom, a "wisdom" that belongs to the old age dominated by the στοιχεῖα τοῦ κόσμου and leads only to corruption (2:20–23). This deceptive philosophy with its decrees and false wisdom belongs to τὰ ἐπὶ τῆς γῆς, "the things upon the earth" (3:2b).[30] The faithful, rather, are to "set their minds on" (φρονέω; cf. Rom 8:5) the treasures of wisdom that are found in Christ and that are in accord with the new age. They are to be careful to make sure that such thinking should lead

---

[27] Arnold, *Colossian Syncretism*, 306.

[28] On this text, see the excellent exegetical work of Sappington, *Revelation and Redemption at Colossae*, 186–90, who interprets it within the framework of an eschatological context. He defines τέλειος as "free from blame or accusation at the last judgment" (189–90).

[29] Andrew T. Lincoln, *Paradise Now and Not Yet: Studies in the Role of the Heavenly Dimension in Paul's Thought with Special Reference to His Eschatology* (SNTSMS 43; Cambridge: Cambridge University Press, 1981), 133.

[30] So also Wolter, *Der Brief an die Kolosser*, 167.

to a life lived out ethically in accord with the new heavenly existence (3:12–17). Such a life will be pleasing to God (1:10a).

Psalm 110:1 in the Rest of the NT and in the Early Fathers

David Hay has compiled a list showing that Ps 110:1 is quoted or alluded to twenty-three times in the NT.[31] Hay writes that five of these are quotations,[32] leaving eighteen allusions.[33] As stated above, this frequency of citation crowns Psalm 110:1 as the most oft-referenced OT text in the NT.

Hay explains that Ps 110:1 functions in four different ways in the NT. He understands it 1) to express the exalted status of Jesus or Christians as they sit at God's right hand, 2) to support particular christological titles, 3) to affirm the subjection of powers to Christ, and 4) to explain his heavenly intercession as priest.[34] He argues further, however, that "these [four] functions may be collapsed into one: early Christians chiefly employed the psalm to articulate the supreme glory, the divine transcendence, of Jesus, through whom salvation was mediated."[35]

The text of Ps 110:1 is also quoted frequently in the early church fathers. The earliest use surfaces at *1 Clem.* 36:5 (ca. 95 C.E.). The quotation is actually of Heb 1:13, which itself is a quotation of Ps 110:1. It is, of course, applied to Christ, and the enemies are identified as any people who are wicked and resist the will of God. The next earliest, extant extra-biblical use of Ps 110:1 is found in *Barn.* 12:10 (70–135 C.E.). The author probably has employed it in light of the Synoptic account's use and ties a quotation of Isa 45:1 with it (see v. 11). Justin Martyr (ca. 165 C.E.) takes up Ps 110:1 to demonstrate that God would raise his Christ to heaven after he had raised him from

---

[31] David M. Hay, *Glory at the Right Hand: Psalm 110 in Early Christianity* (SBLMS 18; Nashville: Abingdon, 1973), 163–64. His tally includes the allusion in the longer ending of Mark at 16:19.

[32] Mark 12:36//Matt 22:44//Luke 20:42–43; Acts 2:34–35; Heb 1:13.

[33] Hay's list of allusions includes: Mark 14:62//Matt 26:64//Luke 22:69; Mark 16:19; Acts 2:33, 5:31, 7:55–56; Rom 8:34; 1 Cor 15:25; Eph 1:20, 2:6; Col 3:1; Heb 1:3, 8:1, 10:12–13, 12:2; 1 Peter 3:22; and Rev 3:21.

[34] Hay, *Glory at the Right Hand*, 52–153, 155. In his study, he also includes early extra-biblical Christian use of Ps 110:1, such as *1 Clem.* 36:5 and *Barn.* 12:10; see pp. 164–65 for these and others.

[35] Hay, *Glory at the Right Hand*, 155.

the dead.[36] Elsewhere he quotes it to prove Christ's divinity.[37] Irenaeus applies it to Christ as the "Word," adding that believers are still on earth and must wait to sit on this throne together with Christ.[38] He later appropriates it to prove Christ is God, and the Son of God.[39]

Tertullian (d. after 220 C.E.) frequently quotes or alludes to Psalm 110:1. He interpreted Christ to be at the right hand after his first coming, but that his enemies would be only finally subdued under his feet at the end of time, in his return.[40] For Tertullian the text can support both the distinction of persons within the Trinity[41] as well as affirm the unity of the Godhead.[42] He also argued that God spoke the Psalm directly to Christ, rejecting the popular Jewish interpretation of his day that the Psalm was addressed to Hezekiah.[43]

Hippolytus (d. 235 C.E.) wrote that God spoke Ps 110:1 to Christ at the time of his resurrection.[44] Novatian (d. after 251 C.E.) quoted it, along with Gen 1:26, 19:24, Ps 2:7–8, and Isa 45:1, to defend the distinct personhood of the divine Christ against the doctrines of the Sabellians.[45]

Hermeneutical and Theological Reflections

Psalm 110 stands as a prophetic announcement bequeathed to a Davidic king. It envisions a day when YHWH's sovereign reign will extend from Zion to encompass all nations through his exalted Davidic king-priest. The apostle Paul at Col 3:1 reveals that he understood the prophetic announcement of Ps 110 to have found its fulfillment in Jesus Christ.

---

[36] *First Apology* 45 (*ANF* 1:178).

[37] *Dialogue with Trypho* 56 (*ANF* 1:224); cf. chapter 127 (*ANF* 1:263).

[38] *Against Heresies* 2.28.7 (*ANF* 1:401).

[39] *Against Heresies* 3.10.5 (*ANF* 1:426), 3.16.3 (*ANF* 1:441).

[40] *Against Hermogenes* 11 (*ANF* 3:483); *The Resurrection of the Flesh* 22 (*ANF* 3:561); *Against Praxeas* 30 (*ANF* 3:627).

[41] *Against Praxeas* 11 (*ANF* 3:606).

[42] *Against Praxeas* 13 (*ANF* 3:607).

[43] *Against Marcion* 5.9 (*ANF* 3:448).

[44] *Fragments from Commentaries*, Genesis 49:21–26 (*ANF* 5:166–67); cf. Cyprian (d. 258 C.E.), *The Treatises of Cyprian* 12.2.26 (*ANF* 5:525–56); Lactantius (d. 330 C.E.) *The Divine Institutes* 4.12 (*ANF* 7:111); idem, *Epitome of the Divine Institutes* 47 (*ANF* 7:241; with Dan 7:13–14); *Apostolic Constitutions* 6.6.30 (*ANF* 7:464).

[45] *Treatise Concerning the Trinity* 26 (*ANF* 5:636–37). In chapter 9 of this same treatise, Novatian quotes Ps 110:1 in a cantata of OT texts that are all interpreted in a redemptive-historical and frequently in a typological manner.

Christ had been enthroned upon the advent of his resurrection, and was sitting at the right hand of God and ruling with him, as God continued to subdue Christ's enemies under his feet.

Paul's echo of Ps 110:1 reveals that he presupposed Christ to be the promised Davidic king of Ps 110, and probably reveals also that the apostle interpreted the "enemies" mentioned in the psalm to include any demonic spiritual beings that animate deceptive philosophies rivaling the gospel (cf. 1 Cor 15:24–25; Eph 1:20–21). Paul's messianic interpretation accords with a major strand of Jewish interpretation of Ps 110 in the first century c.e.

Paul's theological lines that surface at 3:1 also accord well with the echoes of 2 Sam 7 in Col 1:13 that were detected and investigated in chapter six of this study. There it was seen that God had promised David an everlasting royal dynasty of sons who would sit upon the throne of the kingdom of Israel. Paul believed that this promise had come to its ultimate fulfillment in Jesus, a genuine descendant of David, whom God installed as king forever upon the event of his resurrection. Psalm 110 expands upon this promise to show that the enduring kingship, promised to David at 2 Sam 7, would find its fulfillment in one ideal, messianic figure, whose reign would extend universally from Zion and for whom God would crush all enemies who aligned themselves against the LORD and his anointed vicegerent.

CHAPTER THIRTEEN

THE SCRIPTURES OF ISRAEL IN COLOSSIANS 3:5–17: THE ALLUSION TO GENESIS 1:26–27 IN 3:10

Comparison of Textual Versions and Evaluation

Genesis 1:26–27 MT	Genesis 1:26–27 LXX	Colossians 3:10
וַיֹּאמֶר אֱלֹהִים נַעֲשֶׂה אָדָם בְּצַלְמֵנוּ כִּדְמוּתֵנוּ ...וַיִּבְרָא אֱלֹהִים אֶת־הָאָדָם בְּצַלְמוֹ בְּצֶלֶם אֱלֹהִים בָּרָא אֹתוֹ זָכָר וּנְקֵבָה בָּרָא אֹתָם:	καὶ εἶπεν ὁ θεός ποιήσωμεν ἄνθρωπον κατ᾽ εἰκόνα ἡμετέραν καὶ καθ᾽ ὁμοίωσιν... καὶ ἐποίησεν ὁ θεὸς τὸν ἄνθρωπον κατ᾽ εἰκόνα θεοῦ ἐποίησεν αὐτόν ἄρσεν καὶ θῆλυ ἐποίησεν αὐτούς	καὶ ἐνδυσάμενοι τὸν νέον [ἄνθρωπον] τὸν ἀνακαινούμενον εἰς ἐπίγνωσιν κατ᾽ εἰκόνα τοῦ κτίσαντος αὐτόν

This proposal meets our three criteria necessary for an allusion: 1) availability, 2) word agreement, and 3) essential interpretive link. Regarding *availability*, Paul quoted Gen 2:7 LXX at 1 Cor 15:45 and Gen 2:24 LXX at 1 Cor 6:16, which demonstrates that the Genesis account of creation was known by him.[1] Regarding *word agreement*, the two texts share three words verbatim (κατ᾽ εἰκόνα, ἄνθρωπον) and another two conceptually (ὁ θεός = τοῦ κτίσαντος αὐτόν; ἐποίησεν = κτίσαντος).[2] Regarding an *essential interpretive link*, Paul has intended to communicate an Adam-Christ comparison through the allusion, which was to inform the reader's understanding of what he intended by his "old" and "new" man language. The Adam-Christ comparison and the redemptive-historical slant is lost if the reader fails to catch Paul's

---

[1] See also 1 Cor 11:7b–9, 15:21–22, 47; 2 Cor 4:6, 11:3; Rom 5:12–14; cf. 1 Tim 2:13–14; Eph 5:31.

[2] Though the LXX offers ποιέω all three times as the translation for ברא at Gen 1:27, the Greek versions Aquila, Symmachus, and Theodotion read κτίζω. Cf. the use of κτίζω elsewhere in early Judaism to signify the creation of man: Wis 2:23, 10:1; Sir 17:1, 33:10; cf. Eccl 12:1 LXX; Matt 19:4 (which has both verbs).

allusion to Gen 1:26–27, and the reader is left with the "un-allusive" sense or surface-level meaning of the text.[3]

Numerous other scholars have already detected Gen 1:26–27 in Col 3:10.[4] It appears that Paul has pulled once again from Gen 1.[5]

Old Testament Context: Genesis 1:26–27

The mention of the creation of man in the image of God occurs on the sixth day of the creation account of Gen 1:1–2:3. The creation of man as God's "image" stands as the apex of God's creating work in the account. The narrative's goal is to explain man's relation both to the rest of creation and to the one God, and also to present humanity's reason for existence. The sixth day (Genesis 1:24–31) was investigated in chapter three, and the results will not be repeated in detail here. To summarize our earlier investigation of the text: the consequence for humanity being made in the image of God was that they were to rule over all the rest of creation by filling the earth with their progeny through procreation (Gen 1:26, 28). The mandate could be accomplished, because God had endued them with the ability to do so ("he blessed them," v. 28) and had already provided all the food necessary for humanity to complete it (Gen 1:29–30).

The task here is to look more closely at Gen 1:26–27 and to discern what was meant by describing man to be created "in the image of God." God makes man—male and female—"in our image," "according to our likeness" (v. 26), "in his image," "in the image of God" (v. 27). The

---

[3] See p. 30n.73.

[4] Gregory of Nyssa (d. 394 c.e.), *On the Making of Man* 30.33–34 (*NPNF*[2] 5:427); Calvin, *Colossians*, 212n.1; Hühn, *Citate*, 198; Lightfoot, *Colossians*, 215–16; Abbott, *Colossians*, 284; Moule, *Colossians*, 120; Eltester, *Eikon im Neuen Testament*, 163; Jervell, *Imago Dei*, 231–32; Edvin Larsson, *Christus als Vorbild: Eine Untersuchung zu den paulinischen Tauf- und Eikontexten* (ASNU 23; Uppsala: Gleerup, 1962), 188; Ellis, *Paul's Use of the Old Testament*, 154; Caird, *Paul's Letters from Prison*, 205; Hugedé, *Colossians*, 176; Lohse, *Colossians*, 142; Martin, *Colossians*, 107; Ernst, *An die Kolosser*, 226; Schweizer, *Colossians*, 198n.55; Gnilka, *Der Kolosserbrief*, 188; O'Brien, *Colossians*, 191; Bruce, *Colossians*, 147 ("...it is impossible to miss the allusion to Gen. 1:27"); Furter, *Colossiens*, 173; Barth and Blanke, *Colossians*, 64n.98, 414; Aletti, *Colossiens*, 232n.45; Wolter, *Der Brief an die Kolosser*, 180; Patzia, *Colossians*, 76; Dunn, *Colossians*, 221–22; Hübner, *An die Kolosser*, 104; MacDonald, *Colossians*, 138; Hay, *Colossians*, 126; Lincoln, "Colossians," 644; Fee, "Old Testament Intertextuality in Colossians," ad loc.; Beale, "Colossians," ad loc.; see NA[27] side margin; UBS[4] bottom note at Col 3:10.

[5] See chapter three above on the echo of Gen 1:28 in Col 1:6, 10.

two key words, "image" (צֶלֶם; LXX: εἰκών) and "likeness" (דְּמוּת; LXX: ὁμοίωσις), overlap semantically, mutually reinforcing and strengthening each other in meaning.[6] From the immediate context of Gen 1:26–27 little can be learned about what humanity's creation in the image of God might exactly signify. The *consequence*, as we have seen, was that humanity was to rule over the rest of creation.

Genesis 5:1–3, however, furnishes a significant clue as to what being created in the image means for humanity as humanity. The text intentionally recalls Gen 1:26–27 at 5:1–2 ("This is the book of the generations of Adam. When God created man, he made him in the likeness of God. Male and female he created them, and he blessed them and named them Man when they were created" RSV; ESV). Then immediately at v. 3 it narrates that Adam begat his son Seth "in his likeness, according to his image." This is another clear allusion to Gen 1:26–27, and the common interpretation of the passage is that the author was explaining that the image of God was passed on to Adam's children. More likely, the point with the obvious allusion back to Gen 1:26–27 is that as Seth is the son of Adam, *so Adam is the son of God*. This point is not made until Gen 5, well after the fact is established that humanity is creature, not deity, in order to prevent the misunderstanding that Adam as "son" of God was therefore somehow divine. The author iterates that Adam begot Seth (ילד; LXX: ἐγέννησεν), but God *created* man (ברא; LXX: ἐποίησεν) to make clear that man is creature and to deny to the human imagination any fancies of sharing in divinity. Note that Seth is not described as the image of God, but as the image *of Adam*. The obvious implication of Seth's birth in Adam's likeness and image as Adam's son[7]—and the point is made in the way of excellent, indirect, biblical narrative and not with explicit propositional statement—is that Adam therefore *must* have been the son of God, that he *is* the son of God. (This narrative theology was not lost upon the author of Luke's gospel; see Luke 3:38). The narrative looks back and with literary

---

[6] This is supported by the fact that the LXX translates both בְּצֶלֶם אֱלֹהִים at 1:27 and the Hebrew בִּדְמוּת אֱלֹהִים at 5:1 with κατ᾽ εἰκόνα θεοῦ. Cf. H. Wildberger, "צֶלֶם" *TLOT* 3:1082: "The meanings of the two terms [צֶלֶם and דְּמוּת] are...doubtless quite close."

[7] Cf. Gen 4:25, where Seth is explicitly mentioned as the "son" (בֵּן) that Eve "bore" (ילד) to Adam with the language of 5:3: "When Adam had lived 130 years, he begat (ילד) in his likeness, according to his image, and he called his name Seth" (my translation of MT). The LXX translator missed the narrative's repetitional signals and translated ילד with two different words in Greek, possibly for stylistic variation.

mastery communicates profound theological truth by expanding upon Gen 1:26–27 even as it almost casually narrates that Adam begat a son in his own likeness.[8]

In the HB, the word צֶלֶם ("image") occurs seventeen times total, twelve times if one excludes the extraordinary uses found in Gen 1:26, 27 (twice), 5:3 and 9:6. Of these remaining twelve at least five, and possibly six, serve to signify a physical representation of a god, i.e., an idol.[9] The three uses in 1 Samuel denote the physical representations of the mice and boils made to depict the true ones that were plaguing the Philistines.[10] The use in Ezek 23:14 connotes a pictorial representation of Chaldean officers on a wall.[11] The two occurrences in the Psalms belong together in relative isolation from the rest of the uses, connoting something like "shadow."[12] In the Aramaic section of Daniel, the cognate צְלֵם occurs seventeen times, sixteen of which signify a statue or a physical representation of a god.[13] Stendebach is probably correct to say that צֶלֶם is not a technical term for a physical representation of a god; the word is semantically more flexible than that.[14] The word and its cognates among Israel's neighbors nevertheless could and did commonly signify this meaning.[15]

ANE evidence reveals that Gen 1:26–27 has probably tapped into its surrounding religious and cultural environment to make a point about God's creation of humanity.[16] In Assyria and especially Egypt, kings

---

[8] Note the further literary link between both "fathers," God and Adam, seen in the fact that the same formulaic phraseology is used to narrate the naming of their progeny: God creates man (male and female) and "calls their name man" (וַיִּקְרָא אֶת־שְׁמָם אָדָם; 5:2b), and Adam begets a son and "calls his name Seth" (וַיִּקְרָא אֶת־שְׁמוֹ שֵׁת). Those who would object that nowhere does the narrative explicitly call God a father or Adam a son miss the point; biblical narrative is at its best when it teaches indirectly with allusions, puns, and repetitions. See for its overall arguments about how Hebrew narrative works the study by Robert Alter, *The Art of Biblical Narrative* (New York: Basic Books, 1981). For a quick overview, see L. D. Hawk, "Literary/Narrative Criticism," *DOTP* 536–44.

[9] Num 33:52; 2 Kgs 11:18//2 Chr 23:17; Ezek 7:20; Amos 5:26. The sixth is Ezek 16:17.

[10] 1 Sam 6:5 (twice), 11.

[11] Note that in Ezek 23:15, דְּמוּת is employed as an interchangeable synonym with צֶלֶם of v. 14 (cf. again with Gen 1:26–27).

[12] Pss 39:6 [ET 39:7], 73:20; cf. NRSV translation.

[13] Dan 2:31 (twice), 32, 34, 35, 3:1, 2, 3 (twice), 5, 7, 10, 12, 14, 15, 18.

[14] F. J. Stendebach, "צֶלֶם," *TDOT* 12:391.

[15] Stendebach, *TDOT* 12:389; Wildberger, *TLOT* 3:1080; *HALOT*, "צֶלֶם."

[16] See the numerous references in Hans Wildberger, "Das Abbild Gottes: Gen. 1, 26–30," *TZ* 21 (1965): 245–59, 481–501; D. J. A. Clines, "The Image of God in Man," *TynBul* (1968): 53–103.

were often described as the "image" of their supreme deity. Wildberger offers several examples, including the two given below, which praise the pharaoh in relation to his god as the "beloved, bodily *Son* of Re, Lord of the foreign lands…the good god, the *creation* of Re, the *ruler* who has come out of the body already strong; *image* of Horus upon the *throne* of his father; great in strength…."[17] In a second text, Amun, king of the gods, declares of pharaoh Amenophis III that he is "my beloved, bodily *Son*…, my *living image, creation* of my members, whom Mut, the mistress…*gave birth* to me, and whom has been raised up as the only *Lord* of men."[18]

Clines also offers several ANE parallels, including this one spoken by the god Amon-Re to pharaoh Amenophis III: "You are my beloved *son*, who came forth from my members, my *image*, whom *I have put on earth. I have given to you to rule the earth* in peace."[19] The affinities of these texts with Gen 1:26–27 are striking. Those who object[20] to this evidence on the grounds that the inscriptions are not set within the context of the creation of man in a creation account miss that the creation theme is at least present ("creation of Re," "creation of my members"). The pharaoh is described by several titles and descriptions: son, image, creation, lord and/or ruler of the earth. In light of our discussion above on Gen 5:1–3 and the implication of the text that Adam was the (created, not begotten) son of God, then all the same titles or descriptions likewise apply to Adam and to all humanity (including "ruler" as seen in the command "and let them rule…over all the earth"; Gen 1:26, 28). Ian Hart expands on the ANE evidence and sums up the point of Gen 1:26–27 well:

> In the Ancient Near East it was widely believed that a god's spirit lived in any statue or image of that god, with the result that the image could function as a kind of representative of or substitute for the god wherever it was placed. It was also customary in the ANE to think of a king as a representative of a god; obviously the king ruled, and the god was the ultimate ruler, so the king must be ruling on the god's behalf.…This background makes it likely that when the author of Genesis 1 claimed that man was made as the image of God, he meant that man was to be God's representative on earth, ruling…on God's behalf, like a king. In other words, the idea of the image of God was "democratized"—the

---

[17] Wildberger, "Das Abbild Gottes," 485 (emphases mine).
[18] Wildberger, "Das Abbild Gottes," 485–86 (emphases mine).
[19] Clines, "Image of God in Man," 85 (emphasis mine).
[20] Such as Westermann, *Genesis 1–11*, 153–54.

Egyptian and Mesopotamian concept of a king being the god's image was broadened to make mankind in general such an image.[21]

The implication, therefore, is that as humanity fulfilled the mandate to "be fruitful and multiply" and thus expanded in ever-increasing circles upon the earth, God as King would be laying claim to the area to which they had attained, because they served as his living statues, the physical representatives of his reign.[22] They would serve as his vicegerents. The ANE evidence and the later narrative context of Gen 1:26–27 at 5:1–3 confirm that humans are God's royal sons and daughters. According to Gen 1, the purpose of humanity is to fill the earth with the royal reign of its Creator and King, to establish the created world as the realm of the kingdom of God.

Genesis 1:26–27 and Its Exegetical Tradition in Early and Late Judaism

The Genesis 1 "image" tradition appears frequently in the early Jewish literature. Often the language is tied to the idea of Adam as king over all of the created order, as seen, for example, in *2 En.* 30:12: "And I assigned him to be a king, to reign on the earth, and to have my wisdom."[23] This text also highlights Adam's extraordinary wisdom, which is another theme that surfaces occasionally in the literature.[24] Allusions to Gen 1:26–27 are elsewhere connected to statements which claim that God created everything for humanity's sake.[25] Adam is the very representation of God; to insult a human is to insult God.[26] Adam's honor and

---

[21] Ian Hart, "Genesis 1:1–2:3 as a Prologue to the Book of Genesis," *TynBul* 46 (1995): 318–19; cf. Wildberger, "Das Abbild Gottes," 489.

[22] Cf. Hans Walter Wolff, *Anthropology of the Old Testament* (trans. M. Kohl; Philadelphia: Fortress, 1974), 160:

> In the ancient East the setting up of the king's statue was the equivalent of the proclamation of his domination over the sphere in which the statue was erected (cf. Dan. 3.1, 5f.). When in the thirteenth century B.C. the Pharaoh Ramesses II had his image hewn out of rock at the mouth of the *nahr el-kelb*, on the Mediterranean north of Beirut, the image meant that he was the ruler of this area. Accordingly man is set in the midst of creation as God's statue. He is evidence that God is the Lord of creation; but as God's steward he also exerts his rule, fulfilling his task not in arbitrary despotism but as a responsible agent.

[23] *2 En.* 31:3, 44:2, 58:3; *Sib. Or.* fragment 3.12–14; *4 Ezra* 6:53–54; *Jub.* 2:14; Wis 10:2; 4Q504 fragment 8, lines 4–6; Sir 17:2–3.

[24] Philo, *Creation* 148; see also 4Q504 fragment 8, lines 4–6, with its explicit mention of Adam's "understanding and knowledge" (בינה ודעת).

[25] *2 En.* 65:2; *4 Ezra* 8:44. Elsewhere in *4 Ezra*, the opinion is put forward that the world was made especially for Israel as her inheritance (6:55–59).

[26] *2 En.* 44:1–3, 52:2; cf. *T. Isaac* 6:33–34.

beauty was incomparable to anything else in creation. He is gloriously exalted and even the angels were bid to worship him as the image of God.[27] In paradise, Adam enjoyed an open heaven where he might behold the angels, and which was opened up to the third heaven until he sinned.[28] He and Eve wore a covering or stole of glory before they sinned.[29] For some writers, the image consisted of the soul, or spirit, or reason of man,[30] but for others the image appeared to include the physical aspect of man.[31]

Although humanity as God's image was created for incorruption,[32] a blanket of death enveloped all of humanity, and some early Jewish writers held Adam responsible due to his transgression in the garden.[33] At the same time, some of these same texts recognized that individuals were yet responsible for incurring punishment or judgment after their own death.[34] Of significant interest for this present study is the thought on Adam and his descendants found in *4 Ezra* 3:20–22:

> Yet you did not take away from [the sons of Israel] their evil heart, so that your Law might bring forth fruit in them. For the first Adam, burdened with an evil heart, transgressed and was overcome, as were also all who were descended from him. Thus the disease became permanent; the law was in the people's heart along with the evil root, but what was good departed, and the evil remained.[35]

The reason given for why all of humanity, including God's special people, Israel, succumbed to transgression was due to the permanent disease of an evil heart inherited from Adam. Although the Law was present, the heart churned out only evil (cf. *4 Ezra* 4:30). No solution is given for the dilemma. The text only goes on to state that this evil heart was the cause for Israel's exile of 587 B.C.E. (*4 Ezra* 3:23–27).

While Josephus was silent with regard to explicit mention of humanity's creation in the image of God, Philo frequently discusses the concept. Philo held that man existed as "an image of an image." The divine Word or Wisdom existed as the "image of God," and man was

---

[27] *L.A.E.* 13:1–15:3; *2 En.* 30:10–12; *Sib. Or.* 1.23.

[28] *2 En.* 31:1–2, 42:3, 71:28.

[29] *Hist. Rech.* 12:3.

[30] Ps.-Phoc 105–6; *Sib. Or.* 8.402. See especially on Philo below.

[31] *Sib. Or.* 1.23; *T. Isaac* 6:33–34.

[32] Wis 2:23.

[33] *2 Bar.* 17:2–3, 23:4, 48:42–43, 54:15; *4 Ezra* 3:5–7, 7:116–18; cf. *T. Ab.* 8:9.

[34] *2 Bar.* 54:15, 19; *4 Ezra* 7:118; cf. *T. Isaac* 4:32.

[35] B. M. Metzger, "The Fourth Book of Ezra," *OTP* 1:529.

forged as the *cast* of this image, that is, "according to the image."[36]
Philo taught that there were two types of men (he does so inconsis-
tently, however). There exists the man of Gen 1:26–27 made "after
the image": this man is heavenly and incorruptible, consists of the
mind or reason, and does not share in anything earthly or corruptible
(including a body). The second is the man of Gen 2:7, formed out of
clay. This man is corruptible, and is not fashioned according to the
image of God.[37] For Philo, the image of God in man consists of the
rational part of the soul, or the mind (νοῦς).[38] The first man is exalted
because of his pedigree of noble birth: God himself was his father.[39]
Philo asserted also that God "by express mandate appointed [Adam]
king" over all creation and "charged him with the care of animals and
plants, like a governor subordinate to the chief and great King."[40] As
king, the first man was also full of extraordinary wisdom.[41] For Philo,
humanity was "that highest form of life, which has received dominion
over everything whatsoever upon earth, born to be the likeness of
God's power and image of His nature, the visible of the Invisible, the
created of the Eternal."[42]

In later (rabbinic) Judaism, humanity is considered beloved of God
due to its creation in the image of God,[43] and at one point the image
language is interpreted to mean that God originally created humanity
to live and endure forever, as God himself exists.[44] Adam's wisdom
surpasses that of the angelic hosts and is displayed in his ability to
name the animals.[45] In one text, the angelic host nearly mistook Adam

---

[36] *Creation* 25, 146 (cf. 139); *Heir* 231; *QG* 2.62; *Planting* 19–20; *Spec. Laws* 3.83,
3.207; *Alleg. Interp.* 3.96.

[37] *Alleg. Interp.* 1.31, 2.4; *Creation* 134.

[38] *QG* 2.62; *Heir* 231; *Planting* 20; *Names* 223 (λογισμός; "reasoning"); *Spec. Laws* 1.171,
3.207; *Virtues* 204; *Creation* 69, 146; *Worse* 83–84.

[39] *Virtues* 204.

[40] *Creation* 84, 88 (see 83–88; Colson, Whitaker, and Marcus, LCL); see also *Creation*
148.

[41] See again p. 236 and n. 24 above.

[42] *Moses* 2.65 (Colson, Whitaker, and Marcus, LCL). The second-to-last phrase
of the quotation literally reads "the visible image of the invisible nature": ἐικὼν τῆς
ἀοράτου φύσεως ἐμφανής; cf. Col 1:15. This statement seems to contradict elsewhere
Philo's limitation of the image in man to the rational part of the soul or mind (see
n.38 above).

[43] See *m. Avot* 3.15.

[44] *Midr. Rabbah* Numbers 16.24.

[45] *Midr. Rabbah* Genesis 17.4; *Midr. Rabbah* Numbers 19.3; *Midr. Rabbah* Ecclesiastes
7.23; *Pesiqta Rabbati*, Piska 14.9.

for God and worshipped him because he was his exact representation.[46] Through parabolic comparisons, the rabbis also exhibit awareness that the "image" language of Gen 1:26–27 implies that man is likened to a physical representation or statue of God the King.[47] Because man is the representative of God, the rabbis, teaching from Gen 1:26–27, spoke against shaming a man in retaliation for a wrong, out of fear of shaming God.[48] Others taught that the divine image in man could be diminished either by murder or failure to sexually reproduce in marriage.[49] At one point, the plural in the phrase "Let us make man" is ascribed to God speaking to the Torah, viewed as the instrument by which God made creation.[50] Elsewhere, the phrase that God created man in his own image is interpreted to mean that Adam came into the world circumcised.[51]

New Testament Context: Genesis 1:26–27 in Colossians 3:10

The imperatives of Col 3:5–11 flow out of the indicative reality described in 3:1–4 (which, in turn, builds upon Col 2:9–15, 20). The Colossians have died and been raised together with Christ and now their life is hidden with him "in God" (3:3b). They no longer live in the old world or age dominated by the στοιχεῖα τοῦ κόσμου ("the elemental spirits of the universe" RSV, NRSV; 2:20). Since this is so, they are to set their minds on the things "above," on the things of God and of heaven, where Messiah is. They must not set their minds on τὰ ἐπὶ τῆς γῆς, "the things upon the earth," the worldview and ways of the old, στοιχεῖα-dominated age and sphere (3:1–2). They must instead put to death anything that remains of their thinking and conduct that belongs to this lower sphere (3:5a). The apostle immediately offers a list of five vices to explain what types of things he has especially in view (v. 5b). On account of such vices, Paul avows that "the wrath of God is coming," that is, the universal and eschatological judgment of YHWH

---

[46] *Midr. Rabbah* Genesis 8.10.
[47] *Midr. Rabbah* Exodus 30.16; *Midr. Rabbah* Leviticus 34.3; *Midr. Rabbah* Deuteronomy 2.30; *Midr. Rabbah* Genesis 8.8.
[48] *Midr. Rabbah* Genesis 24.7.
[49] *t. Yevamot* 8:7; cf. *Midr. Rabbah* Genesis 17.2, 34.14; *Midr. Rabbah* Ecclesiastes 9.9 §1 (p. 239).
[50] *Pirqe Rabbi Eliezer*, p. 76.
[51] *Avot of Rabbi Nathan*, chapter 2, section 5; cf. *Midr.* Psalms 9.7.

promised through the ΟΤ prophetic movement (3:6a).[52] Paul mentions
the impending day of God's wrath to provide a motivating basis for why
the Colossians must be rid of such conduct.[53] As pagan gentiles, they
once walked and lived in these vices (3:7). The "but now" (νυνὶ δέ; cf.
1:22) of v. 8, however, signals as a "classic Pauline way of indicating
the transition of the old life to the new"[54] the shift from living in the
old sphere dominated by sin to that of the new, where Christ is all in
all (3:11). The Colossian church therefore is to live in these vices no
longer. At 3:8–9a, Paul further adds a second list of five vices that he
demands the faithful "to take off," rounding it off with a prohibition
that forbids lying to another. Paul then in 3:9b-11 provides the basis
for *why* the Colossians must "take off" such conduct through the use of
two aorist participles: they have "stripped off" (ἀπεκδυσάμενοι) the old
man with all his practices and have "clothed themselves" (ἐνδυσάμενοι)
with the new man.[55] What is meant by the language of the old and new

---

[52] See e.g., Isa 13:9–16, 24:1–6, 17–23; 66:18–24; Dan 7; Mal 4:1–6. Paul does
not appear to have any *one* of these texts specifically in mind; rather the apostle has
been influenced by the theme as a whole as it arises from such texts as these. In light
of our chapter on methodology, we may well label such influence on the apostle as a
"strong genealogical parallel" (see p. 25 of this study).

[53] The text of 3:6 that the editors of both the NA^{27} as well as the UBS^4 have placed
in brackets ("upon the sons of disobedience") reflects the uncertainty on their part
as to whether the text is original or not. It is possible that the longer reading is the
original, and that the shorter reading came about through the scribal error known as
homoioarchton ("similar beginning"). It is more probable however, that the omission is
the original reading. Regarding the external evidence, the earliest witnesses attest to
the omission ($\mathfrak{p}^{46}$, about 200 C.E.; Cyprian, who died 258 C.E.). The uncial B, another
outstanding witness, likewise attests to the omission (4th century C.E.). The excellent
witnesses ℵ (4th century C.E.) and A (5th century C.E.) support the longer reading, as
do numerous other uncials, minuscules, and versions. Many of these other witnesses,
however, are of a later date and of less trustworthy text traditions (or "families"), such
as the Byzantine.

Regarding the internal evidence, the omission is by far the superior reading. The omission is both the shorter and the more difficult reading. The omission leaves a statement
that is readable but somewhat awkward. A scribe, recognizing the parallel statement at
5:6 in the sister letter to the Ephesians, inserted into Col 3:6 the second half of Eph 5:6
to smooth out the statement of Col 3:6 and complete its thought. Cf. the conclusions
of Gnilka, *Der Kolosserbrief*, 183; Hugedé, *Colossiens*, 171n.48; Lohse, *Colossians*, 139n.30;
Masson, *Colossiens*, 143n.2; O'Brien, *Colossians*, 173. For a different opinion, see Aletti,
Colossiens, 226; Wright, *Colossians*, 135n.1; Hübner, *An die Kolosser*, 102.

[54] Wright, *Colossians*, 136.

[55] Against Lohse, *Colossians*, 141, the participles are not imperatival in force; cf. Jervell,
Imago Dei, 235–36; Masson, *Colossiens*, 143n.6; O'Brien, *Colossians*, 188–9; Wolter, *Der
Brief an die Kolosser*, 178. On the use of the adverbial participle with a causal force,
see Daniel B. Wallace, *Greek Grammar Beyond the Basics: An Exegetical Syntax of the New
Testament* (Grand Rapids: Zondervan, 1997), 631–32.

"man" (τὸν παλαιὸν ἄνθρωπον...τὸν νέον)?[56] First, it should be noted that the ethical imperatives flow out of the indicative reality that the Colossian faithful have acquired a new identity. They are not exhorted to clothe themselves in the new man, but rather are forbidden to speak lies precisely because they are clothed in the new man already. Their ethical conduct flows out of the indicative reality of their new identity, and thus Paul exhorts the Colossians to act in accord with the new man that they have donned as a garment.

The key to unlocking the identification of what Paul signifies when he mentions the old and new man is found at Col 3:10–11. The new man is being renewed κατ᾽ εἰκόνα τοῦ κτίσαντος αὐτόν ("according to the image of the One who created him"), which is language that serves as a direct allusion to the creation of the first man in his pre-fall state as found at Gen 1:26–27 LXX. The "new man" is not quite to be equated with Christ himself, but is rather the resurrected existence of the new age that is acquired by *incorporation* or *union with the risen Christ.*[57] In the sphere of the new man or humanity, there are no racial or class distinctions, and certainly no more divisions as demarcated by one's circumcision status (3:11; cf. Gal 3:28).

The "old man" is the "body of flesh" of 2:11, the body inherited from Adam, the fallen body of the old and dying age.[58] This body was removed by divine circumcision. Note again the parallel between 2:11b and 3:9b:

Col 2:11: ἐν τῇ ἀπεκδύσει   τοῦ σώματος τῆς σαρκός
Col 3:9: ἀπεκδυσάμενοι   τὸν παλαιὸν ἄνθρωπον

The old man is depicted as a garment that has been removed. With the removal of the old man go the practices that accompanied it (3:9b). When the Colossians "heard and came to understand truly the grace of God" (1:6c), their Adamic bodies were "cut off" in Messiah's circumcision (i.e., his death) and they were raised up by God to new life together with him (2:11–13). This inward spiritual event of death and resurrection with Messiah is vividly captured and portrayed in the initiate's outward experience of the water rite of baptism (Col 2:12).[59] They

---

[56] Cf. Rom 6:6; Eph 4:22, 24.

[57] Cf. Gal 3:27, Rom 13:14.

[58] See discussion on pp. 174–176 of this study.

[59] Several commentators have argued for a baptismal background to explain the clothing imagery in the use of the words ἀποτίθημι, ἀπεκδύομαι, and ἐνδύω found in Col 3:8–10, 12 (e.g., Jervell, *Imago Dei*, 235–36; Lohse, *Colossians*, 141–42; Wolter, *Der*

donned a new garment, the new humanity via their union with Christ, who is the "new man" or new last Adam (3:10–11). Nevertheless, the believer's "new man" experiences the "already–not yet" eschatological tension and is in a continual process of renewal (ἀνακαινούμενον).[60] This renewal process is recreating the pre-Fall image of God in the believer, restoring him or her to a state of "true righteousness and holiness."[61] In the sphere of this new humanity, Christ is all things and in all things (3:11), the head (1:18), prototype (1:15), and mediator (1:15–20) of this recreated new humanity of the inaugurated new creation. The Colossians' donning of the new man as a garment serves as the basis for Paul's subsequent positive imperatives in vv. 12–14 (cf. the οὖν in v. 12a): the church's attitudes and actions are to reflect their identity transformation and are to include such things as compassion, humility, and forbearance, with love the band that ties it all together. The Colossian faithful are to actualize who they are in their union with Messiah, the last Adam and head of the new humanity.

In light of Col 1:15 and 3:10, Paul appears to hold to an "image of an image" theology.[62] Christ *is* the image of God (ὅς ἐστιν εἰκὼν τοῦ θεοῦ, Col 1:15; cf. 2 Cor 4:4; Rom 8:29), while believers are being recreated "*according to* the image" (κατ᾿ εἰκόνα) of God (3:10).[63] That is, believers are being recreated according to the pattern of Christ. This is very close in thought to Philo's image theology: man is made after the image of the divine Word or Wisdom.[64] As we have argued previously, Paul borrowed a hymn at 1:15–20 that depicts Christ as

---

Brief an die Kolosser, 178–79; Aletti, *Colossiens*, 229–31). For the most recent and fullest argument see Jung Hoon Kim, *The Significance of Clothing Imagery in the Pauline Corpus* (JSNTSup 268; London & New York: T&T Clark, 2004), 152–75.

[60] Note both the present tense as well as the passive voice, which is a divine passive: God is continually at work in the believer, effecting the renewal process. Cf. 2 Cor 4:16: "Therefore we do not lose heart, but though our outer man is decaying, yet our inner man is being renewed day by day" (NASB).

[61] Eph 4:24 RSV, NRSV, ESV, NIV.

[62] See also Gnilka, *Der Kolosserbrief*, 188: "Der neue Mensch ist Bild des Bildes, Abbild des Urbildes"; cf. Moule, *Colossians*, 120; Ernst, *An die Kolosser*, 226–27; R. Martin, *Colossians*, 107–8; Furter, *Colossiens*, 173; Dunn, *Colossians*, 222; O'Brien, *Colossians*, 191; Hay, *Colossians*, 126–27. Hübner, *An die Kolosser*, 104, in defense of Gnilka's comment asserts that "ist es äußerst unwahrscheinlich daß 3,10 nach der Intention des AuctCol ohne Bezug auf 1,15 sein sollte." For a dissenting view, see Lightfoot, *Colossians*, 216; Abbott, *Colossians*, 285; Wolter, *Der Brief an die Kolosser*, 180.

[63] Cf. 1 Cor 15:49; Rom 8:29; 2 Cor 3:18; Eph 4:24; see James 3:9. Though some have interpreted the subject of the phrase "of the one who created him" to be Christ, this is unlikely; see O'Brien, *Colossians*, 191; Lohse, *Colossians*, 143n.65.

[64] *Alleg. Interp.* 3.96; *Creation* 25; cf. *Confusion* 146–47. See chapter seven, pp. 125, 126 and 126n.56 for the text of these passages.

personified Wisdom, the mediator of both the original as well as the new creation (see chapter seven). Again, Christ is both the prototype (1:15) and mediator (1:15–20) of this recreated new humanity of the inaugurated new creation.

"Die Erneuerung hat als unmittelbares Ziel die Erkenntnis (εἰς ἐπίγνωσιν)."[65] But to what knowledge does Paul refer? The immediate context of the letter itself provides the answer. The cryptic εἰς ἐπίγνωσιν of 3:10 is shorthand for the fuller ἐπιγνώσει τοῦ θεοῦ ("knowledge of God") of 1:10, the ἐπίγνωσιν τοῦ θελήματος αὐτοῦ ("the knowledge of [God's] will") of 1:9, and the ἐπίγνωσιν τοῦ μυστηρίου τοῦ θεοῦ, Χριστοῦ ("the knowledge of the mystery of God, Christ") of 2:2. This phrase "knowledge of God" has OT roots (LXX: ἐπίγνωσις θεοῦ) and there often carries overtones of covenantal obedience (see Hos 4:1, 6, 6:6; cf. Isa 11:9). It includes the cognitive element of what God is like and what he requires of his covenant people, but goes beyond it to include a life conducted faithfully before God in light of that knowledge and in light of the redemption in Christ.[66] The goal of God's renewal of fallen humanity through Messiah, according to Col 3:10 via the allusion to Gen 1:26–27, is that their may be a people who know God. When Christ is revealed and his followers are revealed together with him (3:4), the Colossian redeemed will faithfully represent God with their whole life and conduct in the renewed creation as his vicegerents and children (recall the exegesis above on Gen 1:26–27). They had begun to do this even in their own day (Col 2:5; cf. Eph 5:1 in light of Eph 4:24).

In the early Church Fathers, Gen 1:26–27 is cited to make several different points. The earliest citation of it outside the NT is found at *1 Clem.* 33:5 (ca. 95 C.E.). Origen (d. 253/4 C.E.) quoted it to argue that, though humanity is already in God's "image," perfection as the "likeness" awaits the consummation.[67] Already in *Barn.* 5:5, 6:12 (ca. 70–135 C.E.) Christ is viewed as the one God addressed when he declared "let *us* make man in *our* image."[68] Tertullian cited it as the ground for sexual

---

[65] Gnilka, *Der Kolosserbrief*, 189; cf. Hugedé, *Colossiens*, 176; O'Brien, *Colossians*, 192; Bruce, *Colossians*, 148.

[66] Cf. O'Brien, *Colossians*, 192: "This true knowledge leads to a conduct that is in conformity with the Creator's will."

[67] *First Principles* 3.6.1 (*ANF* 4:344). Origen maintains this distinction between "image" and "likeness" elsewhere (*Against Celsus* 4.30 [*ANF* 4:509]).

[68] See likewise Justin (d. ca. 165 C.E.), *Dialogue with Trypho* 62 (*ANF* 1:228); Irenaeus, *Against Heresies* 4.20.1 (*ANF* 1:467–68; cf. 1:463); Tertullian (d. after 220 C.E.), *The Resurrection of the Flesh* 6 (*ANF* 3:549); idem, *Against Marcion* 5.8 (*ANF* 3:445); idem, *Against*

purity: the body as God's image is for God.[69] Clement of Alexandria (d. before 215 c.e.) held to an "image of an image" theology: Christ as the Word is the image of God and man is the image of the Word.[70]

Hermeneutical and Theological Reflections

Paul appears to employ Gen 1:26–27 typologically at Col 3:10. The first man, Adam, was made according to the image of God and served as head of the original humanity. Through his transgression, however, sin entered the world, and death through sin. Humanity was at enmity with God and its heart produced only evil continually. The last Adam, Messiah Jesus, *is* the image of God and serves as the head and prototype of the new humanity of the new creation.[71] This new humanity was salvaged from the old and is in process of being recreated to function rightly as God's image-bearers. As the original pre-fall humanity was patterned after the image of God, so the new humanity is in process of being recreated according to that same image as it existed before the fall. The image as stamped upon Adam in his pre-fall state serves as the example or pattern for the new humanity of the new creation. It is in this broad sense that Paul's use of Gen 1:26–27 at Col 3:10 can be classified as a typological use, since a type is a biblical event, person, or institution that serves as a pattern for other events, persons, or institutions.[72] It is not merely an analogical comparison ("this is like that"), since there is also present a real and fundamental historical correspondence between original humanity of the first creation and the renewed humanity of the new creation.[73]

In this inaugurated new creation, the renewed humanity is also in process of attaining to the knowledge of God. In the OT, this true knowledge encompassed an understanding of God and of his will that

---

Praxeas 12 (*ANF* 3:606–7); Novation (d. after 251 c.e.), *Treatise Concerning the Trinity* 26 (*ANF* 5:636); Origen, *Against Celsus* 5.37 (*ANF* 4:560); *Apostolic Constitutions* 5.1.7 (*ANF* 7:441), 8.2.12 (*ANF* 7:487).

[69] Tertullian, *Modesty* 16 (*ANF* 4:91).

[70] *Exhortation to the Greeks* 10 (*ANF* 2:199); cf. Tertullian, *Against Praxeas* 12 (*ANF* 3:606–7).

[71] Cf. Paul's Adam-Christ comparisons elsewhere at Rom 5:12–21; 1 Cor 15:20–22, 42–49.

[72] Baker, "Typology," 327. See again p. 39n.89 of this study.

[73] Baker, "Typology," 327, writes that "typology implies a real correspondence. It is not interested in parallels of detail but only in agreement of fundamental...structure."

was actualized faithfully in life and conduct. This knowledge had been escalated in Christ's first coming and would be fully realized in the consummated new creation (see again chapter four). Then the sweeping, original vision of Gen 1 will be realized, as creation—filled with a renewed humanity that faithfully exercises their delegated authority—flourishes and stands forever established as the realm of the kingdom of God.

CHAPTER FOURTEEN

THE RAMIFICATIONS OF THE INVESTIGATION

This study has discerned that Paul has alluded to or echoed eleven texts from the OT.[1] These include three from Genesis (Col 1:6; 2:13; 3:10), two from Isaiah (Col 1:9–10; 2:22), and two from the Psalms (Col 1:19; 3:1). The list is rounded out by a reference each to 1) the exodus deliverance found in the Pentateuch (Col 1:12–14), 2) Deuteronomy (Col 2:11), 3) 2 Samuel (Col 1:13), and 4) Proverbs (Col 1:15–20). The detection of, arguments for, and collection of these findings in one place constitutes a contribution to 'Old Testament in the New' scholarship in and of itself. The discoveries, however, lend themselves to further observations and contributions, as will be discussed below.

Ramifications for the Overall Understanding of Colossians

What is striking about several of the allusions or echoes of the OT in Colossians is that they consistently touch upon the specific theme of new creation. Of the eleven allusions/echoes proposed in this study, four presuppose this framework and build upon it, three directly: Gen 1:28 in Col 1:6, 10, Prov 8:22–31 in Col 1:15–20, and Gen 1:26–27 in 3:10, and one indirectly: Isa 11:2, 9 in 1:9–10. At Col 1:6, Paul echoes the "be fruitful and multiply" language from the creation account of Gen 1 to depict firstly the *numerical* growth and worldwide expansion of the gospel (1:6a), with the emphasis then shifting to communicating the growth of *internal* spiritual fruit—like love and faith and knowledge of God (1:4, 8, 10)—among the Colossians in 1:6b and especially 1:10, where the echo is repeated explicitly (the phrase is simply assumed in 1:6b).

Furthermore, this Gen 1:28 "be fruitful and multiply" tradition is interwoven with echoes of Isa 11 at Col 1:9–10 ("Spirit-given wisdom

---

[1] In the case of the reference to the Hebrew exodus from Egypt in Col 1:12b–14a, Paul has echoed the foundational *event* of the OT, and not necessarily any one individual text. In the case of the reference to Prov 8, the echo is of this text as it stood *in its first century C.E. interpretive development*.

and understanding") in a mutually interpretive, intertextual web.[2]
Isaiah 11:1–9 portrays the future and ideal Davidic king (interpreted by
early Judaism as a reference to the coming Messiah), who, by means of
his endowment with the Spirit that grants him abundant wisdom and
understanding and knowledge of God, establishes the new creational
kingdom of God and fills the earth with the knowledge of God. The
reader will recall our discussion also of the intertextual conversation
between Isa 11:1–9 and Isa 65:17–25, of which the latter explicitly
mentions the "new heavens and earth."[3] According to Paul in Colossians, Jesus Christ is this long-awaited Davidic Messiah, who is, in
accordance with the prophecy, filling the earth (ἐν παντὶ τῷ κόσμῳ,
Col 1:6) with Spirit-wrought wisdom, understanding, and knowledge of
God (Col 1:9–10; see again Isa 11:9; cf. Hab 2:14). The presupposition
is that God had inaugurated the end-time new creation of the age-to-
come. In Paul's view, the age of fulfillment of all the OT expectations
and promises had begun, because Messiah had arrived on the scene
of human history (cf. 2 Cor 1:20).

The new creation theme is continued by the apostle's insertion of a
hymn at Col 1:15–20, which describes Christ in the language of the
Wisdom figure of Prov 8:22–31 as that tradition stood in its first century exegetical development. Christ is the reality foreshadowed by the
Prov 8 literary personification. He served as God's agent of creation,
through whom all the original creation was made and is sustained
(1:15–17), including the spiritual beings that threaten the Colossian
Christ-followers. Yet Paul also describes Christ as the agent of the *new*
creation, a reality established through his crucifixion and resurrection
(1:18–20). Through Christ, God has effected cosmic reconciliation (1:20;
cf. vv. 21–22). Messiah holds preeminence in this new creation by virtue
of his resurrection, for his resurrection is God's first act of the new
creation. Christ himself is the "beginning" of the new creation as the
firstborn from the dead (1:18).

The imagery of the new creation in Colossians continues on after the
hymn of 1:15–20 at 3:10. Here Paul alludes to Gen 1:26–27 and to the
creation account of the first man made "according to the image of

---

[2] The language belongs to Timothy W. Berkley, *From a Broken Covenant to Circumcision
of the Heart: Pauline Intertextual Exegesis in Romans 2:17–29* (SBLDS 175; Atlanta: SBL,
2000), 204, as he describes the interrelationship between the various OT texts Paul has
built upon in Rom 2:17–29.

[3] See p. 66 of chapter four of this study.

God." The Colossians have put on the "new man," wherein Christ is all in all (3:11), having taken off the "old man with his practices" and donned the "new man being renewed unto knowledge in accordance with the image of the one who created him" (3:10). This "old man–new man" language, in light of the allusion to Gen 1:26–27, almost certainly presupposes "first Adam–last Adam" Christology, which Paul has discussed elsewhere (Rom 5:12–21; 1 Cor 15:20–22, 42–49). Raised with Christ, the Colossians have stripped off the "old man." The "old man," as was argued, is the body inherited from Adam, the mortal and fallen existence of the old age. The Colossians had donned the "new man," the resurrection existence of the new age and new creation, albeit in its "already–not yet" eschatological development, for the new creation is inaugurated but not consummated. The "new man" donned by the Colossians is not quite to be equated with Christ himself, but is rather the resurrection existence of the new age that is acquired by incorporation or union with the risen Christ.

A second benefit from detecting the allusions and echoes of the OT in Colossians is gained in the area of the letter's Christology. Three echoes refer back to OT texts that speak of the Davidic lineage and that presuppose the promise YHWH made to David of an everlasting line on the throne over Israel. 2 Samuel 7:12–18, the foundational text that narrates this promise, is echoed in Col 1:13b ("kingdom of the son of his love"). Colossians 1:9 echoes Isa 11:1–9, a text that begins its prophecy with "a shoot shall come out from the stump of Jesse" (11:1a) and that assumes the promise-to-David tradition of 2 Sam 7. Colossians 3:1 echoes Ps 110:1 ("where Christ is, sitting at the right hand of God"), which likewise presupposes the Davidic-promise tradition. Psalm 110 portrays an ideal Davidic priest-king through whom YHWH will extend his dominion over all nations, beginning from Zion. The imagery corresponds to none of the depictions of David or to any of his sons in the Hebrew Bible's historical books. The psalm's original intention encompasses an ideal, messianic, and universal scope. The apostle Paul applies it directly to Christ, implying that he viewed Christ as the long-awaited and ultimate son of the lineage of David.

Of course, however, the Christological gold-mine is found at Col 1:15–20. Here Paul has possibly borrowed a hymn (and thereby endorsed its teaching) that alludes to the Prov 8 personified Wisdom interpretive tradition. Christ is described in the language of this pre-existent figure, through whom God created the world. Yet God did not merely create all things through the agency of Christ, but the hymn declares that Christ is the ultimate goal for which all was created (1:16). This is language reserved elsewhere in the NT for God alone (see Rom 11:36; 1 Cor 8:6; Heb 2:10). Here Christ is also described as the "image" of God (1:15a), which is language that contributes to the overall allusion to the Prov 8 tradition as found in early Judaism of the first century. The language is yet also ultimately based upon Gen 1, where humanity is said to be made "according to the image" of God and as such serves as God's visible representation and vicegerent.[4] These same undertones permeate Col 1:15a, and the latter notion of vicegerency and rule is supported by the parallelism with the title "firstborn of all creation" at 1:15b. The language of "firstborn" first of all communicates primacy in rank over any would-be contender for supremacy in the cosmos (see Col 1:16, 18d). Christ as the "image" of God is the supreme representation of God and his appointed vicegerent over all.

Our understanding of the Christology of the letter to the Colossians further advances in a significant way by recognition of the echo of Ps 67:17 LXX [ET 68:16] at Colossians 1:19. The echo is embedded in the hymn found at 1:15–20. As argued previously, the hymn breaks down into two basic parts: Christ preeminent in creation (vv. 15–17), and Christ preeminent in the renewed creation (vv. 18–20). The echo of Ps 67:17 LXX therefore informs especially how Christ is preeminent in the renewed creation. With this echo, the hymn portrays Christ as the locus of the divine presence of the new creational age. As God resided at Mt. Zion in the temple, so God has come to reside in Christ in his incarnation ("bodily"; see 2:9). Christ is depicted as the "temple" of the new age, the locus of the divine presence in the renewed creation.

Detection of the OT echoes and allusions provides a third contribution to our overall understanding of Colossians by providing possible light on the identity of the opponents. The present study has served to highlight the Jewishness of the encroaching "deceptive philosophy" (2:8). By echo and allusion as well as explicit statement, Paul undermines the perceived sufficiency of the Torah, the Jerusalem temple, circumcision, Sabbath, the Torah-prescribed festivals, and the dietary laws. The chart below demonstrates what Paul has done with the OT institutions and where in Colossians he has done it:

---

[4] See chapter thirteen of this study.

OT Institution	Jewish Understanding	Paul in Colossians
Torah	Torah is Wisdom	Col 1:15–20: Wisdom finds its reality in Christ
Temple	Jerusalem Temple locus of the divine presence	Col 1:19: Christ is the new and greater locus of the divine presence
Circumcision	Physical circumcision necessary for incorporation into the people of God	Col 2:11–13: Physical circumcision relativized: divinely wrought spiritual circumcision mark of true people of God
Sabbath, New Moons, and Festivals	Sacred days to be kept	Col 2:16–17: Reality found in Christ of the new age
Torah-prescribed dietary regulations	Clean and unclean food laws to be maintained	Col 2:16–17: Reality found in Christ of the new age

At Col 1:15–20, as mentioned already, the Prov 8 Wisdom development is alluded to and its language applied to describe Christ, whereas the Judaism of the first century identified the Torah or Law of Moses with Wisdom. Therefore, Col 1:15–20 probably stands—at least in part—as a polemic against the sufficiency of the revelation of God found in the Mosaic Law. At 1:19, Paul echoes Ps 67:17 LXX, presenting Christ as the "temple" of the new creational age and implying that the Jerusalem Temple is no longer the locus of the divine presence. The detection of the echo of Gen 17 and the echo of Deut 30:6 at Col 2:11, 13 imply the inadequacy of physical circumcision for incorporation into the people of God: a divine circumcision that removes the fallen, mortal body of Adamic flesh is required.[5] At 2:16–17, Paul asserts that Torah-prescribed dietary regulations, festivals, and Sabbath days are shadows that pointed to the reality of Christ in the age-to-come.

---

[5] Note also how physical circumcision is relativized at Col 3:11, when it declares that the categories of "circumcision" and "uncircumcision," i.e., Jew and Greek, are excluded from the new humanity in Christ.

Most scholarship understands the false teaching at Colossae to be a syncretism of pagan and Jewish elements. This work highlights in a new way the Jewishness of the teaching. The tentative conclusion of this study is that the philosophy is an apocalyptically-oriented, ascetic Hellenistic Judaism shaped strongly by a wisdom emphasis. The asceticism goes beyond OT teaching. There seems to be little need or basis to posit an additional *significant* Hellenistic pagan or Gnostic element to the "philosophy" that would justify the label of the system as a "syncretism."

Ramifications of the Investigation for the Relationship Between the Testaments

The above paragraph has already introduced the question of how awareness of the OT allusions and echoes in Colossians can further our understanding of the relationship between the testaments. Regarding this connection, many scholars are in agreement that the basic Pauline understanding of the relationship between the testaments is that of promise and fulfillment.[6] In his 1976 study, David Baker concluded his investigation on the relationship between the Old and New by stating that the framework of promise-fulfillment stands as the most common way of describing the relationship of the OT to the NT *as a whole* among biblical scholars who had studied the subject. He writes:

> It has been shown that the formula "promise and fulfilment" is the most popular way of expressing the relationship between the Testaments today. Sometimes the old formula "prophecy and fulfillment" is still used, often with much the same meaning as "promise and fulfillment," and occasionally other terms such as "expectation" and "announcement" are substituted for "promise".... In general terms this understanding of the relationship has been accepted, though it has been pointed out that there is more to the Old Testament than promise, and that the New Testament's fulfilment goes far beyond the expectations of the Old.[7]

---

[6] So, e.g., Fee, *God's Empowering Presence*, 905, writes that Paul looks "at things in terms of "promise" (the Old Testament) and "fulfillment" (Christ and the Spirit)."

[7] D. L. Baker, *Two Testaments, One Bible: A Study of Some Modern Solutions to the Theological Problem of the Relationship between the Old and New Testaments* (Downers Grove: InterVarsity, 1976), 373.

As a recent example that the promise-fulfillment schema continues to remain attractive, Charles Scobie has selected it for his massive biblical theology project. Through it he runs his four major themes of "God's Order," "God's Servant," "God's People," and "God's Way" from the OT first on through to the NT.[8]

In light of this, we are not out of bounds to affirm likewise that Paul's echoes and allusions of Israel's Scripture in Colossians fit well into the promise-fulfillment framework. Prophetic fulfillment can be discerned in five of the eleven references to Scripture detected in Colossians: Isa 11:1–9 at Col 1:9–10, the exodus-second exodus imagery at 1:12–14, 2 Sam 7 at Col 1:13b, Deut 30:6 at 2:11, and Ps 110:1 at 3:1. Paul believed that the messianic son of David had arrived in the person of Jesus, as God had promised in Isa 11, 2 Sam 7, and Ps 110:1. His arrival inaugurated the promised second exodus (Col 1:12–14) and the circumcision of the heart that would accompany it and finally secure the full covenant obedience that God required and desired (2:11).

The concept of typology is also given due attention in the works of Baker and Scobie.[9] Likewise, typological fulfillment has emerged as a major Pauline hermeneutical factor in the present study of Colossians.[10] The reader will recall the definition of typology presented at the beginning of this study and borrowed from Baker:

> a *type* is a biblical event, person, or institution which serves as an example or pattern for other events, persons, or institutions; *typology* is the study of types and the historical and theological correspondences between them; the *basis* of typology is God's consistent activity in the history of his chosen people.[11]

---

[8] Charles H. H. Scobie, *The Ways of our God: An Approach to Biblical Theology* (Grand Rapids: Eerdmans, 2003), 91–99 ("proclamation/promise: fulfillment/consummation").

[9] Baker, *Two Testaments, One Bible*, 237–70, 368–69; Scobie, *The Ways of our God*, 89–90. For a thorough and excellent discussion on what typology is and is not, see Baker, *Two Testaments, One Bible*, 237–70.

[10] Goppelt, *Typos*, 198, concludes his investigation on typology this way:
our study of OT typology in the NT has introduced us to a comprehensive and profound view of redemptive history.... In contrast to most of the earlier works mentioned in the Introduction, we have not sought simply to present a plausible explanation for the use of the OT in the NT. We have been determined to present the NT's own view. Although we may have modified the question and restricted its scope, we can still affirm that *typology is the method of interpreting Scripture that is predominant in the NT and characteristic of it* (emphasis mine).

[11] Baker, "Typology and the Christian Use of the Old Testament," 327–28.

Baker contends also that the correspondences are both historical and real, and argues that "[typology] is not interested in parallels of detail but only in agreement of fundamental principles and structure."[12]

A typological hermeneutic emerges in the present study at five of the eleven references detected in Colossians: Gen 1:28 in Col 1:6, the exodus imagery at 1:12–14,[13] the allusion to the Prov 8 Wisdom development in Col 1:15–20, the echo of Ps 68:16 [67:17 LXX] at Col 1:19, and Gen 1:26–27 at 3:10. The humanity created according to the image of God and given the mandate to "be fruitful and multiply" serves as the pattern for the new humanity of the new creation (Col 3:10). This new humanity was growing numerically as the gospel of truth rung out across the world from Jerusalem, "bearing fruit and multiplying" (Col 1:6; cf. Acts 1:8). Through this proclamation, God was bringing this new humanity into existence through a second exodus. This time the slave-master is not Egypt, but the "authority of darkness" (Col 1:13). At Col 1:15–20, Paul describes Christ in the language of the Prov 8 Wisdom development in order to make clear that all the wisdom and revelation that the Colossians needed to please God as part of this new humanity was to be found in Christ (cf. Col 2:2–3). Moreover, in the midst of this new humanity of the new creation, God was pleased to transfer his divine presence in order to dwell in Christ. Christ has become the "temple," the locus of the divine presence among the newly recreated people of God (Col 1:19).

Regarding the rest of the uses, one of the eleven has been classified as a sort of analogical use, a general "this is like that" (Isa 29:13 at 2:22). The study classified the echo of Gen 17:11 at 2:13 as an intentional rhetorical play on a phrase that produced a transformation in meaning. In a subtle but brilliant play on words, Paul refers not primarily to the Colossians' physical uncircumcision, but to their previous *spiritual*

---

[12] Baker, "Typology and the Christian Use of the Old Testament," 327.

[13] The careful reader will have noticed that I have classified the echo of the exodus event at Col 1:12–14 both as a prophetic fulfillment and also as a typological fulfillment. The reason for this is because the OT itself promised a second, greater exodus. Thus Col 1:12–14 would be a prophetic fulfillment of this specific promise. The language of the exodus imagery at Col 1:12–14, however, stems directly from the original exodus event and the Pentateuch, wherein no promise of a second exodus exists. The language of the original event has been picked up and a typological relationship produced at Col 1:12–14. Therefore, the exodus imagery at Col 1:12–14 can be reasonably understood to be *both* a prophetic fulfillment of a specific promise of God as well as a typological fulfillment of a non-prophetic event of OT history.

uncircumcision—their state of deadness in trespasses and exclusion from God's (new) covenant people.

It should be mentioned here that Paul's echoing activity in Colossians, a phenomena which was produced often unintentionally or unconsciously, nevertheless frequently reveals Paul's hermeneutical presuppositions with regard to the OT text in question. For example, even though it was classified merely as an echo, the reference to Deut 30:6 at Col 2:13 reveals that Paul presupposed that this prophecy had come to some kind of fulfillment among the Christians of Colossae. Likewise, the detection of Isa 11:2, 9 at Col 1:9–10 reveals that Paul presupposed that this prophecy likewise had come to initial fulfillment in Jesus Christ. In short, the detection of even the echoes in Colossians provides insight into Paul's hermeneutical presuppositions as to how he approached the OT.

In sum, by detecting how Paul echoed or alluded to the OT in Colossians, the present study contributes to our understanding of how Paul related the two testaments and highlights what hermeneutical procedures the apostle presupposed in his approach to the OT. These contributions can be added to other studies to help formulate a full picture for Pauline, NT, and biblical theologies.

How Many of Paul's References Would his Audience Have Actually Detected?

In chapter three of his 2004 book entitled *Arguing with Scripture*, Christopher Stanley questions nine assumptions that he believes shape discussions of Paul's references to Scripture and that require re-examination.[14] Especially relevant here is the question he raises about how many in Paul's audience would have actually recognized and appreciated the apostle's quotations, allusions, and echoes.[15] The query is an excellent one, although it stands as an *audience*-oriented question, not an *author*-oriented one, a distinction of which Stanley is cognizant and appreciates.[16] The focus of our present study, made clear at its beginning,

---

[14] Christopher D. Stanley, *Arguing with Scripture: The Rhetoric of Quotations in the Letters of Paul* (New York: T&T Clark, 2004), 38–61. The chapter is a slightly revised update of his previous article, "'Pearls Before Swine': Did Paul's Audiences Understand His Biblical Quotations?" *NovT* (1999): 124–44.

[15] Stanley, *Arguing with Scripture*, 46–48.

[16] Stanley, *Arguing with Scripture*, 46–47.

is with the *author*-oriented question of what Paul *as author* had done in his letter to the Colossians.[17] It nevertheless would be helpful to discuss briefly the concern Stanley has raised.

Stanley is probably correct to say that the only references "that Paul's first-century audience *definitely* would have recognized are those that are marked as such within the text" (e.g., as with "an explicit quotation formula").[18] The literary capability of Paul's gentile audiences would vary considerably within a congregation. Competence would range from the biblically knowledgeable and functionally literate on the one hand, to the biblically ignorant and functionally illiterate on the other. It is likely that many even of the biblically literate would have failed to catch many of the echoes in Colossians on a first or even second hearing or reading. Therefore, Stanley is right to caution "against the presumption that Paul's first-century audience recognized and appreciated his many unmarked references to the biblical text."[19] Stanley is also correct that the presence of such unmarked references "reveals the literary capabilities not of the audience, *but of Paul himself*, whose engagement with the Jewish Scriptures was such that his thinking and mode of expression were shaped and reshaped by the symbolic universe of the Bible and the language of specific passages."[20]

One response that may be raised in light of Stanley's concerns is whether Paul would have been satisfied with biblically illiterate congregations. Of course, many converts coming to faith in Christ out of pagan backgrounds would have had little if any biblical literacy. Over time, however, through corporate worship and regular teaching of Scripture in the community, one can easily envision a situation where ex-pagan converts grew into maturity and gradually adopted the "symbolic universe" of the Scriptures, possibly even memorizing portions of them.[21] The functionally illiterate could readily adopt this symbolic

---

[17] See pp. 13–15 of chapter 2 of this study.

[18] Stanley, *Arguing with Scripture*, 47; emphasis mine.

[19] Stanley, *Arguing with Scripture*, 47.

[20] Stanley, *Arguing with Scripture*, 48; emphasis mine.

[21] Stanley, *Arguing with Scripture*, 46n.26, questions whether non-Jews "were taught to memorize specific passages of Scripture in the Pauline churches" and whether the Scriptures were even read in the public worship of Paul's churches. Stanley may be right to assert that we have no specific evidence for scriptural memorization in the Pauline churches, but it appears certain that memorization *was* taught to non-Jews in at least one Pauline circle, when at Col 3:16a the author admonishes the gentile church to "let the word of Christ dwell in/among you richly, teaching and instructing

universe and memorize Scripture as well as the literate, if taught. So, for example, an illiterate ex-pagan that had faithfully followed the Christian faith in public worship and biblical teaching for a decade, upon hearing Paul's letter to the Colossians, may well have detected some of the echoes and many or all of the allusions of the letter. It is also possible that Paul wrote with especially the functionally literate in view, some of whom would certainly have held leadership roles in the churches, and expected of them to teach and explain his message to the rest of the congregation, including its OT foundations.

Ramifications of the Investigation for the Question of Paul's Use of the OT in Relation to the Original Context of Scripture

Stanley also questions the assumption that Paul himself knew and took into account the original context of his biblical references. Stanley questions this assumption on two grounds: 1) some of Paul's quotations "[bear] little evident relation to the apparent sense of the original passage" and 2) biblical scrolls would have been largely inaccessible to the apostle, so that he would have had to work from a list of proof texts he had jotted down in a sort of notebook of papyrus or parchment when the scrolls *were* accessible to him.[22]

---

each other." The "word of Christ" is almost certainly the content of the gospel and would have included words that Jesus spoke ("Jesus tradition"; Dunn, *Colossians*, 236; cf. Lohse, *Colossians*, 150; O'Brien, *Colossians*, 206–7). And how else would the "psalms, hymns, and spiritual songs" (Col 3:16b) have been sung in corporate worship but by memorization? The printing press and thus hymnals did not exist.

Regarding the reading of Scripture in public worship, it seems unlikely that ex-pagan converts would be exposed to Scripture in any other way. How then, would they obtain the even rudimentary biblical literacy Paul expected of his audience for even basic comprehension of his letters? Paul simply assumes that his gentile audience in Rome will know who Abraham is (Rom 4), or how the creation-Adam-fall narrative of Gen 1–3 runs (Rom 5:12ff.). At Corinth he expected them to know what a "Passover" sacrifice was, offering no explanation of the otherwise baffling concept (1 Cor 5:7), as well as the person and ministry of Moses, including details of the exodus narrative (1 Cor 10:1–10). The examples could be listed one after another. Moreover, Paul asserts that "what was written [in the Old Testament] was for our instruction [ἐγράφη δὲ πρὸς νουθεσίαν ἡμῶν], upon whom the ends of the ages had come" (1 Cor 10:11). If Paul viewed the OT as *written for the gentiles* of the inaugurated new age, then certainly the onus is on others to supply the reason why Paul would not have expected and ordered that Scripture be taught whenever the community gathered for worship.

[22] Stanley, *Arguing with Scripture*, 53–54.

To reply to Stanley's first objection would take a series of major monographs, because every single instance of OT quotation in Paul would have to be investigated, in accordance with *first-century presuppositions*, not ours of the twenty-first century, to discern whether any of the apostle's use of quotation violated the original sense, as that would have been understood in Paul's day.[23]

In light of the second objection, it appears that Stanley has not considered the role that extensive memorization of Scripture may have played in Paul's quotations of Scripture. Memorization of large swaths of Scripture (not just sentence snippets as proof-texts) would preserve the broad context of a given quotation of Scripture and could have inoculated the apostle from the very criticism that would otherwise render his argument worthless, namely, that he misinterpreted Scripture. Though they may not have made up the bulk of the church, biblically and functionally literate members, some serving as leaders in the congregations, would have been able to check up on Paul's arguments from Scripture. Paul was not the only one "learned in the Scriptures" among the synagogues and churches of the Roman Empire (cf. e.g., Acts 17:2, 10–11, 18:24, 28). The Jews of Berea "examined the scriptures every day" to cross-examine Paul's gospel message in order to see if it cohered with Scripture (Acts 17:11 NRSV). They serve as an example that cautions against positing too quickly that Paul could have readily gotten away with misuse of Scripture. The Jews of Berea would not have been the only Jews of Asia Minor that would have examined the Scriptures to test the legitimacy of Paul's message.

Knowledge of Paul's education is meager. The apostle wrote autobiographically about his former life in Judaism that "as to the law," he was a "Pharisee" (Phil 3:5 NRSV) and that "I advanced in Judaism beyond many among my people of the same age, for I was far more zealous for the traditions of my ancestors" (Gal 1:14 NRSV; cf. Acts 22:3). This latter statement indicates at the least that Paul attended secondary school, probably from ten to thirteen years of age, "to study the oral Torah in the forms of midrash...and mishnah."[24] But

---

[23] Stanley himself has done work in this area. His 1992 monograph *Paul and the Language of Scripture: Citation Technique in the Pauline Epistles and Contemporary Literature* (SNTSMS 74; Cambridge: Cambridge University Press, 1992) in part studies this subject to see what would have been considered acceptable quotation practice in Paul's time.

[24] Duane F. Watson, "Education: Jewish and Greco-Roman," *Dictionary of New Testament Background* (ed. Craig A. Evans and Stanley E. Porter; Downers Grove: InterVarsity,

to attend secondary school in the Jewish educational system almost certainly presupposes a *primary* education in the Jewish educational system. Here, at the primary level, the *written* Torah, the Hebrew Bible, stood as the textbook of the curriculum.[25] It is difficult to see how a Jew with no primary education in the Hebrew Bible, but trained only in the Greco-Roman system, would be allowed to jump into advanced Jewish study of the oral Torah at the secondary level. The foundation of the Hebrew Bible would be missing. It is therefore probable that Paul had a thorough education in the Hebrew Bible, and early on in his childhood, as was typical for a male Jew.[26]

In this primary education, the boys learned Hebrew (girls did not typically attend) and then jumped immediately into reading Scripture. Watson writes

> Instead of dictation the class read small scrolls with passages of Torah written on them (*megillah*) and eventually entire books. Students began reading portions of Leviticus and then turned to Genesis. They eventually read all the books of Scripture in this order: Torah, Prophets and Writings. *Memorization of large portions of the texts read was the desired result.*[27]

Paul's education impressed the "symbolic universe" of Scripture upon him; indeed, the ex-Pharisee would have almost certainly memorized "large portions" of the Hebrew Bible. That the quotation data in his letters reflects that Paul had mastered the Greek OT does not detract from this fundamental fact.[28] The upshot, against Stanley, is that Paul

---

2000), 312; John T. Townsend, "Education (Greco-Roman)," *ABD* 2:316, writes likewise that Paul's statement at Gal 1:14 "indicates that [Paul] reached at least the second level of Jewish education."

[25] Watson, "Education," 312; S. Safrai, "Education and the Study of the Torah," in *The Jewish People in the First Century: Historical Geography, Political History, Social, Cultural and Religious Life and Institutions* (ed. S. Safrai and Michael Stern; 2 vols; CRINT; Assen: Van Gorcum, 1987), 2:950–51; Martin Hengel, *Judaism and Hellenism: Studies in their Encounter in Palestine during the Early Hellenistic Period* (trans. John Bowden; 2 vols.; Philadelphia: Fortress, 1974), 1:81–83 ("Instead of Homer [as in the Hellenistic educational system], the Hebrew Bible, and especially the Pentateuch, held pride of place in instruction"[p. 82]); Townsend, "Education," 2:316; Eliezer Ebner, *Elementary Education in Ancient Israel During the Tannaitic Period (10–220 C.E.)* (New York: Bloch, 1956), 69, 77–80.

[26] Safrai, "Education and the Study of the Torah," 949, writes that "as a rule, [Jewish] children did attend school, learned to read the books of the Bible and acquired the basic knowledge which enabled them to participate in Jewish life."

[27] Watson, "Education," 312 (emphasis mine); Safrai, "Education and the Study of the Torah," 950–51; Ebner, *Elementary Education in Ancient Israel*, 90–93.

[28] Martin Hengel, *The Pre-Christian Paul* (trans. John Bowden; Philadelphia: Trinity Press International, 1991), 18–42, discusses Paul's education and confirms the lines of

simply would not have needed a notebook of proof-texts at his side for quotation in the composition of his letters. He had stored up large swaths of the Scriptures of Israel in his head and heart, as his religion commanded (Deut 6:6–9; Josh 1:8; Pss 1:2, 119:11). As a result, the broad contours of the original context of his quotations should have been at hand for him. He therefore would not be nearly so prone to quote out of context as Stanley's hypothesis would necessarily imply. It is not as though the apostle *couldn't* quote poorly; the possibility yet exists that he could, but the evidence has to be examined carefully to discern what kind of sensitivity Paul's uses reflect. His childhood training, however, makes it reasonable to infer that Paul should have been able to quote with contextual awareness on a fairly consistent basis, without the need for any aids such as a "notebook" of isolated proof-texts.[29]

Why Are There No Explicit Quotations of Scripture in Colossians?

In the light of our study, the question naturally arises as to why Paul did not explicitly quote from Scripture in Colossians. The question becomes all the more acute in light of the apostle's other letters, such as Romans and 1 Corinthians, where the apostle has quoted the Old Testament 59 and 18 times, respectively.[30]

---

my own thinking taken above. Elsewhere Hengel writes, "As a student in Jerusalem, Paul may have worked with both the Hebrew and the Greek texts in accordance with the bilingual milieu in the Jewish capital, where the Hellenists had their own synagogues." Hengel further argues that the preponderance of the LXX in Paul's letters is for the sake of his Greek-speaking audience (Martin Hengel, *The Septuagint as Christian Scripture: Its Prehistory and the Problem of its Canon* [trans. Mark E. Biddle; Grand Rapids: Baker Academic, 2002, 108]). Due to the quotation data embedded in his history, Hengel presents Josephus as another first-century Jew who knew both the Hebrew and Greek biblical texts, yet who "increasingly employed the Greek translation for the sake of his readers" (102).

[29] Again, when we say "contextually," we must define what is "contextual" according to the accepted norms of Paul's day, not ours. Moreover, Paul's hermeneutical toolbox included a typological approach, which the apostle had learned from the example set by the OT itself (e.g., creation → new creation [Gen 1 → Isa 65–66]; exodus → second exodus [Exod 12–19 → Isa 11:10–16, 43:16–21, etc.]; David → another "David" [2 Samuel → Ezek 34:23–24]). This presupposition has to be factored in to the discussion of what would have been considered a "contextual" read by a first-century Jew steeped in the Scriptures.

[30] These counts are taken from Silva's tally of Paul's quotations of Scripture ("Old Testament in Paul," *DPL* 631).

It may be unhelpful, however, to compare Colossians (four chapters) with the likes of Romans (sixteen chapters) and 1 Corinthians (sixteen chapters), and more appropriate to place it side by side with other authentic Pauline letters of a more similar size, such as Philippians (four chapters) and 1 Thessalonians (five chapters). Significantly, Paul does not explicitly quote Scripture either in Philippians or in 1 Thessalonians.[31] In light of this evidence, Paul's decision not to quote in a letter the size of Colossians is not a new and mysterious phenomenon, but something the apostle has done on other occasions in letters of similar size.

David Hay has argued that Paul's lack of scriptural quotation in Colossians "is strong evidence that the Error was not primarily a form of Judaism."[32] But this does not necessarily follow. As we have seen in this study, Paul has relativized the significance of Torah, the temple, circumcision, Sabbath, and the Torah-prescribed Jewish festivals and dietary regulations through both his use of allusion to and echo of the OT, as well as through direct statement (e.g., Col 2:16–17). This trend certainly suggests that the "philosophy" was predominantly Jewish, though perhaps not exclusively so. Paul's alluding and echoing activities, as well as his direct statements, suggest that the philosophy consisted in some form of an apocalyptically-oriented, ascetic Hellenistic Judaism shaped strongly by a wisdom emphasis. The evidence, however, does not allow us to suggest anything more specific.

Any answer as to why Paul "avoided" quoting Scripture explicitly is mere speculation (if putting it this way is even correct). One possible explanation (and admittedly, very speculative), however, is that Paul may have wanted to avoid confusing his audience. If, as this study has argued, Paul has depicted Christ as Wisdom, and the "philosophy" had argued that Torah was Wisdom, then Paul has supplanted Torah with Christ and exalted him to the place of preeminence. Christ himself is the storehouse of all wisdom and understanding (Col 2:3). In light of this, for Paul then to quote from Torah as a source of authority and wisdom could have created confusion in the congregation. One can

---

[31] Scholars have nevertheless detected allusions and echoes to Scripture in both of these letters. See, e.g., on the letter to the Philippians, Silva, "Old Testament in Paul," 634–35; see now also the *Commentary on the New Testament Use of the Old Testament* (ed. G. K. Beale and D. A. Carson; Grand Rapids: Baker Academic, 2007), which has separate chapters on the use of the OT in both Philippians and 1 Thessalonians.

[32] Hay, *Colossians*, 27.

imagine the response to the quotation of Torah in the letter to run
along the lines of "if Christ, and not Torah, is Wisdom, then why did
Paul just quote from Torah as his source of authority and wisdom?
Has he changed his mind? Torah must really still be an essential place
for finding divine wisdom." For the sake of the preeminence of Christ
as the climax of divine revelation and the ultimate source of divine
wisdom, Paul may well have avoided quotation of Scripture (Torah),
lest the initial rhetorical effect of his argument fail to convince his
audience of the exclusive supremacy of Christ.[33] Paul had never met
the Colossians and was imprisoned at the time of writing his letter to
them. The apostle had to make his point and had no opportunity to
instruct on how Torah still could serve the community as a faithful,
though incomplete, source of revelation and wisdom. Paul had to make
his one point clear and hammer it home hard: Christ holds the place
of preeminence as the climax of revelation and stands as the ultimate
source of divine wisdom; the Colossians must hold fast to him alone
(Col 2:6–8). The congregation as a whole had not yet veered off course
(Col 2:5), but the threat stood close by (Col 2:4, 8), and Paul desired
to cut it off before it influenced them to their harm.

Ramifications of the Investigation for the Issue of Authorship

Of some significance is the observation that seven of the texts that
Paul has alluded to or echoed in Colossians have surfaced elsewhere
in his other letters of Romans and 1–2 Corinthians. The chart below
shows what texts and where:

---

[33] In light of the fact that I have proposed two allusions in this study (the Prov
8 interpretive tradition in Col 1:15–20 and Gen 1:26–27 in Col 3:10), and have
argued that allusions are *intentional* attempts to refer an audience to a previous "text"
(understood broadly; see my discussion in chapter two of this work with regard to the
nature of allusion), the objection may be raised that the reason for Paul's omission
of any quotation of ΟΤ Scripture would apply also to any allusions. This may be so,
but allusion is an indirect mode of reference, whereas a quotation is direct, and this
indirect nature of allusion can create a literary "space" that distances the author
from the precursor text even as the precursor is brought to the audience's attention.
Moreover, in both allusions detected and defended in this study, neither is appealed
to by Paul as an authority. Instead, the imagery is picked up to help convey reality in
the language of the symbolic universe that Paul assumes that he shares in common
with his audience.

OT Reference	Location in Colossians	Location in Paul's Letters[34]
Genesis 1:26–27	3:10	1 Cor 11:7
Genesis 17:11	2:13	Rom 2:17–29[35]
		(cf. Rom 4:9–17)
The Exodus Event	1:12b–14a	1 Cor 10:1–11;
		cf. 1 Cor 5:6–8
Deuteronomy 30:6	2:11	Rom 2:29[36]
2 Samuel 7:12–18	1:13b	2 Cor 6:18[37]
Isaiah 11:1–9	1:9–10	Rom 15:12 (Isa 11:10)[38]
Isaiah 29:13	2:22	1 Cor 1:19 (Isa 29:14)[39]

The observations within the chart are notable, and they stand as a contribution to the study of the Pauline use of Scripture. Are there, however, any implications of the common use of these same source texts for the discussion on the authorship of Colossians? At first glance, it appears that the evidence would further confirm that Colossians is an authentic letter of Paul. The apostle has echoed language once again from the same source texts he is known to have referenced elsewhere in his letters. The argument could, however, cut the other way. A master disciple of Paul would have known Paul's favorite passages of Scripture, and it is highly probable that he would have made many of them his own. Therefore, there is possibly little here that furthers the debate concerning the authorship of Colossians.

---

[34] Because the purpose of this chart is to highlight the similarities between Colossians and those letters considered by critical scholarship to be authentic letters of Paul, I have excluded from this list the disputed letters of 2 Thess, Eph, and the Pastorals.

[35] For defense of this allusion in Rom 2, see now Berkley, *From a Broken Covenant to Circumcision of the Heart*, 95–98.

[36] For defense of this allusion, see now Berkley, *From a Broken Covenant to Circumcision of the Heart*, 98–107. Note also that Paul quotes Deut 30:12–14 at Rom 10:6–8.

[37] The Pauline authorship of this verse is debated (as is the authenticity of the entire section of 2 Cor 6:14–7:1). For a discussion of the evidence and the arguments both for and against Pauline authorship, see Thrall, *Second Epistle to the Corinthians*, 1:25–36. Thrall herself concludes that "neither contextual nor theological arguments are sufficient to prove conclusively that 2 Cor 6.14–7.1 is non-Pauline" (35)

[38] Isa 11:10 reads, "On that day the root of Jesse shall stand as a signal to the peoples," tying it tightly to Isa 11:1–9, which begins at v. 1 with "a shoot shall come out of the stump of Jesse, and a branch shall grow out of his roots" (NRSV).

[39] Cf. Rom 11:8 (combined quotation of Deut 29:3 and Isa 29:10).

*Ramifications of the Investigation for the Relationship
Between Colossians and Ephesians*

While there is no space to argue for the presence of the allusions and
echoes in Ephesians here, many have seen those listed in the chart
below.[40] Our study further contributes to the continuing discussion of
the relationship between the letters of Colossians and Ephesians. It is
widely acknowledged that these two letters share an especially close
relationship of some sort. In the chart below, the references to Scripture
that are shared by Colossians and Ephesians are listed:

OT Reference	Location in Colossians	Location in Ephesians
Genesis 1:26–27	3:10	4:24
Psalm 110:1	3:1	1:20
Psalm 68:16	1:19	4:8 (Psalm 68:18)
Isaiah 11:2	1:9–10	1:17

What, if any, implications do these findings have for contributing to the
understanding of the relationship between these two letters? One major
view holds that the author of Ephesians borrowed from Colossians.[41]
If this is so, then the author of Ephesians may not have detected the
echoes of Gen 1:26–27, Ps 110:1, or Isa 11:2 in Colossians, but instead
merely imitated the language and incorporated it into his own letter.
This, however, could not be the case with the echo of Ps 68:16 [67:17
LXX] at Col 1:19, for the author of Ephesians explicitly quotes Ps 68,
displaying full awareness of the source with his use of a quotation formula (διὸ λέγει; "therefore it says"). He therefore did not merely imitate
any language from Colossians. It is noteworthy that no portion of Ps 68
is quoted anywhere else in the NT. Could it be only mere coincidence
that both Colossians and Ephesians refer to the same stanza of Ps 68
(i.e., vv. 15–18 ET) when the letters possess such an obvious literary

---

[40] Including, e.g., the NA[27] side margin apparatus and the UBS[4] bottom notes. The
quotation of Ps 68:18 ET at Ephesians 4:8 is explicit and widely recognized.

[41] Thus Victor Paul Furnish, "Ephesians, Epistle to the," *ABD* 2:540, can write that
"there can be little doubt that the author of Ephesians has borrowed ideas and even
terminology from Colossians."

relationship of some kind? But then how does one explain the explicit quotation of Ps 68:18 at Eph 4:8? Did the author of Ephesians detect the echo at Col 1:19 and subsequently decide to employ the stanza for his own particular purpose in a full-blown explicit quotation? Or, does the borrowing run the other way?[42] Or, do the letters somehow stem from the same author at a time when the entire stanza was fresh in his mind? The least plausible explanation is that the phenomenon is to be chalked up to mere coincidence.

---

[42] This option is unlikely. The majority view is that the author of Colossians borrowed a hymn and inserted it at 1:15–20. Therefore, the echo of Ps 68 at Col 1:19 has come with the hymn and *its* author, and not from the author of Colossians. The author of Colossians, then, did not borrow the idea for the use of Ps 68 from Ephesians. Of course, this argument is valid unless the majority view is *incorrect* and the author of Colossians is in fact the author of the hymn of 1:15–20 as well.

CHART SUMMARY OF THE ALLUSIONS AND ECHOES OF SCRIPTURE DETECTED IN PAUL'S LETTER TO THE COLOSSIANS

The study detected eleven allusions and echoes of Scripture. For the convenience of the reader, they are listed and arranged by their shared thematic idea below:

New Creation

OT Reference	Colossians	Mode of Reference	Shared Language/ Concepts	Hermeneutical Presupposition
Genesis 1:28	1:6, 10	Echo	"bearing fruit and increasing in all the world"	typological
Isaiah 11:2, 9 (see 11:1–9)	1:9–10	Echo	"Spirit-given wisdom and understanding"; "knowledge of God"; "all the world" (Col 1:6) (see also below in **Christ as Messianic son of David**)	direct prophetic fulfillment
Proverbs 8:22–31 Jewish exegetical Development	1:15–20 ("the Christ-hymn")	Allusion	a) Titles of "Firstborn," "Image," "Head," "Beginning" b) existence *before* all of creation c) *agent* of creation d) *sustainer* of creation e) locus of the divine presence f) *agent of reconciliation and peace* between God and humanity	typological
Genesis 1:26–27	3:10	Allusion	"according to the image of the one who created him"	typological

Christ as Messianic son of David

OT Reference	Colossians	Mode of Reference	Shared Language/ Concepts	Hermeneutical Presupposition
Isaiah 11:2, 9 (11:1: "shoot of Jesse"; cf. 11:10)	1:9–10	Echo	Assumes the Promise-to-David tradition preserved at 2 Sam 7 (see above in chart on **New Creation**)	direct prophetic fulfillment
2 Samuel 7:12–18	1:13b	Echo	"kingdom of the son of his love"	direct prophetic fulfillment
Psalm 110:1	3:1	Echo	"sitting at the right hand"	direct prophetic fulfillment

Temple

OT Reference	Colossians	Mode of Reference	Shared Language/ Concepts	Hermeneutical Presupposition
Psalm 68:16 [LXX 67:17]	1:19	Echo	"in it/him all the fullness/God was pleased to dwell"	typological

The exodus motif

OT Reference	Colossians	Mode of Reference	Shared Language/ Concepts	Hermeneutical Presupposition
The narrative of the exodus in the Pentateuch and promises of a second exodus in the prophets	1:12b–14a	Echo	"the Father, who had made you fit for a <u>share of the inheritance</u> of the saints in the light, <u>who delivered us</u> from the domain of darkness and <u>transferred us into the kingdom</u> of the son of his love, in whom we have <u>redemption</u>"	both typological and direct prophetic fulfillment

Circumcision

OT Reference	Colossians	Mode of Reference	Shared Language/ Concepts	Hermeneutical Presupposition
Genesis 17:11, 14, 23, 24, 25	2:13	Echo	"[you shall circumcise] the flesh of your foreskin"; cf. Col 2:11	rhetorical (play on the words that produced transformation in meaning)
Deuteronomy 30:6	2:11	Echo	Divinely wrought spiritual circumcision	direct prophetic fulfillment

Idolatry

OT Reference	Colossians	Mode of Reference	Shared Language/ Concepts	Hermeneutical Presupposition
Isaiah 29:13	2:22	Echo	"in accordance with the commandments and teachings of men"	analogical

APPENDIX TWO

PROVERBS 2:2–6 IN COLOSSIANS 2:2–3?

Comparison of Textual Versions and Evaluation

Proverbs 2:2–6 MT	Proverbs 2:2–6 LXX	Colossians 2:2–3
² לְהַקְשִׁיב לַחָכְמָה אָזְנֶךָ תַּטֶּה לִבְּךָ לַתְּבוּנָה: ³ כִּי אִם לַבִּינָה תִקְרָא לַתְּבוּנָה תִּתֵּן קוֹלֶךָ: ⁴ אִם־תְּבַקְשֶׁנָּה כַכָּסֶף וְכַמַּטְמוֹנִים תַּחְפְּשֶׂנָּה: ⁵ אָז תָּבִין יִרְאַת יְהוָה וְדַעַת אֱלֹהִים תִּמְצָא: ⁶ כִּי־יְהוָה יִתֵּן חָכְמָה מִפִּיו דַּעַת וּתְבוּנָה:	² ὑπακούσεται <u>σοφίας</u> τὸ οὖς σου καὶ παραβαλεῖς καρδίαν σου εἰς <u>σύνεσιν</u> παραβαλεῖς δὲ αὐτὴν ἐπὶ νουθέτησιν τῷ υἱῷ σου ³ ἐὰν γὰρ τὴν <u>σοφίαν</u> ἐπικαλέσῃ καὶ τῇ <u>συνέσει</u> δῷς φωνήν σου [τὴν δὲ αἴσθησιν ζητήσῃς μεγάλη τῇ φωνῇ]¹ ⁴ καὶ ἐὰν ζητήσῃς αὐτὴν ὡς ἀργύριον καὶ ὡς <u>θησαυροὺς</u> [τὰ <u>ἀπόκρυφα</u>]² ἐξερευνήσῃς αὐτήν ⁵ τότε συνήσεις φόβον κυρίου καὶ <u>ἐπίγνωσιν</u> <u>θεοῦ</u> εὑρήσεις ⁶ ὅτι κύριος δίδωσιν <u>σοφίαν</u> καὶ ἀπὸ προσώπου αὐτοῦ <u>γνῶσις</u> καὶ <u>σύνεσις</u>	εἰς πᾶν πλοῦτος τῆς πληροφορίας τῆς <u>συνέσεως</u>, εἰς <u>ἐπίγνωσιν</u> τοῦ μυστηρίου <u>τοῦ</u> <u>θεοῦ</u>, Χριστοῦ, ³ ἐν ᾧ εἰσιν πάντες οἱ <u>θησαυροὶ</u> τῆς <u>σοφίας</u> καὶ <u>γνώσεως</u> <u>ἀπόκρυφοι</u>.

This proposal meets the two criteria of our first tier for the establishment of an echo: 1) availability and 2) word agreement. Regarding *availability*, Paul displays acquaintance with the book of Proverbs elsewhere in his

---

¹ Vaticanus (B) and Sinaiticus (S or ‎א) omit this bracketed line; cf. MT. The line is found in Origen's fifth column and Alexandrinus (A).

² Symmachus and Theodotion read τὰ ἀπόκρυφα instead of καὶ ὡς θησαυρούς. The words were often used together, as seen in LXX Isa 45:3, 1 Macc 1:23, Josephus, *Ant.* 12.250, even as they are today in modern usage ("hidden treasure(s)").

letters (Rom 2:6, 12:20; 2 Cor 9:7). With regard to *word agreement*, Col 2:2–3 shares five words in common with Prov 2:2–6: θησαυρός (both texts have the plural), σοφία, σύνεσις, γνῶσις, and ἐπίγνωσις. Indeed, a comprehensive search in the *TLG* search engine on its entire corpus in the time before and up to the date of the letter to the Colossians found only three texts that had even the first *three* of these words together within a space of six lines of text. The three texts were Jer 28:15–16, Sir 1:25–26, and Prov 2:4–6, all texts from the LXX. Only Prov 2:4–6 and Col 2:2–3 share all *five* words out of the entire *TLG* corpus up to the time of Paul (with a given limit of six lines of text). As relatively common as most of the words may be, they only cluster together like this in these two texts. In light of this evidence, the least that can be said is that the language of Col 2:2–3 is *biblisch*, stemming from the Greek OT.[3]

Our second tier of evidence ("confirmatory observations") further strengthens the proposal that Prov 2:2–6 has been echoed in Col 2:2–3. The third criterion of this second tier asks whether other allusions or echoes from the same OT book in question have been verified elsewhere in the letter to the Colossians (see p. 33). If so, this increases the probability that the apostle pulled another reference from that same OT book or even from that same section in that book. In the case in question, we have argued that the Prov 8:22–31 personified Wisdom interpretive tradition has been alluded to at Col 1:15–20 (see chapter seven). This thereby strengthens the proposal that Prov 2:2–6 has been echoed at Col 2:2–3.

Significantly, Prov 2:2–6 LXX belongs to the few texts in Proverbs that discuss personified Wisdom. While not necessarily the case in the MT, in the LXX there are explicit repetitions of verbs in 2:2–4 from 1:24–28 that literarily connect the two units of 1:20–33 and 2:1–6 together and consequently give the impression that the elaboration upon Lady Wisdom in 1:20–33 is carried on through to about 2:6 (after which she fades from view until later).[4] In Prov 1:24, Lady Wisdom asserts that she called out to the fools, but they did not "listen" (ὑπακούω) to her; at

---

[3] Some similar phraseology can be found outside the LXX: Plato, *Philebus* 15 E (LCL); Xenophon (d. ca. 354 B.C.E.), *Memorabilia*, 4.9; Philo, *Unchangeable* 92; *Posterity* 62; *Prelim. Studies* 127.

[4] A couple of later interpreters connected Prov 2:6 with the Prov 8:22 personified Wisdom figure (*Midr. Rabbah* Leviticus 11.3; Clement of Alexandria, *Exhortation to the Greeks*, 8 (*ANF* 2.194).

2:2 the father urges his son to "listen" (ὑπακούω) to "wisdom" (σοφία). At Prov 1:28, Lady Wisdom warns the fools that because they did not heed her, she will not listen when they "call upon" (ἐπικαλέω) her in the day disaster strikes; in 2:3 the father pleads with his son to "call upon" (ἐπικαλέω) "wisdom" (τὴν σοφίαν) to avert disaster (2:12–22). At Prov 1:28, Lady Wisdom warns the fools that, although they will "seek" (ζητέω) her in the day of their disaster, they will not find her; in 2:4 the father urgently appeals to his son to "seek" (ζητέω) "her" (αὐτήν), that is, "wisdom."

More evidence can be adduced for this echo. The first criterion of the second tier of evidence asks whether other scholars have seen Prov 2:2–6 behind Col 2:2–3 (see p. 32). This question can be answered in the affirmative.[5]

There are, however, reasons to pause before accepting the conclusion that Prov 2:2–6 has been echoed in Col 2:2–3. First, while several scholars have claimed to see Prov 2 in Col 2:2–3, many of these also posit other literary references here at the same point. The most common and notable suggestions are Isa 45:3 LXX, Sir 1:24–25, and *1 En.* 46:3. Other scholars offer Job 28:21 (e.g., Toy) and Dan 2 (e.g., Beale). In my opinion, a reference to Isa 45:3 LXX is dubious at best.[6] And while Sir 1:24–27 and *1 En.* 46:3 probably can serve as relevant and helpful background material, it is unlikely that either is in view at Col 2:2–3.

---

[5] Toy, *Quotations in the New Testament*, 201, 292 (with Job 28:21); R. Martin, *Colossians*, 76: "the whole train of ideas and words suggests a conscious indebtedness to the figure of wisdom in Proverbs 2:3ff."; Wright, *Colossians*, 95: "Christ sums up in himself all that the Jews predicated of 'Wisdom' (*cf.* Pr. 2:1–8, whose LXX translation is echoed several times in our present passage)"; Lindemann, *Der Kolosserbrief*, 37 (with Isa 45:3); Barth and Blanke, *Colossians*, 64n.98 (with Isa 45:3); Schnabel, *Law and Wisdom from Ben Sira to Paul*, 259–60; Beale, "Colossians," ad loc.; NA[27] side margin (with Isa 45:3, Sir 1:24f., and 1 *En.* 46:3). The 16th edition of the Nestle Greek NT (1936) posted Col 2:3 as a *quotation* of Prov 2:3 (and Isa 45:3); cf. Schweizer, *Colossians*, 118n.6: "The language is biblical. In Prov. 2:3–6 θησαυροί, σοφία, γνῶσις are found, as also are σύνεσις, ἐπίγνωσις θεοῦ (Col. 2:2)…"; cf. O'Brien, *Colossians*, 96; Moule, *Colossians*, 87, who says of Prov 2:3 that it is "suggestive enough, if the reader continues on through the succeeding verses." Lohse, *Colossians*, 82n.117, however, is adamant that "the text neither contains an OT quote nor is any allusion to an OT passage intended." It may be worthy to note also that Fee, "Old Testament Intertexuality in Colossians," does not offer this echo.

[6] So also Bruce, *Colossians*, 91n.12: "Despite the collocation of θησαυρός and ἀπόκρυφος, it is doubtful whether there is a conscious reminiscence here of Isa. 45:3." Contrast Beare, "Colossians," 186; Ellis, *Paul's Use of the Old Testament*, 154; Pokorný, *Colossians*, 107n.19 (it "may be an allusion to Is. 45:3"); Barth and Blanke, *Colossians*, 64 and n.98.

Additional scholarly conjectures of other texts such as these force the question, "Have we overheard correctly, or are we reading something into the text that is not there?" This is the ever present question in positing echoes. These other, widely divergent, scholarly conjectures dampen the force of the argument for accepting Prov 2 as the text behind Col 2:2–3.

The second reason for the hesitation to offer the echo is because the shared words are used differently in Col 2:2–3 than they are in Prov 2:2–6. Yes, the words are the same words; there is a definite "word cluster" common to both texts. The similarities, however, seem to end there. The words neither occur in the same order as in the LXX, nor are they clumped together in the same way in their phrases. For example, the word γνῶσις is clumped with σύνεσις in the phrase καὶ ἀπὸ προσώπου αὐτοῦ γνῶσις καὶ σύνεσις at Prov 2:6, but γνῶσις is clumped with σοφία instead in the phrase οἱ θησαυροὶ τῆς σοφίας καὶ γνώσεως at Col 2:3. There is, moreover, a lack of any structural correspondences between the two texts (as say, e.g., that the verbal hendiadys, "bearing fruit and multiplying" of Col 1:6 shares with the Gen 1:28 phrase "be fruitful-and-multiply"). It is due to this lack of correspondence in word order, similar phraseology, and structure that casts some doubt as to the veracity of the proposed echo of Prov 2:2–6 in Col 2:2–3. The language in Col 2:2–3 surely stems from the biblical wisdom literature, but the question as to whether we can pin the source of it down to any *one* particular text within that literature probably should remain open.

APPENDIX THREE

THE PROBABLE TEXT-FORMS BEHIND THE DETECTED
ALLUSIONS AND ECHOES IN PAUL'S LETTER
TO THE COLOSSIANS

Chapter	Old Testament Text	Location in Colossians	Probable (Proto-) Text-Form
3	Genesis 1:28	1:6	"Paul has probably rendered his own Greek translation of the original Hebrew...under the partial influence of the LXX wording...." (see pp. 52–55)
4	Isaiah 11:2, 9	1:9–10	LXX
5	The exodus motif	1:12–14	LXX
6	2 Samuel 7 Promise-to-David Exegetical Tradition	1:13	LXX
7	Proverbs 8:22–31 Interpretive Development	1:15–20	LXX
8	Ps 68:16 [67:17 LXX]	1:19	LXX
9	Deuteronomy 30:6	2:11	MT
10	Genesis 17	2:13	LXX
11	Isaiah 29:13	2:22	LXX
12	Psalm 110:1 [109:1 LXX]	3:1	LXX
13	Genesis 1:26–27	3:10	LXX

SELECTED BIBLIOGRAPHY

Primary Sources

Aland, Kurt, Barbara Aland, Johannes Karavidopoulos, Carlo M. Martini, and Bruce M. Metzger, eds. *Novum Testamentum Graece*. 27th ed. Stuttgart: Deutsche Bibelgesellschaft, 1993.

Barthélemy, D., and J. T. Milik. *Qumran Cave 1*. DJD 1. Oxford: Clarendon, 1955.

Braude, William G. *The Midrash on Psalms*. Edited by Leon Nemoy. 2 vols. Yale Judaica Series 13. New Haven: Yale University Press, 1976.

———. *Pesikta Rabbati: Discourses for Feasts, Fasts, and Special Sabbaths*. Edited by Leon Nemoy. 2 vols. Yale Judaica Series 18. New Haven: Yale University Press, 1968.

Braude, William G., and Israel J. Kapstein. *Pesikta de-Rab Kahana: R. Kahana's Compilation of Discourses for Sabbaths and Festal Days*. Philadelphia: Jewish Publication Society of America, 1975.

———. *Tanna Debe Eliyyahu: The Lore of the School of Elijah*. Philadelphia: Jewish Publication Society of America, 1981.

Brooke, Alan England, Norman McLean, and Henry St John Thackeray, eds. *The Old Testament in Greek: According to the Text of Codex Vaticanus, Supplemented from other Uncial Manuscripts, with a Critical Apparatus Containing the Variants of the Chief Ancient Authorities for the Text of the Septuagint*. 3 vols. Cambridge: Cambridge University Press, 1906–1940.

Bushell, Michael S., and Michael Tan. *Bibleworks 6*. Norfolk, Va.: Bibleworks LLC, 2003.

Charles, R. H., ed. *The Apocrypha and Pseudepigrapha of the Old Testament: In English with Introductions and Critical and Explanatory Notes to the Several Books*. 2 vols. Oxford: Clarendon, 1913.

Charlesworth, James H., ed. *The Old Testament Pseudepigrapha*. 2 vols. ABRL. New York: Doubleday, 1983.

Cohen, A., ed. *The Minor Tractates of the Talmud*. 2 vols. 2nd ed. London: Soncino, 1971.

Colson, F. H., G. H. Whitaker, and Ralph Marcus. *Philo*. 10 volumes and 2 supplements. LCL. Cambridge, Mass.: Harvard University Press, 1929–1953.

Danby, Herbert. *The Mishnah*. Oxford: Oxford University Press, 1983.

Denis, Albert-Marie. *Concordance Grecque Des Pseudépigraphes D'Ancien Testament*. Louvain-la-Neuve: Université Catholique De Louvain, 1987.

Elliger, K., and W. Rudolph, eds. *Biblia Hebraica Stuttgartensia*. Stuttgart: Deutsche Bibelgesellschaft, 1977.

Epstein, Isidore, ed. *The Babylonian Talmud*. 35 vols. London: Soncino, 1935–1952.

Freedman, H., and Maurice Simon, eds. *Midrash Rabbah: Translated into English with Notes, Glossary and Indices*. 10 vols. London: Soncino, 1961.

Friedlander, Gerald. *Midrash Pirke de Rabbi Eliezer*. 4th ed. New York: Sepher- Hermon, 1981.

Grossfeld, Bernard. *The Targum Onqelos to Genesis*. ArBib 6. Wilmington, Del.: Michael Glazier, 1988.

Hallo, William W., ed. *The Context of Scripture*. 3 vols. Leiden: Brill, 1997– .

Hammer, Reuven. *Sifre: A Tannaitic Commentary on the Book of Deuteronomy*. Edited by Leon Nemoy. Yale Judaica Series 24. New Haven: Yale University Press, 1986.

Harmon, A. M., K. Kilburn, and M. D. MacLeod. *Lucian*. 8 vols. LCL. Cambridge, Mass.: Harvard University Press, 1913–1967.

Holmes, Michael W., ed. *The Apostolic Fathers*. Translated by J. B. Lightfoot and J. R. Harmer. 2nd ed. Grand Rapids: Baker, 1989.

Kovacs, David. *Euripides*. 6 vols. LCL. Cambridge, Mass.: Harvard University Press, 1994–2002.

Lauterbach, Jacob Z. *Mekilta de-Rabbi Ishmael*. 3 vols. JPS Library of Jewish Classics. Philadelphia: Jewish Publication Society of America, 1933–1935.

Levertoff, Paul P. *Midrash Sifre on Numbers*. Translations of Early Documents, Series III: Rabbinic Texts. London: Golub, 1926.

Levey, Samson H. *The Targum of Ezekiel: Translated, with a Critical Introduction, Apparatus, and Notes*. Edited by Kevin Cathcart, Michael Maher, and Martin McNamara. ArBib 13. Wilmington, Del.: Michael Glazier, 1987.

Martínez, Florentino García, and Eibert J. C. Tigchelaar, eds. *The Dead Sea Scrolls Study Edition*. 2 vols. Leiden: Brill and Grand Rapids: Eerdmans, 1997–1998.

McNamara, Martin. *Targum Neofiti 1: Genesis*. ArBib 1A. Collegeville, Minn.: Liturgical Press, 1992.

McNamara, Martin, Kevin Cathcart, and Michael Maher, eds. *The Aramaic Bible: The Targums*. 19 vols. Wilmington, Del.: Michael Glazier, 1987– .

Neusner, Jacob. *The Tosefta: Translated from the Hebrew with a New Introduction*. 2 vols. Peabody, Mass.: Hendrickson, 2002.

Rahlfs, Alfred, ed. *Septuaginta*. Stuttgart: Deutsche Bibelgesellschaft, 1979.

Roberts, Alexander, and James Donaldson, eds. *Ante-Nicene Fathers*. 10 vols. 1885 1887. Reprint, Peabody, Mass.: Hendrickson, 1994.

Schaff, Philip, ed. *Nicene and Post-Nicene Fathers: First Series*. 1886–1889. 14 vols. Reprint, Peabody, Mass.: Hendrickson, 1994.

Schaff, Philip, and Henry Wace, eds. *Nicene and Post-Nicene Fathers: Second Series*. 1890–1900. 14 vols. Reprint, Peabody, Mass.: Hendrickson, 1994.

Thackeray, H. St. J. et al. *Josephus*. 10 vols. LCL. Cambridge, Mass.: Harvard University Press, 1926–1965.

Townsend, John T. *Midrash Tanhuma: Translated Into English with Introduction, Indices, and Brief Notes*. 2 vols. Hoboken, N.J.: KTAV, 1989–1997.

Vince, J. H. et al. *Demosthenes*. 7 vols. LCL. Cambridge, Mass.: Harvard University Press, 1930–1949.

Visotzky, Burton L. *The Midrash on Proverbs: Translated from the Hebrew with an Introduction and Annotations*. Edited by Sid Z. Leiman. Yale Judaica Series 27. New Haven: Yale University Press, 1992.

Yonge, C. D. *The Works of Philo: Complete and Unabridged*. Peabody, Mass.: Hendrickson: 1996.

Ziegler, Joseph, et al., eds. *Septuaginta Vetus Testamentum Graecum: Auctoritate Societatis Litterarum Gottingensis editum*. 16 vols. Göttingen: Vandenhoeck & Ruprecht, 1931– .

Secondary Literature

Abbott, T. K. *A Critical and Exegetical Commentary on the Epistles to the Ephesians and to the Colossians*. ICC. Edinburgh: T&T Clark, 1897.

Aletti, Jean-Noël. *Saint Paul Épitre Aux Colossiens*. ÉB. Paris: Gabalda, 1993.

Allen, Leslie C. *Psalms 101–150*. WBC 21. Waco, Tex.: Word, 1983.

Alter, Robert. *The Art of Biblical Narrative*. New York: Basic Books, 1981.

Altick, Richard D., and John J. Fenstermaker. *The Art of Literary Research*. 4th rev. ed. New York: W. W. Norton & Company, 1993.

Anderson, A. A. *The Book of Psalms*. 2 vols. NCB. Grand Rapids: Eerdmans, 1972.

———. *2 Samuel*. WBC 11. Dallas: Word, 1989.

Anderson, Bernhard W. "Exodus Typology in Second Isaiah." Pages 177–95 in *Israel's Prophetic Heritage: Essays in Honor of James Muilenburg*. Edited by Bernhard W. Anderson and Walter Harrelson. New York: Harper & Brothers, 1962.

——. *Out of the Depths: The Psalms Speak for Us Today.* 3rd ed. Louisville: Westminster John Knox, 2000.

Anderson, F. I. "2 (Slavonic Apocalypse of) Enoch." Pages 91–213 in vol. 1 of *The Old Testament Pseudepigrapha.* Edited by James H. Charlesworth. 2 vols. ABRL. New York: Doubleday, 1983.

Arav, Rami. "Hermon, Mount." Pages 158–60 in vol. 3 of *The Anchor Bible Dictionary.* Edited by David Noel Freedman. 6 vols. New York: Doubleday, 1992.

Archer, Gleason L., and Gregory Chirichigno. *Old Testament Quotations in the New Testament.* Chicago: Moody, 1983.

Arnold, Clinton E. *The Colossian Syncretism: The Interface Between Christianity and Folk Belief at Colossae.* WUNT 2/77. Tübingen: J. C. B. Mohr (Paul Siebeck), 1995. Reprint, Grand Rapids: Baker, 1996.

Astour, Michael C. "Melchizedek." Pages 684–86 in vol. 4 of *The Anchor Bible Dictionary.* Edited by David Noel Freedman. 6 vols. New York: Doubleday, 1992.

Augustine. *Expositions on the Book of Psalms.* Vol. 8 of *The Nicene and Post-Nicene Fathers,* Series 1. Edited by Philip Schaff. 1886–1889. 14 vols. United States: Christian Literature Publishing Co., 1888. Reprint, Peabody, Mass.: Hendrickson, 1994.

Baker, Carlos. *The Echoing Green: Romanticism, Modernism, and the Phenomena of Transference in Poetry.* Princeton, N.J.: Princeton University Press, 1984.

Baker, David L. *Two Testaments, One Bible: A Study of Some Modern Solutions to the Theological Problem of the Relationship between the Old and New Testaments.* Downers Grove: InterVarsity, 1976.

——. "Typology and the Christian Use of the Old Testament." Pages 313–30 in *The Right Doctrine from the Wrong Texts?: Essays on the Use of the Old Testament in the New.* Edited by G. K. Beale. Grand Rapids: Baker, 1994. Reprint from *SJT* 29 (1976): 137–57.

Baltzer, Klaus. *The Covenant Formulary in Old Testament, Jewish, and Early Christian Writings.* Translated by David E. Green. Philadelphia: Fortress, 1971.

Bandstra, A. J. *The Law and the Elements of the World: An Exegetical Study in Aspects of Paul's Teaching.* Kampen: Kok, 1964.

Barrett, C. K. *The First Epistle to the Corinthians.* BNTC. London: A&C Black, 1968. Reprint, Peabody, Mass.: Hendrickson, 1996.

Barth, Markus, and Helmut Blanke. *Colossians: A New Translation with Introduction and Commentary.* Translated by Astrid B. Beck. AB 34B. New York: Doubleday, 1994.

Bassler, Jouette. *Divine Impartiality: Paul and a Theological Axiom.* SBLDS 59. Chico, Calif.: Scholars, 1982.

Bauer, Jean B. "Encore une fois Proverbes viii 22." *VT* 8 (1958): 91–92.

Beale, G. K. *The Book of Revelation.* NIGTC. Grand Rapids: Eerdmans, 1999.

——. "Did Jesus and his Followers Preach the Right Doctrine from the Wrong Texts? An Examination of the Presuppositions of Jesus' and the Apostles' Exegetical Method." Pages 387–404 in *The Right Doctrine from the Wrong Texts?: Essays on the Use of the Old Testament in the New.* Edited by G. K. Beale. Grand Rapids: Baker, 1994. Reprint from *Them* 14 (April 1989): 89–96.

——. *John's Use of the Old Testament in Revelation.* JSNTSup 166. Sheffield: Sheffield Academic Press, 1998.

——. "The Old Testament Background of Paul's Reference to "the Fruit of the Spirit" in Galatians 5:22." *BBR* 15.1 (2005): 1–38.

——. "The Old Testament Background of Reconciliation in 2 Corinthians 5–7 and its Bearing on the Literary Problem of 2 Corinthians 6:14–7:1." Pages 217–47 in *The Right Doctrine from the Wrong Texts?: Essays on the Use of the Old Testament in the New.* Edited by G. K. Beale. Grand Rapids: Baker, 1994. Reprint from *NTS* 35 (1989): 550–81.

——. "Colossians." Pages 841–870 in *Commentary on the New Testament Use of the Old Testament.* Edited by G. K. Beale and D. A. Carson. Grand Rapids: Baker Academic, 2007.

———. Review of Jon Paulien, *Decoding Revelation's Trumpets: Literary Allusions and Interpretation of Revelation 8:7–12*. *JBL* 111 (1992): 358–61.

———. *The Use of Daniel in Jewish Apocalyptic Literature and in the Revelation of St. John*. Lanham, Md.: University Press of America, 1984.

Beare, Francis W. "The Epistle to the Colossians." Pages 133–241 in vol. 11 of *The Interpreter's Bible*. Edited by George Arthur Buttrick. 12 vols. New York: Abingdon, 1955.

Beasley-Murray, Paul. "Colossians 1:15–20: An Early Christian Hymn Celebrating the Lordship of Christ." Pages 169–83 in *Pauline Studies: Essays Presented to Professor F. F. Bruce on his 70th Birthday*. Edited by Donald A. Hagner and Murray J. Harris. Grand Rapids: Eerdmans, 1980.

Beaudet, Roland. "La typologie de l'Exode dans le Second-Isaïe." Pages 11–21 in *Etudes Theologiques*. Edited by Roy Lorenzo. Québec: Presses de l'Université Laval, 1963.

Beker, J. Christiaan. "Echoes and Intertextuality: On the Role of Scripture in Paul's Theology." Pages 64–69 in *Paul and the Scriptures of Israel*. Edited by Craig A. Evans and James A. Sanders. JSNTSup 83. Sheffield: JSOT Press, 1993.

Benoit, P. "'Ἅγιοι en Colossiens 1.12: Hommes ou Anges?" Pages 83–101 in *Paul and Paulinism: Essays in Honour of C. K. Barrett*. Edited by M. D. Hooker and S. G. Wilson. London: SPCK, 1982.

Ben-Porat, Ziva. "The Poetics of Literary Allusion," *PTL: A Journal for Descriptive Poetics and Theory of Literature* 1 (1976): 105–128.

Berkley, Timothy W. *From a Broken Covenant to Circumcision of the Heart: Pauline Intertextual Exegesis in Romans 2:17–29*. SBLDS 175. Atlanta: SBL, 2000.

Best, Ernest. *A Critical and Exegetical Commentary on Ephesians*. ICC. Edinburgh: T&T Clark, 1998.

Bevere, Allan R. *Sharing in the Inheritance: Identity and the Moral Life in Colossians*. JSNTSup 226. London: Sheffield Academic Press, 2003.

Bieder, Werner. *Der Kolosserbrief*. Zürich: Zwingli-Verlag, 1943.

Black, Jeremy. "Ashur (god)." Page 36 in *Dictionary of the Ancient Near East*. Edited by Piotr Bienkowski and Alan Millard. Philadelphia: University of Pennsylvania Press, 2000.

Blenkinsopp, Joseph. "Scope and Depth of Exodus Tradition in Deutero-Isaiah 40–55." Pages 41–50 in *The Dynamism of Biblical Tradition*. Edited by Pierre Benoit, Roland E. Murphy, and Bastiaan Van Iersel. Concilium, vol. 20. New York: Paulist, 1967.

Böhl, Eduard. *Die Alttestamentlichen Citate im Neuen Testament*. Vienna: Braumüller, 1878.

Borgen, Peder. "Philo of Alexandria." Pages 333–42 in vol. 4 of *The Anchor Bible Dictionary*. Edited by David Noel Freedman. 6 vols. New York: Doubleday, 1992.

Botterweck, G. J. and H. Ringgren, eds. *Theological Dictionary of the Old Testament*. Translated by J. T. Willis, G. W. Bromiley, and D. E. Green. 13 vols. Grand Rapids: Eerdmans, 1974–.

Bratcher, Robert G., ed. *Old Testament Quotations in the New Testament*. 3rd rev. ed. UBS Handbook Series. New York: United Bible Societies, 1984.

Braulik, G. "Die Ausdrücke für "Gesetz" im Buch Deuteronomium." *Bib* 51 (1970): 39–66.

Briggs, C. A. *A Critical and Exegetical Commentary on the Book of Psalms*. 2 vols. ICC. Edinburgh: T&T Clark, 1907.

Bright, John. *A History of Israel*. 3rd ed. Philadelphia: Westminster, 1981.

Brown, Colin, ed. *New International Dictionary of New Testament Theology*. 4 volumes. Grand Rapids: Zondervan, 1975–1985.

Brown, Raymond E. *An Introduction to the New Testament*. ABRL. New York: Doubleday, 1997.

———. *The Gospel According to John*. 2 vols. AB 29. Garden City: Doubleday, 1966.

———. *The Semitic Background of the Term "Mystery" in the New Testament*. Biblical Series 21. Philadelphia: Fortress, 1968.

——. *The "Sensus Plenior" of Sacred Scripture*. Baltimore: St. Mary's University, 1955.
Bruce, F. F. *The Epistles to the Colossians, to Philemon, and to the Ephesians*. NICNT. Grand Rapids: Eerdmans, 1984.
Bryan, Steve. *Jesus and Israel's Traditions of Judgement and Restoration*. SNTSMS 117. Cambridge: Cambridge University Press, 2002.
Buis, Pierre. "La Nouvelle Alliance." *VT* 18 (1968): 1–15.
Burnett, F. W. "Wisdom." Pages 873–77 in *Dictionary of Jesus and the Gospels*. Edited by Joel B. Green and Scot McKnight. Downers Grove: InterVarsity, 1992.
Burney, C. F. "Christ as the ΑΡΧΗ of Creation (Prov. viii 22, Col. i 15–18, Rev. iii 14)." *JTS* 27 (1925–6): 160–77.
Caird, G. B. *Paul's Letters from Prison*. New Clarendon Bible. Oxford: Oxford University Press, 1976.
Calvin, John. *The Epistles of Paul the Apostle to the Galatians, Ephesians, Philippians, and Colossians*. Translated by T. H. L. Parker. Calvin's New Testament Commentaries 11. Grand Rapids: Eerdmans, 1965.
Carroll, Robert P. *The Book of Jeremiah*. OTL. Philadelphia: Westminster, 1986.
Cazelles, Henri. "Sacral Kingship." Pages 863–66 in vol. 5 of *The Anchor Bible Dictionary*. Edited by David Noel Freedman. 6 volumes. New York: Doubleday, 1992.
Childs, Brevard S. *Biblical Theology of the Old and New Testaments: Theological Reflection on the Christian Bible*. Minneapolis: Fortress, 1992.
Christ, Felix. *Jesus Sophia: Die Sophia-Christologie bei den Synoptikern*. ATANT 57. Zürich: Zwingli-Verlag, 1970.
Ciampa, Roy E. *The Presence and Function of Scripture in Galatians 1 and 2*. WUNT 2/102. Tübingen: J.C.B. Mohr (Paul Siebeck), 1998.
Clement, Ronald E. "The Book of Deuteronomy: Introduction, Commentary, and Reflections." Pages 269–538 in vol. 2 of *The New Interpreter's Bible*. 12 vols. Nashville: Abingdon, 1994–2002.
Clines, D. J. A. "The Image of God in Man." *TynBul* (1968): 53–103.
Cohen, Jeremy. *"Be Fertile and Increase, Fill the Earth and Master It": the Ancient and Medieval Career of a Biblical Text*. Ithaca: Cornell University Press, 1989.
Collins, John J. *Daniel: A Commentary on the Book of Daniel*. Hermeneia. Minneapolis: Fortress, 1993.
——. "Sibylline Oracles." Pages 317–472 in vol. 1 of *The Old Testament Pseudepigrapha*. Edited by James H. Charlesworth. 2 vols. ABRL. New York: Doubleday, 1983.
Comfort, P. W. "Temple." Pages 923–25 in *Dictionary of Paul and His Letters*. Edited by Gerald F. Hawthorne and Ralph P. Martin. Downers Grove: InterVarsity, 1993.
Conzelmann, Hans. "Der Brief an die Kolosser." Pages 176–202 in *Die Briefe an die Galater, Epheser, Philipper, Kolosser, Thessalonicher und Philemon*. Edited by Gerhard Friedrich and Peter Stuhlmacher. 16th edition. NTD 8. Göttingen: Vandenhoeck & Ruprecht, 1985.
Craigie, Peter C. *The Book of Deuteronomy*. NICOT. Grand Rapids: Eerdmans, 1976.
Cranfield, C. E. B. *The Epistle to the Romans*. 2 vols. ICC. Edinburgh: T&T Clark, 1975.
Dahood, Mitchell. *Psalms III, Psalms 101–150*. AB 17A. Garden City, N.Y.: Doubleday, 1970.
Daly-Denton, Margaret. *David in the Fourth Gospel: The Johannine Reception of the Psalms*. AGJU 47. Leiden: Brill, 2000.
Das, A. Andrew. *Paul, the Law, and the Covenant*. Peabody, Mass.: Hendrickson, 2001.
Davies, W. D. *Paul and Rabbinic Judaism: Some Elements in Pauline Theology*. 4th ed. Philadelphia: Fortress, 1980.
Delamarter, Steve. *A Scripture Index to Charlesworth's The Old Testament Pseudepigrapha*. London: Sheffield Academic Press, 2002.
DeMaris, Richard E. *The Colossian Controversy: Wisdom in Dispute at Colossae*. JSNTSup 96. Sheffield: JSOT Press, 1994.

Dibelius, Martin. "The Isis Initiation in Apuleius and Related Initiatory Rites." Pages 61–121 in *Conflict At Colossae: A Problem in the Interpretation of Early Christianity Illustrated by Selected Modern Studies*. Edited and translated by Fred O. Francis and Wayne A. Meeks. Rev. ed. Missoula, Mont.: Scholars Press and SBL, 1975.

Dibelius, Martin, and D. Heinrich Greeven. *An die Kolosser, Epheser, an Philemon*. 3rd ed. HNT 12. Tübingen: J. C. B. Mohr (Paul Siebeck), 1953.

Dittmar, Wilhelm. *Vetus Testamentum in Novo: Die alttestamentlichen Parallelen des Neuen Testaments im Wortlaut der Urtexte und der Septuaginta*. 2 vols. Göttingen: Vandenhoeck & Ruprecht, 1903.

Dodd, C. H. *The Interpretation of the Fourth Gospel*. Cambridge: University Press, 1968.

Donaldson, T. L. "Parallels: Use, Misuse and Limitations." *EvQ* 55 (1983): 193–210.

Drummond, James. *Philo Judaeus; or, The Jewish-Alexandrian Philosophy in its Development and Completion*. 2 vols. London: Williams and Norgate, 1888.

Dunn, J. D. G. *Christology in the Making: A New Testament Inquiry into the Origins of the Doctrine of the Incarnation*. 2nd ed. Grand Rapids: Eerdmans, 1996.

———. *The Epistles to the Colossians and to Philemon*. NIGTC. Grand Rapids: Eerdmans, 1996.

———. *Romans 9–16*. WBC 38B. Dallas: Word, 1988.

Ebner, Eliezer. *Elementary Education in Ancient Israel During the Tannaitic Period (10–220 C.E.)*. New York: Bloch, 1956.

Eissfeldt, Otto. *The Old Testament: An Introduction*. Translated by Peter R. Ackroyd. New York: Harper and Row, 1965.

Ellis, E. Earle. *Paul's Use of the Old Testament*. Grand Rapids: Eerdmans, 1957.

Els, P. J. J. S. "אהב." Pages 277–99 in vol. 1 of *New International Dictionary of Old Testament Theology and Exegesis*. Edited by W. A. VanGemeren. 5 vols. Grand Rapids: Zondervan, 1997.

Eltester, Friedrich-Wilhelm. *Eikon im Neuen Testament*. BZNW 23. Berlin: Töpelmann, 1958.

Ernst, Josef. *Die Briefe an die Philipper, an Philemon, an die Kolosser, an die Epheser*. RNT. Regensburg: Pustet, 1974.

Esler, Philip F. *Galatians*. London and New York: Routledge, 1998.

Eslinger, Lyle. "Inner-Biblical Exegesis and Inner-Biblical Allusion: The Question of Category." *VT* 42 (1992): 47–58.

Evans, Craig A. "The Colossian Mystics." *Bib* 63 (1982): 188–205.

———. "Listening for Echoes of Interpreted Scripture." Pages 47–51 in *Paul and the Scriptures of Israel*. Edited by Craig A. Evans and James A. Sanders. JSNTSup 83. Sheffield: JSOT Press, 1993.

———. "New Testament Use of the Old Testament." Pages 72–80 in *New Dictionary of Biblical Theology*. Edited by T. Desmond Alexander and Brian S. Rosner. Downers Grove: InterVarsity, 2000.

Evans, Craig A., and James A. Sanders. *The Function of Scripture in Early Jewish and Christian Tradition*. JSNTSup 154. Sheffield: Sheffield Academic Press, 1998.

———. *Luke and Scripture: the Function of Sacred Tradition in Luke-Acts* Minneapolis: Fortress, 1993.

Falk, Daniel K. *Daily, Sabbath, and Festival Prayers in the Dead Sea Scrolls*. STDJ 27. Leiden: Brill, 1998.

Fallon, F. "Theodotus." Pages 785–93 in vol. 2 of *The Old Testament Pseudepigrapha*. Edited by James H. Charlesworth. 2 vols. ABRL. New York: Doubleday, 1985.

Fee, Gordon D. *The First Epistle to the Corinthians*. NICNT. Grand Rapids: Eerdmans, 1987.

———. *God's Empowering Presence: The Holy Spirit in the Letters of Paul*. Peabody, Mass.: Hendrickson, 1994.

———. "Old Testament Intertextuality in Colossians: Reflections on Pauline Christology and Gentile Inclusion in God's Story." In *History and Exegesis: New Testament Essays in*

Honor of Dr. E. Earle Ellis on his 80th Birthday. Edited by S. Aaron Son. T&T Clark, 2006.

———. "Wisdom Christology in Paul: A Dissenting View." Pages 251–79 in *The Way of Wisdom: Essays in Honor of Bruce K. Waltke.* Edited by J. I. Packer and Sven K. Soderlund. Grand Rapids: Zondervan, 2000.

Fekkes, Jan, III. *Isaiah and Prophetic Traditions in the Book of Revelation: Visionary Antecedents and their Developments.* JSNTSup 93. Sheffield: JSOT Press, 1994.

Fensham, F. Charles. "Father and Son as Terminology for Treaty and Covenant." Pages 121–35 in *Near Eastern Studies in Honor of William Foxwell Albright.* Edited by Hans Goedicke. Baltimore: John Hopkins, 1971.

Feuillet, A. *Le Christ Sagesse de Dieu d'après les Épitres Pauliniennes.* ÉB. Paris: Gabalda, 1966.

Fiensy, D. A., and D. R. Darnell. "Hellenistic Synagogal Prayers." Pages 671–97 in vol. 2 of *The Old Testament Pseudepigrapha.* Edited by James H. Charlesworth. 2 vols. ABRL. New York: Doubleday, 1985.

Fishbane, Michael. "The "Exodus" Motif/The Paradigm of Historical Renewal." Pages 121–40 in *Text and Texture: Close Readings of Selected Biblical Texts.* New York: Schocken, 1979.

Fitzmyer, Joseph A. *Romans: A New Translation and Commentary.* AB 33. New York: Doubleday, 1993.

Fox, Michael V. *Proverbs 1–9.* AB 18A. New York: Doubleday, 2000.

———. "The Sign of the Covenant: Circumcision in the Light of the Priestly *ʾôt* Etiologies." *RB* 81 (1974): 557–96.

———. "*tôb* as Covenant Terminology." *BASOR* 209 (1973): 41–42.

France, R.T. *Jesus and the Old Testament: His Application of Old Testament Passages to Himself and His Mission.* Downers Grove: InterVarsity, 1971; Reprint, Vancouver, British Columbia: Regent College Publishing, 1998.

Francis, Fred O. "The Background of EMBATEUEIN (Col 2:18) in Legal Papyri and Oracle Inscriptions." Pages 197–207 in *Conflict At Colossae: A Problem in the Interpretation of Early Christianity Illustrated by Selected Modern Studies.* Edited and translated by Fred O. Francis and Wayne A. Meeks. Rev. ed. Missoula, Mont.: Scholars Press and SBL, 1975.

———. "Humility and Angel Worship in Col 2:18." Pages 163–95 in *Conflict At Colossae: A Problem in the Interpretation of Early Christianity Illustrated by Selected Modern Studies.* Edited and translated by Fred O. Francis and Wayne A. Meeks. Rev. ed. Missoula, Mont.: Scholars Press and SBL, 1975.

———. "A Re-examination of the Colossian Controversy." Ph.D. diss., Yale University, 1965.

Furnish, Victor Paul. *II Corinthians.* AB 32A. Garden City, N.Y.: Doubleday, 1984.

———. "Ephesians, Epistle to the." Pages 535–42 in vol. 2 of *The Anchor Bible Dictionary.* Edited by David Noel Freedman. 6 vols. New York: Doubleday, 1992.

Furter, Daniel. *Les Épîtres de Paul aux Colossiens et à Philémon.* CEB. Vaux-sur-Seine: Edifac, 1987.

Gnilka, Joachim. *Der Kolosserbrief.* HTKNT 10/1. Herder: Freiburg, 1980.

Goodenough, Erwin R. *An Introduction to Philo Judaeus.* 2nd ed. Oxford: Basil Blackwell, 1962.

Goppelt, Leonhard. *Typos: The Typological Interpretation of the Old Testament in the New.* Translated by Donald H. Madvig. Grand Rapids: Eerdmans, 1982.

Gough, Henry. *The New Testament Quotations.* London: Walton and Maberly, 1855.

Green, William Scott. "Doing the Text's Work for It: Richard Hays on Paul's Use of Scripture." Pages 58–63 in *Paul and the Scriptures of Israel.* Edited by Craig A. Evans and James A. Sanders. JSNTSup 83. Sheffield: JSOT Press, 1993.

Grinfield, Edward. *Scholia Hellenistica in Novum Testamentum.* 2 vols. London: Pickering, 1848.

Hafemann, Scott J. *Paul, Moses, and the History of Israel: the Letter/Spirit Contrast and the Argument from Scripture in 2 Corinthians 3*. WUNT 81. Tübingen: J. C. B. Mohr (Paul Siebeck), 1995. Reprint, Peabody, Mass.: Hendrickson, 1996.

——. "Paul's Use of the Old Testament in 2 Corinthians." *Int* 52 (1998): 246–57.

Hall, Robert G. "Circumcision." Pages 1025–31 in vol. 1 of *The Anchor Bible Dictionary*. Edited by David Noel Freedman. 6 vols. New York: Doubleday, 1992.

Hanson, Anthony Tyrrell. *The Living Utterances of God: The New Testament Exegesis of the Old*. London: Darton, Longman, and Todd, 1983.

——. *Studies in Paul's Technique and Theology*. Grand Rapids: Eerdmans, 1974.

Harmon, Matthew S. "The Influence of Isaiah 40–66 in Galatians." Unpublished dissertation proposal. Wheaton College Graduate School, 2004.

Hart, Ian. "Genesis 1:1–2:3 as a Prologue to the Book of Genesis." *TynBul* 46 (1995): 315–36.

Hawk, L. D. "Literary/Narrative Criticism." Pages 536–44 in *Dictionary of the Old Testament Pentateuch*. Edited by T. Desmond Alexander and David W. Baker. Downers Grove: InterVarsity, 2003.

Hay, David M. *Colossians*. ANTC. Nashville: Abingdon, 2000.

——. *Glory at the Right Hand: Psalm 110 in Early Christianity*. SBLMS 18. Nashville: Abingdon, 1973.

Hays, Richard B. *The Conversion of the Imagination: Paul as Interpreter of Israel's Scripture*. Grand Rapids: Eerdmans, 2005.

——. *Echoes of Scripture in the Letters of Paul*. New Haven: Yale University Press, 1989.

——. "On the Rebound: A Response to Critiques of *Echoes of Scripture in the Letters of Paul*." Pages 70–96 in *Paul and the Scriptures of Israel*. Edited by Craig A. Evans and James A. Sanders. JSNTSup 83. Sheffield: JSOT Press, 1993.

Hengel, Martin. *Judaism and Hellenism: Studies in their Encounter in Palestine during the Early Hellenistic Period*. Translated by John Bowden. 2 vols. Philadelphia: Fortress, 1974.

——. *The Pre-Christian Paul*. Translated by John Bowden. Philadelphia: Trinity Press International, 1991.

——. *The Septuagint as Christian Scripture: Its Prehistory and the Problem of its Canon*. Translated by Mark E. Biddle. Grand Rapids: Baker Academic, 2002.

Hirsch, E. D., Jr. *Validity in Interpretation*. New Haven: Yale University Press, 1967.

Hirsch, Emil G. "Shemoneh 'Esreh." Pages 270a–282b in vol. 11 of *The Jewish Encyclopedia*. Edited by Isidore Singer. 12 vols. New York: Funk and Wagnalls, 1925.

Holladay, William L. *Jeremiah 1*. Hermeneia. Minneapolis: Fortress, 1986.

——. *Jeremiah 2*. Hermeneia. Minneapolis: Fortress, 1989.

——. *The Root šûbh in the Old Testament: with Particular Reference to its Usages in Covenantal Contexts*. Leiden: Brill, 1958.

Hollander, John. *The Figure of Echo: A Mode of Allusion in Milton and After*. Berkeley: University of California Press, 1981.

Hooker, Morna D. "Were there False Teachers in Colossae?" Pages 315–31 in *Christ and Spirit in the New Testament: Studies in Honour of Charles Francis Digby Moule*. Edited by Barnabas Lindars and Stephen S. Smalley. Cambridge: Cambridge University Press, 1973.

Hoppe, Rudolf. *Epheserbrief, Kolosserbrief*. SKKNT 10. Stuttgart: Verlag Katholisches Bibelwerk, 1987.

Horne, Thomas Hartwell. *An Introduction to the Critical Study and Knowledge of the Holy Scriptures*. 2 vols. 8th ed. New York: Robert Carter, 1847.

Hübner, Hans. "New Testament, OT Quotations in the." Pages 1096–104 in vol. 4 of *The Anchor Bible Dictionary*. Edited by David Noel Freedman. Article translated by Siegfried S. Schatzmann. 6 vols. New York: Doubleday, 1992.

——. *An Philemon. An die Kolosser. An die Epheser*. HNT 12. Tübingen: J. C. B. Mohr (Paul Siebeck), 1997.

——. *Vetus Testamentum in Novo: Band 2, Corpus Paulinum*. Göttingen: Vandenhoeck & Ruprecht, 1997.

Hugedé, Norbert. *Commentaire de L'Épître aux Colossiens.* Geneva: Labor et Fides, 1968.

Hühn, Eugen. *Die alttestamentlichen Citate und Reminiscenzen im Neuen Testamente.* Tübingen: J. C. B. Mohr (Paul Siebeck), 1900.

Isaac, E. "1 (Ethiopic Apocalypse of) Enoch." Pages 5–89 in vol. 1 of *The Old Testament Pseudepigrapha.* Edited by James H. Charlesworth. 2 vols. ABRL. New York: Doubleday, 1983.

Ishida, Tomoo. "Solomon." Pages 105–13 in vol. 6 of *The Anchor Bible Dictionary.* Edited by David Noel Freedman. 6 vols. New York: Doubleday, 1992.

Jenni, Ernst, and Claus Westermann, eds. *Theological Lexicon of the Old Testament.* Translated by Mark E. Biddle. 3 vols. Peabody, Mass.: Hendrickson, 1997.

Jervell, Jacob. *Imago Dei: Gen 1, 26f. im Spätjudentum, in der Gnosis und in den paulinischen Briefen.* FRLANT 76. Göttingen: Vandenhoeck & Ruprecht, 1960.

Jobes, Karen H., and Moisés Silva. *Invitation to the Septuagint.* Grand Rapids: Baker Academic: 2000.

Joüon, Paul. *A Grammar of Biblical Hebrew.* Roma: Editrice Pontificio Istituto Biblico, 1993.

Kee, H. C. "Testaments of the Twelve Patriarchs." Pages 775–828 in vol. 1 of *The Old Testament Pseudepigrapha.* Edited by James H. Charlesworth. 2 vols. ABRL. New York: Doubleday, 1983.

Keener, Craig S. *The Gospel of John: A Commentary.* 2 vols. Peabody, Mass.: Hendrickson, 2003.

Keesmaat, Sylvia C. "Exodus and the Intertextual Transformation of Tradition in Romans 8.14–30." *JSNT* 54 (1994): 29–56.

Kelly, J. N. D. *Early Christian Creeds.* 2nd ed. London: Longman's, 1960.

Kidner, Derek. *Psalms 73–150.* TOTC. London: Inter-Varsity, 1975.

Kim, Jung Hoon. *The Significance of Clothing Imagery in the Pauline Corpus.* JSNTSup 268. London: T&T Clark, 2004.

Kim, Seyoon. *The Origin of Paul's Gospel.* WUNT 2/4. Tübingen: J. C. B. Mohr (Paul Siebeck), 1981. Reprint, Grand Rapids: Eerdmans, 1982.

Kimball, Charles A. *Jesus' Exposition of the Old Testament in Luke's Gospel.* JSNTSup 94. Sheffield: JSOT Press, 1994.

Kissane, Edward J. *The Book of Psalms.* Dublin: Browne and Nolan, 1964.

Kitchen, K. A. "Exodus, The." Pages 689–708 in vol. 2 of *The Anchor Bible Dictionary.* Edited by David Noel Freedman. 6 vols. New York: Doubleday.

Kittel, G., and G. Friedrich, eds. *Theological Dictionary of the New Testament.* Translated by G. W. Bromiley. 10 vols. Grand Rapids: Eerdmans, 1964–1976.

Kline, Meredith G. *By Oath Consigned: A Reinterpretation of the Covenant Signs of Circumcision and Baptism.* Grand Rapids: Eerdmans, 1968.

———. *Treaty of the Great King: The Covenant Structure of Deuteronomy.* Grand Rapids: Eerdmans, 1963.

Knox, W. L. *St. Paul and the Church of the Gentiles.* Cambridge: University Press, 1939.

Koch, Dietrich-Alex. *Die Schrift als Zeuge des Evangeliums: Untersuchungen zur Verwendung und zum Verständnis der Schrift bei Paulus.* BHT 69. Tübingen: J. C. B. Mohr (Paul Siebeck), 1986.

Kodell, J. "'The Word of God Grew': The Ecclesial Tendency of Λόγος in Acts 1,7; 12,24; 19,20." *Bib* 55 (1974): 505–19.

Kraus, Hans-Joachim. *Psalms 60–150.* Translated by Hilton C. Oswald. CC. Minneapolis: Fortress, 1993.

Kümmel, Werner Georg. *Introduction to the New Testament.* Translated by Howard Clark Kee. Rev. ed. Nashville: Abingdon, 1975.

Lamp, Jeffrey S. "Wisdom in Col. 1:15–20: Contribution and Significance." *JETS* 41 (March 1998): 45–54.

Lang, Bernhard. "Wisdom." Pages 900–5 in *Dictionary of Deities and Demons in the Bible*. Edited by Karel van der Toorn, Bob Becking, and Pieter W. Van der Horst. 2nd revised ed. Leiden: Brill/Grand Rapids: Eerdmans, 1999.

Larsson, Edvin. *Christus als Vorbild: Eine Untersuchung zu den paulinischen Tauf- und Eikontexten.* ASNU 23. Uppsala: Gleerup, 1962.

Leaney, A. R. C. *The Rule of Qumran and Its Meaning: Introduction, Translation, and Commentary.* NTL. Philadelphia: Westminster, 1966.

Le Déaut, R. "Le Thème de la Circoncision du Coeur (Dt. XXX 6; Jér. IV 4) dans les Versions Anciennes (LXX et Targum) et à Qumrân." Pages 178–205 in *Congress Volume (Vienna 1980)*. VTSup 32. Leiden: Brill, 1981.

Lightfoot, J. B. *Saint Paul's Epistles to the Colossians and to Philemon*. Rev. ed. Classic Commentary Library. MacMillan and Co., 1879. Reprint, Grand Rapids: Zondervan, 1886.

Lincoln, Andrew T. "The Household Code and Wisdom Mode of Colossians." *JSNT* 74 (1999): 93–112.

——. "The Letter to the Colossians." Pages 552–669 in vol. 11 of *The New Interpreter's Bible*. 12 vols. Nashville: Abingdon, 1994–2002.

——. *Paradise Now and Not Yet: Studies in the Role of the Heavenly Dimension in Paul's Thought with Special Reference to His Eschatology*. SNTSMS 43. Cambridge: Cambridge University Press, 1981.

Lindars, Barnabas. "The Place of the Old Testament in the Formation of New Testament Theology." *NTS* 23 (1977): 59–66.

Lindemann, Andreas. *Der Kolosserbrief*. ZBKNT 10. Zürich: Theologischer Verlag, 1983.

Litwak, Kenneth D. "Echoes of Scripture? A Critical Survey of Recent Works on Paul's Use of the Old Testament." *CurBS* 6 (1998): 260–88.

Llewelyn, S. R., ed. *New Documents Illustrating Early Christianity*. 9 vols. Sydney, Australia: Macquarie University, 1981–.

Lohmeyer, Ernst. *Die Briefe an die Philipper, Kolosser und an Philemon*. KEK. Göttingen: Vandenhoeck & Ruprecht, 1964.

Lohse, Eduard. *Colossians and Philemon*. Translated by William R. Poehlmann and Robert J. Karris. Hermeneia. Philadelphia: Fortress, 1971.

Longenecker, Bruce W. *The Triumph of Abraham's God: The Transformation of Identity in Galatians*. Nashville: Abingdon, 1998.

MacDonald, Margaret Y. *Colossians and Ephesians*. SP 17. Collegeville, Minn.: Liturgical Press, 2000.

Manning, Gary T. *Echoes of a Prophet: The Use of Ezekiel in the Gospel of John and in Literature of the Second Temple Period*. JSNTSup 270. London: T&T Clark, 2004.

Martin, Ralph P. *Colossians and Philemon*. Revised ed. NCB. London: Oliphants, 1978.

Martin, Troy W. *By Philosophy and Empty Deceit: Colossians as Response to a Cynic Critique*. JSNTSup 118. Sheffield: Sheffield Academic Press, 1996.

Masson, Charles. *L'Épitre de Saint Paul aux Colossiens*. CNT 10. Neuchatel: Delachaux, 1950.

Maurer, C. "Der Hymnus von Epheser 1 als Schlüssel zum ganzen Brief." *EvT* 11 (1951/52): 151–72.

McCarter, P. Kyle, Jr. *II Samuel: A New Translation with Introduction, Notes and Commentary*. AB 9. New York: Doubleday, 1984.

McCarthy, Dennis J. "Notes on the Love of God in Deuteronomy and the Father-Son Relationship between Yahweh and Israel." *CBQ* 27 (1965): 144–47.

——. *Old Testament Covenant: A Survey of Current Opinions*. Richmond, Va.: John Knox, 1972.

——. *Treaty and Covenant: A Study in the Ancient Oriental Documents and in the Old Testament*. AnBib 21A. Rome: Biblical Institute Press, 1978.

McKane, William. *A Critical and Exegetical Commentary on Jeremiah*. 2 vols. ICC. Edinburgh: T&T Clark, 1996.

——. *Proverbs*. OTL. Philadelphia: Westminster, 1970.

Melick, Richard R., Jr. *Philippians, Colossians, Philemon*. NAC. Nashville: Broadman, 1991.

Mendenhall, George E. *Law and Covenant in Israel and the Ancient Near East*. Pittsburgh: The Presbyterian Board of Colportage, 1955.

Metzger, Bruce M. "The Fourth Book of Ezra." Pages 517–59 in vol. 1 of *The Old Testament Pseudepigrapha*. Edited by James H. Charlesworth. 2 vols. ABRL. New York: Doubleday, 1983.

Michaelis, Wilhelm. "πρωτότοκος." Pages 871–81 in vol. 6 of *Theological Dictionary of the New Testament*. Edited by G. Kittel and G. Friedrich. Translated by G. Bromiley. 10 vols. Grand Rapids: Eerdmans, 1964–1976.

Michel, Otto. *Paulus und Seine Bibel*. BFCT 2/18. Gütersloh: Bertelsmann, 1929. Reprint, Darmstadt: Wissenschaftliche Buchgesellschaft, 1972.

Milgrom, Jacob. *Leviticus 1–16*. AB 3. New York: Doubleday, 1991.

Miller, Patrick D. *Deuteronomy*. IBC. Louisville: John Knox, 1990.

Miner, Earl. "Allusion." Pages 38–39 in *The New Princeton Encyclopedia of Poetry and Poetics*. Edited by Alex Preminger and T. V. F. Brogan. Princeton, N. J.: Princeton University Press, 1993.

Moo, Douglas J. *The Epistle to the Romans*. NICNT. Grand Rapids: Eerdmans, 1996.

——. "Israel and the Law in Romans 5–11: Interaction with the New Perspective." Pages 185–216 in *Justification and Variegated Nomism, volume 2: the Paradoxes of Paul*. Edited by D. A. Carson, Peter T. O'Brien, and Mark A. Seifrid. WUNT 2/181. Tübingen: Mohr Siebeck, 2004.

——. "The Problem of *Sensus Plenior*." Pages 175–212 in *Hermeneutics, Authority, and Canon*. Edited by D. A. Carson and John D. Woodbridge. Grand Rapids: Academie Books, 1986. Reprint, Grand Rapids: Baker, 1995.

Moran, William J. "The Ancient Near Eastern Background of the Love of God in Deuteronomy." *CBQ* (1963): 77–87.

Moritz, Thorsten. *A Profound Mystery: The Use of the Old Testament in Ephesians*. NovTSup 85. Leiden: Brill, 1996.

Morris, Leon. *The Apostolic Preaching of the Cross*. 3rd rev. ed. Grand Rapids: Eerdmans, 1965.

Moule, C. F. D. *The Epistles of Paul the Apostle to the Colossians and to Philemon: An Introduction and Commentary*. CGTC. Cambridge: Cambridge University Press, 1957.

Moyise, Steve. *The Old Testament in the Book of Revelation*. JSNTSup 115. Sheffield: Sheffield Academic Press, 1995.

——. *The Old Testament in the New: An Introduction*. Continuum Biblical Studies Series. London and New York: Continuum, 2001.

Murphy, Roland E. *Proverbs*. WBC 22. Nashville: Thomas Nelson, 1998.

Myers, Jacob M. *1 Chronicles*. AB 12. Garden City, N.Y.: Doubleday, 1965.

O'Brien, Peter T. *Colossians, Philemon*. WBC 44. Waco, Tex.: Word, 1982.

——. *Introductory Thanksgivings in the Letters of Paul*. NovTSup 49. Leiden: Brill, 1977.

Oden, Thomas C., ed. *Colossians, 1–2 Thessalonians, 1–2 Timothy, Titus, Philemon*. ACCS 9 (NT). Downers Grove: InterVarsity, 2000.

Overfield, P. D. "Pleroma: A Study in Content and Context." *NTS* 25 (1979): 384–96.

Pao, David W. *Acts and the Isaianic New Exodus*. WUNT 2/130. Tübingen: J. C. B. Mohr (Paul Siebeck), 2000. Reprint, Grand Rapids: Baker Academic, 2002.

Pate, C. Marvin. *The End of the Age Has Come: the Theology of Paul*. Grand Rapids: Zondervan, 1995.

Patzia, Arthur G. *Ephesians, Colossians, Philemon*. NIBCNT 10. Peabody, Mass.: Hendrickson, 1995.

Paulien, Jon. *Decoding Revelation's Trumpets: Literary Allusions and Interpretation of Revelation 8:7–12*. Andrews University Seminary Doctoral Dissertation Series, vol. 11. Berrien Springs, Mich.: Andrews University Press, 1988.

——. "Elusive Allusions: The Problematic Use of the Old Testament in Revelation." *BR* 33 (1988): 37–53.

Perri, Carmela. "On Alluding." *Poetics* 7 (1978): 289–307.

Pokorný, Petr. *Colossians: A Commentary*. Translated by Siegfried S. Schatzmann. Peabody, Mass.: Hendrickson, 1991.

Porter, Stanley E. "The Use of the Old Testament in the New Testament: A Brief Comment on Method and Terminology." Pages 79–96 in *Early Christian Interpretation of the Scriptures of Israel: Investigations and Proposals*. Edited by Craig A. Evans and James A. Sanders. JSNTSup 148. Vol. 5 of *Studies in Scripture in Early Judaism and Christianity*. Sheffield: Sheffield Academic Press, 1997.

Ringgren, Helmer. "גשׁ." Pages 215–19 in vol. 9 of *Theological Dictionary of the Old Testament*. Edited by G. J. Botterweck and H. Ringgren. Translated by J. T. Willis, G. W. Bromiley, and D. E. Green. 13 vols. Grand Rapids: Eerdmans, 1974–.

Rogers, Cleon L., III. "The Meaning and Significance of the Hebrew Word אמון in Proverbs 8,30." *ZAW* 109 (1997): 208–21.

Rosner, Brian S. *Paul, Scripture, and Ethics: A Study of 1 Corinthians 5–7*. AGJU 22. Leiden: Brill, 1994. Reprint, Grand Rapids: Baker, 1999.

Rowland, Christopher. "Apocalyptic Visions and the Exaltation of Christ in the Letter to the Colossians." Pages 220–29 in *The Pauline Writings: A Sheffield Reader*. Edited by Stanley E. Porter and Craig A. Evans. Sheffield: Sheffield Academic Press, 1995. Reprint from *JSNT* 19 (1983): 73–83.

Safrai, S. "Education and the Study of the Torah." Pages 945–70 in vol. 2 of *The Jewish People in the First Century: Historical Geography, Political History, Social, Cultural and Religious Life and Institutions*. Edited by S. Safrai and Michael Stern. 2 vols. CRINT. Assen: Van Gorcum, 1987.

Sahlin, Harald. "The New Exodus of Salvation According to St Paul." Pages 81–95 in *The Root of the Vine: Essays in Biblical Theology*. New York: Philosophical Library, 1953.

Sakenfeld, Katharine Doob. *The Meaning of Hesed in the Hebrew Bible: A New Inquiry*. HSM 17. Missoula, Mont.: Scholars Press, 1977. Reprint, Eugene, Oreg.: Wipf & Stock, 2002.

Sanday, William, and Arthur C. Headlam. *A Critical and Exegetical Commentary on the Epistle to the Romans*. ICC. New York: Charles Scribner's Sons, 1896.

Sanders, E. P. "Literary Dependence in Colossians." *JBL* 85 (1966): 28–45.

Sanders, James A. "Canon." Pages 837–52 in vol. 1 of *The Anchor Bible Dictionary*. Edited by David Noel Freedman. 6 vols. New York: Doubleday, 1992.

Sandmel, Samuel. "Parallelomania." *JBL* 81 (1962): 1–13.

——. *Philo of Alexandria: An Introduction*. New York: Oxford University Press, 1979.

Sappington, Thomas J. *Revelation and Redemption at Colossae*. JSNTSup 53. Sheffield: JSOT Press, 1991.

Sarna, Nahum M. *Exploring Exodus: The Heritage of Biblical Israel*. New York: Schocken Books, 1987.

——. "Psalm 89: A Study in Inner Biblical Exegesis." Pages 29–46 in *Biblical and Other Studies*. Edited by Alexander Altman. Studies and Texts 1. Cambridge: Harvard University Press, 1963.

Sasson, Jack M. "Circumcision in the Ancient Near East." *JBL* 85 (1966): 473–76.

Savignac, Jean de. "Note sur le sens du Verset viii 22 des Proverbes." *VT* 4 (1954): 429–32.

Schnabel, Eckhard J. *Law and Wisdom from Ben Sira to Paul: A Tradition Historical Inquiry into the Relation of Law, Wisdom, and Ethics*. WUNT 2/16. Tübingen: J. C. B. Mohr [Paul Siebeck], 1985.

Schniedewind, William. *Society and the Promise to David: The Reception History of 2 Samuel 7:1–17*. New York: Oxford University Press, 1999.

Schweizer, Eduard. *The Letter to the Colossians: A Commentary*. Translated by Andrew Chester. Minneapolis: Augsburg, 1982.

——. "Slaves of the Elements and Worshippers of Angels: Gal 4:3, 9 and Col 2:8, 18, 20." *JBL* 107 (1988): 455–68.

Scobie, Charles H. H. *The Ways of our God: An Approach to Biblical Theology.* Grand Rapids: Eerdmans, 2003.

Scott, James M. *Adoption as Sons of God: An Exegetical Investigation into the Background of* ΥΙΟΘΕΣΙΑ *in the Pauline Corpus.* WUNT 2/48. Tübingen: J. C. B. Mohr [Paul Siebeck], 1992.

——. "Heavenly Ascent in Jewish and Pagan Traditions." Pages 447–52 in *Dictionary of New Testament Background.* Edited by Craig A. Evans and Stanley E. Porter. Downers Grove: InterVarsity, 2000.

——, ed. *Exile: Old Testament, Jewish, and Christian Conceptions.* JSJSup 56. Leiden: Brill, 1997.

——, ed. *Restoration: Old Testament, Jewish, and Christian Perspectives.* JSJSup 72. Leiden: Brill, 2001.

Scott, Martin. *Sophia and the Johannine Jesus.* JSNTSup 71. Sheffield: JSOT Press, 1992.

Scott, R. B. Y. "Wisdom in Creation: The ʾĀmôn of Proverbs VIII 30." *VT* 10 (1960): 213–23.

Seifrid, Mark A. *Christ, our Righteousness: Paul's Theology of Justification.* NSBT 9; Downers Grove: InterVarsity, 2000.

Seitz, Christopher R. *Isaiah 1–39.* Interpretation. Louisville: John Knox, 1993.

Seow, C. L. "Ark of the Covenant." Pages 386–93 in vol. 1 of *The Anchor Bible Dictionary.* Edited by David Noel Freedman. 6 vols. New York: Doubleday, 1992.

Skehan, Patrick W. and Alexander A. Di Lella. *The Wisdom of Ben Sira.* AB 39. New York: Doubleday, 1987.

Shaw, Harry. *Dictionary of Literary Terms.* New York: McGraw-Hill, 1972.

Shogren, Gary S. "Presently Entering the Kingdom of Christ: The Background and Purpose of Col 1:12–14." *JETS* 31 (1988): 173–80.

Shutt, R. J. H. "Letter of Aristeas." Pages 7–34 in vol. 2 of *The Old Testament Pseudepigrapha.* Edited by James H. Charlesworth. 2 vols. ABRL. New York: Doubleday, 1983.

Silva, Moisés. "Old Testament in Paul." Pages 630–42 in *Dictionary of Paul and his Letters.* Edited by Gerald F. Hawthorne and Ralph P. Martin. Downers Grove: InterVarsity, 1993.

Silva, Moisés and Karen H. Jobes. *Invitation to the Septuagint.* Grand Rapids: Baker, 2000.

Slayton, Joel C. "Bashan." Pages 623–24 in vol. 1 of *The Anchor Bible Dictionary.* Edited by David Noel Freedman. 6 vols. New York: Doubleday, 1992.

Sommer, Benjamin D. "Exegesis, Allusion and Intertextuality in the Hebrew Bible: A Response to Lyle Eslinger." *VT* 46 (1996): 479–89.

Spicq, Ceslas. *Theological Lexicon of the New Testament.* Translated and edited by James D. Ernest. 3 vols. Peabody, Mass.: Hendrickson, 1994.

Stanley, Christopher D. *Arguing With Scripture: The Rhetoric of Quotations in the Letters of Paul.* New York: T&T Clark International, 2004.

——. *Paul and the Language of Scripture: Citation Technique in the Pauline Epistles and Contemporary Literature.* SNTSMS 74. Cambridge: Cambridge University Press, 1992.

——. "'Pearls Before Swine': Did Paul's Audiences Understand His Biblical Quotations?" *NovT* 41 (1999): 124–44.

Sterling, Gregory E. "Prepositional Metaphysics in Jewish Wisdom Speculation and Early Christian Liturgical Texts." Pages 219–38 in *Wisdom and Logos: Studies in Jewish Thought in Honor of David Winston.* Edited by David T. Runia. Studia Philonica Annual 9. Atlanta: Scholars Press, 1997.

Stone, Michael E., and Jonas C. Greenfield. "The Prayer of Levi." *JBL* 112 (1993): 247–66.

Strauss, Mark L. *The Davidic Messiah in Luke-Acts: the Promise and its Fulfillment in Lukan Christology*. JSNTSup 110. Sheffield: Sheffield Academic Press, 1995.

Stuart, Douglas. *Hosea–Jonah*. WBC 31. Waco, Tex.: Word, 1987.

Stuhlmacher, Peter. *Paul's Letter to the Romans: A Commentary*. Translated by Scott J. Hafemann. Louisville: Westminster/John Knox, 1994.

Stuhlmueller, Carroll. *Creative Redemption in Deutero-Isaiah*. AnBib 43. Rome: Biblical Institute Press, 1970.

Sweeney, Marvin A. *Isaiah 1–39: with an Introduction to Prophetic Literature*. FOTL 16. Grand Rapids: Eerdmans, 1996.

———. "Jesse's New Shoot in Isaiah 11: A Josianic Reading of the Prophet Isaiah." Pages 103–18 in *A Gift of God in Due Season: Essays on Scripture and Community in Honor of James A. Sanders*. Edited by Richard D. Weis and David M. Carr. JSOTSup 225. Sheffield: Sheffield Academic Press, 1996.

Swete, Henry B. *An Introduction to the Old Testament in Greek*. Cambridge: Cambridge University Press, 1902. Reprint, New York: KTAV, 1968.

Tate, Marvin E. *Psalms 51–100*. WBC 20. Dallas: Word, 1990.

Tennyson, Hallam. *Alfred Lord Tennyson: A Memoir*. 2 vols. New York: MacMillan, 1898.

Thiele, Edwin R. *The Mysterious Numbers of the Hebrew Kings*. Rev. ed. Grand Rapids: Eerdmans, 1965.

Thielman, Frank. *Paul & the Law: A Contextual Approach*. Downers Grove: InterVarsity, 1994.

Thompson, J. A. *Deuteronomy*. TOTC. London: Inter-Varsity, 1974.

———. "Israel's 'Haters.'" *VT* 29 (1979): 200–05.

Thompson, Michael. *Clothed with Christ: The Example and Teaching of Jesus in Romans 12.1–15.13*. JSNTSup 59. Sheffield: JSOT Press, 1991.

Thrall, Margaret E. *A Critical and Exegetical Commentary on the Second Epistle to the Corinthians*. 2 vols. ICC. Edinburgh: T&T Clark, 1994.

Tigay, Jeffrey H. *Deuteronomy*. JPS Torah Commentary. Philadelphia: Jewish Publication Society, 1996.

Tomson, Peter J. *Paul and the Jewish Law: Halakha in the Letters of the Apostle to the Gentiles*. CRINT 3/1. Assen/Maastricht: Van Gorcum, 1990.

Townsend, John T. "Education (Greco-Roman)." Pages 312–17 in vol. 2 of *The Anchor Bible Dictionary*. Edited by David Noel Freedman. 6 vols. New York: Doubleday, 1992.

Tov, Emanuel. "Textual Criticism." Pages 393–412 in vol. 6 of *The Anchor Bible Dictionary*. Edited by David Noel Freedman. 6 vols. New York: Doubleday, 1992.

Toy, Crawford Howell. *Quotations in the New Testament*. New York: Charles Scribner's Sons, 1884.

Turpie, David McCalman. *The Old Testament in the New: A Contribution to Biblical Criticism and Interpretation*. London: Williams and Norgate, 1868.

VanderKam, James C. "Covenant." Pages 151–55 in vol. 1 of *Encyclopedia of the Dead Sea Scrolls*. Edited by Lawrence H. Schiffman and James C. VanderKam. 2 vols. Oxford: Oxford University Press, 2000.

VanGemeren, W. A., ed. *New International Dictionary of Old Testament Theology and Exegesis*. 5 vols. Grand Rapids: Eerdmans, 1997.

Van Leeuwen, Raymond. "The Book of Proverbs: Introduction, Commentary, and Reflections." Pages 17–264 in vol. 5 of *The New Interpreter's Bible*. 12 vols. Nashville: Abingdon, 1994–2002.

Van Ruiten, J. T. A. G. M. "The Intertextual Relationship Between Isaiah 65,25 and Isaiah 11,6–9." Pages 31–42 in *The Scriptures and the Scrolls: Studies in Honour of A. S. Van Der Woude on the Occasion of His 65th Birthday*. Edited by F. García Martínez, A. Hilhorst, and C. J. Labuschagne. VTSup 49. Leiden: Brill, 1992.

Vaux, Roland de. *Ancient Israel: Its Life and Institutions*. Translated by John McHugh. New York: McGraw-Hill, 1961.

Vawter, Bruce. "Prov 8:22: Wisdom and Creation." *JBL* 99 (1980): 205–16.

Venard, L. "Citations de l'Ancien Testament dans le Nouveau Testament." Pages 23–51 in vol. 2 of *Dictionnaire de la Bible: Supplément.* Edited by L. Pirot and A. Robert. 11 volumes. Paris: Librairie Letouzey et Ané, 1928–.

Vollmer, Hans. *Die Alttestamentlichen Citate bei Paulus: Textkritisch und biblisch theologisch gewürdigt nebst einem Anhang Ueber das Verhältnis des Apostels zu Philo.* Freiburg and Leipzig: J. C. B. Mohr (Paul Siebeck), 1895.

Wagner, J. Ross. *Heralds of the Good News: Isaiah and Paul "in Concert" in the Letter to the Romans.* NovTSup 101. Leiden: Brill, 2002.

Wakefield, Andrew H. *Where to Live: The Hermeneutical Significance of Paul's Citations from Scripture in Galatians 3:1–14.* Academia Biblica 14. Leiden: Brill, 2003.

Wall, Robert W. *Colossians & Philemon.* IVPNTC. Downers Grove: InterVarsity, 1993.

Wallace, Daniel B. *Greek Grammar Beyond the Basics: An Exegetical Syntax of the New Testament.* Grand Rapids: Zondervan, 1997.

Wallis, Gerhard. "אהב." Pages 99–118 in vol. 1 of *Theological Dictionary of the Old Testament.* Edited by G. J. Botterweck and H. Ringgren. Translated by J. T. Willis, G. W. Bromiley, and D. E. Green. 13 vols. Grand Rapids: Eerdmans, 1974–.

Waltke, Bruce K. "Micah." Pages 591–764 in *Obadiah, Jonah, Micah, Nahum, and Habakkuk.* Edited by Thomas Edward McComiskey. Vol. 2 of *The Minor Prophets: An Exegetical and Expository Commentary.* Grand Rapids: Baker, 1993.

———. *Proverbs: Chapters 1–15.* 2 vols. NICOT. Grand Rapids: Eerdmans, 2004.

———. "Samaritan Pentateuch." Pages 932–38 in vol. 5 of *The Anchor Bible Dictionary.* Edited by David Noel Freedman. 6 vols. New York: Doubleday, 1992.

Waltke, Bruce K., and Cathi J. Fredricks. *Genesis: A Commentary.* Grand Rapids: Zondervan, 2001.

Waltke, Bruce K., and M. O'Connor. *An Introduction to Biblical Hebrew Syntax.* Winona Lake, Ind.: Eisenbrauns, 1990.

Washburn, David L. *A Catalog of Biblical Passages in the Dead Sea Scrolls.* SBL Text-Critical Studies 2. Atlanta: SBL, 2002.

Watson, Duane F. "Education: Jewish and Greco-Roman." Pages 308–13 in *Dictionary of New Testament Background.* Edited by Craig A. Evans and Stanley E. Porter. Downers Grove: InterVarsity, 2000.

Watson, Francis. *Text and Truth: Redefining Biblical Theology.* Grand Rapids: Eerdmans, 1997.

Watts, Rikki E. *Isaiah's New Exodus and Mark.* WUNT 2/88. Tübingen: J. C. B. Mohr (Paul Siebeck), 1997. Reprint, *Isaiah's New Exodus in Mark.* Grand Rapids: Baker Academic, 2000.

Weinfeld, Moshe. *Deuteronomy 1–11: A New Translation with Introduction and Commentary.* AB 5. New York: Doubleday, 1991.

Weiss, H. "The Law in the Epistle to the Colossians." *CBQ* 34 (1972): 294–314.

Wenham, Gordon J. *Genesis 16–50.* WBC 2. Dallas: Word, 1994.

Westermann, Claus. *Genesis 1–11: A Commentary.* Translated by John J. Scullion. Minneapolis: Augsburg, 1984.

Wilcox, Max. "On Investigating the use of the Old Testament in the New Testament." Pages 231–43 in *Text and Interpretation: Studies in the New Testament Presented to Matthew Black.* FS. Edited by Ernest Best and R. McL.Wilson. Cambridge: Cambridge University Press, 1979.

Wildberger, Hans. "Das Abbild Gottes: Gen. 1, 26–30." *TZ* 21 (1965): 245–259, 481–501.

———. *Isaiah 1–12.* Translated by Thomas H. Trapp. CC. Minneapolis: Fortress, 1991.

———. *Isaiah 28–39.* Translated by Thomas H. Trapp. CC. Minneapolis: Fortress, 2002.

Williams, H. H. D. *The Wisdom of the Wise: The Presence and Function of Scripture within 1 Cor 1:18–3:23.* Leiden: Brill, 2001.

Williams, Ronald J. *Hebrew Syntax: An Outline.* 2nd ed. Toronto: University of Toronto, 1976.

Wisdom, J. R. *Blessing for the Nations and the Curse of the Law: Paul's Citation of Genesis and Deuteronomy in Gal. 3.8–10.* Tubingen: Mohr Siebeck, 2001.

Wiseman, D. J. "Abraham Reassessed." Pages 141–60 in *Essays on the Patriarchal Narratives.* Edited by A. R. Millard and D. J. Wiseman. Winona Lake, Ind.: Eisenbrauns, 1983.

Wolff, Hans Walter. *Anthropology of the Old Testament.* Translated by Margaret Kohl. Philadelphia: Fortress, 1974.

Wolfson, Harry Austryn. *Philo: Foundations of Religious Philosophy in Judaism, Christianity, and Islam.* 2 vols. Rev. ed. Cambridge: Harvard University Press, 1948.

Wolter, Michael. *Der Brief an die Kolosser. Der Brief an Philemon.* ÖTKNT 12. Gütersloh: Mohn, 1993.

Wright, N. T. *The Climax of the Covenant: Christ and the Law in Pauline Theology.* Minneapolis: Fortress, 1993.

———. *Colossians and Philemon.* TNTC. Grand Rapids: Eerdmans, 1986.

———. *Jesus and the Victory of God.* Vol. 2 of *Christian Origins and the Question of God.* Minneapolis: Fortress, 1996.

———. *The New Testament and the People of God.* Vol. 1 of *Christian Origins and the Question of God.* Minneapolis: Fortress, 1992.

Wright, R. B. "Psalms of Solomon." Pages 639–70 in vol. 2 of *The Old Testament Pseudepigrapha.* Edited by James H. Charlesworth. 2 vols. ABRL. New York: Doubleday, 1983.

Yates, Roy. *The Epistle to the Colossians.* Epworth Commentaries. London: Epworth, 1993.

———. "'The Worship of Angels' (Col 2:18)." *ExpTim* 97 (1985): 12–15.

Yee, Gale A. "An Analysis of Prov 8 22–31 According to Style and Structure." *ZAW* 94 (1982): 58–66.

INDEX OF ANCIENT SOURCES

1. *Old Testament*

2. *OT Apocrypha*

3. *OT Pseudepigrapha*

4. *Qumran*

5. Josephus

6. *Philo*

7. New Testament

8. *Targums*

9. *Rabbinic Writings*

10. *Apostolic Fathers*

11. Early Church Fathers

INDEX OF AUTHORS

INDEX OF GREEK AND HEBREW WORDS AND PHRASES

INDEX OF SUBJECTS

CPSIA information can be obtained
at www.ICGtesting.com
Printed in the USA
BVHW071928271221
624891BV00001B/20